02/29/00
70
ABH-2179

Women and the Death Penalty
in the United States, 1900–1998

Women and the Death Penalty in the United States, 1900–1998

KATHLEEN A. O'SHEA

Foreword by Ann Patrick Conrad

Westport, Connecticut
London

Library of Congress Cataloging-in-Publication Data

O'Shea, Kathleen A.
  Women and the death penalty in the United States, 1900–1998 /
Kathleen A. O'Shea ; foreword by Ann Patrick Conrad.
    p.   cm.
  Includes bibliographical references and index.
  ISBN 0–275–95952–X (alk. paper)
    1. Women prisoners—United States—History—20th century—Case
studies.   2. Death row inmates—United States—History—20th
century—Case studies.   3. Capital punishment—United States—
History—20th century—Case studies.   4. Executions and
executioners—United States—History—20th century—Case studies.
I. Title.
HV9466.O74   1999
364.66′082′0973—dc21   98–23550

British Library Cataloguing in Publication Data is available.

Library of Congress Catalog Card Number: 98–23550
ISBN: 0–275–95952–X

First published in 1999

Praeger Publishers, 88 Post Road West, Westport, CT 06881
An imprint of Greenwood Publishing Group, Inc.

Printed in the United States of America

The paper used in this book complies with the
Permanent Paper Standard issued by the National
Information Standards Organization (Z39.48–1984).

10 9 8 7 6 5 4 3

For Beverly, who fills my life with love and laughter

"Wherever you go, I will go, wherever you live, so shall I live; your people will be my people, and your God will be my God too."

—*Book of Ruth, 1:16*

Contents

Foreword

In American society, it is generally held that the level of criminal punishment should be proportional to the crime that is prosecuted according to conditions of due process. Penalties fall into the broad categories of those which are retributive (designed to punish the perpetrator) and those which are restitutive (designed to restore in some measure that which has been taken from another).

From a social justice perspective, any consideration of the death penalty raises questions about the right of society to take the life of a person. Some hold that there is never a valid reason to do so, while others contend that the death penalty is valid because it can act as a deterrent. More recently, however, the televising of criminal trials, and the televised countdown to executions (as in the case of Karla Faye Tucker, 1998) have raised questions among the general public about the objectivity of due process. As a result, the subjective dimensions of prosecution and sentencing, as well as execution have come into question. With it has come a renewed sensitivity to the fallibility of human decision making particularly with respect to such irreversible choices as the enactment of the death penalty.

In recent years, the experiences of women have been observed and studied from a variety of unique perspectives. This work examines the plight of women who have faced the death penalty in the past and women who are currently facing the death penalty. By forcing us to confront the cyclical nature of violence, it raises questions as to who are the victims and who are the perpetrators in many cases. Multiple cases cited show the lives of women victimized by societal, familial, and spousal abuse who victimized others in response. Racism, domestic violence, and lack of respect for the dignity of persons are dominant themes in the transformation from victim to perpetrator.

From a societal perspective, the structure and management of America's prisons, as well as their economic position in society have taken on a new significance in the late twentieth century. Private for-profit prison management based on economies of scale have made prison expansion a lucrative prospect for business and an exciting new market for stockholders. Thus, the newly emerging prison industry reinforces retributive punishment. Within this economic context, the added resources needed to include rehabilitative services become a profit liability in the short run and an uncertain product line as far as long range planning is concerned.

Regardless of the reader's philosophic or moral perspective on capital punishment, this book introduces its audience to the experiences of women we seldom hear about and are rarely forced to consider: women sentenced to death. A closer look at their stories shows that at some level their hopes, desires, and worries are remarkably similar to their free counterparts. At the same time, their existence as incarcerated persons sentenced to death ensures lives of continual uncertainty.

Whether your response is one of horror or one of "Except for the grace of God there go I," this book provides some unforgettable insights into the criminal justice process as well as the economic, social, and interpersonal factors that influence the daily existence of a woman on death row.

Ann Patrick Conrad, DSW
Dean and Associate Professor
National Catholic School of Social Service
The Catholic University of America
Washington, DC

Preface

As of July 1998, there were forty-seven women on death row in the United States. Karla Faye Tucker (TX) and Judi Buenoano (FL) were both executed in 1998 and three women, in Arkansas, Illinois and Texas, were given the death penalty. This is the largest group of condemned women on death row at any one time in our history. No other "advanced" country, in time of peace, has had more.

Still, information on this phenomenon is scarce. In 1990, Professor Victor Streib, the most noted scholar currently studying women and the death penalty, indicated that the primary goal of his research was to "document each and every lawful American execution of a female offender since the earliest European settlement of this country." Due largely to his efforts, we now know a great deal more than we ever did. In his writings, Professor Streib (1990a) recognizes the work of Watt Espy (*The Espy File*, 1987), who has documented executions in the United States since 1608, as a primary resource.

Poignantly, in her 1984 study *Female Crime and Delinquency*, Coramae Richey Mann included a section about women on death row in a chapter entitled "The Most Forgotten Female Offenders." While it is true that we hear of these women when they are executed as well as when their crimes outrage or offend certain segments of society, by and large we know little about women on death row. And we know even less about how the death penalty has been applied to and enacted upon women throughout our history.

So far, thirty-one states — that is two thirds of the American jurisdictions that support the death penalty — have legally executed women at some time in their history. As Streib points out (1990b), this would seem to indicate a rather broad acceptance of the practice.

Between 1899 and 1953 eight women were sent to the electric chair at Sing Sing located in Ossining, New York, and sometime between 1893 and 1996 four women were executed at San Quentin in California. There have also been numerous documented and undocumented lynchings of women of whom we know almost nothing at all. This book documents the lives of one-hundred and seventy-five women who were given the death penalty in the United States since 1900. Only states that gave women the death penalty are considered here.

In the modern era of capital punishment (1973 to present), 113 women have been sentenced to death (Streib, 1990b). Of this number three, Velma Barfield in North Carolina (1984), Karla Faye Tucker in Texas (1998), and Judi Buenoano in Florida (1998), have been executed. Given today's climate (470 executions since 1976) it is very likely we will see another woman executed soon.

Texas, for example, which has been called the capital of capital punishment and appears to thrive on executions, carried out thirty-seven in 1997 alone. As of July 1998, it had executed 155 prisoners since the death penalty was reinstated in that state and there are seven women on death row in Texas as this book goes to print.

Pennsylvania, which has four women on death row, recently carried out its first two executions since the death penalty resumed in 1977. Of the fifty-six executions carried out in 1995, forty-three were in states that have women on death row.

To fully understand the history of women in our criminal justice system, we need to look at women who have been given the death penalty and at the circumstances surrounding their sentencing and deaths. The reality is that in the seventeen states that have women on death row today, women may be hanged, shot by a firing squad, given cyanide gas to inhale, electrocuted, or given poison through an intravenous drip. And despite continuous rhetoric, none of these practices has proven to be painless or particularly "humane."

In hanging, the length of the drop is estimated by a person's weight. If the drop is too short, the person dies slowly and agonizingly by strangulation. If it is too long, the person's head is torn off, as was the case with Eva Dugan in Arizona in 1930. The fact that she was beheaded during hanging caused this method of execution to be banned in Arizona.

Also in 1930, a man named Eddie Ives, who was sentenced to hang for two murders in Colorado, had to be hanged twice because of his weight. Ives, who weighed only 97 pounds, was no match for the 500-pound weight attached to the rope that was supposed to hang him. The drop did not snap his neck but only threw him 8 feet into the air before the rope came off its pulley and dropped Ives head-first onto the prison's concrete floor still alive. On the second try, the rope held and Ives died 15 minutes after being hanged. One hanging in Washington state in 1910 took 22 minutes.

An execution by hanging can be traumatic for everyone involved, including the prison staff, witnesses, and the executioner. Prison staff, in states where hanging has been used, have reported suicidal thoughts, depression, and other psychological problems.

To be executed by a firing squad, a method still retained in two states (Idaho and Utah), one with a woman on death row (Idaho), the prisoner is strapped into a chair and hooded. A target is pinned on the person's chest and five marksmen, one with blanks, aim and fire. The person may die instantly or may linger until she/he bleeds to death. Such was the case of Gary Gilmore, executed in Utah in 1977. Although he sustained four bullet wounds directly to his heart, he did not die instantly. The purpose of using blanks is to prevent anyone from knowing who is responsible for a person's death. However, several marksmen have noted that anyone who has ever shot a rifle knows whether they are firing blanks or not.

Some say the era of the electric chair may be over. But it still exists in states: Florida, Alabama, Georgia, Tennessee, South Carolina, and Nebraska. And despite years of practice, we have not yet perfected how to legally murder human beings. Innumerable stories of botched electrocutions exist. The most recent one was the execution of Pedro Medina on March 25, 1997, in the electric chair at Starke, Florida. According to the *Tampa Tribune* (1997), a six-inch flame and a cloud of smoke shot from Medina's head as the execution began; a Florida Department of Corrections spokesperson said the malfunction sent a thick cloud of smoke smelling of burnt flesh through the execution chamber, forcing security officers to open windows to let out the stench.

A similar malfunction had occurred seven years earlier, in 1990, with the same chair. In that execution, flames erupted from the headpiece the prisoner was wearing after the first jolt of electricity. Amid the smell of burning flesh and the confusion as to what should be done, it was discovered that the prisoner was still alive and three more jolts of electricity were required to stop the prisoner's breathing, even though the chair was on fire. Bills have been introduced in all the states that still have the electric chair to change the method of execution to lethal injection. Prior to the 1998 execution of Judi Buenoano in Florida, her daughter begged the state to allow her mother to be executed by lethal injection to avoid the chance that she might be burned. The state, of course, executed Judi Buenoano in the electric chair and afterwards assured everyone she felt no pain.

The gas chamber, though never really popular, was adopted after World War I, and was thought to be "more humane" than hanging or electrocution. For execution by gas, the prisoner is strapped to a chair with a container of sulfuric acid underneath. The execution room is sealed, and cyanide is dropped into the acid to form lethal gas. In 1960, before he was executed by the state of California, Caryl Chessman arranged with a reporter to communicate from behind the glass wall of the gas chamber. As the cyanide pellets mingled with the sulfuric acid, the convicted murderer moved his head up and down violently in a last nod. Yes, he was saying, it hurts. The reporter wrote "Whatever medicine says, the eyes of Chessman did not die quickly, not even gracefully, after his twitching reflexes took over from a dead brain" (*Lexington Herald-Leader,* 1961).

In 1983, in Mississippi, prison officials had to clear the witness room 8 minutes after the gas was released because the prisoner was still alive and his desperate gasps for air repulsed everyone. At its height, in the 1930s and 1940s the gas chamber was used by only nine states. Today it is still used in Arizona, North Carolina, and Maryland. Two of these, Arizona and North Carolina have women on death row.

When the gas chamber was used in Colorado, Wayne Patterson, the prison warden during Colorado's 1967 execution of Luis Monge, was the person who lifted the lever that dropped the cyanide pellets. Of this experience he said, "An execution is an execution. You're dead when it's all done, doesn't make any difference how you do it. As far as I was concerned, every person that voted for it in Colorado had his hand on the lever, same as I did" (*Denver Post,* 1997).

The most recent method of execution, lethal injection, represents an evolution of sorts, that is, the medicalization of the death penalty. For this method everything is prepared as if one is in an operating room, and many prisons even have their execution chambers in the medical wing, where one can't help wonder how physicians balance the concepts of *primum non nocere* (first do no harm) and execution.

A gurney is there, white sheets and rubber gloves, catheters, IV drip, needles, tranquilizers, and physicians. An hour or two before execution the prisoner is given a physical and declared "fit to be executed." In executions by lethal injection, physicians participate both passively, by preparing drugs and training staff and actively, by supervising executions and keeping inmates in good health until they can be executed. Medical associations in some states have objected to the fact that a physician must be present to declare a person dead after an execution and if the person is not dead, the physician is then required, in effect, to tell the state to kill him/her.

In Stephen Trombley's film *The Execution Protocol,* Warden Paul Delo informs viewers that dying by lethal injection is "very similar to getting an anesthetic prior to an operation, and it's about the same amount of drama" (Lanier, 1994).

First used in Texas, lethal injection has also had its drawbacks. In 1989 a Texas inmate had a violent reaction to the mixture of drugs used for his execution. His chest heaved and he choked and gasped for breath. It was so grueling that one of the witnesses fainted. It was also in Texas in 1988 that two minutes into the execution of a prisoner by lethal injection, the syringe came out of the prisoner's vein and a stream of chemicals shot across the room. The execution team had to reinsert the needle, during which time the curtain through which the witnesses were watching was closed for 14 minutes. Although the inmate was alive, witnesses could not observe what was going on. When the curtain was finally opened the execution resumed and the prisoner was pronounced dead 40 minutes after he had been strapped to the gurney.

In a recent turn of events, attorneys for Miguel Richardson in Texas challenged the manner in which Texas performs executions by lethal injections.

According to Richardson's lawyers, the lack of written guidelines regulating the chemical dosages and the way they're administered, as well as a lack of training for corrections personnel regarding proper catheter insertion, could result in extreme pain and suffering by the inmate.

Deborah Denno (Simpson, 1997), a Fordham University law professor, makes an argument against lethal injection in an article in the *Iowa Law Review* that chronicles 23 lethal injections, 11 of them in Texas, that in her opinion went wrong. Most of the problems she cites were from difficulties in finding usable veins in prisoners with long-term drug abuse problems, clogged tubes, and malfunctions of automated lethal injection machines. However, the state of Texas does not feel anything has gone wrong in their executions, since, as they point out, none of the inmates they've executed have walked away.

Jim Brazil (Simpson, 1997), a Baptist chaplain for Texas death row inmates said, "It's as humane as any form of death you can find." He said, "Basically, they go to sleep first it's very clean, very clinical." But, of course, all the people who feel that way are alive.

Dr. Edward Brunner (Groner, 1995), a professor at Northwestern University Medical School in Chicago and an anesthesiologist with a doctorate in pharmacology, stated, "What the use of these drugs does is sanitize the killing, so that it appears to the observers that everything is being done mercifully."

Brunner further stated that the use of the drug sodium pentothal, which we are told makes the inmate unconscious, could, if not given the right dosage, merely paralyze the person so that they are fully aware. In such a state you feel like a 10-ton weight is on your chest, you're unable to breathe and suffering excruciating pain. You are literally being suffocated to death with a burning sensation running through you as potassium chloride is injected. Until it reaches the person's heart and kills him/her, the pain is intense.

To the observer, the person being executed appears to be peaceful and still because he/she is paralyzed. Brunner said that the drugs used for lethal injections are approved by the FDA for humanitarian reasons. The FDA requires that people who manufacture drugs test them before they are used and nobody has ever tested the drugs for executions. What wardens do, according to Brunner, is actually "unauthorized experimentation on human beings."

In 1888 when New York was considering the most humane means of administering the death penalty, the medical profession so strongly opposed the use of a hypodermic needle that the idea was dropped. Nevertheless, since 1991, 80 percent of all executions nationwide have been by lethal injection.

In a 1994 report *Breach of Trust: Physician Participation in Executions in the United States* (Nelson, 1994), four organizations criticized state laws that require medical personnel to participate in executions. The report stated, in part, "Execution is not a medical procedure and is not within the scope of medical practice." It further stated "Physicians are clearly out of place in the execution chamber, and their participation subverts the core of their professional ethics."

According to the 1991 guidelines (Nelson, 1994) of the American Medical Association Council on Ethical and Judicial Affairs, medical participation in an execution would include:

- Selecting lethal injection sites;
- Starting intravenous lines to serve as conduits for lethal injections;
- Prescribing or administering pre-execution tranquilizers or other psychotropic agents;
- Inspecting, testing, or maintaining lethal injection devices;
- Consulting with or supervising lethal injection personnel;
- Monitoring vital signs on site or remotely (including electrocardiograms);
- Attending, observing, or witnessing executions as a physician;
- Providing psychiatric information to certify competence to be executed;
- Soliciting or harvesting organs for donation from condemned or executed prisoners.

When Dr. Ralph Gray assisted at the first execution by lethal injection in Texas in 1982, he was responsible for finding the correct veins for the lethal injection, monitoring the inmate's heartbeat during the execution, and informing everyone when the inmate was dead. A couple of times during the execution he shook his head indicating the inmate needed more time to die (Nelson, 1994).

The 1994 report, which took no position on capital punishment, was prepared in part by the American College of Physicians, Human Rights Watch, Physicians for Human Rights, and the National Coalition to Abolish the Death Penalty. In 1992 the American Medical Association (AMA) stated that "An individual's opinion on capital punishment is the personal moral decision of the individual. A physician as a member of a profession dedicated to preserving life when there is hope of doing so, should not be a participant in a legally authorized execution." The AMA first announced its position in 1980, disturbed by the similarities between the lethal injection gurney and an operating table. In 1983 the American Nurses Association declared any participation in executions by nurses as a "breach of the ethical tradition of nursing."

So we have come full circle and are working our way back. From the most barbaric times when undesirables were stoned or fed to the lions, to the Middle Ages when they were burned at the stake drawn and quartered, to the eighteenth century when they were guillotined, to the present with the most medical of methods, lethal injection. And recently, in 1996, Georgia lawmaker Doug Teper (D) proposed a bill to replace the electric chair with the guillotine (which chops a person's head off). Teper's reasoning for his proposal was that it would allow death-row inmates the freedom to become organ donors since the "blade makes a clean cut and leaves vital organs intact" (Amnesty

International, 1996). One can only wonder the effect this might have on witnesses and what kind of person might volunteer to be the executioner.

In 1764, the Italian jurist Cesare Beccaria asserted that "The death penalty cannot be useful, because of the example of barbarity it gives." In 1972 Chief Justice Thurgood Marshall postulated that given enough information about the death penalty, "The great mass of American citizens would conclude that the death penalty is immoral and, therefore, unconstitutional" (*Furman v. Georgia,* 408 US 238). It is not the purpose of this book to decide whether or not either of these assertions is true.

The main purpose of this work is to put a human face on the death penalty. The old adage "out of sight, out of mind" is true. It is not by accident that we do not find women on death row down the street from us. Most prisons with women on death row are in isolated and godforsaken areas. In Florida, for example, the Broward Correctional Institution where four women are now on death row is at the end of the Everglades in the middle of nowhere. In her book on Karla Faye Tucker, Beverly Lowry describes the Mountain View Unit where women are held on death row in Texas in the words of a correctional officer who said, "I don't know whether the Texas Department of Corrections chooses the worst places in the world to build [prisons] or if they just get that way." States with women on death row do not advertise the fact, and lawyers who represent women on death row often caution them against speaking to anyone, lest they jeopardize their appeals. In writing this book I had several experiences with such lawyers who threatened me with everything from supoenas to jail.

The truth is that because executions are held behind locked doors, in dark places, and before extremely small audiences, the vast majority of people who favor the death penalty are never touched by it personally. The likelihood of any of us knowing a woman on death row in our lifetime is actually quite rare. Unlike fires, accidents, cancer, or heart attacks, the death penalty does not usually happen to women in our family. Yet women are increasingly sentenced to death.

Specifically, this book looks at the states that currently have women on death row and gives information about their death penalty process, and about the women themselves where it was available. It also presents information about states, such as Georgia, that do not currently have women on death row, but have had in the past. I begin this journey in the year 1900. I arbitrarily chose that as a beginning, recognizing that there were women given the death penalty and executed before then (see Chapter 1).

Most of the information in this book is available in bits and pieces elsewhere. Some, contributed by those involved, is not. But, it seemed to me that in order to view the whole picture, the death penalty information we have about women, such as it is, should be compiled somewhere in one place. My hope is that as time goes on there will be nothing to add to this piece of history. However, even as this book goes to press, there are a number of capital cases involving women in the system.

I am not a lawyer, nor do I pretend to be an expert in the intricacies of death penalty laws, so it is not about the law. Nor is it a death penalty debate. It is, in part, about the telling of stories, an ancient and womanly thing to do, and about passing our stories on.

In writing this book, I put my life on hold, and attempted to contact every woman currently on death row, in order to give each the opportunity to speak for herself, from her own experience. I was not funded for this project nor did I receive any kind of an advance. Everything I have done has been at my own expense. Once I started to do this, I was unable to stop. I knew I had to see it through whatever the cost.

Prison officials, including those one would imagine most supportive such as chaplains, and lawyers do not make contact with women on death row an easy thing. Nor do they encourage it. It was not unusual for me to travel hundreds of miles to arrive at a prison where I had negotiated a visit over a period of months to be put in a waiting room for two or three hours without an explanation. By the time the woman I was supposed to see was brought in, only an hour of visiting time remained. On one occasion, I was locked in a visiting booth (built especially for visits with death row inmates) about the size of two telephone booths for three hours alone just waiting. After three hours, I was allowed to speak to the woman I went to see for forty-five minutes. On another occasion, I spent countless hours in phone calls and letters to set up an interview which I had to travel half way across the United States (from where I live) to do. Negotiations went on for months. When everything was finally set up, I made the trip and arrived at the prison to find out the prisoners status had changed and I was denied the interview.

Letters were returned and phone calls thwarted or evaded. Every state has its own set of rules about how to visit someone on death row. If I was not successful in my attempts, I did not give up. I contacted prisoners rights organizations in various states to find out why the women were not allowed to receive letters or visitors, and quite often, they helped me get through. And the women themselves often led me to other women.

This book has been a long process. Through correspondence, phone calls, and personal interviews, I have become saturated with the despair and longing for the truth most of these women experience, both the truly guilty and those who were found guilty but are not. Often I found myself gasping for breath and had to step aside and allow my spirit to heal and regenerate my sense of commitment to this project.

Where it was possible, I have included the words of the women who are currently or have been on death row to whom I spoke or with whom I corresponded. Where direct quotes by women on death row are used, the pages were edited by the women themselves. Many have been told they are monsters — some told me "I am the monster you've read about." As these women age in isolation (Faye Copeland, on death row in Missouri, will be 80 when this book is published), most have given up trying to set the records straight.

I have listened to and understand the arguments about women getting the death penalty less frequently than men in this country, and I acknowledge and recognize the large number of men on death row in our country today. I do not wish to ignore them or their plight. But this is an exposé about the women. Few though their numbers may be, they are on death row, and for the most part terribly isolated, invisible, and alone. They do think about dying and this, in part, is what they've asked me to say.

Acknowledgments

Even as I felt driven to bring this book to fruition, it would not have been possible without the loving support of my partner, Beverly Fletcher. I acknowledge and thank her for believing that this research was possible and necessary, for sacrificing her own time and space to ensure it would happen, and for spending countless hours at the most unusual times and in unpredictable places, listening to the horrors of execution practices and the despair with which women on death row speak of their lives.

I am equally grateful to Hannelore Hahn and the women of the International Women's Writing Guild for planting the seed that would flourish as a writer and for nurturing it for oh, so many years, in dry as well as seasons of plenty.

A special thanks to my long-time friend, Susan Baugh, of Atkins House, who initiated the process of interviewing the women on death row in Pennsylvania and who through her position on the Women's Advisory Council of the Commissioner of the Department of Corrections in Pennsylvania has given me a unique insider's perspective. She has personally supported and encouraged my writing for many years, and her dedication and work with and for women prisoners and ex-prisoners is a daily inspiration.

I express my gratitude to my friend and sister, Suzanne Tewawina, for the Native American perspective on this project and for the constancy of her strength and healing in counseling Native American women prisoners. I also thank her for her willingness to give her time to accompany me to various prison sites.

I thank my community of colleagues, professors, and students, at the National Catholic School of Social Service at the Catholic University of America in Washington, DC for their support and insights and for working with me to see this project come to light.

Of all of the families who have shared their pain and sorrow, I am especially grateful to Renate Janka who opened her heart to me, and to her support group throughout the world in particular Kirk Fowler and Anders Rosenquist who have worked tirelessly donating countless hours of personal time in pursuit of truth and justice. Pat Galbraith and Clara Boggs have kept my e-mail box supplied with relevant articles and occasional jokes and for that I give thanks.

A special thanks to Audrey Kaufman, Chair of Life Lines Ireland, who is working on her own book and shared information on various women she knew and interviewed.

Alex Wallner and her husband, John, allowed me to use their "upper room" as a space to write and complete some of this book and Alex accompanied me through the dank dark halls of Eastern State Penitentiary while John shared his personal insights on serving as the foreman of a capital jury in Pennsylvania. For these, I am also grateful.

My thanks to Jennie Brown for her information on early executions in America, and for allowing me to use details from the hanging of her grandfather in Montana.

Brother Patrick Byrd of the Discalced Carmelite Monastery in San Antonio, Texas, recently deceased, was especially helpful in providing the mailing addresses and prison numbers of several women on death row. May he rest in peace.

The women residents and staff of Atkins House in York, PA, particularly Doris Gray and Nancy Reisinger, were most gracious in providing their personal information and observations about women's prisons. For their information and time, my thanks.

Librarians who offered me assistance include Carol Bontempo of the Missouri Department of Corrections, who provided information on Bonnie Brown Heady. Tom Davis of the North Carolina Supreme Court Library offered useful information on the death penalty in North Carolina. Paul Carnahan of the Vermont historical library is responsible for the information on Mary Rogers. John Fougere of the Missouri Department of Corrections provided information on the death row population in Missouri. Vera Nichols of the California State Library provided death penalty references for California. Penny Gibson of the University of Alabama School of Law Library was most helpful in providing information on women and the death penalty. Ms. Nola Crawford of the New Jersey State Law Library provided references on the death penalty in New Jersey. Cassie Pierson of the Legal Services for Prisoners in California provided a variety of articles, fact sheets, and listings of resources on the death penalty and women in California.

A note of gratitude to Joan Brett and Rick Halperin for faithfully posting the *Death Penalty News & Updates* on the Net. And to the *women2women* community (http://www.women2women.com), especially the owners, Sue Boettcher and Eva Shaderowfsky who featured me for two weeks before my book was even published. I am also grateful to Eva for having me as a guest in her AOL chat room *Evenings With Eva,* to discuss my book with her net-guests. In this same group, I am indebted to the editors and owners of the *Women's International Network* (WIN Magazine), Judith Culp Rubin, and Janice Wasser for publishing my story about interviewing a woman on death row for their net readers (http://www.winmagazine.base.org).

My thanks to the women currently on death row who took a chance and shared information about themselves with me. I also thank the wardens and their assistants who allowed me access to the women on death row and helped me with that process.

I would like to acknowledge the following individuals who granted me permission to quote material for use in this book: Mary Leftridge Byrd, Ana Cardona, Louise Harris, Donetta Hill, Andrea Jackson, Renate Janka, Audrey Kaufman, Virginia Larzelere, Lynda Lyon, Debra Milke, Kelley O'Donnell, Dolores Rivers, Robin Row, and Karla Windsor.

Finally, I would like to thank Nita Romer, my acquisitions editor, for her enthusiasm in taking on this project and her willingness to work with me and my production editor, Elizabeth Meagher for everything.

Last, but not least, a word of gratitude to my writing group, Lucia Edmonds, Beverly Fletcher, and Barbara Greig, the trinity of women, who mean so very much to me.

1

History and the Execution of Women

> The calculated killing of a human being by the state involves, by its very nature, an absolute denial of the executed person's humanity. The vilest murder does not, in my view, release the state from constitutional restraint on the destruction of human dignity.
>
> — *U.S. Supreme Court Justice William Brennan*

> If the action of the death penalty is genuine "compassion" for both the victims and the accused it could be appropriate. But that takes a society without revenge.
>
> —*JW, Foreman of a capital jury*

Although only three women, Margie Velma Barfield in North Carolina, Karla Faye Tucker in Texas, and Judi Buenoano in Florida have been executed since the Supreme Court authorized executions in 1976, there is a historic precedent for executing women in the United States.

Since the first European settlers arrived in America the death penalty has been accepted as just punishment for women (Baird & Rosenbaum, 1995). Capital punishment had long been the practice in England and throughout Europe. Gatrell (1994) and Linebaugh (1992) present numerous cases between 1770 and 1868 of women who were executed in England for things as minor as stealing a bolt of cloth. Examples include women like Mary Dutton, who was hanged in 1742 for stealing a watch and Elizabeth Fox who was hanged for stealing five Portuguese coins (Linebaugh, 1992). Of Fox we are told "she walked the streets, robbed, stole, and took everything she could lay hold on, being one of the most scandalous creatures and notorious pickpockets in town"(140). Hannah Wilson, a vendor of peas and beans, was hanged at the age of 25 for stealing clothes, and Mary Standford was hanged for picking a pocket of a handkerchief and 4 guineas. Linebaugh (1992) lists 92 women hanged between 1703 and 1772 in Tyburn. Among them, Mary Goddard was hanged for picking a pocket and Elizabeth Price for burglary. Susan Perry for murdering a child, and Sarah Clifford for stealing 13 flounder and mackerel in the streets "when those fish were in season"(144). Ann Mudd was hanged for murdering her husband and Mary White for stealing an apron. According to a statistical analysis of London indictments for the year 1740, the one felony for which a larger number of women than men were hung was receiving stolen goods (Linebaugh, 1992).

Potter (1993) indicates that the work of John Locke, the leading apologist of the new Protestant order in England, was largely responsible for such uses of the death penalty. Locke's writings emphasized repeatedly that the sole purpose of the state was the preservation of property and that the state could use whatever punishment it deemed necessary to protect that goal, including the death penalty. Although Locke believed that citizens had an inalienable right to life, he also believed that right was forfeited by criminal acts against property. According to Potter (1993), this doctrine of forfeiture was very influential in English law and justified the death penalty for even trivial property offenses.

Aside from petty thievery, 10 percent of the women hanged at Tyburn were hanged for infanticide (Linebaugh, 1992), though none after 1849, and the practice ended entirely with the passing of the Infanticide Act in England.

Mary Ellenor and Agatha Ashbrook were both hanged in 1708 for infanticide (Linebaugh, 1992). In 1734, Judith Leford was hanged for killing her newborn. Elizabeth Ashbrook, in 1735, and Jane Cooper, in 1737, were both hanged for infanticide. Sarah Allen, who suffocated her infant child, was hanged in 1738, and Elizabeth Harwood, who drowned her child, was hanged in 1739. Sarah Wilmhurst was hanged in 1743, and in 1752 Ann Wallsam was also hanged for infanticide. A common thread running through the tapestry of all these women's lives was that they were poor and considered immoral in some way by the general public.

In the English statutes the listing of crimes punishable by execution was accompanied by an appropriate biblical quotation (Baird & Rosenbaum, 1995), to bring home the idea that individuals were punished severely not only because they had broken a civil law, but also because they were morally unfit to remain alive. A customary method of execution and retribution was to hang a woman until she was dead and then burn her body at the stake, in full view of the public.

Gatrell (1994) tells us that well into the nineteenth century, criminal women were deemed monsters in England, which is, perhaps, one reason executions were such a public spectacle. Even though abolitionists were afoot, invitations to executions were often published on billboards and flyers, and individual curiosities were titillated with gruesome details of what could be expected. The younger and prettier the condemned, the more thrilling the sight.

A poster in 1847 announced the execution of a young girl, 16 years of age (Gatrell, 1994) as a "Grand Moral Spectacle." The same announcement went on to say she was to be "publicly strangled," attended by a Minister of the Church of England and the hangman, The Great Moral Teacher. The hangman, it explained, after "fastening her arms to her side and putting a rope round her neck would strike the scaffold from under her." And if her neck didn't break after that he would "pull the legs of the miserable girl until by his weight and strength united he strangled her" (164).

The 1786 execution of Phoebe Harris, who was hanged for the crime of coining silver, was witnessed by a crowd of some 20 thousand people (Gatrell, 1994). An account of her execution revealed that she was led to a wooden stake, where she stood on a stool with the noose of a rope attached to an iron bolt driven into the top of the stake around her neck. The stool was then removed and as her body convulsed, she "noisily" choked to death for several minutes. About half an hour later her body was chained to the stake and the executioner placed two cartloads of branches and twigs around it and set them on fire. Her body then burned for over two hours (Gatrell, 1994).

Although, by all accounts, everyone loved a hanging, two years after Phoebe's hanging, when Margaret Sullivan was hanged and burned, an article in the paper noted, "There is something inhuman in burning a woman" (Gatrell, 1994).

Nevertheless, some people defended the practice of burning women's bodies, saying that although it was a horrible spectacle, there was no pain involved since the woman was already dead. An account in one newspaper from the day of Margaret Sullivan's hanging supported the abolition of public burning, saying the smoke was a nuisance that made people who were already ill in the neighborhood much sicker.

Aside from the burning of women's dead bodies, women were also burnt alive for certain crimes such as treason. The last woman publicly burned alive in England was Catherine Hayes in 1726, and an account of it (Gatrell, 1994) indicates that this was because the executioner accidentally set the fire before he had hanged her. In 1790 Sir Benjamin Hammett asked Parliament to abolish the practice of burning women "post mortem" in the cause of humanity. He said, in effect, that the practice was a disgrace. The English Parliament officially abolished the burning of women in May 1790.

The similarities between Gatrell's accounts of women executed in England and accounts of the executions of women, mostly black, by lynching, in the United States cannot be ignored. Although the method of execution, hanging and burning, was often the same, by the 1900s, with racism fueling the flames, stories of the cruelty and barbarity of American southern lynchings are unequaled by any English accounts. The case of one woman in Georgia reprinted by Radford and Russell (1992) is particularly stark.

In 1918, in Brooks County, Georgia, a black woman by the name of Mary Turner was lynched because she protested the hanging of her husband. Guilty of no crime, he was lynched because an angry mob could not find the person really responsible for shooting and killing a local farmer. After hanging her husband the men heard that Mary had expressed anger and grief at what had happened and they decided to "teach that nigger a lesson" (55). Family members hid her for a time but the men eventually found her and, even though she was pregnant, hanged her.

They bound her ankles together and hanged her upside down from a tree and while she was hanging they doused her with gasoline and oil and set her on fire. As she screamed and writhed in pain a man stepped from the bloodthirsty crowd and ripped open her abdomen with his knife. According to a published account of the day, her unborn child tumbled out. Witnesses said the child cried once before the man crushed it to death with the heel of his boot.

In January 1923, Edith Thompson was hanged in England. Her lover had killed her husband and, though some suggested conspiracy, many believed she was hanged for adultery as much as for murder. Her death was seen as the result of a "kind of frozen moral inertia" (Potter, 1993) which "seized those whose business and responsibility it should have been to avoid an act that was essentially unjust" (121). It is not known when the last woman will be hanged in America, but in England, Ruth Ellis, who was hung at Holloway Prison in North London on July 13, 1955, closed the books on that chapter of English history.

In America women represent 2.5 percent of all persons executed under state and local authority after 1608 (Schneider & Smykla, 1991). Ninety percent of these women were executed under local authority (counties, townships, villages), and the majority (87%) prior to 1866 (Schneider & Smykla, 1991). The two most common crimes for which women received the death penalty in America prior to 1866 were murder (76%) and witchcraft (7%) and a significant number who were executed for murder, murdered their husbands. The most common method used by wives to murder their husbands was poisoning.

The first recorded execution of a woman in the United States was that of Jane Champion, in James City, Virginia, in 1632. She was hanged for an unknown crime, and her age was not listed (Schneider & Smykla, 1991). The youngest person on record executed in the United States was Hannah Ocuish, a Native American child, who was said to have been retarded; she was 12 years of age when she was executed. She was hanged in New London County, Connecticut, on December 20, 1786, for the alleged murder of a 6-year-old white girl.

The Espy File (Espy & Smykla, 1987) contains 14,570 cases of documented executions in the United States between 1608 and 1987. Of this number, 1,749 were slave executions. Of the slave executions 189 were known to be women. Ten of the women were juveniles. Of the juveniles, nine were women of color. Eight were black and one was Native American. One female juvenile was white.

Two women slaves whose executions were documented were Marja Lamb, burned for arson in Suffolk County, Massachusetts, on September 22, 1681, and Amy Spain, a 17-year-old woman hanged on March 10, 1865, in Arlington

County, South Carolina, for an unknown crime. The oldest woman executed in early American history was a 65-year-old woman who was a slave and is remembered only by the surname Greene. She was hanged in Prince William County, Virginia, on February 13, 1857, for murder (Schneider & Smykla, 1991).

The most common crimes for which black women slaves were executed were homicide, arson, and assault (Streib, 1990b). Streib (1990b) notes that women slaves were also executed for "conduct unbecoming a slave" (853), such as rebellion or petty treason. White women who were executed during this time were almost always executed for witchcraft.

Early executions in America, as in England, were public. They were usually held in town squares and attended mostly by men. Before being executed, women were paraded in thin gowns before large crowds gathered for the sport. Far from being somber events, those in attendance could be counted on to be cruel and rowdy individuals who frequently shouted obscenities at the condemned. As in Gatrell's accounts of women's hangings in England, one could expect there were "execution-groupies" who attended every hanging or burning because it was the thing to do, or because they were perversely drawn to such events. Women executed in this fashion often died facing a sea of men without ever seeing the face of another woman. In those days, executions were carried out almost immediately after a death sentence had been imposed, or, at the very least within a few days, so that, the concept of death row, as we know it today, did not exist.

In her forthcoming work *Too Late For Sympathy Now*, Jennie Brown paints a picture of the excitement surrounding the public execution by hanging of her grandfather, Clinton Dotson, in 1901 in Montana. Invitations were mailed out to witness the event. Jennie reports that "By July 25th, 1901, hundreds of applications for cards of admission had been received by the officials." And "It became an arduous task for the sheriff to sort through and determine who would receive the invitations."

The invitations, which were enhanced with pictures of the condemned, read "Mr._____ You are invited to witness the execution of James Fleming (alias James McArthur) and Clinton Dotson on Friday, September 6, 1901 at 10:00 a.m. at the Powell County Jail in Deer Lodge, Montana." According to Brown, the invitations were signed by the sheriff of Powell County, Montana, and were considered a prize worth having. Requests for permits to the execution accelerated daily. Not since the street fair and carnival held in Butte on July 14 of the same year had such a festive air prevailed.

On the actual day of the execution, the *Butte Miner*, a local paper, reported the mood of the town in this way:

No trains had run into Deer Lodge the night before and many people who had wanted to come from Butte to Anaconda had been disappointed. They were coming in on Friday morning's train instead and Chief of Police Reynolds and Sheriff Furey, along with other prominent officials, asked Sheriff McMahon to postpone the hanging until the train from Butte arrived to which he agreed. In keeping with the festive air surrounding the jail, the prison band was called upon to give a concert to entertain the visitors awaiting the execution. When the train from Butte pulled into the station, an estimated two hundred people piled off and proceeded to the scene of the hanging.

Clinton Dotson was hanged at 11:29 a.m., his last words being "Catch hold of me, I'm going to fall." The *Butte Miner* reported:

It was a gruesome sound to hear the baying of a hound shortly after Dotson had been sent on his way to eternity. The dog was evidently just outside the stockade surrounding the scaffold and as soon as the rope holding the weight had been cut, the animal began to moan and cry like a man wounded to the death and crying in his agony for assistance. Many spoke of it and several who were superstitiously inclined explained the meaning of the bad omen.

Brown concludes her account of the event by noting "All in all," the *Butte Miner* reported, "the execution was one of the most successful ever carried out in the state of Montana."

LYNCHING OF WOMEN

Ida B. Wells, a brilliant African-American journalist, human rights activist, and investigative reporter, is responsible for many of the documented accounts of lynchings in the United States. Born in 1862 to parents, who were slaves, she attended a school in Holly Springs, Mississippi, established by the Freedmen's Bureau for the education of former slaves. In 1878, at the age of 16, Ida lost both parents to Yellow Fever. She then took on the responsibility of raising her five brothers and sisters and supported them by becoming a country schoolteacher.

In 1884, on her way to work aboard the Chesapeake, Ohio, and Southwestern Railroad, the conductor ordered Ms. Wells to give her seat to a white man. He told her she would have to leave first class where she was sitting, because due to the railroad's new "Separate but Equal" policies. "Coloreds" had to sit in the forward coach

In her autobiography Ms. Wells wrote: "I refused him, saying that the car was a smoker, and, as I was in the ladies' car, I proposed to stay." With that the conductor grabbed her by the arm and tried to drag her out. Bracing her feet against the back of the chair in front of her, Ida bit him and he let go of her. When he returned with help Ms. Wells was dragged from the train amidst the applause and cheers of white passengers.

Ida saw the "Separate but Equal" statutes and Black Codes which had been spreading through the South after Reconstruction as attempts to re-establish the racial inequalities that had existed during slavery, and she sued the railroad for illegally discriminating against her. The Supreme Court reversed a decision by a local court in her favor in 1887. Ms. Wells expressed her outrage at this through a series of articles in a church newspaper where she wrote of her intentions to defy the Black Codes whenever and wherever she could. She urged all her readers to do the same. Eventually, her newspaper column became so popular she was offered an editorship at a small black newspaper in Memphis, Tennessee. She accepted the offer and in her position as editor continued to write "bold" editorials that doubled the paper's circulation. Eventually, however, she was fired from both the editorship and her Memphis teaching position.

In 1892, three of Ida's friends were lynched in events surrounding the opening of a black-owned grocery store across the street from a white-owned grocery in Memphis. Her editorials at the time against white public officials in Memphis who permitted and tolerated racism and lynchings resulted in the destruction of her newspaper office by an angry white mob. Had Ida been in her office that day she probably would have been hanged. After the fire, Ms. Wells moved to New York and became a correspondent for several black newspapers, ceaselessly launching attacks on lynching and its perpetrators.

Ida usually found out about lynchings almost as soon as they occurred from numerous contacts she maintained throughout the states. When she heard of one she would immediately travel to where it had taken place and interview eyewitnesses to find out what events had led up to it. From this information she wrote detailed reports about the more primitive and evil nature of lynch mobs.

She always took the position that African Americans of her day were destined to re-enslavement unless they protested against the boundaries imposed on their lives by whites. It was her belief that the major impediment to the protest process was the threat of lynching. Her articles were the first to accurately describe events leading up to lynchings, events that people in the South knew about and lived with, but which had never been reported to outsiders. She documented the fact that African Americans were being lynched for registering to vote, for testifying in court, for not being deferential to whites, and even for knowing or being related to someone who had displeased a white person. African-American women were often lynched with their children because a husband had already been lynched or was suspected of doing something for which he would be lynched.

Archivist, Daniel Williams of Tuskegee University, a historically black college near Montgomery, Alabama, is currently responsible for more than 60 boxes and files of original records of documented mob lynchings in the United States since 1882. Of the Tuskegee collection, James Roark, a professor of Southern history at Emory University, said, "It is crucial that this repository be preserved. The pictures in the files are gruesome and the stories they detail are worse. But we must recognize these were grim realities. The scholarly significance of this collection is immeasurable."

Among the documents are thousands of original newspaper articles published by white and black owned presses detailing the events leading up to individual lynchings, the actual lynchings, and their immediate aftermath. There are also reports from the turn of the century telling blacks about the counties and states where they and their families would be safe, as well as a 1930 study warning people of the signs or symptoms of racial disharmony that precede lynchings. Studies from the 1920s about the economic, demographic and geographic makeup of mobs are also included.

The documented executions of women by lynching in the United States, lest they be forgotten, include the following:

1632	Jane Champion	Hanged in James City, VA
1660	Mary Dyer	Hanged in Boston
1681	Marja Lamb	A slave woman burned at the stake in Suffolk County, MA
1735	Patience Boston	First woman hanged in ME
1767	Venus	A 17-year-old black woman hanged in NY
1786	Hannah Ocuish	A Native American child hanged in New London, CT
1851	Juanita aka Josefa	A woman from Mexico hanged in CA
1857	A woman named Greene	65-year-old slave woman hanged in Prince William County, VA
1865	Amy Spain	17-year-old slave hanged in Arlington County, SC
1868	Cummin's daughter	A black woman lynched in Pulaski County, KY
1870	Mrs. John Simes	A black woman lynched in Henry County, KY
1872	Mrs. Hawkins	A black woman lynched in Fayett County, KY

1876	Mrs. Ben French	A black woman lynched in Gallitin County, KY
1880	Milly Thompson	A black woman lynched in Clayton County, GA
1889	Rose Etheride	A black woman lynched with Five black men in Phoenix, SC
	A white woman	Lynched with two men in Tiptonville, TN
	Mary Puckett	Lynched with her husband at Lynn Creek in the Oklahoma Territory
	Ella Watkins aka "Cattle Kate"	Hanged in Sweetwater, WY
	An unnamed woman	A white woman lynched with A black man in Spring Place, GA
1891	A woman named "Baker"	A white woman lynched in Northern Arkansas
	Rose Eliot	A black woman lynched in Centerville, AL
	Lousie Stevenson	A black woman lynched in Hollandale, MS
1892	Mary Briscoe	A black woman lynched with Her husband and son in AR
	Daughter of John Hastings	Lynched with her brother in Calahoula, LA
	Ella	A black woman lynched in Rayville, LA
	Eliza Lowe and Ella Williams	Wives lynched with their husbands in AL
	Mrs. Martin	A black woman lynched in Sumner County, TN

1893	Emma Fair	A black woman lynched in Carrolton, AL
	Mahala Jackson	A black woman lynched in Jackson, MS
	Mother of Phil Evans	A black woman lynched with her daughter and grand-daughter in Bardstown, KY
1895	Mary Deane	A black woman lynched in Greenville, AL
	Alice Green	A black woman lynched in Greenville, AL
	Martha Green	A black woman lynched in Greenville, AL
	Mollie Smith	A black woman lynched in Trigg County, KY
	Harriet Talley	A black woman lynched in Petersburg, TN
1897	Amanda Franks	A black woman lynched in Jefferson, AL
	Hannah Kearse	A black woman lynched in Colton County, SC
1898	Dora Baker	A black woman lynched with her husband in Lake City, SC
	Eliza Goode	A black woman lynched in Greenwood, SC
	Mary Pearson	A white woman lynched near Natchez, MS
	May Queen	A black woman lynched in Phoenix, SC
1901	Ballie Crutchfield	Abducted and lynched in Rome, TN

1901	Mary Hearn	A white woman lynched in Osceola, AR
	Dee Mayes	Lynched in Selma, AL
	An unnamed black woman	Lynched in Smith County, MS with four black men
	Three unnamed black women	Stripped and flogged by a mob of fifty men in MS
1902	Belfied, Betsy, and Ida McCray	Three black women lynched Carrolton, MS
	Bell Duly	A black woman lynched in Fulton, KY
	Mrs. Wideman	A black woman lynched in Troy, SC
1903	Jennis Steers	A black woman hanged near Shreveport, LA
	Dora Wright	Hanged for murder in Oklahoma
1904	Mrs. Luther Holberts	A black woman burned at the stake with her husband near Doddsville, MS
	Rebecca Scott	A black woman lynched in Georgia
	Marie Thompson	A black woman lynched in Lebanon Junction, KY
1907	Two unnamed black women	Lynched in Stamps, AR
	Mrs. Sam Padgett	Lynched in Tatnall County, GA with her son
1908	Dee Dawson	A black woman lynched in Hickory, MS

1908	Mrs. David Wallace	A black woman from Hickory Grove, KY lynched with her husband and five children
1910	Laura Porter	A black woman lynched in Monroe, AL
	Hattie Bowman	A black woman lynched in Graceville, FL
1911	Laura Nelson	A black woman and her son lynched in Okemah, OK
1912	Ann Bostwick	A black woman lynched in Crisp County, GA
	Belle Hathaway	A black woman lynched with three black men in Hamiliton, GA
	Mary Jackson	A black woman lynched in Marshal, TX
1913	Mrs. J. Perry and child	A woman and her child who were killed after kerosene was poured on their home and set on fire.
1914	Rose Carson	A black woman lynched in Elloree, SC
	Jennie Collins	A young black woman from Shaw, MS who was lynched
	Marie Scott	A black woman abducted from a Muskogee, OK jail by a mob of men and hanged from a telephone pole.
	An unnamed black girl	17-year-old lynched near Wagner, OK
	Paralee Parker	A young black woman lynched in West Plains, MO

1914	Mrs. Fred Sullivan	A black woman hanged with her husband in Byhalia, MS
1915	Eula and Ella Charles	Lynched in Monticello, GA with two black men
	Cordella Stevenson	Hanged in Columbia, MS
1916	Mary Connell	A black woman lynched with ten black men in Brooks County, GA
	Mary Dennis	A black woman lynched with three black men in New-berry, FL
1917	Emma Hooper	Lynched in Hammond, LA
1918	Bessie, Sarah, and Tenola Cabaniss	Three black women lynched in Huntsville, TX with three black men of the same family
	Maggie House	A black woman lynched in Shubuta, MS
	Mary Turner	A black woman lynched with ten black men in Brooks County, GA
1920	Minnie Ivory	A black woman hanged in Coffee County, GA
1924	Penny Westmoreland	A black woman lynched in Spalding County, GA
1926	Bertha Lowman	A black woman lynched in Aiken, SC with her brother
1930	An unnamed woman	Lynched in Emell, AL with three black men
	Holly White	A black woman lynched in Scooba, MS
1946	Two black women	Lynched with their husbands by a mob near Monroe, GA

The *Time Line of African American History, 1881–1900* and the *Time Line of African American History, 1901–1925* give the following statistics for known lynchings in the United States. These figures almost certainly reflect scores of unnamed African American women:

1882	Forty-nine African Americans lynched
1883	Fifty-three African Americans lynched
1884	Fifty-one African Americans lynched
1885	Seventy-four African Americans lynched
1886	Seventy-four African Americans lynched
1887	Seventy African Americans lynched
1888	Sixty-nine African Americans lynched
1890	Eighty-five African Americans lynched
1891	One hundred and thirteen lynched
1892	One hundred and sixty-one lynched
1893	One hundred and eighteen lynched
1894	One hundred and thirty-four lynched
1895	One hundred and thirteen lynched
1896	Seventy-eight African Americans lynched
1897	One hundred and twenty-three lynched
1898	One hundred and one African Americans lynched
1899	Eighty-five African Americans lynched
1900	One hundred and six African Americans lynched
1901	One hundred and five African Americans lynched
1902	Eighty-five African Americans lynched
1903	Eighty-four African Americans lynched
1904	Seventy-six African Americans lynched
1905	Fifty-seven African Americans lynched
1906	Sixty-two African Americans lynched
1907	No statistics
1908	Eighty-nine African Americans lynched
1909	Sixty-nine African Americans lynched
1910	Sixty-seven African Americans lynched
1911	Sixty African Americans lynched
1912	Sixty-one African Americans lynched
1913	Fifty-one African Americans lynched
1914	Fifty-one African Americans lynched
1915	Fifty-six African Americans lynched
1916	Fifty African Americans lynched
1917	Thirty-six African Americans lynched
1918	Sixty African Americans lynched
1919	Seventy-six African Americans lynched
1920	Fifty-three African Americans lynched
1921	Fifty-nine African Americans lynched
1922	Fifty-one African Americans lynched
1923	Twenty-nine African Americans lynched
1924	Sixteen African Americans lynched

By the 1830s legal outdoor executions became a mote in the public eye. To appease abolitionists, state legislatures moved them behind prison walls (Mackey, 1976; Masur, 1989). The 1840s saw the rise of the anti-gallows societies in America, and in 1847 a group of Philadelphia women petitioned the state legislature with over 10,000 signatures to abolish capital punishment (Masur, 1989) completely. What they stated then seems by all accounts to hold true today: it is the poor who are executed, while the wealthy universally escape this form of punishment.

The first execution by electrocution took place in New York in 1890, and by 1896, Ohio introduced electrocution. Massachusetts began executing by electrocution in 1898, New Jersey in 1906, Virginia in 1908, and North Carolina in 1910. At least twenty other states adopted the use of the electric chair soon afterward, making electrocution the most popular means of execution in America at the time.

The heyday of the death penalty in the United States was in the 1930s; the executioners' busiest year was 1935, with a total of 199 legal executions. According to McCafferty (1960), 1930 was the first year when there was complete coverage of all the executions carried out in state institutions, as well as those by sheriffs in state and local facilities.

There were fewer executions in the 1940s and fewer still in the 1950s. In 1965 a commission revising the New York State Penal Code wrote, "whatever aspect of the death penalty one examines, one finds nothing but obstruction, confusion and waste."

Today, the 1972 Supreme Court ruling in *Furman v. Georgia* [408 US 238, 92 S.Ct. 2726 (1972)] remains a focal point of death penalty discussions. In this decision, by a narrow and fractured 5–4 majority, capital punishment was banned in all states where it was then being practiced. In its ruling, the Court stated that under the existing laws, "The imposition and carrying out of the death penalty constituted cruel and unusual punishment in violation of the Eighth and Fourteenth amendments to the Constitution of the United States." The majority of the Court concentrated its objections on the way death-penalty laws were then applied in individual states. Existing death penalty statutes of the time were found to be unconstitutional because they were "arbitrary, capricious, and discriminatory" in their application. The court ultimately decided that states had insufficient procedural checks on their sentencing practices when the decisions they were making meant life or death.

Two justices, Justice William Brennan and Justice Thurgood Marshall, held that capital punishment per se is unconstitutional. Justice Brennan wrote that capital punishment depended on "a system in which the punishment of death is invariably and swiftly imposed" and "our system, satisfies neither of these." He went on to say "A rational person contemplating a murder is confronted, not with the certainty of a speedy death, but with the slight possibility that he will be executed in the distant future." Although Brennan and Marshall said the death penalty was unconstitutional under any circumstances, the other seven justices did not agree with them and encouraged the states with death penalty statutes to rewrite their laws.

Justice William O. Douglas wrote the death penalty was unconstitutionally discriminatory because of its disproportionate impact on minorities and individuals of lower socioeconomic means. He summed up his opinion by saying, "No standards govern the selection of the death penalty. People live or die, dependent on the whim of one man or twelve." Justices Potter Stewart and Byron White cited the "freakish and arbitrary manner" in which the death penalty was imposed "as a problem." The Chief Justice at the time, Warren Burger, wrote the dissenting opinion, joined by Justice William Rehnquist, that the majority decision left the death penalty in "an uncertain limbo" and suggested that state legislatures "bring their laws into compliance by providing standards for judges and juries to follow." But even as he wrote, Burger said he doubted that anyone could define adequate standards. He felt that defining which cases should get the death penalty in advance had "been uniformly unsuccessful."

At the time of this decision there were over 600 persons under death sentences in 32 states (Bedau, 1984). Although the ruling was not definitive, it reversed all pending death sentences and invalidated the capital punishment laws of the federal government, the District of Columbia, and all the states that had retained the death penalty. None of the prisoners on death row at the time could be executed, nor could anyone be sentenced to death. The immediate effect of the *Furman* decision was that states began revising their death penalty statutes to conform to constitutional standards and the Supreme Court's concerns.

Unfortunately, although *Furman v. Georgia* ended the existing death-penalty practices, it did not provide any guidance to individual states about how to go about drafting new statutes. It merely told them they should. States, therefore, turned to the American Law Institute's Model Penal Code, written in the 1950s (Weschler, 1959), which basically had two requirements for how capital trials and sentencing should be conducted. First, the sentencing part of the trial should be separate from the guilt-innocence phase (bifurcated); and second, some type of guidance should be given to those responsible for sentencing, so that they could make a reasonable decision about who should or should not be sentenced to death.

The thinking on the first requirement, that is, separating the two parts of a trial, was that before *Furman* many states had a system where the jury would give the verdict and the sentence in one trial and there was no opportunity for the defendant to present mitigating circumstances.

As for the second requirement, that is, instructions about what to consider before deciding a sentence, it was suggested that juries be given lists of aggravating or mitigating circumstances, so they could know what they were supposed to be considering.

Florida had new statutes within six months, followed by Texas, Georgia, and Louisiana. Finally, in 1976 with *Gregg v. Georgia* [428 US 153,96 S.Ct. 2909 (1976)] the Supreme Court ruled on the two basic approaches to sentencing, which were, "Mandatory" and "Discretionary." Some states, such as North Carolina and Louisiana, had made the death penalty mandatory for first-degree murder, while other states, such as Florida, Georgia, and Texas, had adopted a process called "Guided Discretion." This meant that the judge and the jury had to weigh every capital defendant's case on a balance of aggravating and mitigating circumstances.

Mandatory death sentences were eventually ruled unconstitutional, but guided discretion was accepted, and in July 1976 (*Gregg v. Georgia*) the Supreme Court upheld the death penalty decision of the state of Georgia indicating that with the new standards of a bifurcated trial and a mandatory appeals process, the death penalty, in effect was constitutional and did not violate the eighth and fourteenth amendments. With the decision in *Gregg v. Georgia* the Supreme Court sent a strong message that "It's OK to execute people again because we have laws that will help judges and juries decide what to do." In effect, it declared that the death penalty as it stood would not be unfair, arbitrary, racist, or discriminatory against anyone.

Because of the Guided Discretion mandate juries in capital cases were required to consider aggravating and mitigating circumstances. Aggravating circumstances might include whether or not the defendant had a prior record, if she/he had committed murder in the course of another felony, or if a crime was "heinous, atrocious or cruel." If the defendant was very young, the product of abuse, or under the influence of a threatening accomplice, these would be mitigating circumstances. If the aggravating circumstances outweighed the mitigating circumstances, the death penalty could be imposed. The state Supreme Court was then required to review the decision to assure that it met the standards of the law.

In this stage of a trial prosecutors present aggravating factors and defense attorneys are supposed to present "mitigating factors." This is a crucial stage in a trial for those whose lives hang in the balance. For women, as a result of the Violence Against Women Act of 1994, states are now permitted to present evidence of battered women's syndrome at this phase in a trial, and more than half of the women on death row today have histories of abuse.

Despite the implications, investigating abuse is time-consuming and expensive. It frequently requires the services of social workers, psychologists, and special investigators who must all be paid, out of funds public defenders usually do not have.

Judith Haney, a woman who spent ten years on death row in Alabama for the murder of her husband, appealed her death sentence because her court-appointed trial lawyers failed to obtain hospital records of her treatment for injuries that were inflicted by her husband. Faye Copeland, the oldest woman on death row today, also appealed her case on the grounds of abuse. In Judith's case, aside from the abuse appeal, one of her lawyers was held in contempt of court and jailed for being intoxicated during her trial. Some death row inmates have been successful in appealing their cases on the grounds of ineffective counsel, but most have not. Judith Haney was given a life sentence in 1997, but Faye Copeland sits on death row in Missouri today.

According to Bryan Stevenson (1996), between 1976 and 1982, 70 percent of the death sentences imposed were reversed by federal courts due to fundamental constitutional violations. It gradually became obvious that most states were not able to meet the basic constitutional requirements in capital cases. Due to this inability to avoid constitutional errors at the state level, the responsibility to guarantee fairness in almost every single death penalty case fell, for the most part, on the federal courts. By the mid-eighties, this prompted the Supreme Court to begin limiting the power of the federal courts. Eventually, the Supreme Court could ignore everything, including evidence of innocence, if a lawyer did not comply with ever-increasing federal guidelines.

Harold G. Clarke, a Chief Justice of the Georgia Supreme Court who reviewed many death sentences in his career said, "This is a highly specialized area of law, and even good criminal lawyers may not have had much experience in capital cases" (Lacayo, 1992). A study of the Texas judicial system found that three out of four convicted murderers with court-appointed lawyers were sentenced to death, as opposed to one out of three with private attorneys (Amnesty International, 1992). Aside from lack of experience, court appointed lawyers work for very little pay, under extremely stressful circumstances, and it is safe to assume, that few, if any, know much about why women commit capital crimes.

In 1989 the American Bar Association (ABA) published the *Guidelines for the Appointment and Performance of Counsel in Death Penalty Cases* urging all jurisdictions with the death penalty to use them. The guidelines called for the appointment, by a committee, of two experienced attorneys at each stage of a capital case. The specific duties of the committee would be to identify the attorneys credentials, experience, and skills, making the need for a "specialized practice of capital representation" clear. The guidelines also stated that lawyers assigned to capital cases should receive a "reasonable rate of hourly compensation" reflective of the responsibilities death penalty litigation entails.

In actual practice, however, a number of death-penalty states, including several southern states with the nation's highest execution rates, use a system where lawyers are appointed from a list of local attorneys fresh out of law school or older ones who specialize in areas as far removed from murder as title searches and divorce litigation. For this reason, it is rare to find a court-appointed lawyer who is skilled in all the complexities of capital cases. Generally, volunteer lawyers handle habeas appeals and, according to Benavid (1996), representing "dead men walking" is complicated, time-consuming, and emotionally draining.

Within four years after the Furman decision, more than 600 persons had been sentenced to death and twenty years after *Gregg,* the Supreme Court continues to make procedural rulings on the death penalty based on what is required by the eighth amendment.

CAPITAL PUNISHMENT TODAY

In a 1997 study, Professor Michael Radalet, chairman of the University of Florida's Department of Sociology, surveyed 67 current and former presidents of the top three criminology professional organizations, The American Society of Criminology, the Academy of Criminal Justice Sciences, and the Law and Society Association. Results showed that 90 percent of the country's top criminology experts believe that imposing the death penalty in an effort to deter crime is a waste of time and money.

According to Radalet, these experts believe the death penalty never has been, is not now, and never will be a deterrent to homicide over and above life imprisonment. And he said it is highly unusual to see a 90 percent agreement on any issue among these experts.

With approximately 3,365 people on death row (1998) in the United States today, executions are moving at an alarming pace. There have been 470 executions since 1976, with 156 of these in Texas alone, 37 in 1997. Despite this high number the fact remains that if we executed one person a day for 365 days out of each year, it would take over 8½ years to empty our death rows provided no one else was sentenced to death during that time. Statistics show that in the ten-year period, between 1987 and 1997 roughly 1,000 people, or 100 a year, were added to death rows throughout the United States. Assuming this rate continued, 8 years from now we can count on at least 800 new death row inmates, at the very least.

In 1996 151 bills relating to the death penalty were submitted to 50 state legislatures. Seventeen bills were submitted in Tennessee, 13 in New York, and 11 in Illinois. These bills were directed at expanding the reach of the death penalty and at speeding up executions.

New York and Kansas have recently adopted the death penalty and there are now only twelve states that do not have it; Alaska, Hawaii, Iowa, Maine, Massachusetts, Michigan, Minnesota, North Dakota, Rhode Island, Vermont, West Virginia, and Wisconsin.

On April 24, 1996, President Clinton signed the Anti-terrorism and Effective Death Penalty Act (AEDPA). This death penalty reform act reduced the amount of habeas relief available to state prisoners on death row by establishing tighter filing deadlines for lawyers and requiring federal courts to give more deference to state court decisions.

Under the old federal statutes, federal district judges were required to review any and all claims in capital cases independently of a state court's findings to determine whether there were any constitutional violations. At the discretion of a federal judge, the decision on whether or not to hold an evidentiary hearing was made. This decision depended on the existence of one or all of eight circumstances that a prisoner had to show:

- That the merits of the factual dispute were not resolved in state court, That the fact-finding procedure used by the state was not adequate to afford a fair hearing;
- That the material facts were not adequately developed in state court;
- That the state court did not have jurisdiction over the subject matter or over the prisoner;
- That the prisoner was indigent and the state court did not appoint counsel to represent him/her;
- That the prisoner did not receive a full, fair, and adequate hearing in the state court;
- That the prisoner was otherwise denied due process of law; and/or
- The federal court concluded that the state determination was not fairly supported by the record.

Since the framing of our Constitution, lawyers have used the writ of *habeas corpus,* to delay or stop executions of death row inmates and for years Congress has tried to put restrictions on how it can be used. Now, with the signing of the AEDPA, federal judges in most cases must defer to state courts' interpretations of the federal Constitution. The act says that "State courts shall be presumed to be correct" and that prisoners "shall have the burden of rebutting the presumption of correctness by clear and convincing evidence."

The AEDPA effectively does away with repeated habeas filings. Any prisoner who has had one completed federal habeas proceeding (a decision from the district court, a decision from the court of appeals, and a chance to solicit review on certiorari to the Supreme Court) cannot file a second petition without getting "permission" from the Court of Appeals to do so. This means a prisoner must file a "request for permission to file" in the Court of Appeals, and if a three-judge panel grants permission to file, then the prisoner can file a petition in the district court. If the court refuses permission for the prisoner to file a second petition, that decision cannot be changed. The judges who decide whether the petition should be considered are supposed to base their decisions on whether or not (1) the claim is on a new rule of constitutional law that is retroactive to cases on review by the Supreme Court; (2) facts presented could not have been discovered or known before; and (3) facts, if true, will prove the person not guilty.

If the three-judge panel denies an application, that application cannot be appealed anywhere. Time limits on habeas petitions for death row inmates have been narrowed to six months (180 days) if the states where they reside have adopted the recommended procedures for appointing and paying competent counsel to handle state, though not federal, post-conviction work (Yaffe, 1996).

Recently, the Supreme Court ruled that portions of the 1996 law placing restrictions on the ability of state prison inmates, including those on death row, to receive a hearing in federal court does not apply retroactively to the petitions for writs of habeas corpus that were already pending in federal court when the law took effect. This decision overturned a ruling by the U.S. Court of Appeals for the Seventh Circuit. The decision did not rule on the substance of the law, but only on the question of retroactivity.

One former death penalty law clerk in California had a capital case with 11,000 pages in the case record. She estimated that, even if she did nothing but read all day, she wouldn't finish reading the transcripts for six weeks, which is a large part of a six-month filing time. This type of intensive labor is a major problem for attorneys who take on capital cases. According to the same clerk, by the time you finish reading the case, "You haven't talked to your client, done any investigation, or started writing." So if attorneys have any other kind of practice it's next to impossible to do a good job anywhere. In the worst case scenario a death row inmate may not have a lawyer or be able to find one before the one-year time limit for habeas petitions expires.

Among other things, the new crime bill did away with funding for Post-Conviction Defender Organizations (PCDOs), which after 1988 represented almost half of the inmates currently on death row throughout the United States. Eliminating funding for these 20 special offices nationwide tightened the process for the attorneys who depended on them. Those in favor of closing the offices said they were taxpayer-funded think tanks through which inmates were allowed endless habeas appeals. Supporters said they provided immeasurable assistance to overburdened lawyers.

At a recent conference on the death penalty in the twenty-first century (1995), it was pointed out that one of the many things that makes the death penalty arbitrary in our country today is the fact that the quality of counsel in capital cases is so irregular. It has been shown that over 90 percent of death row inmates are represented by public defenders, and that real criminal defense lawyers do not take capital cases unless there is big money involved. But, even if all the capable criminal lawyers in the country decided to work on capital cases, there just aren't enough lawyers. In Harris County, Texas, for example, there are more than 180 capital cases in the court system right now.

For this reason, the American Bar Association (ABA), which has never taken a position on the death penalty, has recommended a moratorium on capital punishment. According to the ABA, "efforts to forge a fair capital punishment jurisprudence have failed." The measure, without taking a stand on capital punishment, calls for executions to be halted until:

There is competent counsel for all capital defendants. Most, jurisdictions do not have the kind of legal services that can afford to give defendants charged with capital crimes an adequate defense. Many death penalty states do not even have working public defender systems. For the most part, capital cases are still assigned to under-qualified and overburdened lawyers, who may have little or no experience with criminal law, let alone capital cases which involve a complex body of constitutional laws and unusual procedures that do not apply in other criminal cases. Poor representation at trials increases the risk of convicting innocent people and is very costly to the taxpayer.

There is a federal review of state prosecutions. The Supreme Court has put numerous procedural barriers in place for claiming that death sentences are unconstitutional or that they were imposed in violation of the federal law. New restrictions on habeas appeals make it more likely that constitutional violations will go undetected and unremedied. Aside from this, Congress eliminated the organizations that provided expert advice and assistance to lawyers dealing with death penalty cases. Federal courts are under time limitations to rule on capital cases. The new law requires that capital cases "be given priority by the district court and by the court of appeals over all non-capital matters." A district court judge has 180 days to review and rule on capital habeas applications. The court of appeals has 120 days to make its ruling. Within these time constraints, they must fit the "preparation of all pleadings and briefs, and if necessary, an evidentiary hearing." The U.S. Congress has made the Administrative Office of the U.S. Courts the watchdog for ensuring compliance with these new time limits.

There is a notable effort made to eliminate racial discrimination in capital sentencing. No effort has been made to remedy this situation or to confront racial bias in death sentencing, even though numerous studies and reports have confirmed that it exists. The most recent study *The Death Penalty in Black and White: Who Lives, Who Dies, Who Decides* (Dieter, 1998) released by the Death Penalty Information Center in Washington, DC looks at two studies on racial disparity in death sentencing. The first study of 1,000 homicide cases in Philadelphia over a period of 10 years found that black defendants are 4 times more likely to be sentenced to death than white defendants. The second study looks at the key players who decide whether or not a person will be sentenced to death. Of the chief District Attorneys in counties using the death penalty in the United States, nearly 98 percent are white and only 1 percent is African-American or persons of color.

The ABA has also called for the elimination of executions of mentally retarded defendants and juveniles.

A 1998 report from the Death Penalty Information Center indicated that public support for the death penalty dropped below 50 percent when voters were offered alternative forms of sentencing. According to the report, more people support life without parole plus restitution to the victim's family than the death penalty. A 1995 Gallup Poll involving a randomly selected sample of 1000 adults in the U.S. reported that 77 percent favored the death penalty, responding to the question "Are you in favor of the death penalty for a person convicted of murder?" Of the 769 favoring the death penalty in this poll, the question was asked, "Some experts estimate that one out of a hundred people who have been sentenced to death was actually innocent. If that estimate is right, would you still support the death penalty for a person convicted of murder?" Of these people 74 percent responded yes, they would still support it;

20 percent said no; and 4 percent said it would depend. Of all respondents 57 percent remained in favor of the death penalty even if mistakes are made.

Likewise, a survey in April–May of 1996 by the Virginia Tech Center for Survey Research polled 1,168 adult Virginians on the death penalty. Of the respondents 76 percent favored the death penalty for convicted murderers, although a majority, 57 percent, would favor abolishing capital punishment if the option of life without parole existed.

In response to the statement "There should be a death penalty for convicted murderers," the range of responses was:

- Strongly agree   57%
- Somewhat agree   26%
- Somewhat disagree   8%
- Strongly disagree   6%
- Don't know   4%

To understand this, it is, perhaps, important to look at who has full discretion in capital cases. According to Nakell and Hardy (1987) in a typical capital punishment state, full discretion is given to:

THE POLICE who can
- fail to identify the perpetrator
- fail to apprehend the perpetrator
- decide that the homicide was justifiable or excusable, or
- decide to charge a degree of homicide less than capital (i.e.less than first-degree)
- decide whether or not to arrest a suspect on a first-degree murder charge

THE DISTRICT ATTORNEY who makes the decision whether to indict the defendant for first-degree murder can
- decide whether or not to make a charge of first-degree murder
- indict to trial or to reduce or dismiss the charge with or without plea negotiations
- decide whether or not to present the first-degree murder charge to a grand jury or to reduce or dismiss it
- decide whether or not to submit the first-degree murder charge to the jury
- decide whether to convict on the first-degree murder charge
- decide whether or not to ask for a death sentence
- decide whether or not to affirm the conviction and death sentence
- decide whether or not to execute the death sentence

Other decision-makers involved in this process are:

THE PROSECUTING ATTORNEY who, with or without negotiating with the defendant, can

- decide not to seek an indictment because she/he believes the evidence as to homicide or the evidence identifying the perpetrator is insufficient or that homicide was justifiable and thus excusable
- decide to seek an indictment for a degree of homicide less than first-degree murder
- decide after indictment to accept a guilty plea to a degree of homicide less than first-degree or to some other crime (i.e. armed robbery) committed by the defendant, or
- decide to pursue at trial a charge less than first-degree murder

THE GRAND JURY which might
- decide to return an indictment for a degree of homicide less than first-degree murder
- decline to indict for homicide, or
- indict

THE TRIAL JUDGE who can rule on
- the admissibility of evidence, or
- what degree of homicide, if any, the jury will be allowed to consider, or
- whether to grant a new trial after a guilty verdict
- the punishment the jury can recommend
- whether or not to impose the death penalty

THE SENTENCING JURY which might find
- that no aggravating circumstances exist, or
- that mitigating circumstances outweigh any aggravating circumstances, or
- that, based on the aggravating and mitigating circumstances the recommended sentence should be life or death

THE STATE SUPREME COURT which can
- reverse the conviction, or
- reverse the death penalty, but not the conviction

THE GOVERNOR who can
- grant pardon
- grant commutation

Discretion describes a wide range of autonomy (Nakell & Hardy, 1987), but there is a legal context that imposes limits on its range. Discretion in the criminal process is the difference between formal law and law in action. Although laws are written by legislators and interpreted by courts, they are applied by human beings who are ultimately individuals acting largely on their own personal interpretation of a situation.

PROSECUTORS

According to Stephen Bright (1995) of the Southern Center for Human Rights in Atlanta, the "Two most important decisions in any death penalty case are the prosecutor's initial decision whether or not to seek the death penalty and his/her subsequent decision whether or not to allow a plea for a sentence less than death." "And," says Bright, "it's completely subjective."

On a daily basis, prosecutors make life and death decisions based on their personal beliefs about the evidence presented, about the credibility of witnesses, about the law, about burden of proof and many other factors, and no one disputes their judgments in these matters.

A former federal prosecutor in Richmond, Virginia said, "Prosecutorial discretion is a recognized aspect of the law. Sometimes it's arbitrary. When death is an option, it looks real arbitrary. I don't think we should give people, especially elected officials, the power to make those kinds of subjective decisions."

As a society, we choose to believe that people on death row, including women, are there because they have committed the most horrible and unspeakable crimes. However the reality, for most women on death row, is that they have committed the kinds of crimes that cannot be easily distinguished from the crimes of hundreds of other individuals. The difference is, the other individuals are living out life terms in our state and federal prisons or walking the streets of our cities as free men and women.

In many cases, two people equally involved in the same felony murder are given different sentences. As a society we need to ask why. According to the International Commission of Jurists (*Human Rights Quarterly,* 1997), one of the main reasons is that "there is no judicial or administrative control over the prosecutorial discretion of District Attorneys" who are empowered to seek the death penalty. Another reason is that "Decisions concerning which defendants shall live and which shall die are left to the uncontrolled and unbridled discretion of individual prosecutors." One criminal lawyer, who represented about 20 capital defendants, said the whole process is arbitrary and capricious and depends on the prosecutor, the city and, the victim.

Professor Edward Chikofsky, who teaches courses on capital punishment at Fordham University, said at a 1995 conference on the death penalty, "I am unaware of any jurisdiction that has any kind of formalized guidelines or oversight review about how an individual prosecutor's office decides whether or not to seek the death penalty in a particular case." Death sentencing continues to be a game where winners and losers are determined by the luck of the draw. The ethnic and economic backgrounds of the accused, the region in which the crime occurred, the dispositions of the police and prosecutors, the skills of the court-appointed lawyers, and the personal prejudices of judges and juries are all variables in the game.

JUDGES

Most judges in the United States are elected to office. They run for office on political platforms and, in some states, party affiliation. This means, in effect, that a judge's campaign money comes from individuals he will later be required to make decisions about or pass judgment on.

With little interference or interest from higher courts, no two judges and no two juries are alike. Applications of the law vary from county to county, from court to court, from state to state. Judges have no clear rationale for their sentencing practices, nor do federal or state laws provide adequate guidelines for them to follow. Some judges, known as "hanging judges" hand out the death penalty more than others. Federal Judge Marvin E. Frankel, a prominent critic of sentencing practices, asserted that nothing in a judges training or experience prepares him or her for understanding criminals (1973). According to Frankel, judges are not uniformly humane and compassionate. He said relatively few judges have any experience in defending criminals, and almost no judges have experienced the socioeconomic conditions under which the vast majority of offenders live. This lack of parallel experience should be cause for concern, since judges make irrevocable decisions about people's lives.

To further complicate matters, a judge's decisions are based on circumstances that are not always clear-cut, such as, the extent to which a woman/man participated in a crime, whether she/he was provoked, and whether she/he poses a future threat to society. Although many women on death row today are convicted of being the actual perpetrators of their crimes, some are there for conspiracy to commit murder, and others were given the death penalty for merely being at the scene of a crime committed by someone they accompanied.

Recently, Florida Supreme Court Chief Justice Gerald Kogan, who presided over some 1,200 capital cases in his career, said he had three objections to capital punishment in Florida, which he believes is not working: (1) innocent people are executed, (2) it is not a deterrent to crime, and (3) it places a tremendous burden on the court system.

JURIES

A much-debated concept that arose out of the desire for fairness in death penalty sentencing is that of "death qualified jurors." The Sixth Amendment to the U.S. Constitution guarantees everyone the right to a trial by an impartial jury; and for a death sentence to be imposed, a jury must unanimously agree to recommend it. Yet, to avoid the possibility that any juror would vote against the death penalty simply because she/he opposes capital punishment, all jurors in capital cases must indicate that they are willing to vote to impose the death penalty in at least some circumstances [*Witherspoon v. Illinois*, 391 US 510, 88 S.Ct. 1770 (1968)]. Jurors who agree to this are called "death qualified jurors." Individuals who cannot agree to recommend the death penalty under any circumstance are called "excludables" and are prohibited from serving on capital juries. Research has shown that death-qualified jurors are more prone to conviction than death penalty excludables (Blankenship et al., 1997), which is one argument against a process that supposedly guarantees fairness.

In a 1997 report on the Administration of the Death Penalty in the United States (*Human Rights Quarterly,* 1997), the International Commission of Jurists stated that the practice of "death-qualification" is a useful tool with which the prosecutor can create a jury predisposed to convict. Because of this, the Commission found that the requirement of death-qualified juries introduces an element of unfairness into the death sentencing process. Since, ideally, a jury represents a cross section of the entire community, in capital sentencing, a death-qualified jury represents only a cross section of those who would, given the right circumstances, impose the death penalty. The Commission felt that this is very close to creating a "hanging jury" where a sentence of death is the inevitable outcome and, in actual practice, "death-qualified" juries become "death-determining juries."

Most recently, in an article in the *Journal of the American Statistical Association* (Stasny, Kadane, & Fristsch, 1998) research showed that excluding people opposed to the death penalty from serving on juries in trials where the defendant may be sentenced to death can bias the results of the trials.

Five capital punishment states (AL, FL, DL, IN, CO), also have a jury override provision which means if a jury in a capital trial recommends one sentence, state law empowers the trial judge to override the recommendation of the jury and impose another. Although the jury override was created to allow a judge to overrule a jury's recommendation of death (Lafferty, 1995), in actual practice the jury override has been used by judges to impose a sentence of death over a jury's recommendation of life. According to Lafferty (1995), between 1972 and 1982 one of every five death sentences in Florida involved an override of a jury's life recommendation by a judge imposing death.

In describing his experience as foreman of the jury in a capital trial, one former juror explained:

We were instructed to use the information we were given. We could not ask questions either from the judge, witnesses, or attorneys. We could not take notes. What you heard is what you made use of. You had to decide as to what you felt was evidence. I can say that I felt the information would have been different had the accused had money.

The same individual went on to explain that since it must be a total agreement of all twelve jurors in a capital case, for twelve people to say "death" to another human being is a very intense thing. In commenting on his personal philosophy, he stated

As a Buddhist, I can't say take a life but there seems to be the possibility that some people could have such disregard for murder and suffering that it is for other's protection and benefit that a person needs to be stopped. So the negative Karma can be broken.

THE SUPREME COURT

In 1998, the Supreme Court used the case of convicted murderer and rapist Thomas Thompson to rebuke the Ninth U.S. Circuit Court of Appeals for delaying executions. The justices were divided in their ruling by a 5–4 vote. Justice Anthony Kennedy presented a 26-page majority opinion that stated, in effect, that executions are going too slowly. "Finality is essential to both the retributive and deterrent functions of criminal justice" Kennedy wrote (Carelli, 1998). Justices David Souter, John Paul Sevens, Ruth Bader Ginsburg, and Stephen G. Breyer dissented.

Also in 1998 the Supreme Court ruled on limiting how death row inmates challenge the applicability of the Anti-terrorism and Effective Death Penalty Act of 1996. Under the Act only states that provide post-conviction legal help to death row inmates qualify to impose new deadlines. Troy Ashmus, a death row prisoner in California sued in federal court to disqualify the state of California from the new deadlines and a federal trial judge ruled that California had not met the act's requirements. The Ninth Circuit Court of Appeals upheld the ruling. Nevertheless, the U.S. Supreme Court overturned both decisions. Chief Justice William H. Rehnquist wrote that Ashmus' lawsuit was "not a justiciable case within the meaning of Article III (of the U.S. Constitution)." Thus, according to the Supreme Court, the federal courts do not have authority to rule on it. Rehnquist further explained that federal courts have the power to rule on "controversies" but not to hand down advisory opinions. According to the Court, the "controversy" between Ashmus and California was whether he was entitled to have a federal court overturn his conviction or death sentence. The question of whether or not California qualified for the expidited law had to be decided in an inmate's appeal not in a preliminary challenge (*Calderon v. Ashmus,* 97–391).

At a 1997 meeting in Portland, Oregon, of about 450 judges, court officials and lawyers in the Ninth Circuit Court of Appeals, U.S. Supreme Court Justice Sandra Day O'Connor said the flurry of last-minute appeals as executions approach is "one of the most worrisome aspects" of her job. She said that the Supreme Court would appreciate it if states would stop setting executions for as late as midnight.

Executions in western states, many of which are in the Ninth Circuit, are often at midnight Pacific Time, which leaves the U.S. Supreme Court dealing with matters as late as 3 a.m. Eastern Standard Time. Justice O'Connor said that dispensing justice at that time of day is difficult at best.

In 1991 Chief Justice William H. Rehnquist called for changes in the death penalty appeals process. He said then that the system invited delays in executions that extended for years. More than 11,000 federal appeals had been filed the year before.

In response to this call, the Supreme Court reversed its own commitment to reviewing cases to ensure that innocent men and women are not put to death. In 1993, the case of *Herrera v. Collins* [506 US 390, 113 S.Ct. 853 (1993)], the Court held that the Constitution does not protect condemned state prisoners from execution *even if there is new evidence of innocence*. In his opinion, Chief Justice Rehnquist wrote of "the very disruptive effect that entertaining claims of actual innocence would have on the need for finality in capital cases." In other words, it is much less disruptive to execute someone than to entertain the possibility that she/he might be innocent — even if there is evidence that she/he is. A strange theory of justice, indeed.

Justice William Brennan was one of the last true liberals to sit on the Supreme Court of the United States. His tenure in the Supreme Court spanned eight presidencies. Many of his decisions infuriated conservatives, but nowhere was his activism more evident than in his opinions on capital punishment. Brennan thought the death penalty was unconstitutional not just when it was unfairly applied, but always. He never stopped speaking out against it and on his ninetieth birthday, he called capital punishment "a barbaric and inhuman punishment that violates our Constitution." He based his opinion on the Eighth Amendment, which states "Excessive bail shall not be required, nor excessive fines imposed, nor cruel and unusual punishments inflicted." Justice Brennan felt that the execution of a person by the state cannot be anything other than cruel and unusual.

Former Supreme Court Justice Lewis Powell, a Nixon appointee and a once staunch supporter of capital punishment, said he would change his decisions in all cases in which he voted to uphold the death penalty, if he could because "it serves no useful purpose and brings discredit on the whole legal system."

Shortly before his retirement, Supreme Court Justice Harry A. Blackmun, who for more than 20 years voted to enforce the death penalty in scores of cases, vowed, "From this day forward, I shall no longer tinker with the machinery of death. I feel morally and intellectually obligated simply to concede that the death penalty experiment has failed and no combination of procedural rules or substantive regulations can ever save the death penalty from its inherent constitutional deficiencies."

And Chief Justice William O. Douglas commented in *Furman v. Georgia* that "one searches our chronicles in vain for the execution of any member of the affluent strata of this society" (1972, p. 2733).

DISCRIMINATION

In 1987 the Supreme Court ruled that statistical evidence of discrimination was insufficient to render the death penalty statutes unconstitutional in the case of Warren McCleskey, a black man who was executed in the electric chair in Georgia for killing a white Atlanta policeman in the robbery of a furniture store in 1978.

In 1987 McCleskey [*McCleskey v. Kemp,* 481 US 279, 107 S.Ct. 1756 (1987)], the defendant, argued that Georgia's use of the death penalty was racially biased. He based his claim on a study conducted by a University of Iowa Professor, David Baldus (1990). This study established that defendants accused of killing whites are 4.3 times more likely to receive the death penalty than defendants accused of killing African Americans, and black defendants are more likely to be executed.

In a 5–4 opinion written by Justice Powell, the Supreme Court accepted the data that documented racial bias in Georgia's death penalty but also upheld McCleskey's death sentence. Powell said, in effect, that inequities based on race are "inevitable" in the administration of capital punishment, and this is something state legislatures need to address. After retiring from the Supreme Court upon being asked if he had any regrets, former Chief Justice Powell indicated that if he could change one decision he made, it would be McCleskey. Warren McCleskey, of course, did not benefit from this afterthought since he was executed.

Regional differences are powerful factors in death sentencing and executions. Since the 1880s executions in southern states have exceeded the numbers in other regions (Schneider & Smykla, 1991). From 1935 to 1969, southern states executed 1,887 persons, the highest numbers being from Georgia, Texas, and Florida (Zimring & Hawkins, 1986). Although studies are yet to appear about how southern attitudes toward women may influence the likelihood of a woman being sentenced to death, it is worth noting that 23 of the 47 women currently on death row are in southern states.

Researchers have long been aware of patterns in death-sentencing practices in the United States. Quite often a death sentence depends not so much on the crime as on where it was committed and who committed it (Gross & Mauro, 1983). Across the board, African Americans are punished more severely than whites, the poor more severely than the rich.

During the 1970s and 1980s about half of the people on death row at any given time were African American (Bedau, 1984). In Texas, African Americans who kill whites are six times more likely to receive death sentences than African Americans whose victims are African American. In Florida, African Americans who kill whites are 40 times more likely to end up on death row than whites who kill African Americans (Bedau, 1984). Bedau (1984) noted that of the 3,862 persons executed between 1930 and 1980 in the United States, 2,077, or 54 percent, were African Americans.

Professor David Baldus (1990) proposed the idea of limiting the death sentence to cases where it would be applied to everyone guilty of certain crimes. In other words, have state courts devise a way of identifying what they consider more serious murder cases, and only those that fit their strict criteria could be tried as capital cases. This would limit the amount of discretion open to prosecutors and juries and reduce the influence of factors such as race. The result would be a more uniform application of the death penalty. However, while agreeing in theory, Stanford Law Professor Samuel Gross suggested that determining which murders are more heinous and which are less might not be an easy task.

Gross was responsible for an eight-state study confirming Baldus's finding that the race of a murder victim plays a determinative role in who gets the death penalty when the defendant is black and the victim is white. Professor Richard Berk of the University of California, Santa Barbara, did a similar study in Mississippi confirming both the Baldus and Gross findings.

Richard Broday of the NAACP Legal Defense and Educational Fund said, "You can't have a death penalty without racism. The only way to eliminate racism in the death penalty is to eliminate the death penalty itself."

In 1991 the Justice Department reported that blacks made up a much larger percentage of death-row inmates than of the nation's population and in 1991 blacks comprised 40 percent of prisoners awaiting execution.

MENTAL RETARDATION

To date, 18 mentally retarded offenders have been executed. The states with statutes forbidding execution of the mentally retarded are Arkansas, Colorado, Georgia, Indiana, Kansas, Kentucky, Maryland, New Mexico, New York, Tennessee, Washington, and the federal system.

THE COST

In his concurring opinion in *Furman v. Georgia* (1972), Chief Justice Thurgood Marshall wrote, "When all is said and done, there can be no doubt that it costs more to execute a man than to keep him in prison for life."

A number of studies have shown that the expense of putting someone to death is greater than the expense of keeping him/her in prison for the rest of his/her life at every stage, from the pretrial investigations to the ultimate execution. The reported cost of the trial and conviction of Timothy McVeigh, convicted in the Oklahoma bombing, was $50 million. This included the costs of the prosecution, the government, the FBI, and the defense. In 1992, the Administrative Office of the U.S. Courts estimated the cost per defendant in death penalty cases was $337, 500.

An execution in Florida costs about $3.2 million for each death penalty case, as opposed to $700,000 to house an inmate for life, that is, until she/he dies of natural causes. And a recent study of two capital cases in Kentucky (Blakely,

1990) estimated a cost of approximately $2.5 million and $7 million each, as opposed to approximately $700,000 to $800,000 to imprison for life.

In New York, the latest state to reactivate its capital punishment statutes, the New York State Defender's Association projected the potential cost of litigating a capital case through a trial and the appeals conservatively at $1.8 million (Graddess, 1988).

Professor J.W. Vanderhoof, Professor of Criminal Justice Studies at the University of North Carolina in Pembroke, said, "I tell my students that the most important financial decision in a death penalty case is that of the prosecutor. It is that decision — and whatever motivated it — to seek the death penalty which is the combination to the treasury."

The death penalty is a statement society makes to show it has a response to those who harm the most vulnerable and innocent. But, because we are human, whether or not it is a wise and appropriate response will continue to fuel debates for many years to come.

2

Alabama: Electrocution

The state of Alabama has sentenced ten women to death since 1900. Three of these, Selena Gilmore, Earle Dennison, and Rhonda Belle Martin were executed. There are three women on death row in Alabama today.

Alabama began using the electric chair, its "Yellow Momma" (nicknamed because of its bright yellow color), in 1927. The first chair was built by a Ed Mason a prisoner and cabinetmaker who was serving a sixty-year sentence for theft and grand larceny. It was installed in Kilby Prison in 1923 because that was the main prison in the state at the time. It remained there until 1970, when it was moved to Holman Prison where it now sits in a room by itself with the control mechanisms in an adjoining room. Between 1930 and 1976 there were 135 executions (107 black, 28 white). The last woman executed in Alabama was Rhonda Belle Martin in 1957. Since 1977, there have been 17 executions in the state.

The minimum age for execution in Alabama is 16, and seven of the prisoners currently on death row were 16 or 17 years old at the time of their crime.

EXECUTIONS IN ALABAMA

Alabama changed to electrocution from hanging in 1923 and it is still the only official method of carrying out a sentence of death specified in the Alabama Code. As early as 1983 the state Senate Judiciary Committee voted in favor of using lethal injection in place of electrocution, however, that bill ultimately failed. Again in 1997 a bill was discussed which would allow those scheduled to die the option of lethal injection. In discussing the proposed change, Representative Paul Parker (D) said, "Lethal injection would be less unsettling to executioners, and would leave the condemned killers' bodies more intact for funerals and lessen the risk of a botched execution."

In its death penalty history, Alabama has experienced some troubling executions. For example, in April 22, 1983, when John Evans was hit with the first jolt of electricity, which lasted 30 seconds, his body tensed up, causing the electrode on his left leg to snap off. Within seconds smoke and flames shot out from under the hood that covered his head, and when two physicians entered the death chamber they found him still alive. Ignoring his lawyer's plea, a third jolt of electricity was applied and he died. The execution took 14 minutes and left Evans' body charred and smoldering. Alabama law allows application of electricity to a condemned person until the person is dead, regardless of how long that takes.

Alabama also has a history of executing retarded inmates (Applebome, 1989). In 1989 the state executed Horace Dunkins, who according to court records had an IQ of 69, despite the fact that another man had pleaded guilty to the crime. Dunkins was convicted of murdering Lynn McCurry, a 26-year-old mother of four, who was found tied to a tree behind her home and stabbed 66 times. The man who pleaded guilty to the murder is serving a life sentence for it today.

In Dunkins's execution the first jolt of electricity only knocked him unconscious. The warden, Charles Jones, said that because the jacks connecting the electricity to the chair had been reversed, there was not enough voltage to kill him on the first try. Somewhat apologetically, the warden explained that even though they check the equipment all the time, these things do happen. It took 19 minutes for Horace to die (Tran, 1989).

When the state of Alabama electrocuted Edward Horsley, Jr., shortly after midnight on February 16, 1997, his last statements were inaudible because the prison had yet to install a speaker in the room. But, according to the NAACP, as Horsley was being electrocuted, the Deputy Commissioner of Prisons, E.G. "Red" Sanders, was having a loud, jovial telephone conversation which everyone present could hear. First he swapped a meat loaf recipe and then went on to discuss a football game. The warden finally interrupted his phone call to inform him that the prisoner had been executed. Horsley's attorney, Steve Hawkins, and three friends witnessed the execution.

In 1998 Steven Allen Thompson waived his appeals saying he wanted to spare his victim's family and his own family any further pain and was executed in Alabama's electric chair on Friday, May 8. He had been found guilty of the brutal murder of 25-year-old Robin Balarzs of Huntsville. She was bound, gagged, beaten, raped, stabbed and then dragged 300 feet behind a car after Thompson robbed her of $1 and an engagement ring. Ms. Balarzs had a 3-year-old son at the time she was killed. Her mother attended the execution saying it was not for vengeance but to show that someone cared about her daughter.

Executions in Alabama take place at midnight and cost the taxpayers about $10,000 in overtime for each one. State officials say that setting executions for 12:01 a.m. gives the state the maximum time to carry out an execution on a 1-day death warrant.

RACIAL DISCRIMINATION IN ALABAMA

Recently (September 1997) the Alabama Supreme Court reinstated the capital murder conviction of Levi Pace in a 7–1 ruling. Previously, Pace had shown that Morgan County, Alabama, where he was being tried, had a lengthy history of racial discrimination in the selection of grand jury forepersons and that prosecutors had acted wrongly in excluding blacks from serving as head of the grand jury that indicted him. In its ruling, the Supreme Court stated that the discrimination involved did not amount to a "plain error" which would be a violation of Pace's rights, and thus reversed the previous decision of the Alabama Court of Criminal Appeals that had overturned Pace's conviction.

The Supreme Court agreed that Pace's constitutional right to equal protection was violated due to racial discrimination, but since Pace did not file a motion in time to prevent his indictment, the court had to decide whether the violation was severe enough to have violated his due process rights. The court decided it was not severe enough for two reasons, written and presented by Justice Terry Butts:

Jury forepeople are chosen after a grand jury is impaneled and since there was no question in Pace's case that the jury was properly constituted, the fact that the foreperson was wrongly chosen was not a severe error, and

The role of the foreperson in Alabama courts is largely a clerical position with little power to affect the outcome of a grand jury.

Since the death penalty resumed in 1975, 77 percent of those executed in Alabama have been black men. In recent years, Alabama state courts have had to reverse 18 capital cases due to overwhelming evidence of racial bias.

In Birmingham recently (1997), Pierre Sane, the head of Amnesty International, said that Alabama's death penalty laws are just as racist today as they were in the years of segregation. He said, "Although the practice of excluding blacks from juries has been ruled unconstitutional by the Supreme Court, Alabama continues to systematically engage in this practice especially when defendants are black."

In another unprecedented case, the execution of Henry Hays in 1997 was Alabama's first execution in eighty-four years for a crime in which the defendant was white and the victim black. Black people in Alabama make up 26 percent of the population, 2 percent of the prosecutors, 4 percent of the criminal court judges, and 66 percent of the prison inmates.

Although less than 11 percent of all murders committed by black defendants in Alabama involve white victims and 60 percent of black death row inmates are awaiting execution for white victim cases. Each year in Alabama, 67 percent of all homicide victims are black, yet less than 23 percent of capital cases involve black victims.

Walter McMillan spent six years on Alabama's death row because the state built a case against him on perjured testimony, and it withheld crucial evidence that would have proven his innocence. McMillan believes he was given the death penalty because he was a black man in a relationship with a white woman and because his son is married to a white woman, both racial and sexual taboos in Alabama.

In Monroeville, Alabama, known as the home of Harper Lee's *To Kill a Mockingbird*, Rhonda Morrison, an 18-year-old white woman was murdered in a dry cleaning store in 1986. The police had no suspects until eight months after the crime when Ralph Myers, a 30-year-old man with a long criminal record, was arrested for another murder. Under intense grilling by the police Myers told them that McMillan had murdered the girl some seven months earlier and that he had witnessed the murder (Applebome, 1993). Walter McMillan, who had two jobs, no criminal record, and no history of violence, was arrested immediately and, in an unusual move, sent to Alabama's death row in Holman State Prison. By profession, he was a pulpwood worker; he was married and had nine children. In a trial that lasted one-and-a-half days he was convicted on the testimony of three state witnesses.

The state's key witness, Ralph Myers, said that McMillan had asked him for a ride to the dry cleaners the day of the murder and while they were there he saw McMillan murder Rhonda. Friends and relatives of Walter testified that he was at a fish fry on the day and at the time of the murder. No physical evidence ever linked McMillan to the crime, and all three of the witnesses received favors from the state for incriminating him.

The jury recommended a sentence of life-without-parole; however, Judge Robert E. Lee Key changed the sentence to death saying it was a "vicious and brutal killing of a young lady in the first full flower of adulthood."

When Brian Stevenson, head of the Alabama Equal Justice Initiative, got involved in the case he found numerous incidences of lies and missing evidence. After listening to a tape of the testimony against McMillan someone flipped it over to the other side and heard a key witness complain about being pressured by the police to frame McMillan. Eventually all three prosecution witnesses recanted their testimony, and every element of the prosecution's case was discredited. In March 1993, all charges against McMillan were dismissed and he was freed (Casteneda, 1993), but his six years on death row will not soon be forgotten.

THE DEATH PENALTY IN ALABAMA TODAY

Governor Fob James, the 55th Governor of Alabama and the only Alabaman who was first elected governor as a Democrat (1978) and then re-elected as a Republican (1994), counts among his accomplishments the revision of the Alabama Criminal Code, making it one of the toughest in the nation. He also boasts of the construction of three prisons to house dangerous criminals, and of the fact that he was governor when the death penalty was legalized in Alabama.

After the execution of Karla Faye Tucker in Texas in 1998, Governor James was quoted as saying that gender would not make any difference to him in weighing whether or not to spare a condemned killer from the electric chair. "Every case has to be measured on its own merits regardless of gender," he said. However, with three women still on death row in his state, Governor James may have to consider the issue in the near future. In Alabama the governor can decide independently of the Board of Pardons and Parole whether to commute a sentence.

Jimmy Fry, a popular Alabama district attorney, said, "I'm a typical Southern conservative — so there are some things you generally believe in, and the death penalty is one of them. If you ask me if its more likely that a poor person will go to the electric chair than a wealthy person, then I'll say yes every time. Poor people are also more likely not to have good teeth. It's not fair, but life's not fair. If all the people on death row were killed tomorrow we would be a safer nation."

J. D. White, a former death row warden in Alabama, stated, "There is no such thing in our country as swift and sure punishment. We have the best system in the world, but no swift or sure punishment. We tend to perform executions quietly behind closed doors, for the deterrent effect. I think it should be a swift, public affair."

The Equal Justice Initiative (EJI) of Alabama was conceived and incorporated in Montgomery. Funds were provided through a McArthur Foundation Grant given to Attorney Bryan Stevenson to continue providing legal services to death row prisoners and capital defendants after the Alabama Capital Representation Resource Center was forced to close due to the withdrawal of federal funds. As such, the EJI has attempted to maintain many of the services previously provided by the Resource Center.

In the initial regrouping, the staff was reduced from thirteen to nine. While the number of attorneys available to work on capital cases decreased, the actual number of capital cases increased. As of 1996, 240 people were awaiting capital murder trials in Alabama.

There are many cases in Alabama where the accused have been sent to death row without due process. In Alabama's counsel assignment system, inexperienced attorneys are frequently assigned to cases in small towns where they know everyone and are afraid of reprisals if they become tough advocates for their clients. Alabama pays court-appointed lawyers who represent indigent death row inmates $20.00 per hour for all out-of-court work. This fee hasn't been changed since 1981. The state caps attorney compensation at $1,000 or 50 hours. Experts and those who have been through the process estimate the minimum number of hours needed to prepare a capital case is 500.

As part of the solution, capital cases in Alabama have been farmed out. Currently, law firms outside the state represent approximately 35 out of 150

Alabama death row cases. To accomplish this, Bryan Stevenson goes on recruiting trips to places such as New York, Philadelphia, and Boston, where he addresses bar associations. Outside law firms also hook up with the Alabama project through such things as the American Bar Association's Post-Conviction Death Penalty Representation Project. These firms usually take cases that are in the appeals process and do the bulk of their work on federal appeals. One New Jersey firm explained they took a case of two men accused of murder and sentenced to death because there "seemed to be a very compelling case for the innocence of both men."

It seems such a commitment is necessary since most death penalty defenses have very little glamour. For example, Attorney David Wadyka of the firm of Hannoch Weisman said that Hannoch spent about $1 million in attorney time since 1991, using a team of five attorneys and a paralegal for a client, Richard Townes, who was executed on January 23, 1996. Looking back, Wadyka said the benefit of the case was the satisfaction that Townes "got the best representation he could possibly have gotten. We could not have done anything more than we did."

JUDICIAL OVERRIDE IN ALABAMA

Alabama's capital sentencing scheme, like that of Florida, has a judicial override (Russell, 1993). Both states require trial by jury and jury participation in the sentencing process, but both give the ultimate sentencing authority to the trial judge. A sentence of death in both states is subject to automatic appellate review.

However, the two states differ in one important aspect. The Florida Supreme Court requires that the trial judge give *great weight* to the jury's recommendation and she/he may not override the advisory verdict of life unless the facts suggesting a sentence of death are so clear and convincing that virtually no reasonable person could doubt it. This is referred to as the Tedder Standard [*Tedder v. State,* 322 So. 2d, at 910] and also applies to a jury's recommendation of death.

In Alabama, the capital sentencing statute requires only that the judge *consider* the jury's recommendation, and Alabama courts have refused to put the Tedder Standard into their statute. This basic difference between the two states was the source of the controversy about whether the Eighth Amendment to the Constitution required a sentencing judge to give any particular weight to the recommendations of a jury. In resolving this question, the Supreme Court acknowledged that while sentencing power resides with the jury in most states, when a state reaches a decision about how best to administer its criminal laws the Eighth Amendment is not violated. It, therefore, rejected the idea that Alabama should be made to change its laws and make the jury the final arbitrator of life or death (Russell, 1993).

There have been 55 jury overrides from a life without parole recommendation to a death sentence since capital punishment resumed in Alabama. In nearly 25 percent of all death cases, the trial judge overrode the jury's sentencing verdict of life imprisonment without parole. Out of 55 jury overrides, 53 defendants were male and 2 were female.

WOMEN SENTENCED TO DEATH IN ALABAMA

The prison where women are held on death row in Alabama, Tutwiler Correctional Facility, is named after Julia Strudwick Tutwiler (1841–1916), who was said to have been born fifty years ahead of her time. Known for her work in both education and the prison system, she was a poet and author, and one of her poems became the Alabama state song in 1931.

Julia Tutwiler was well known to state legislators and governors of her day, and through her forceful persuasion, the state prison system underwent a complete renewal. It was through her efforts that separate prisons for men and women were built, and it was Julia who succeeded in getting juveniles separated from hardened criminals. She also established the first prison board and the first sanitation program responsible for inspecting all the state prisons; she also initiated schools and religious services in Alabama prisons which she herself attended each Sunday morning.

1930

Selena Gilmore: Black; Executed, 1930. Silena Gilmore herself believed that corn liquor was her downfall. After several hours of heavy drinking one night, she went into a restaurant and ordered some food to go. When she was told she'd have to wait for her order, she became loud and rowdy, and was ultimately asked to leave.

Accordingly, she went home, loaded her shotgun, returned to the restaurant and shot the waiter who had thrown her out. She was black, the waiter was white. On January 24, 1930, she was executed, singing hymns and telling others to beware of the evils of corn liquor.

1953

Earle Dennison: White; Executed, September 4, 1953. Earle Dennison was convicted of first-degree murder in the death of her 2½-year-old niece, Shirley Dianne Weldon, by giving her arsenic. Everyone agreed that Earle was never quite herself after the death of her husband. She was a trained nurse and had worked for more than 25 years on the nursing staff at the Wetumpka General Hospital, where she was employed up until the time of her arrest.

After her arrest Earle confessed her crime to two different people. One confession was to Mrs. Edwina Mitchell, who was the superintendent of the

Julia Tutwiler Prison for Women in Wetumpka. Apparently, after Earle was arrested she took an overdose of sleeping pills with the intention of committing suicide. The attempt was not successful, and Earle was in Wetumpka Hospital for four days and then transferred to the hospital ward at Tutwiler. When Superintendent Mitchell asked her if she had anything to say after she woke up, she made a confession that Mitchell wrote down and Earle signed. In it she said she had given her niece poison in a glass of orange juice, and that after her niece got sick and vomited, she gave her Coca-Cola that also had arsenic in it. This too made her niece sick, and when she vomited again Earle took her to the hospital. By then it was too late and the child died a few hours later.

Her second confession was made on the same day as the first to the toxicologist, Dr. Rehling, who performed the autopsy on her niece and affirmed that she had died of arsenic poisoning. Traces of arsenic were found on a measuring cup, the Coca-Cola bottle, and her niece's dress. Dr. Rehling summarized Earle's confession and gave it to her to sign, which she did.

Before her niece died in the hospital, Earle paid a $500 premium on the child's life insurance for a policy in the amount of $5,000, for which Earle was the principal beneficiary.

Earle was the first white woman executed in Alabama, which the governor said he deeply regretted but could find no basis for preventing. Male family members were the only witnesses at her execution.

1957

Rhonda Belle Martin: White; Executed, October 11, 1957. Rhonda Belle Martin was tried and convicted of poisoning her fourth husband. She signed a confession after his death saying that she had put poison in his coffee over a period of several months preceding and during his fatal illness. She ultimately admitted poisoning several people including three husbands, her mother, and three of her daughters over a number of years.

During her trial, much was made of the fact that she had married her husband's son after her husband's death, and there was a great deal of discussion about whether or not such a relationship was incestuous according to Alabama law. The prosecution felt strongly that a desire to marry her stepson might have been sufficient motive for Rhonda to poison her husband.

Her principal defense was that she was insane at the time of the murder. A psychiatrist testified that he had examined Rhonda and that in his opinion she was schizophrenic. Her lawyers, therefore, tried to prove that because of her schizophrenia Rhonda was not responsible for her actions.

Before her execution, she left a note asking that her body be left to science so someone could find out why she committed the crimes. She said she couldn't understand it herself, because she had no reasons that she knew of for doing it.

1978

Debra Bracewell: White; Reversed in 1981. Debra Bracewell was sentenced to death for murder in May 1978. She was on death row for three years when her sentence was reversed in 1981.

1981

Patricia Thomas: White; Reversed in 1990. Patricia Thomas was sentenced to death for murder in December 1981. She was on death row for nine years before her sentence was reversed in 1990.

1983

Judith Ann Neelley: White; Currently on death row. Judith Ann Neelley was 17-years-old when her attorney dubbed her the "Bride of Frankenstein." This was a reference to her association with her husband, Alvin Neelley with whom she is believed to have participated in at least fifteen murders in three states (Alabama, Tennessee, and Georgia). Alvin was 12 years older than Judith and an ex-con who had been incarcerated for shooting his first wife. In their exploits together, the two of them called themselves "Night Rider" and "Lady Sundance."

During a time when Judith was incarcerated for armed robbery, she gave birth to twins, and when she and Alvin were on their crime sprees the twins were often with them, in the back seat of the car.

In September 1982, Judith kidnapped 13-year-old Lisa Ann Millican from a shopping mall in Rome, Georgia because, she said, Alvin told her he wanted her to find him a woman. Later she said that she had picked Lisa because her husband had specified he wanted "a virgin" and Lisa looked like Richie Cunningham's sister.

Lisa Millican was a resident of a facility for neglected girls in Georgia and was out on a shopping trip with a supervisor and other residents on the day she encountered Judith Neelley. Judith and Alvin each had their own cars and when they were out looking for victims they would keep in touch by CB radio. Judith usually drove around in a Brown Dodge with her twins in the back so she looked like a typical mother, which made it easier to convince people to go with her. When Lisa got in her car, Judith took her to a motel room where Alvin was waiting and the two of them molested her repeatedly over a period of days. When they decided they'd finished with her and wanted to move on, Judith handcuffed Lisa to her in the front seat of her Dodge and took off with the twins following Alvin who was in his red 1975 Ford Granada. They stopped at a secluded picnic area in a place called Little River Canyon where Judith injected Lisa with Liquid Plumber and Drano, saying it would put her to sleep so they could escape. Judith had heard that a mixture of the two would effectively kill someone and it would appear to be a heart attack. But, it did not work on Lisa, who was left instead writhing in pain from the torture in the motel room, from fear, and from having the solution injected in her neck, arms, and buttocks.

According to the record, Alvin was upset that the solution had not killed Lisa and told Judith to go get the gun and shoot her. At his bidding, Judith got a gun and took Lisa to the edge of the cliff where she told her to look out over the canyon. When Lisa started begging for her life Judith shot her in the head. Her body did not fall into the canyon as Judith had hoped it would, but rather fell backwards. So Judith dragged the body over to the edge and rolled it off. She then threw the syringes, Drano can, and her blue jeans, which had been splattered with Lisa's blood, into the canyon with Lisa's body.

A few days later, seemingly unaffected by previous events, Judith was out looking for a new victim for Alvin and approached John Hancock and his roommate Janice Chatman as they were returning from a visit with Janice's mother. Judith saw them walking down the street and drove up and told them she was from out of town and wanted to ride around and talk. The two of them agreed to ride around with her for a while. After they got in the car, she drove to a rural area in Georgia where Alvin was waiting. During the drive Judith talked to Alvin on her CB and later Hancock remembered their handles were "Night Rider" and "Lady Sundance."

When John got out of the car to relieve himself Judith pulled a gun on him and told him to start walking. She then shot him in the back. The bullet hit him in his right shoulder, and he immediately fell and pretended to be dead. Leaving him for dead, Judith and Alvin took Janice to a motel where they spent the night raping her. The next day Judith shot Janice and began once more to look for a new victim.

For reasons that have never been established, after Lisa Millican's murder, Judith called the police and told them where they could find Lisa's body and then called a local radio station and told them about it, adding that the perpetrator had been an officer at a local juvenile facility. The police were finally able to tie Judith Neelley to the case when they looked at a list of former residents of the juvenile home and Judith's name was on it. One of the things John Hancock told the police was that the woman was riding around with twin babies in the car and one of the workers at the juvenile home remembered that Judith had given birth to twins when she was 15 years old.

When the police started looking for Judith and Alvin they found them already in custody in Murfreesboro, Tennessee where they had been jailed for passing bad checks. John Hancock was able to identify them and after their arrest they confessed to a number of crimes and provided the police with details of certain crimes that only the perpetrators could know. Both gave the police full confessions.

Judith claimed that as a battered wife she was forced to do her husband's bidding and that he had forced her to participate in his crimes. Alvin, on the other hand, claimed it was actually Judith who planned and executed their victims. But, regardless of what was said, John Hancock positively identified

Judith Neelley as the one who shot him in the back.

After pleading guilty, Alvin Neelley was given two life sentences in Georgia and Judith was tried in Alabama for the murder of Lisa Millican. On March 22, 1983, a jury found her guilty of capital murder but recommended that she be spared the electric chair. A judge overruled the decision and sentenced her to death.

In 1998 Judith Neelley was nearing the end of years of challenges to her conviction. After Karla Faye Tucker's execution in Texas, Alabama State Senator Lowel Barron (D) said that while Karla's case may have brought some attention to Judith Neelley, he strongly believed she deserved to be executed and would oppose any effort to spare her.

"I have a feeling for everyone including Judith Ann Neelley," Barron said. "But, I also remember vividly how she and Alvin subjected 13-year-old Lisa to sexual torture for hours in a Scottsboro motel, then carried her over to Little River Canyon, injected lye in her veins, shot her, and threw her off. Anyone who commits a heinous crime like that should be put to death."

1988

Judie M. Haney: White; Reduced to life in prison without parole, 1997. Judie Haney admitted paying her brother-in-law to kill her husband in 1984. She said her motive was more than 15 years of physical abuse. Court records show that Judie told her sister and brother-in-law that she would give them all the money she had if they would make sure her husband did not bother her any more. After that, her brother-in-law, Jerry Henderson, shot Jerry Haney to death.

Judie's attorneys later claimed that her court-appointed lawyers failed to obtain hospital records of treatment for injuries that were inflicted by her husband. "If the jury had appreciated the role of the abuse Judie Haney and her children had suffered, it would have been a very strong mitigating factor," said Judie's attorney, Stephen Bright.

A hospital worker initially said Judie's treatment records could not be found, but one of the trial attorneys, Gould Blair, located them — after Judie had already been sentenced. During her trial, Blair was held in contempt and jailed for a night after the judge concluded he was intoxicated in the courtroom. "This kind of trial has no place in the legal system," Bright said. But the jury members did not witness Blair's drunkenness and were not told about it. Later, Blair said he deeply regretted the drinking incident. He insisted, however, that Judie Haney undermined her own defense by taking the stand, against his advice, and leaving the impression that she had masterminded the crime. He said, "She was not underrepresented one bit."

In October 1997 Judie's sentence was reduced to life without parole with the agreement of the state prosecutors and the family of the victim, Jerry Haney. The agreement had several conditions, including one that Judie cannot have the sentence reduced any further. If she fails to comply with the terms the state may reimpose the death penalty.

1988

Altione Walker: White; Reversed in 1992. Altione Walker was sentenced to death in December 1988 for hiring two of her nephews to kill her lover, William Berry, for $100. She had been trying to end her abusive relationship with Berry and testified she was afraid he would kill her because he had already killed one woman he had abused and had served six years for manslaughter. Berry was shot with a 12-guage shotgun and a hand pistol and his body was found in a forest. Both Altione and one of her nephews, James Charles Lawhorn were sentenced to death. Altione spent four years on death row and her sentence was reversed in 1992.

1989

Louise Harris: Black; Currently on death row. Louise Harris was convicted and given the death penalty for planning the murder of her husband, a deputy sheriff. At the time of his death, it was said she was having an affair with a man named Lorenzo McCarter, whom she supposedly asked to find someone to kill her husband. According to court documents, McCarter approached a co-worker about the murder, but the co-worker refused and reported McCarter to his supervisor. Later, McCarter found two men who were willing to do it, Michael Sockwell and Alex Hood. Sockwell and Hood were each given $100 and a promise of more money to come after the murder.

It was reported that on the night of the murder, Louise Harris called McCarter on his beeper when her husband left work. McCarter and Hood then waited in a parked car on a nearby street, and Sockwell hid in the bushes next to a stop sign. When Harris's husband stopped his car at the intersection, Sockwell jumped out and shot him, point blank, with a shotgun.

Louise was arrested for murder, after questioning, and McCarter agreed to testify against her about the conspiracy in exchange for the prosecutor's promise not to seek the death penalty in his case. Thus, McCarter testified that Louise had asked him to kill her husband so they could both share in his death benefits, which totaled about $250,000.

With McCarter's testimony, the jury convicted Louise of capital murder. At the sentencing hearing, a number of witnesses attested to Louise's goodness and strong character. She was raising seven children, held three jobs simultaneously, and participated actively in her church. Because of this, the jury recommended by a 7–5 vote, that she be imprisoned for life without parole. However, the trial judge exercised the Alabama jury override in deciding to sentence her to death.

The judge said he found one aggravating circumstance, that the murder was committed for money, and one statutory mitigator, that Louise Harris had no prior criminal record. The judge also said a non-statutory mitigating circumstance was that Louise Harris was a hardworking, respected member of her church and community. Nevertheless, noting that Louise had planned the crime and financed its commission and stood to benefit the most from her husband's murder, the judge concluded that the one statutory aggravating circumstance outweighed all of the non-statutory mitigating circumstances, and that the sentence ought to be death.

In separate proceedings, all the conspirators were convicted of capital murder. McCarter and Hood received prison terms of life without parole; Sockwell, the triggerman, was sentenced to death after the trial judge rejected a jury recommendation, again by a 7–5 vote, of life imprisonment. The Alabama Court of Criminal Appeals affirmed Louise Harris's conviction and death sentence in 1992.

Louise Harris's case was argued before the U.S. Supreme Court on December 5, 1994 [*Harris v. Alabama* 632 So.2d 503 (1992)] and decided on February 22, 1995 (Muallem, 1996). Justice Sandra Day O'Connor delivered the opinion of the Court stating that the compatability of Alabama's death penalty scheme with the protection granted by the Eighth Amendment was examined, and that since the Alabama death penalty scheme allows a trial judge to override a jury's recommendation, the Supreme Court upheld the decision. The Supreme Court further noted that there is not one correct way for a state to set up its death penalty scheme and that there is no constitutional requirement of a specific method for balancing mitigating and aggravating factors in considering a death penalty. Nevertheless, statistics reveal that Alabama trial judges overrides are consistently biased and overwhelmingly work to the detriment of defendants. From death row in Alabama, Louise said:

There are victims on both sides when a person is locked up away from their family especially the children. They hurt having to deal with where their mother is at and what she is accused of. Because all they know is this is my mother and I love her. Prison life is no fun. It is a nightmare the only difference is you are awake.

Regarding her life on death row, Louise says:

The rules change all the time. You never know what to expect. There is never any privacy. They know what you have all the time...how much of it you got...and take what you have if they want to and it is nothing you can do about it. And people say inmates have it made in prison. Not in Alabama prison...and I believe why people that get out of prison commit more crimes is because they leave prison with a lot of hate that has built up — because jail and prison change a person to be very mean from the way they are treated.

1994

Lynda (Block) Lyon: White; Currently on death row. Lynda Lyon and George Sibley, are one of three husband and wife teams on death row in the United

States. Both were convicted of killing Opelika, AL, police officer Roger Lamar Motley in a Wal-Mart parking lot on October 4, 1993. From death row in Alabama, Lynda wrote:

My case is highly political, involving not just Alabama, but Florida, California, and Connecticut as well. I published a political magazine from Orlando and made political enemies in high places. Even now, my husband and I have been warned that there may be attempts on our lives. It is internationally known (we have supporters in 9 other countries) that we are taking our case to Congress.

Lynda is arguing her case on the contention that she fired on Officer Motley in self-defense and to protect her husband when she heard shots ring out and saw the officer shooting at her husband. She says that she and her husband are wrongfully imprisoned and charged with capital murder because, even though it is unconstitutional, public officials are seen to have more rights and more intrinsic worth than other Americans and, therefore, are given preferential treatment.

Lynda, a professional writer and publisher, and George, a legal researcher and counselor, met and were married in Orlando, Florida. In her book *Captive Hearts* (1996) Lynda remembers it like this:

It was fate and a libertarian philosophy that brought George and me together at a Libertarian Party meeting in Orlando, Florida, 1991. George helped me launch a new magazine—*Liberatus*—and we published hard-hitting articles about political corruption. We pioneered a revocation process that eliminated driver's licenses, school board surveillance on my home-schooled son, IRS demands, and state revenue notices.

Lynda was using an outdoor pay phone in front of a Wal-Mart outside of Opelika, AL, when Officer Motley approached the car where Lynda's husband, George, was waiting for her, with her son. Motley had been requested to check them out by a woman who decided, after pulling up alongside of them that they were homeless.

According to Lynda, when George looked in the rearview mirror of their Mustang hatchback and saw the police officer approaching their car, he got out, closed the door, and waited next to the car to see what the officer wanted. When Officer Motley ordered him to produce his driver's license, George said he didn't have one and turned to get his exemption papers out of the car. At this point, for reasons that are still unclear, the officer decided to arrest Sibley and told him to put his hands on the car. When George hesitated the officer reached for his gun and George reached for his at the same time. Motley then ran for cover behind his police car and they started firing at each other.

Lynda reported hearing "popping noises," which she did not, at first, recognize as gunfire. But, when she turned away from the phone and saw Officer Motley in a crouched position behind his car, she realized immediately what was going on. At that point, she dropped the phone, drew her own gun, and fired at Motley from behind. As he turned toward her, one of her bullets struck him in the chest and he fell backward. Then, with his gun still aimed at her, he crawled to his car and somehow managed to get in and drive away, though mortally wounded.

George Sibley had also been shot in the exchange, but he managed to drive their car out of the parking lot. Being unfamiliar with the area, they were unable to avoid traffic and, traveling at speeds of up to 100 mph, they drove until a police roadblock eventually stopped them. Lynda's son, presumably frightened by what had just taken place, was crying in the back seat of their car.

Lynda said her motherly instincts kicked in when she heard her son crying and she rolled down her window, held up her hand, and yelled, "Stop, I have a child in the car." With that she kissed her 9-year-old son goodbye and let him out of the car. As her son walked away, the police shouted for them to surrender, but the two of them held out for four more hours.

According to Lynda, they discussed the shooting and what they planned to do in the future. Neither wanted to spend the rest of their lives in prison and they knew that if Officer Motley died they would be charged with capital murder and most likely given the death penalty. Meanwhile, the police had brought in a negotiator. When he asked them what they wanted, Lynda printed their terms in a notebook, which she held up for them to see:

- To talk to my son
- To talk to the press
- To talk to the clergy of my religion

The negotiator originally agreed to grant all of their requests if they surrendered, but, according to Lynda, they lied to lure the two of them out of the car and, in the end, granted none of their requests. Ultimately, they were surrounded by a SWAT Team, and George told Lynda, "If we surrender, it will take years to resolve this," to which Lynda replied, "At least we'd be fighting it together." Within a few minutes, they kissed each other goodbye and got out of the car with their hands up. Eventually, in two separate trials, both Lynda and George were given the death penalty.

In a November 1995 press release (*The Lyon-Sibley Update*) from death row, George and Lynda indicated that they were using their death sentences to bring to light the unconstitutionality of police privilege. According to their statement, the original recently discovered Thirteenth Amendment, on which they are basing their argument, forbids the acceptance and retaining of titles of nobility and positions of privilege and honor by public officials, so that all those who hold office and hold such positions of privilege must forfeit their citizenship.

In May 1996, Lynda and George bypassed the Alabama appeals courts and all lower federal courts and took their appeal to the Supreme Court stating that their incarceration is unconstitutional and without jurisdiction because they acted in self-defense in the shooting of Officer Motley. They demanded their immediate release on the evidence of three facts:

- That the original Thirteenth amendment forbids retaining titles of nobility and positions of privilege by public officials;

- That the ABA is an unconstitutional monopoly in control of the judiciary;

- That all state and federal laws make the killing of a law enforcement officer a capital offense, because he/she is a law enforcement officer, regardless of any mitigating circumstance. This confers unconstitutional privilege to law enforcement officers in violation of the original Thirteenth amendment, which forbids such privilege.

Because they deliberately bypassed all state and federal courts, they cannot return to those courts. The Supreme Court refused to hear their case, so they are now taking their appeal to Congress, which, under certain constitutional grounds, can take such cases.

The Alabama Court of Criminal Appeals has affirmed the conviction and death sentence of Lynda and George. Both Lynda and George refused to participate in the court's review of their cases and refused to have any attorneys represent them. In 1996, the Alabama Court of Criminal Appeals sent their cases back to Lee County for the trial judge to determine if both knew the consequences of refusing an attorney for their appeals. The court upheld their convictions saying they were satisfied that the two of them fully understood what they were doing when they waived their right to an attorney for their appeals. Thus the Court of Criminal Appeals affirmed their convictions.

Alabama Court of Criminal Appeals Judge Sue Bell Cobb who wrote the opinion in Lynda's ruling, stated that "The appeal of [Lyon's] conviction has been anything but routine." Cobb pointed out that the only procedural difference in the cases of George Sibley and Lynda Lyon is that Lynda acted as her own attorney. George had an attorney during the trial, but he refused to appeal or accept an attorney for an appeal, Cobb wrote.

During the automatic appeal of their cases, neither George nor Lynda filed appellate briefs with the Court of Criminal Appeals. However, both remain on death row in Alabama today, working on their appeals, doing research, and writing documents which, Lynda has indicated, will be presented to Congress at the appropriate time. Regarding this Lynda recently wrote:

We are finishing up the last portion of the Petition to send to Congress. George and I have drafted formal charges of Fraud and Treason against five judges, 3 prosecutors, and an assistant state Attorney General; and have implicated in these charges another judge, 5 lawyers, a court clerk and a court-reporter all of whom were involved in either the Florida or the Alabama cases. These charges are addressed to Congress and will be sent along with the Petition. These are those ABA judges and prosecutors who knowingly committed Fraud against us and Treason against the United States because they were informed of their lack of jurisdiction under the true Thirteenth Amendment, yet disregarded the evidence we presented and proceeded against us anyway; and the lawyers and the court reporters who knowingly participated in the fraud against us. Copies of these charges are being sent to those charged and implicated, and as the ABA judiciary have become aware of our plans to bypass their court altogether and zealously pursue the issue of their treasonous acts under the true Thirteenth Amendment, various members of the judiciary and other ABA agents have been deserting the fight against us.

When George and I withdrew from the Appeals Court, the Court appointed lawyers to take over our appeals, without our knowledge and consent. We immediately charged the lawyers with "barretry." Within a week they begged the Appeals Court's permission to withdraw. The Court reluctantly granted withdrawal and did not attempt to "give" us lawyers again.

After we spurned their attempt to force lawyers upon us, the Appeals Court ordered us to be taken back to the trial judges for a hearing to determine whether we were mentally capable of handling our own appeals. George and I weren't going to play that game. When the judge, in front of a courtroom full of spectators, including the dead officer's family, tried to question us about our education and experience, we refused to answer and only told him that he had no legal standing to force us to participate in his charade. The judge fell into an embarrassed silence, the prosecutor grew apoplectic with rage, and the spectators stared in astonishment. We left a stunned, silent courtroom without having yielded at all. The judges never forced us back to court again.

On September 29, in a TV interview with me which was broadcast on "Inside Edition" I let it be publicly known that George and I were not having any more to do with ABA courts, that we were taking our appeal straight to Congress. The next day, the Assistant State Attorney General who was handling our case for the state of Alabama withdrew from the case and resigned from the Attorney General's Capital Murder division altogether.

When the Appeals Court affirmed my conviction and sentence the newspapers stated that two of the judges had excused themselves from the case, without explanation. Two lawyers, one assistant attorney general, and two appeals court judges have backed away from our case so far. We expect the body count to grow now that we have made formal charges against the principal agents. George and I have always kept in mind that these judges, prosecutors and lawyers are not demi-gods — they are power-hungry mortals used to intimidate the public. They have discovered that they do not intimidate us, that we have seen that they are not the Wizard of Oz, but only small men inside black robes with pious attitudes. We will soon expose them for the imposters they are.

Lynda said two booklets she wrote (*The ABA, America's Shadow Government* and *Captive Hearts*) and intentionally left copyright-free so that they could be distributed without charge have been stolen by a man she describes as a "thief and a cheap hustler." According to Lynda he left her name on the books as the author and is selling them for his own profit.

3

Arizona: Gas/Lethal Injection

The state of Arizona has sentenced three women to death since 1900. One of these women, Eva Dugan, was executed, and there is one woman on death row in Arizona today.

Arizona resumed capital punishment in 1992, and twelve people have been executed in the state since then. Former Governor Fife Symington, convicted of criminal activity himself, proposed and signed into law some of the toughest, most effective criminal justice legislation in the United States. This included a new truth-in-sentencing provision that eliminates parole and mandates that every convict now serve no less that 85 percent of his/her sentence.

The state uses lethal injection to execute condemned inmates sentenced after November 15, 1992 and those sentenced before that date may choose either gas or lethal injection. In June 1998 Arizona held its first daytime execution. Douglas Gretzler was executed at 3:00 p.m. Under a new rule signed by Chief Justice Thomas Zlaket, an execution must take place during a 24-hour-period beginning at whatever time the Director of the Department of Corrections decides. So, for example, if the time is set for 3:00 p.m. the execution can take place anytime until 3:00 p.m. the following day.

A spokesman for the Arizona Department of Corrections reported everything went extremely well with Gretzler's execution saying, "Carrying out an execution in the daytime proved to be a success." Likewise, the state Assistant Attorney General said it was a huge success and much easier to do during regular business hours.

Two weeks prior to an actual execution, the Arizona Department of Corrections conducts a dry-run of the execution process including a "mock" execution using supplies and drugs which have expired. A medical training device is used to practice intravenous insertion. Debra Milke, the only woman on death row in Arizona, recounted the trauma of going through this rehearsal when her last appeal at the state level was rejected.

She was given forms to fill out — what she wanted for her last meal, who the witnesses would be, and what she wanted done with her body after execution. The chaplain visited her and spoke of guilt and atonement, then the prison psychiatrist visited to make sure she was sane enough to be executed, and finally, a doctor who checked her arms and rolled her veins to determine where the best spot for a lethal injection would be.

EXECUTION IN ARIZONA

For an execution in Arizona two "operations teams" are put in place. One team consists of four members who have the responsibility of restraining the condemned person. The other team of four is responsible for the execution itself, including inserting the intravenous lines and administering the drugs. Arizona requires that team members complete a psychological examination and teams are rotated for each execution. Critical stress debriefing is mandatory for the restraining and operations team following an execution.

Three drugs are administered during an execution in the following sequence:

- 5g. with dilutent of sodium pentothal;
- 10mg. of Pavulon (generic name for pancuronium bromide);
- 2mEq/ml of potassium chloride.

Arizona authorizes no more than five witnesses selected by the condemned offender and these must have a letter of invitation from the warden approved by the director of the Arizona Department of Corrections in order to attend. Victim witnesses, media witnesses, and official or state witnesses may attend only if they have a letter of invitation from the director if the Department of Corrections. Witness team escorts are also authorized to attend.

Arizona is one of the states that have executed mentally ill inmates. In 1996 Luis Mata was executed despite being described as suffering from "significant brain damage that affected almost every aspect of his life."

On January 1, 1998, Arizona executed Jose Jesus Cejas, the inmate who had been on death row 23 years, the longest of any inmate in Arizona. He was executed for the 1974 shooting deaths of Randy and Linda Leon, a young Phoenix couple. He had gone to their home with the intention of stealing marijuana. He shot Linda Leon twice in the chest with a .22-caliber pistol, then dragged her body into the bedroom where he used a pillow to muffle four more shots to her head. When Linda's husband came home, Cejas shot him four times. Cejas later attended the funerals of the couple and offered assistance to the police in finding the murderer.

The Arizona Supreme Court rejected an emergency stay of execution shortly after the clemency board voted 4–1 against commuting Cejas's sentence to life imprisonment. Cejas's wife attended his clemency hearing and testified that her husband had told her he planned the robbery and murders. She said he had "no remorse for anything he's done and if he had it to do again, he would." The board also saw letters Cejas had written to his wife threatening to kill her as a punishment.

In a strange turn of events, a former judge, Melvin McDonald, who sentenced Cejas to death twice, filed an affidavit on his behalf in which he said he no longer thought Cejas should be executed. He said that in his 23 years on death row Cejas was a model prisoner who earned his high school equivalency diploma, took college classes, and worked at various prison jobs to stay out of trouble. The former judge said, "Had I an inkling of Cejas's potential for improvement I would have sentenced him to life imprisonment and not death."

About 30 people witnessed the execution, but no family members were present at Cejas's request. The drapes were opened at 12:01 a.m. Cejas had no final words, but he did leave a written statement in which he appealed to attorneys throughout the United States to stop representing clients who may be given the death penalty, as a protest. He lay on the gurney with his arms strapped to his sides and with a white sheet covering him from the waist down. He was given injections in both arms and witnesses said the execution was very subtle. He was pronounced dead at 12:05. State officials classified the execution as "calm, cool, and clinical."

Also on death row in Arizona is Viva LeRoy Nash who is 81 at the writing of this book and is believed to be the nations oldest death row prisoner. He lives in solitary confinement inside an 8 by 9-foot cell at the Arizona State Prison in Florence. He has had five heart attacks over the last 15 years and takes two heart pills and aspirin each day and is on a low-fat diet. He spends his time reading law books and writing to pen pals. Nash has been in and out of prisons since he was 16, when he first served time for stealing a car. When Nash was in his sixties he escaped from the Utah State Prison where he was serving time for aggravated robbery and second-degree murder. While he was on the run, he murdered a Phoenix coin shop employee, for which he was given the death penalty. Nash says he is no threat to society and would like to be transferred to a nursing home.

LEGAL REPRESENTATION IN ARIZONA

In 1998 the appeals process was brought to a halt in Arizona. The state had adopted competency standards for death penalty lawyers after Congress passed the new death penalty law in 1996 and provided for a $7,500 flat fee for anyone representing condemned prisoners in post-conviction appeals. These are the appeals in state court after the Arizona Supreme Court upholds a conviction and death sentence and before a case is appealed in the federal courts.

With fees at a $7,500 cap few lawyers applied for appointment to existing cases and those who did frequently withdrew their applications. The main complaint was that doing a post-conviction appeal could take more than 500 hours of work. Issues not raised at that stage cannot be argued later in federal court. So, if you are going to do it, you need to do it right the first time the lawyers said. They felt that when you are talking about a person's life the responsibility is awesome.

WOMEN SENTENCED TO DEATH IN ARIZONA

1928

Eva Dugan: White; Executed, 1928. At age 52, Eva Dugan was convicted of murder and executed largely on circumstantial evidence. Her alleged victim was her employer, who was also a rancher. People speculated that her motive was the possibility of inheriting his property. However, she fled the state in his car shortly after his death and served a year in New York for car theft.

The body was discovered a full year after the crime, and there was some doubt that Mrs. Dugan was strong enough to have dealt the fatal deathblow. She accused a drifter named Jack of committing the murder, but Jack was never found.

Eva had two children and while she was on death row never divulged the whereabouts of her son, although her daughter wrote to her occasionally. Her main contact was with her elderly father who lived in California.

In her last interview before she was executed, Eva Dugan passed a hat for donations so she could pay for her burial plot and funeral expenses. She had been sewing handmade items to raise money, and her father had sent her his last $50.00 to help out.

In her will she left her son and daughter "A kiss across a thousand miles of heartaches." She also gave "heartfelt thanks" to those who had befriended her, and to those who had been unkind she gave "forgiveness and a wisp of hemp." Cheerful to the end as Mrs. Dugan faced the executioner she shook the warden's hand, kissed each of the prison guards she had grown close to and ascended the steps of the gallows.

When she was hanged, on February 21, 1930, she was decapitated due to a debilitating muscle disease that had weakened her neck. Seeing her executed in this way was so revolting that some witnesses fainted. Her decapitation caused enough public outrage that hanging, as a form of execution, was banned in Arizona.

1933

Winnie Ruth Judd: White; Commuted and sent to a state mental hospital.
Born and raised in a well-to-do Illinois family, Winnie Ruth moved to
California to study nursing. In California she met and married a wealthy
physician, Dr. William Judd. While there she contracted tuberculosis and was
sent to Phoenix in hopes the dry air would cure her condition. In 1931 she
moved in with two friends, 30-year-old Agnes Ann Le Roi and 23-year-old
Hewig Samuelson. The three women shared a bungalow and were happy for a
few months. But then Winnie started thinking that Agnes and Hewig were
stealing her many male admirers.

She was 25, with a good figure, copper hair, large blue eyes; and she had a
number of male suitors. Nevertheless, she confronted her two friends on the
night of October 16, 1931, and asked them why they were interfering with her
love life. Both women laughed at her, she claimed. So, she pulled out a small
revolver and shot them. She then crammed their bodies into a trunk and booked
a reservation on the Golden State Limited, to return to California, planning to
take the bodies with her. When a train porter arrived at the house and told
Winnie that her trunk was too heavy to be shipped as personal luggage, she told
him it was full of medical books belonging to her husband. The porter
suggested she rearrange the books into two trunks and she agreed to do so.

She had the porter take the large trunk to an apartment she had rented and
there she removed Hewig's body and sawed it into pieces so that it would fit
into a smaller trunk and a suitcase. She then shipped the three pieces of
luggage to Los Angeles and climbed aboard the Golden State Limited to head
there herself.

Once she got to Los Angeles, she took a taxi to the University of Southern
California and went to the political science building to see her 26-year-old
brother, Burton, who was teaching there. She begged him to accompany her to
Union Station to retrieve her trunks. "We must take them to the beach and
throw them in the ocean," she told him. She was quite frantic in her
conversation with him and he noticed her hand was bandaged. Later it was
learned she had purposely shot herself after she shot her two roommates hoping
to claim she'd killed them in self-defense.

Burton went with her and at Union Station they claimed the two trunks and a
large suitcase. The baggage clerk noticed one of the trunks smelled like a dead
animal and he suspected Winnie and her brother of being meat smugglers
because deer were being illegally shipped into the Los Angeles area at the time.
He also noticed a dark sticky substance oozing from one of the pieces of
luggage. The baggage clerk told them he had to inspect the luggage before he
could turn it over to them, but Winnie quickly told him her husband had the
only key. Then she left with her brother.

When detectives opened one of the trunks in the station they were shocked to
find Hewig's dismembered corpse. When they picked up Burton, he said his

sister had told him there were "two bodies in the trunks and the less you know, the better off you are."

Police found Winnie hiding in a building at the La Vena sanitarium where she had been a patient. She had been there for three days sneaking into the kitchen at night to get food. During this time her husband had placed an ad in the local newspaper begging her to come home. When Winnie's hand became infected and she needed medical attention, she turned herself in. After being arrested, Winnie was extradited to Arizona to be tried for the murder of her two friends.

At the trial she held up her hand and said that Hewig had shot her and that she'd struggled with her for several minutes. Winnie's mother and other relatives testified that the family had been afflicted with insanity for years. Winnie made a point of looking as crazy as possible by appearing in court with wild hair and by continuously ripping at her clothes and mumbling to herself throughout the trial. Once, she jumped up, pointed to the jury and shouted, "They're all gangsters." Later she told her husband "Let me throw myself out the window." Finally, when she became hysterical, guards removed her from the courtroom. The court agreed she was insane, but the jury nevertheless sentenced her to death. While she was awaiting execution Winnie was declared officially insane by prison doctors and was sent to the Arizona State Mental Asylum, from which she escaped.

In 1952 when Winnie was captured they found a passkey in her hair and a razor under her tongue. She was taken back to the asylum she had escaped from. In 1962 she escaped again and went as far as Concord, California, where she became a live-in housekeeper for Ethel and John Blemer. In December 1971 the Arizona Parole Board commuted Winnie's life sentence to time served, and she was released.

Winnie returned to the home of Ethel and John Blemer, and when Ethel died in 1983 Winnie sued for her estate, claiming the Blemers had kept her as an indentured servant. She was eventually awarded $225,000 plus $1,250 a month for life.

1991

Debra Jean Milke: White; Currently on death row. In 1990 Debra Jean Milke was convicted of first-degree murder, conspiracy to commit first-degree murder, kidnapping and child abuse in the death of her 4-year-old son, Christopher. The child abuse conviction was overturned on appeal. Since 1991 Debra has been the only woman on death row in the state of Arizona.

At the time of her son's death, Debra was living with her son and a roommate, James Lynn Styers. She worked at an insurance company while Styers, a disabled unemployed veteran, watched his 2-year-old daughter and Christopher. The Supreme Court records state that Debra persuaded Styers and his friend Roger Mark Scott to kill her son because she didn't want him to grow up to be like his father and wanted to claim Christopher's insurance money. Debra Milke's Mother, Renate Janka, tells her story this way:

After a disastrous marriage to Mark Milke, who was addicted to both drugs and alcohol, Debbie wanted to forge a new life for herself and their son Christopher. She had been in love with Mark, but his addictions, his physical and sexual abuses, his numerous times in jail leaving Debbie and Christopher without income or any human support made it impossible for her to keep the marriage going and her son safe.

Debbie knew that Christopher loved his father and, for that reason she granted Mark liberal visiting rights, and, it is true "SHE DID NOT WANT HER SON TO GROW UP LIKE HIS FATHER" — after Christopher's murder, this statement Debra made came back to haunt her. It was taken completely out of context and used by the police and the press as a motive for Debbie's alleged conspiracy in the murder of her only and beloved child.

In 1989, after Mark was released from prison, Debbie let him spend a day with Christopher. Later, when she went to pick Chris up, Mark was high and acting irrational, and ended up attacking Debbie. He grabbed her by the throat and tried to choke her and in the struggle, took her car keys and threatened to kill her and take Chris. When he refused to give her car keys back, Debbie took Christopher and ran. Petrified that Mark would come after them, she hid behind a dumpster until she was sure he was not pursuing them. By the time she felt safe enough to come out, it was late at night. She was stranded with her son and without her car. It was then that she found a phone and called Jim Styers whom she had met through her sister Sandy.

She knew Jim did not drink, smoke, or curse, and that he went to church on a regular basis, so she trusted him. When Jim learned of her situation he offered to let Debbie and Christopher share the apartment with him and his 2-year-old daughter. At first, Debbie refused, but she had been staying with Mark's mother, and she was afraid Mark would find her if she returned there, so she agreed to stay with Styers, at least temporarily, until she could find and afford a place of her own.

Debbie was never romantically involved with Jim Styers and at her trial, Debbie testified that they had a strictly business arrangement. Styers, a Vietnam veteran, had killed before and frequently hallucinated about women and children he'd killed in Vietnam. But Debbie did not know that when she agreed to stay with him.

At the time Debbie moved in Styers was undergoing psychiatric treatment and was on heavy medication. Perhaps because of her own state of mind, Debbie didn't notice anything strange about him, and he was always respectful to her. But, her ideas began to change when she found he had purchased a gun and ammunition and had taken the children (who were only 2 and 4 years old) to the desert "snake hunting" with a loaded weapon. She was angry about that and wrote to tell several other people and me what he had done. The gun, which was kept in a holster hidden in Styer's closet, was still there in its normal location the day Chris was reported missing. And when the police asked Debbie if Styers owned a gun she said yes and showed it to them.

She wanted Styers to keep his guns out of the children's reach. For this reason on the night before the murder, when Debbie was sorting laundry and found some bullets in a pair of Styers's blue-jeans, she grabbed them and put them in her purse. Her idea was to dispose of them or to put them where the children would not find them. On the day of her arrest, her stepmother found them and, at Debbie's trial, speculated in the worst possible light about what having them in her purse might mean.

In August 1989, Debbie began working for an insurance company in Tempe. Since Mark had never returned her car, she relied on Styers for transportation. Styers, who was unemployed and living on a government pension, began to see himself as her protector and only hope in a somewhat obsessive way. For her part, Debbie was happy to be working toward supporting herself and her son and was making plans to move out and be on her own. She had started to check out affordable housing in Tempe and had found a good day school for Christopher. Her employer had offered her a benefit package with a rider for a nominal standard life insurance for both her and Christopher, which was another point that was terribly misconstrued by the prosecutors in her trial. Debbie never purchased a separate insurance policy for Christopher, as the press and the prosecutors insisted she did.

In September of 1989, my husband and I visited Debbie and Christopher and were very proud of how she was tackling her life and problems. We wanted to help her out, and we purchased a car for her and she insisted on setting up an account to pay us back, which she did until the time of her incarceration. Debbie also had a new boyfriend at the time, but neither she nor her boyfriend was interested in rushing into a marriage. Both expressed a desire to get their careers on the way and to wait and see what might happen in the future.

During our visit in 1989, we met Jim Styers, and he had a very negative reaction to the way we were encouraging Debbie to set up her life. By then, she had begun to think about moving out on her own and getting a place for her and Chris, although she did not actually begin looking for an apartment until early November when she felt she could afford it. She also felt obliged to give Jim enough time to find someone else to share his household expenses. He had helped her in her time of need and she did not want to leave him stranded. Therefore, in late November after she was approved for an apartment, she told him and us that she would move out in January 1990, which would give him five weeks to find a roommate. Ultimately, Styers begged Debbie to stay with him, which she had no desire to do, and one-week later, her son Christopher, the love of her life, was dead.

There is speculation that Styers may have felt that if Debbie lost the only thing that mattered to her in her life, her son Christopher, she would have no one to turn to except him, but only Styers really knows what he was thinking.

Debbie has always been terribly naive and trusting, and when Styers asked her if he could use her car to go to the mall on December 2, 1989, she readily agreed. Christopher overheard them talking about it that morning and asked his mother if he could go to the mall with Styers and have his picture taken with Santa. Debbie asked Styers if this was O.K. and he agreed. Christopher selected his favorite outfit (for the picture) and dressed himself. Debbie checked to make sure he looked OK and then hugged him good-bye, not knowing she would never see her son again.

Styers left with Christopher in Debbie's car and went to get his friend Scott, whom Debbie knew very little about. He then took Christopher and Scott to get pizza and afterward drove out to the desert. There one of the two men shot Christopher in the back of the head three times, killing him instantly. It is still unclear who actually did the killing because both men deny having pulled the trigger. It was Scott who led the police to Christopher's body.

We now know that after the murder of my grandson the two men drove to the mall and stayed there for a while before Styers drove Scott home. Afterward, Styers went back to the mall and contacted the mall security to say that Christopher was missing, and he called Debbie at 1:00 p.m. and told her that Christopher was nowhere to be found.

I talked to Debbie the same day this happened and she was incoherent and terrified. All of us immediately thought that her ex-husband had kidnapped Christopher. I told Debbie to trust the police (a bad mistake). Debbie thought a child molester might have abducted her son, and never once considered Styers might not be telling the truth. Later, our son-in-law called us with the news that Christopher had been found murdered in the desert and I collapsed at the news. But it got worse a few hours later when we were told that Debbie had "confessed" to Christopher's murder to a Detective Saldate, the homicide investigator. This was completely incomprehensible to me. I knew that could not possibly be true.

The day after Christopher was reported missing Debbie was barely able to function and was with her father and stepmother in Florence, Arizona. At the time, she had no idea that the police had interrogated either Styers or his friend Scott. Detective Saldate flew to Florence to interrogate Debbie and called ahead to tell the Pinal County sheriff's office to take Debbie to the county jail. Before Saldate's arrival Debbie was sick with fear over what might have happened to Christopher.

Once he got to the jail, Detective Saldate excluded all other law enforcement officers from the interrogation and took Debbie into a room with a steel door and closed it. The two of them were completely alone the whole time. Later, Saldate claimed he made notes during their conversation, which he destroyed and never showed to anyone. There was no audio or video recording made during the interrogation either. Later, however, reportedly from memory, Saldate wrote up Debbie's alleged "Confession," a document that Debbie never saw or signed.

Saldate began his interrogation by telling Debbie that Christopher had been murdered. While she was trying to grapple with the impact of this news, Saldate claimed he read her her rights. Of course, no one else was present, so it was her word against his. But, even after Debbie heard the news of Christopher's death, she never grasped that anyone thought she might be implicated in this horrible crime.

In the midst of her grief, Debbie remembers Saldate telling her he was a "friend" and that it would be good to clear her conscience. When she finally realized what he was all about and what he was trying to get her to say, she asked to be allowed to make a phone call and she asked for an attorney, but she was never allowed to contact anyone before, during, or after his interrogation. Saldate later stooped as low as to suggest that Debbie had tried to get on his good side by "exposing herself " to him. One can only imagine the kind of ego needs that would prompt a man in his position (that is, with total power over her) to say such a thing. At the end of his interrogation Saldate told Debbie to speak to no one and he left with her in his patrol car.

Debbie had never been in trouble nor involved with law enforcement officers in her life and was totally ignorant of the whole process. And, I, myself, encouraged her to trust the police, which I truly regret at this point in time.

After interrogating Debbie, Saldate intimidated several prospective witnesses to get them to say things to incriminate her. He went so far as to tell her sister Sandy that he would have her arrested and brought to Phoenix if she did not agree to testify against Debbie. He used the same tactics with other friends of Debbie's.

Debbie has always denied any knowledge or participation in Christopher's death, and she was given a lie detector test that confirmed her statements. But, these results were not admissible in court. Yet a totally fabricated confession built completely on Saldate's memories, a man with known political ambitions, which my daughter never saw or signed, was taken as the gospel truth. It gives one cause to doubt everything about the so-called "Justice" system.

I have learned now that trials are really big boy games. They have very little or nothing to do with the person on trial. Attorneys who make the best moves win and the others lose. Wins often translate into votes and career advancements, and courts reward winners while punishing losers. There is no effort whatsoever to understand or break the cycle of cause and effect that perpetuates crime.

The mass media have immense potential to effect positive change, but they prefer, instead, appealing to our basest instincts, entertaining us with prurient details of brutal crimes and trivializing human suffering. Truth finding takes time and resources, but horror headlines sell. Political ambitions of elected officials in the judicial and law enforcement system are valued higher than human life. Innocent people are sent to death row and the entire legal apparatus covers it up, because politicians will not admit mistakes. I cannot comprehend that this can happen in a democracy. My daughter is innocent, but she is on death row because someone wanted to get ahead politically — someone she never even knew before her son was murdered.

The Supreme Court of Arizona handed down a warrant for Debbie's execution without ever looking at her Appeals Petition. After a Warrant for Execution is handed down, the state automatically appoints two public defenders to work on the habeas for the state Federal Courts. Fortunately, our own lawyer felt uncomfortable working with the appointed public defenders and dismissed them. Then, by coincidence, we found out that one of the public defenders was the son-in-law of a Judge of the Arizona Supreme Court. With these family ties, that "public defender" was not concerned with my daughter's best interest. If our lawyer hadn't dismissed them, Debbie's execution would have been a mere formality like the entire state appeals process.

Today she is a piece of property belonging to the state of Arizona. She lives in a single cell on lock-down 23 hours a day. She is not allowed personal phone calls and is allowed only non-contact visits behind a plastic wall with a prison official present. To see a visitor she is strip searched and shackled and the entire unit has to go on lock-down for her to be able to leave her cell. As she walks across the yard, "Milke's coming" is shouted all over the unit. I can share with you what Debbie wrote to me about her life on death row:

We all cope in different ways and I have learned to cope by being alone. I cannot possibly explain what I feel psychologically, but I know that I (only) feel totally at ease in my room by myself. When I think about or know that I'm to be taken out of my room for some reason, I feel like a defenseless child who is about to be abused and there's nothing I can do about it. Yes, I'm an adult and have a stronger mind than a child, but abuse is abuse whether it happens to a 10-year-old or a 34-year-old. This place is my abuser. The terror and fear inside is overwhelming. No one knows what it feels like. I only feel safe in my room (when nothing is happening). But, I know I won't feel completely right or safe until I'm out of here. I see the chains and shackles and my heart races and I say inside "No, please don't do this to me. I'm not dangerous. Why do I have to go through this?" It's horrible, Mom, absolutely horrible. This is one of the reasons I have so much trouble going up front. It's not because I don't want to see anybody. I often look out my window towards the main building and think about a day when I will be leaving this place. I imagine the scene and even hear myself saying, "This is the last day I'm ever chained up. The pain I feel is indescribable and I'll never be the same again. I will never get over this, ever. My heart has been ripped to shreds."

My daughter is basically a shy person who is petrified at the thought of making a spectacle. Being a "freak show" upsets her so much that she is on a roller coaster of depression. I have only been able to see her once since I arrived in Arizona. Strip searches before and after visits are one of her biggest traumas. She begged me in a letter not to come visit her and to understand how it was not possible for her to appear "upbeat" any longer, even though she would really like to hug me and cry for hours.

A warrant for Debbie's execution was signed and her execution date was set for January 29, 1998. No one can ever know how frightening and torturous that is. She received a stay of execution, but now has only one chance to file a habeas appeal, and the decision on that is at the discretion of one judge who is assigned to review the case and rule on the constitutionality of the proceedings.

I would tell people to believe the incredible happens — in a so-called democracy anyone can be deprived of the most fundamental human rights. This can happen to your child! Debbie's most recent trauma was when they forced her to go through the actual motions of her execution right down to her last meal and what method of execution she would prefer. This is human torture.

My daughter has declined interviews because her first tries at that resulted in tabloid headlines and articles full of misquotes and false statements. She is barely holding on to her sanity and prays daily that her case will be reopened and the true facts established. The most difficult thing for Debbie to endure was to lose her beloved son in a brutal murder. She never had a chance to say goodbye to him or grieve for him in a proper way. Since her incarceration she has lost almost everyone she loved. First, her only child, then her mother-in-law in 1992, her grandparents (my parents) in 1994 and 1996, and now her father — and in his obituary, his family chose not to even mention Debbie among his family survivors.

Debbie has written on her thoughts about facing death — something a mother imagines going through first. Just when she had begun to see a little light at the end of the tunnel in her life, she was abruptly robbed of everything. She was young and these were the most precious years of her life. But even beyond that, she has been portrayed as a depraved monster and is denied the most basic human rights. The system continues to dehumanize her and deny her human dignity. For this sorrow, a mother has no words.

Writing from prison where he sits on death row, Jim Styers asked Debra to read Psalm 51:

Have mercy upon me, O God, in your goodness, in your tenderness wipe away my faults; wash me clean of my guilty, purify me from my sin.

I am well aware of my faults, I have my sin constantly in mind. Having sinned against none other than you. Having done what you regard as wrong.

This is the closest to an admission of guilt that Debra has ever received from Jim Styers. Debra Milke remains on death row in Arizona today.

4

Arkansas: Electrocution/Lethal Injection

The state of Arkansas has sentenced two women to death since 1900. No woman has been legally executed in Arkansas, and there is one woman on death row in Arkansas today.

In 1913 the state of Arkansas adopted electrocution as the official form of execution and in 1996 a bill was introduced in the Arkansas legislature to replace execution with lethal injection. Under the new bill any persons convicted of a capital offense after July 4, 1983 will be executed by lethal injection while those convicted before that date may choose between lethal injection and electrocution. The minimum age for execution in Arkansas is 16 although juveniles can be tried as adults at age 14 if the charge is capital murder.

In 1998, after two boys ages 11 and 13 shot and killed four girls and a teacher and left ten others injured at a local school, Arkansas authorities began to review and question their existing state laws regarding juvenile criminals and capital offenses. The current law states that no one under age 14 may be tried as an adult.

This is not a new discussion. These issues were first considered in Arkansas, 117 years ago in the state Supreme Court. A statute then held that a child under age 12 could not be found guilty of any crime or misdemeanor. Under Arkansas common law if a child indicted for a felony was between the ages of 7 and 13 it was up to the jury to decide whether the "prisoner had a guilty knowledge that he or she was doing wrong" (McFarland, 1998). The presumption of law, according to the courts, was that a child of that age "has not such guilty knowledge, unless the contrary be proven by evidence." The law further stated that in the case of children, who fell into the 12 to 13 years-of-age range, the common law presumption was that the alleged offender "is not capable of discerning between good and evil."

These state laws regarding juveniles continued to be discussed and changed over the years and in 1904 the Arkansas state Supreme Court held that the state has the burden of proving that a juvenile offender has the mental capacity to know right from wrong in relation to his/her offense.

In 1975 a law was passed that juveniles 15 and older could be tried as adults and it was up to the prosecutors to decide if offenders between the ages of 15 and 17 would be charged as adults or juveniles. Again, in 1983, the law was amended to allow prosecutors to charge 14-year-olds as adults in the case of first or second-degree murder and rape. There was a clause in the 1983 law explaining that the change was necessary because there were "many instances in which persons 14 years of age have committed premeditated murder but due to the present law can only be dealt with as juveniles." In 1989 a law was passed allowing offenders as young as 14 to be charged as adults for other crimes including capital murder, kidnapping, aggravated robbery and first-degree battery. More offenses were added to this list later, such as possession of a gun on school property, acts of terrorism, discharging a firearm from a vehicle, and soliciting a minor to join a street gang.

In 1997 legislation was introduced to lower the minimum age at which juveniles could be charged as adults to 12 for capital murder, first and second-degree murder, kidnapping, aggravated robbery, and a host of other offenses. The bill, however, never went forward.

Today, in lieu of the events of 1998, Arkansas states senators Tom Kennedy (D) and Mike Everett (D) are drafting a proposal regarding the crimes of capital murder, first-degree murder, and rape. According to Kennedy, age would not be a factor if the state can prove the individuals charged were old enough and mature enough to know what they were doing. The proposal, however, will not include the death penalty for anyone younger than 14. In the Kennedy-Everett proposal the charges would be at the prosecutor's discretion if the state can prove that the alleged offender:

- Is able to form the criminal intent to commit the felony
- Was able to take substantial steps in furtherance of the act
- Was able to appreciate the consequences of his/her conduct

According to the Senators this proposed bill would be the basis for a legislative study on how to deal with violent juvenile offenders. It will also serve as the impetus for more debates on the issue.

EXECUTIONS IN ARKANSAS

In 1913 the state of Arkansas adopted electrocution as its method of execution because it was thought to be more humane than hanging. This remained the mode of capital punishment until 1996 when then state Attorney

General Steve Clark testified in favor of changing the method of execution to lethal injection finding that to be even more humane. The introduction of lethal injection came about partly because of horror stories circulating for years regarding botched electrocutions in the state.

In the execution of 61-year-old F. G. Bullen in the 1930s, for, example, one witness, a Department of Corrections staff member recalled placing Bullen's body in the coffin after he had been electrocuted. But before the undertaker could close the lid Bullen gasped and started breathing and they realized he was still alive. After the warden was called, guards came and took Bullen's limp body out of the coffin and carried it back to the electric chair for another charge. They strapped him in again and administered the electricity five more times until he was finally pronounced dead.

But execution by lethal injection in Arkansas has had its problems too. In the 1992 execution of Ricky Ray Rector it took medical staff more than 50 minutes to find a suitable vein in Rector's arm. Witnesses were not permitted to view it, but they reported hearing Rector's loud moans throughout the process. During the ordeal, Rector (who was brain damaged from a lobotomy) tried to help his executioners find a vein.

On Wednesday, January 8, 1997, in Varner, Arkansas beginning at 7:09 p.m. three men were executed in the same night. This was the second triple execution in Arkansas' history, the first one was in 1994.

Wilburn A. Henderson, 56, was executed in Arkansas on July 8, 1998 for the murder of a woman in 1980. He was the first condemned prisoner put to death in Arkansas in 1998 and the thirty-sixth in the United States.

All recently condemned inmates in Arkansas have chosen lethal injection.

WOMEN SENTENCED TO DEATH IN ARKANSAS

1984

Patricia Hendrickson: White; Reversed in 1985. Patricia Hendrickson was sentenced to death in Arkansas for murder in 1984. She spent less than a year on death row before her sentence was reversed the following year.

1998

Christina Riggs: White; Currently on death row. At age 26, Christina Riggs was sentenced to death for the murders of her two children, Justin 5, and Shelby 2. She killed them with lethal doses of drugs she took from the hospital where she worked as a nurse and by suffocation. She tried to kill herself at the same time. Her defense unsuccessfully claimed insanity saying Christina, a former resident of Oklahoma, suffered stress from assisting victims of the Oklahoma City bombing in 1995. Prosecutors acknowledged that Christina suffered from depression and antisocial behavior, but said she was a manipulator who killed her children because they had become an inconvenience.

In November 1997, her mother called police to investigate the scene at Christina's home in Sherwood, Arkansas. She had not heard from her daughter and was worried. Upon entering the home they found Christina conscious but unresponsive on the bedroom floor and her children's bodies on the bed in the same room. The County Coroner estimated that the children had been dead from 10 to 14 hours before the police found them. After Christina was released from the hospital she was arrested immediately and charged with the murders of her two children.

At her trial in 1998, Christina admitted killing Justin Thomas, 5, and his sister Shelby Alexis who would have been three a month after her death. She told the court she had given them each a glass of water containing a lethal dose of the antidepressant amitriptyline because she wanted them to fall asleep before she injected them and herself with doses of potassium chloride.

She injected Justin first in the vein on the right side of his neck and when he cried out because the drug caused a burning sensation as it traveled through his body, she gave him some morphine for the pain and held him until he stopped crying. After he stopped crying she smothered him with a pillow. It was then, Christina said, that she decided to smother Shelby also. She said she did not want Shelby to suffer the pain of the injection as Justin had. The medical examiner who performed the autopsies on the children's bodies said that the drugs would have killed the children in about a half an hour whereas death by suffocation was almost immediate. Christina did inject herself with the drugs and potassium chloride, but told the court she didn't die because God had wanted her to live through the next seven months during which time she was baptized.

Christina's lawyers tried to defend her actions using her depression, which they said, was caused by a hereditary chemical imbalance. But probably her description of how she methodically went about killing her children was enough for the jury to find her guilty. In closing arguments the prosecution said there are people who are insane and there are people who do insane things.

In 55 minutes the jury (7 women and five men) found her guilty of two counts of capital murder and rejected lesser offenses of manslaughter and insanity. Upon hearing the verdict, Christina collapsed in the courtroom. During the sentencing phase of the trial she told the jurors "I want to die." She said she loved her children and should have protected them, but didn't and wanted to go and be with them now. She asked her mother to forgive her. When the sentence was read Christina's attorney said she said "Thank you" and squeezed his hand.

Judge Marion Humphrey set Christina Riggs' execution date for August 15, 1998 which her attorney said he would not appeal if Christina did not want to.

5

California: Gas/Lethal Injection

The state of California has sentenced sixteen women to death since 1900. Four women, Ethel Juanita Spinelli, Louise Peete, Barbara Graham, and Elizabeth Ann Duncan were executed in California's gas chamber at San Quentin, and there are 8 women on death row in California today.

California now has the largest death row in the United States, with 494 (July, 1998) condemned and the governor of the state has sole authority to grant clemency.

The Criminal Practices Act of 1851 authorized legal executions in California and capital punishment was incorporated into the California State Penal Code on February 14, 1872. The official statement read, in part:

A judgment of death must be executed within the walls or yard of a jail, or some convenient private place in the county. The Sheriff of the county must be present at the execution, and must invite the presence of a physician, the District Attorney of the county, and at least twelve reputable citizens, to be selected by him; and he shall at the request of the defendant, permit such ministers of the gospel, not exceeding two, as the defendant may name, and any persons, relatives, or friends, not to exceed five, to be present at the execution, together with such peace officers as he may think expedient to witness the execution. But no other persons than those mentioned in this section can be present at the execution, nor can any persons under age be allowed to witness the same.

In the beginning all executions in California were carried out in the counties where the crimes were committed. In 1891 the California state legislature amended the rule to state to read "A judgment of death must be executed within the walls of one of the state prisons designated by the Court by which judgment is rendered."

After this, the warden replaced the sheriff as the person who was required to be present at all executions, and the invitation to attend an execution was extended to the Attorney General of the state rather than to the District Attorney.

At the time of this decree, executions were conducted at both California state prisons, which were San Quentin and Folsom. Hanging was the only method used at the time, and there was no official way of deciding whether a person should be hanged at San Quentin or Folsom. Apparently this was left to the discretion of the presiding judge.

The first state-conducted hanging at San Quentin was that of a man named Jose Gabriel on March 3, 1893, convicted of murdering an elderly farm couple. The first hanging at Folsom was on December 13, 1895. Between 1893 and 1937, when the state legislature replaced hanging with lethal gas as a method of execution, a total of 215 inmates were hanged at San Quentin and 92 were hanged at Folsom. The last execution by hanging at San Quentin was in 1942.

Following a legislative mandate in 1937 to execute by lethal gas, California's only gas chamber was built at San Quentin by the Denver-based Eaton Metal Products Company. On December 2, 1938, the first human execution by lethal gas was carried out. The chamber itself was olive-green in color and had two seats, Chair A and Chair B, where over a period of approximately 30 years, 194 prisoners, four of them women, some alone, some side by side went to their deaths.

The official manual for gassing, which came with the chamber when it was built, recommended a minimum of 10 minutes to kill a person, but said that some cases might take longer. Various eyewitnesses over the years, including doctors and toxicologists, revealed that just moments after the cyanide pellets were dropped prisoners usually struggled against the straps for a few moments and then it would take anywhere from 10 seconds to 8 minutes to lose consciousness.

The first two prisoners executed in California's gas chamber shortly after it was installed in 1938, were Robert Lee Cannon and Albert Kessel. They were convicted of murdering Warden Clarence Larkin. After their execution, four other inmates were executed in connection with the same murder, all within a two-week period.

WOMEN EXECUTED BY GAS IN CALIFORNIA

1941

Ethel Juanita Spinelli: White; Executed, 1941. On November 21, 1941, Ethel Juanita Spinelli, became the first woman executed by lethal gas in California. In his personal memoirs Warden Clinton Duffy (Duffy & Hirschberg, 1962) described her as "the coldest, hardest, character, male or female, I have ever known." She was the leader of a group of gangsters that included her lover, gangster Mike Simeone, her children, and several other young people. Her followers affectionately called her "The Duchess."

Ethel was sentenced to die for ordering the murder of 19-year-old Robert Sherrard, one of her gang members, because she thought Sherrard was going to turn "stoolie" and talk about a previous murder the gang had committed. He was given "knock-out" drops, then bludgeoned to death and dumped in a river. Another gang member, Albert Ives, one of the three men who assisted in the murder, informed. Ives was later declared insane and sent to a state mental hospital for the rest of his natural life. He was the prosecution's star witness. Gordon Hawkins and Mike Simeone, Ethel's common law husband, were the other two who participated in the murder and, like The Duchess, both were given the death penalty.

Ethel Spinelli's death-sentence and pending execution generated heavy publicity that resulted in three different stays of execution, which were uncommon in the 1940s. At the time, Warden Duffy said he felt that "She was receiving special consideration because of her sex; if she were a man, she would have died on schedule," he said. The warden remembered her (Duffy & Hirschberg, 1962) as "homely, scrawny, nearsighted, a sharp-featured scarecrow, with thin lips, beady eyes, and scraggly black hair flecked with gray." He said, "It hardly seemed possible that young punks with neither brains nor character would take orders from her."

Despite Warden Duffy's memories, Ethel Spinelli was so well loved by prison inmates that when she was sentenced to die thirty prisoners signed a petition addressed to the governor asking that one of them be allowed to take her place in the gas chamber. Their petition was, of course, rejected and on November 21, 1941, she was put to death.

Warden Duffy remembered taking the final walk with Ethel. When they arrived at the gas chamber, he said he realized the witnesses had not been seated, so he told her there would be a delay, for which he apologized. He then asked her if she would prefer to return to her cell and wait, but Ethel said no, "We'll just stand here." As the witnesses filed in she remarked, "The sun's out, isn't it, warden?" To which Duffy replied "Yes," and Ethel added, "It's a beautiful day."

Once all the witnesses were inside, Warden Duffy said, "All right, Mrs. Spinelli, it's time." She said, "O.K." and walked quickly into the gas chamber and sat down. Warden Duffy noted in his memoirs that "She was the only person I knew who could stand and talk about the weather while waiting to die."

Even though she was remembered as having led a life of callous indifference, her last request was that the photographs of her three children and an infant grandchild be taped over her heart (Duffy & Hirschberg, 1962). Her request was granted, and that was the way she died.

1947

Louise L. Peete: White; Executed, 1947. On April 11, 1947, At age 50, Louise L. Peete became the second woman executed by lethal gas in California.

Mrs. Peete was born in Bienville, Louisiana, in 1883 and was a cultured and refined woman who was quite confident to the very end that she would receive a commutation of her death sentence. It was her second trip to San Quentin, which she referred to as her "little gray home in the West." On her first stint, she had been convicted of the murder of Jacob Denton, a mining tycoon, after his body was found in his house with a bullet hole in his head. She served her sentence for that and was released on her tenth application for parole. An elderly couple, who knew her, Margaret and Arthur Logan, volunteered and were approved to supervise her parole.

Arthur ended up in a mental institution, and in 1945 Margaret was found dead in her garden with a bullet hole in her head. Louise had been writing checks from the couple's account, living in their home, and writing wonderful parole reports each month on her own behalf. She was convicted of Margaret's murder and sentenced to death.

Just before entering the gas chamber she said, "Governor Warren is a gentleman. No gentleman would send a lady to her death." But when the chivalry of the future Chief Justice of the U.S. Supreme Court failed to materialize, she went to her death with quiet dignity.

1955

Barbara Graham: White; Executed, June 3, 1955. Barbara Graham, known as "Bloody Babs," was the third woman to die by lethal gas in California. She was executed on June 3, 1955. Barbara was born in 1923 in Oakland, California, and when she was 2-years-old her mother, Hortense, was sent to a home for "wayward girls." As a result, Barbara was raised by neighbors and received only a superficial education. As a teenager she was picked up for vagrancy and sent to the same reformatory where her mother had been as a teenager. She was released from there in 1939.

Despite her beginnings, Barbara enrolled in business college, married, and had a child. By 1941 she was divorced, and she traveled aimlessly around California for several years. She was arrested twice in San Diego for "lewd and disorderly conduct" and served two months in jail. She then went to San Francisco, where she married a second time. This marriage lasted only a few months. She was arrested for prostitution in 1944, and by 1946 her only friends were criminals involved in prostitution and gambling. She was involved with some underworld characters at the time although she had no record of violence.

She worked for a while in Chicago as a cocktail waitress, then in 1947 she went to San Francisco, where she worked as a call girl for the infamous Madam Sally Stanford. After a perjury incident Barbara tried to straighten her life out by becoming a nurses' aide in a hospital in Tonapak, Nevada. In 1951 she married a third time and moved to Seattle. There she met and married Henry Graham and stayed with him until 1953, when she had her third child. Graham introduced her to drugs and to a crook named Emmet Perkins.

When she met Emmet Perkins and Jack Santo, they were already in trouble with the law as the heads of a murderous crime gang. She became Perkins's mistress and agreed to accompany him to rob an elderly widow in Malibu who was supposed to have a lot of money in a safe at her home. As it turned out, there was no money in the safe, which made them both angry. John True, a gang member who received immunity for his testimony against them, said that Barbara lost her head and savagely beat the old woman and smothered her with a pillow.

Eventually, she was convicted of murder along with Emmet Perkins and Jack Santo, but she denied her guilt until the very end and many were convinced that she was innocent. Edward S. Montgomery, a reporter who covered the crime, won a Pulitzer Prize for his many articles about her. His writings were the basis for the 1958 movie *I Want to Live* where the grim series of last-minute reprieves and legal maneuverings that Barbara Graham endured are portrayed.

Barbara had three sons, and she swore her innocence on the youngest one's head before she died. Tommy, her son, was only two at the time. During her trial and the other proceedings she expressed a wish to protect her 14-year-old son from publicity because, she said, "They are so sensitive at that age."

Her execution got under the skin of attendant Joe Feretti more than any of the others he'd seen. "God she was a beautiful woman" Feretti remembered. "I was with her all night. We told jokes. What made it real bad was she got two stays right there, that morning. She was just walking into the chamber the first time when the phone rang and she had to wait some more. Then it happened again and she cried out, 'Why do they torture me?' " (Tabor, 1958).

"When she finally started in the third time, she asked for a blindfold," Feretti recalled "She was the only one who ever did. I don't think she wanted to see anyone in the witness room." Feretti strapped Barbara in the chair, patted her knee and said, as he had to the hundred before her, "Now take a deep breath and it won't bother you" to which Barbara replied, "How in the hell would you know?"

1962

Elizabeth Ann Duncan: White; Executed, August 8, 1962. Elizabeth Ann Duncan, known as "Ma Duncan" was the fourth and final woman executed in California's gas chamber, just 3 years after being convicted of murdering her pregnant daughter-in-law. Her own attorney said, "There's nothing good that can be said about Elizabeth Duncan." Hers was the most famous trial in Ventura County, California, and the jury took only 4 hours and 15 minutes to convict her. She went to her death on August 8, 1962.

Elizabeth was born Hazel Sinclair Nigh in Kansas City in 1904. She first married a man named Dewey Tessier at the age of 14. She had a rather chaotic life, marrying at least eleven times, though some suspected it was more like twenty. She married several younger men promising them large sums of money but when she was not forthcoming with the money, the marriages were annulled. A few of her marriages were not valid because they happened while she was still legally married to someone else.

Her son, Frank, was fathered by Frank Law in 1928, but she later changed his last name to Duncan because Duncan was the husband who had the best credit rating of all her husbands.

Elizabeth initiated several scams in her career, such as demanding and receiving child support from her ex-husbands by sending pregnant women claiming to be herself to a doctor to get false documentation of pregnancies. She had a total of five children from her marriages. One died of a brain hemorrhage, and three others were turned over to adoption agencies.

Elizabeth lavished all her love and attention on her son Frank, and by working in bars, restaurants, and stores she put him through college and law school. While she was raising him, in 1953, she was convicted of running a house of prostitution in San Francisco.

As a fifty-four-year-old widow, Elizabeth lived with Frank in Santa Barbara. In November 1957, the two had a fight about buying a beauty parlor and Frank ordered his mother out of the apartment. Elizabeth immediately took an overdose of sleeping pills and had to be admitted to a hospital. While visiting her in the hospital Frank met a nurse named Olga Kupcyzk, a 29-year-old Canadian, and began dating her. Mrs. Duncan strongly opposed their relationship and ordered Olga to stop seeing her son. When Olga told her she would not stop seeing him and was, in fact, going to marry him, Mrs. Duncan screamed (according to witnesses), "You'll never marry my son! I'll kill you first!"

Despite his mother's objections, Frank and Olga were secretly married in June 1958. To keep their marriage a secret, Frank went home to his mother on their wedding night. For several weeks after their marriage the newlyweds lived at Olga's apartment. Then in August, Frank gave in to his mother's repeated requests and the couple moved in with her. It was that same month that Elizabeth began asking some of her son's clients if they knew of anyone who would like to earn a large sum of money. She then recruited a man named Ralph Winterstein to go with her to Ventura County Superior Court, where with Winterstein claiming to be Frank Duncan and Elizabeth saying she was Olga Duncan, she asked for and received a decree of annulment of their marriage.

When Elizabeth learned that Olga was pregnant, she decided she needed to move quickly if she was going to eliminate her. Her idea was that someone would kidnap her daughter-in-law, take her to Mexico, kill her, and then pour lye over her body to prevent identification. Inquiries led her to two men, Luis Moya and Augustine Baldonado, who were a pair of small-time hoodlums who agreed to do the job. Elizabeth gave them a cash advance of $175, which they spent on gloves, adhesive tape, car rental and bullets for a borrowed pistol.

On the night of November 18, Moya and Baldonado drove to Olga Duncan's apartment in Santa Barbara. Moya rang the bell and told Olga that her husband, Frank, was downstairs in the car, unconscious from a car accident. As she ran down to help him, they hit her on the head with a pistol and dragged her into the car. Although she was seven months pregnant, Olga fought her attackers fiercely and once they got her in the car they had to stop repeatedly because of the struggle. They hit her on the head so hard and so often that they broke the gun. When the car began acting up, they abandoned their Mexico plan and drove into the California hills toward Ojai. With Olga still fighting desperately for her life, Moya and Baldonado took turns strangling her, then dug a pit in an orange grove and buried her. They finished at about 2:00 a.m. and went back to Elizabeth for the rest of their money. When she heard what they'd done, she wasn't happy and complained about the sloppy job and about having Olga's body too close. She then gave them $400 and told them that was all the money she could raise.

Olga Duncan's body was discovered two days later, and it didn't take the police long to pick up Moya and Baldonado — who admitted their guilt and quickly implicated Mrs. Duncan. She denied the story, saying the pair were former clients of her son who had come to her threatening to kill him because they were unhappy about the way he had handled their cases. She swore she'd paid them the money to keep them from hurting Frank.

Mrs. Duncan's trial began on February 24, 1959, and, on her behalf, her lawyer pleaded not guilty by reason of insanity. The prosecution, however, presented witness after witness who told about Elizabeth's unhealthy fixation on her son, her repeated death threats to Olga, and her attempts to recruit killers. On March 16, the jury came back with a verdict of guilty of murder in the first-degree. Four days later, after hearing reports from court-appointed psychiatrists, Mrs. Duncan's insanity plea was rejected and a sentence of death was pronounced for all three defendants.

Edmund "Pat" Brown, who was governor of California at the time, summed up his memories of this case and his decision to execute Elizabeth in this way:

The fact that she was a woman, the only woman sentenced to die during my term as governor, and only the fifth woman ever sentenced to death in California history — did have some effect on my thoughts and feelings. I felt a great repugnance about letting a woman die, as I suspect even the toughest death-penalty advocate would. My clemency secretary summed up the case and included all the relevant psychiatric evidence. "From a clinical psychiatric standpoint there is no evidence of mental illness, and she can best be fitted into the category of character behavior neurosis, which is relatively synonymous to a sociopathic personality," one doctor wrote, "every psychiatrist who examined her could find no evidence of psychosis or mental illness in the legal sense sufficient to justify a commutation or an act of clemency in this matter." Elizabeth Duncan was found to be as guilty of the savage murder of Olga Duncan as Luis Moya and Augustine Baldonado were — even more, in that she had brought about the crime by hiring them to commit it. In spite of the fact that she was a woman, and a mother, I knew there was a time in all capital cases when I had to just let it go and move on to other things. I was the head of a growing state, in need of new schools and public health programs, with an election coming up in a few months. I had to say to myself, "I've got lots of good people to take care of; I can't worry about this bad one anymore." (Brown, 1989)

Frank supported his mother throughout her trial and execution, even though it was his pregnant wife she had hired someone to kill. However, Elizabeth Duncan died alone in the San Quentin gas chamber. Her last words were, "I'm innocent. Where's Frank?" Her beloved son Frank was at the California Supreme Court pleading for his mother's life.

THE CALIFORNIA GAS CHAMBER

On April 8, 1967, Aaron Mitchell, convicted of killing a peace officer during a robbery, became the 194th person executed in the gas chamber at San Quentin and the last person executed in California until 1992. He was dragged struggling and screaming to the gas chamber, where the warden read his death warrant and gave the signal to release the gas. Howard Brodie, a journalist who witnessed the execution wrote: "When the gas hit him his head immediately fell to his chest. Then his head came up and he looked directly into the window I was standing next to. For nearly seven minutes, he sat up that way, with his chest heaving, saliva bubbling between his lips. He tucked his thumbs into his fists and finally his head fell down. It took twelve minutes to kill him" (Dietz, 1992).

For 25 years after Mitchell's execution there were no executions in California, and on February 18, 1972, the California Supreme Court declared the death penalty cruel and unusual punishment in violation of the state constitution. As a result of this decision, 107 inmates had their sentences changed and were taken off death row. Thus, death row ceased to exist in California. Nine months later the California electorate amended the state constitution and overruled the decision of the California Supreme Court.

In 1972 the United States Supreme Court held that the death penalty was unconstitutional as it was being administered in some states. This ruling prompted California to pass legislation that same year making the death penalty mandatory in certain cases and under certain conditions. Among the circumstances warranting a death penalty were kidnapping if the victim died, train wrecking if any person died, assault by a life prisoner if the victim died within a year, treason against the state, and first-degree murder under specific conditions (for hire, of a peace officer, of a witness to prevent testimony, if committed during a robbery or burglary, if committed during course of a rape by force, if committed during performance of lewd and lascivious acts upon children, if committed by persons previously convicted of murder).

In late 1976, the California Supreme Court, basing its decision on the United States Supreme Courts' decision in *Furman v. Georgia*, held that the California death penalty statute was unconstitutional because it did not allow defendants the opportunity to present evidence in mitigation. After this ruling 70 inmates had their sentences changed, including the women known as "Charlie's girls" who had been given the death penalty in the Tate-La Bianca murders.

California re-enacted its death penalty statute in 1977 (CAL.PENAL.CODE SS190.1 to 190.6), and under the new statute, evidence in mitigation was permitted and the death penalty was allowed as a possible punishment for first-degree murder under certain conditions. These conditions included: murder for financial gain, murder by a person previously convicted of murder, murder of multiple victims, murder with torture, murder of a peace officer, murder of a witness to prevent testimony, and several other murders under particular circumstances.

The 1979 revision of the California Penal Code included the sentence of life imprisonment without the possibility of parole. With this, the punishment for kidnapping, ransom, extortion, or robbery was changed from death to life without parole. Treason, train derailing or wrecking, and securing the death of an innocent person through perjury became punishable by death or life imprisonment without the possibility of parole. California judges were thus given the option of sentencing convicted capital murderers to life without the possibility of parole. To date over 1,700 people in California have received this alternative sentence which includes a no-appeals process. According to the California Governor's Office, no one sentenced to life without parole has been released since the state provided for this option in 1977.

California currently operates under Proposition 7, a broader statute, which was on the California ballot in November 1978 and superseded the 1977 statutes. Under current state law, whenever a death penalty is given it must be automatically reviewed by the State Supreme Court. If the Supreme Court affirms the death sentence, the inmate can initiate appeals on constitutional issues through writs of *habeas corpus*.

Although the California death penalty was reinstated in 1978, there were no executions in California until April 1992 when Robert Alton Harris was executed for the murders of two San Diego teenagers. Harris was on death row for thirteen years and one month. The California Department of Corrections received more than 1,000 media requests in the six weeks leading up to Harris' execution. In the end, 125 reporters were allowed inside the media center, 26 large broadcast vans were parked in an adjacent parking lot, and 17 journalists were allowed to witness the execution. It took 14 minutes for Harris to die. Judge Marilyn Hall Patel ordered the videotaping of the execution of Harris and placed the tapes under court seal.

In 1992 several death row inmates in California filed a suit [*Fierro v. Gomez*, 790F Sup.Ct. 966 CA (1992)] claiming that the means of execution used in California, the gas chamber, violated the Eighth Amendment's ban on cruel and unusual punishment. The focus of the court was whether the risk of pain was excessive. In considering this case, the court used expert testimony such as witnesses and execution records showing that prisoners took at least two minutes to lose consciousness and that during that two minutes suffered excruciating pain caused by cellular suffocation.

On August 27, 1992 California added lethal injection as a method of execution. Inmates could then choose between lethal injection and gas. In August 1993, David Mason waived both his right to federal appeals and his right to choose between lethal injection and the gas chamber as a method of execution. He was, therefore, put to death in the gas chamber as the California law stipulates, when an inmate does not choose (Paddock, 1993).

In October 1994, a U.S. District Judge in California (San Francisco) ruled that the gas chamber was cruel and unusual punishment, thus barring the state from using it as a method of execution. The ruling was upheld by the U.S. Ninth Circuit Court of Appeals in February 1996. This decision came just as California was preparing to execute its third prisoner since 1976 and was criticized by Governor Wilson as "shortsighted and misguided." He said he believed that California should not be prohibited from using the gas chamber to execute society's most brutal and heinous killers.

The Ninth U.S. Circuit Court of Appeals decision, founded on the 1994 federal ruling, was the first by any U.S. court to declare a method of execution unconstitutional; it was based on evidence that gas chamber deaths are accompanied by prolonged pain. Among other evidence, federal Judge Marilyn Patel — appointed to the bench by former President Regan — allowed testimony from holocaust survivors. Judge Patel then ordered the state to switch to lethal injection, to end the slow suffocation of a condemned person by gassing. "Symptoms of air hunger include intense chest pains, such as felt during a heart attack, acute anxiety, and struggling to breathe," according to Patel.

"It's an important decision in that it prohibits the state from torturing people to death," an ACLU lawyer who represents prisoners challenging the gas chamber stated. "It recognizes that even people on death row who are going to be executed deserve some humanity."

Judge Patel noted that 10 states, including California, used gas as the sole method of execution in 1990, and none use it today. Judge Patel indicated that the trend away from using gas, along with evidence of pain, shows that gas chamber executions violate "evolving standards of human decency" (Doyle, 1993).

The modified California Penal Code was then written to state that if either manner of execution is found to be invalid, the punishment of death should be imposed by the alternative means. Three executions have taken place since it was adopted.

David Mason (8/4/93) was on death row in California for 9 years and 7 months, William Bonin (2/23/96) was on death row for 13 years and one month, and Keith Williams (5/3/96) on death row in California for 17 years.

LETHAL INJECTION IN CALIFORNIA

Serial killer William Bonin, convicted of sexually assaulting and killing fourteen boys in Los Angeles and Orange Counties, was the first to be executed by lethal injection on February 23, 1996. Several hundred people were at San Quentin for the event. Outside, in the cold night air, the pro-death penalty people were carrying signs, some drinking and partying, and some holding candles and praying. Family members of Bonin's victims were also there; a few wanted closure, others revenge, and still others wanted him spared, since the state was doing to him what he had done to their children. A fistfight broke out between people representing both sides of the issue, and several hundred riot police quelled the disturbance by showing their force. Inside, the scene, as described by a Los Angeles Times reporter Ken Elingwood, was quite different.

Fifty witnesses were present. The old gas chamber, looking like a sea-green steel bubble, was converted to a lethal injection room for the occasion by replacing the chair in the center with a table. Witnesses did not see Bonin enter the chamber, nor did they see him while he was being strapped to the table. When the curtain opened, they saw him dressed in fresh denim and gray socks, lying on the table, blinking toward the ceiling.

Bonin never expressed remorse for his crimes. He spent his final hours watching "Jeopardy," eating pizza and ice cream, and chatting with the Catholic chaplain. Prison officials said he walked himself to the table without resistance, but technicians had a difficult time finding a good vein. Officials said that a half hour before his execution, Bonin said, "I would suggest that when a person has a thought of doing anything serious against the law, that before they did that they should go to a quiet place and think about it seriously."

A minute after Bonin breathed his last breath his skin turned blue. Relatives of some of his victims were present. No one from Bonin's family was present. By 12:15 it was over. The prison officials judged California's first execution by lethal injection a success.

In July 1998 a three-judge panel of the Ninth Circuit Court of Appeals ruled that the federal ban on the use of the gas chamber as a form of execution was no longer binding because of new state laws allowing inmates to choose between two methods.

EXECUTION WITNESSES

Two weeks before a scheduled execution in July 1997, Governor Wilson signed legislation on the death penalty requiring prison officials to invite victims' families to witness an execution. In signing the bill Wilson said, "Every day families of victims struggle to overcome the pain and sorrow they feel as a result of these violent predators' heinous acts on their loved ones and families should be entitled to bring closure to their suffering."

On February 28, 1997, in a decision in the case of *California First Amendment Coalition v. Calderon,* filed by the ACLU, the U.S. District Court of California upheld the First Amendment right of the press to witness the entire California execution procedure. The press had filed a complaint indicating they were not allowed to view the first 20 minutes of preparation for an inmate's execution. Arthur Calderon, Director of the California Department of Corrections said that the reasoning behind the restricted viewing was to protect the identity of the executioners. But, the court found that there was no evidence that media presence jeopardizes prison security or the safety of prison personnel. The court ruled that the state's Department of Corrections must allow the procedure to be viewed "at least from the point in time just prior to the condemned being immobilized" until after the prisoner dies.

The state appealed the decision to the U.S. Circuit Court of Appeals and in May 1998 a Federal Judge overturned the ruling. The judge cited a 1974 Supreme Court decision supporting his ruling that the First Amendment does not guarantee the press any special access over and above what is available to the general public. At this point, the case is next slated for presentation to the Supreme Court.

In California the witness area is built so that up to fifty people can witness an execution. Those who may be included are specified in the California Penal Code as:

- Warden
- Attorney General
- 12 Citizens
- 2 Physicians
- 5 Inmate family/friends (if requested)
- 2 Inmate spiritual advisor (if requested)

State procedures allow for:

- 17 News media representatives
- 9 State-selected witnesses
- 4 Staff escorts

LAST 24 HOURS

The day before an execution the warden makes special arrangements for the condemned to have visits from approved family members, spiritual advisors, and friends. Around 6:00 p.m. the day before, the inmate is moved to the death watch cell which is adjacent to the execution chamber, and three staff members are assigned to the deathwatch.

In the deathwatch cell the inmate has his/her last meal of whatever he/she has requested. Between 7:00 and 10:00 p.m. on the day of his/her execution an inmate is allowed visits from the chaplain and the warden. The inmate can read, watch television or listen to the radio while on the deathwatch. He/she may also request food or soft drinks.

Family, spiritual advisors, or friends whom the inmate has selected as witnesses may arrive up to two hours before the execution. About 30 minutes before execution, the inmate is given new prison issue clothes to wear. The inmate is then escorted to the execution chamber a few minutes prior to the appointed time and strapped onto a table. The condemned is then connected to a cardiac monitor that is connected to a printer outside the execution chamber. An IV is started in two usable veins and a flow of normal saline solution is administered at a slow rate. One line is held in reserve in case of a blockage or malfunction in the other. The door is closed. The warden reads the death warrant and issues the execution order.

THE EXECUTION

Prior to an execution, syringes are prepared containing:

- 5.0 grams of sodium pentothal in 20–25 cc of dilutent
- 50 cc of pancuronium bromide
- 50 cc of potassium chloride

Each of these chemicals is lethal in the amounts administered. At the warden's signal, sodium pentothal is administered first, then the line is flushed with sterile normal saline solution. This is followed by pancuronium bromide and a saline flush, and finally, potassium chloride. A physician is required by the California Penal Code to be present when death occurs.

After all the witnesses have left, the body is removed. Typically, the family claims the body. If not, the state makes the arrangements.

THE COST

Capital punishment in California, as in every other state, is more expensive than life imprisonment without parole. In Los Angeles County, the total cost of capital punishment is $2,087,926, while the total cost of life imprisonment without possibility of parole in $1,448,935. A study done by the *Sacramento Bee* (1996) argues that California would save $90 million per year if it were to abolish the death penalty, as this is the amount incurred annually beyond the ordinary costs of the justice system. Of the total amount, $78 million is incurred at the trial level.

THE DEATH PENALTY IN CALIFORNIA TODAY

According to a Field poll released March 13, 1997, 74 percent of Californians support capital punishment (ACLU Abolitionist, April 1997). In 1996 Governor Pete Wilson proposed increasing the number and pay of attorneys who defend death row inmates. Wilson's plan would add more than 100 public defenders to the state's payroll, create an office of Post-Conviction Counsel to handle state and federal appeals, and raise the pay of private counsel handling death row cases from $95 to $125 an hour, the amount paid in California federal courts.

The governor's aim is to speed up executions by eliminating a backlog of 130 death row inmates without attorneys. Since restoring capital punishment in 1978, California has sentenced 514 people to death, but only four have been executed. "We're taking a step toward the day when old age will no longer be the leading cause of death among inmates on death row," Governor Wilson stated.

In 1995, Governor Wilson signed a bill allowing people who commit a murder during a carjacking to be eligible for the death penalty as well as murders committed in drive-by shootings. In 1996 the California legislature discussed allowing voters to approve capital punishment measures involving drive-by shootings, carjackings, and the killing of a juror. Additional death penalty discussions included giving the death penalty for murdering a social worker or child abuse worker engaged in the performance of his/her duties, and of setting time limits on death penalty appeals.

In 1997, a federal appellate court in California ruled that California cannot take advantage of the law to speed up death penalty appeals that came about as a result of the Federal Anti-terrorism and Effective Death Penalty Act of 1996. Under the law repeat appeals are strictly limited if the issue could have been raised in the inmates' initial appeal. But, according to the court, California has not complied with the guidelines they set forth, and, as of last year, more than 130 inmates on California's death row did not have legal representation.

Governor Wilson is now unveiling a package of 20 juvenile justice bills, suggesting that the possibility of applying the death penalty to a 14-year-old murderer should be considered (ACLU Abolitionist, June 1997).

WOMEN SENTENCED TO DEATH IN CALIFORNIA

In 1971 a California jury found three women, Susan Atkins, Patricia Krenwinkle, and Leslie Van Houten, guilty of first-degree murder on seven counts of murder and conspiracy to commit murder and on one count of conspiracy to commit murder because of two successive multiple homicides in which they participated. All three were given the death penalty.

Linda Kasabian, who was granted immunity, also participated in the crimes. All were members of a commune known as "The Family," which was a group of about twenty people gathered together by Charles Manson in Chatsworth, California. The members were mostly young women, three of whom had children. One of the goals of The Family was to reject the conventions and values of society.

At Chatsworth The Family lived in bunkhouses and other buildings that were part of a horse ranch owned and operated by George Spahn. Manson was the undisputed leader of the group, and members understood that membership in the group meant giving their will to him. He often told them, "In order to love someone, you must be willing to die for them and must be willing to kill them and have them kill you. You must be willing to experience anything for them."

In the trial, the People argued that Manson ordered the killings as part of a plan to foment a revolution of blacks against the white establishment from which the family would eventually benefit. Evidence was presented regarding Manson's control over the family and his prophecies of the coming race war, which he named "Helter Skelter" after one of the Beatles songs. His influence ranged from simple to complex matters. He decided where The Family lived, where they slept, what they wore, when they could eat as well as matters such as who would take care of The Family's children and who would have sex with whom.

Manson and his followers referred to the members of the white establishment as "pigs," and the perpetrators of the crimes left writings in the blood of the victims at both crime scenes that included the words "pigs" and "Helter Skelter." Linda Kasabian's testimony was the only direct evidence tying the other three women to the murders.

The California Court of Appeals reversed the judgment of one of the women whose counsel disappeared (Leslie Van Houten) and affirmed the judgment of the others, modifying their sentences to life imprisonment.

THE MURDERS: TATE

Actress Sharon Tate was pregnant and married to movie director Roman Polanski in August of 1969, but Polanski was out of the country and Wojiciech Frykowski and Abigail Folger were living with Sharon at the Polanski residence. Mrs. Winifred Chapman, the cook, was the person who found the bodies when she arrived for work the morning of August 10, 1969.

The police eventually located five bodies on the premises. These were the bodies of Frykowski and Folger who were found on the front lawn, Steve Parent who was found in a car just inside the entrance gate, and Sharon Tate and Jay Sebring who were found in the living room, their bodies connected by a rope. A towel was wrapped around Sebring's neck and covered his face. The word "Pig" was written in blood, later identified as Sharon Tate's, on the front door.

Sharon had suffered 16 stab wounds, Folger was stabbed 27 times, Sebring had 7 stab wounds and one gunshot wound, Frykowski's body had 5 stab wounds and his scalp had 13 lacerations by a blunt instrument plus two gunshot wounds. Parent's body had five gunshot wounds. There was no evidence that anything had been stolen and it was, therefore, assumed the sole motive of the crime was murder.

THE MURDERS: LA BIANCA

On August 10, 1969, Frank Struthers, the 16-year-old son of Rosemary La Bianca, returned home from a trip and found his stepfather, Leno La Bianca, dead. The police reported his body was located in the living room with a blood-soaked pillowcase covering his head. The victim's hands were tied behind his back with a leather thong, and a carving fork was stuck in his stomach. On his stomach was scratched the word "War." There was an electrical cord knotted around his neck. He had 13 stab wounds and 14 puncture wounds and a knife was found protruding from his neck.

Mrs. La Bianca's body was found in the front bedroom. Her hands were tied with an electrical cord. A pillowcase was over her head, and an electrical cord was also wound around her neck. Her body had sustained 41 stab wounds. "Death to the Pigs" was written in blood on a wall in the living room. Over the door "Rise" was written in blood, and, on the refrigerator door "Helter Skelter" was written in blood. As in the previous crime, there was no evidence that anything had been stolen and it was, therefore, assumed the primary motive for the crime was murder.

THE WOMEN

1970
Susan Denise Atkins: White; Commuted to life, 1971. Susan Atkins, known as Sadie in the Manson Family, was twenty-one years old at the time of her arrest. She had grown up in San Jose, California. Her mother had died of cancer while she was in her teens, and after dropping out of high school she went to San Francisco, where she earned a living by hustling. When she joined Charles Manson and his followers, Charlie gave her the name Sadie Mae Glutz, she explained during the trial, to "free herself of her past."

After her arrest, while incarcerated at Sybil Brand Prison awaiting trial, Susan told two female inmates about her participation in the Tate murders and implied that she might have been involved in the La Bianca murders, although it was later determined she was not. A third female inmate testified at the trial that when they heard a broadcast about the murders Susan had remarked "That ain't the way it went down."

Two people testified at the trial that Susan Atkins was the one who killed Sharon Tate. Newspaper accounts said that Susan recalled the killing of Sharon Tate, saying she had an urge to drink her blood, "It was slick and I brought my hand to my face and I could smell the blood. I opened my mouth and licked it off my fingers." She said she thought of carving out Sharon's unborn child and bringing it to Charlie wrapped in a towel. "How proud Charlie would be if I presented him with the baby cut from the womb of a woman." Barbara Hoyt, another Family member, testified that she had overheard Susan say that Sharon Tate was the last to die. But Susan testified before the grand jury that it had actually been Tex Watson who killed Sharon.

Other evidence presented against Susan was hair similar to hers that was found on some discarded bloodstained clothes in the vicinity of Cielo Drive. The blood was later identified as Type B, blood that matched that of Steve Parent. Three letters that Susan wrote from prison while awaiting trial also implicated her in the crimes.

Twenty-seven years in prison has changed Susan. A letter that appeared on the Internet last year, written from prison reads in part:

I greet you in the name of Jesus Christ, my Savior and Lord. I've prayed a great deal and sought God about this letter and pray even as I write it that when you receive it, your spirit will bear witness, by the Holy Spirit, that its contents, intent and purpose is not self motivated, but rather God-directed and anointed to accomplish His will for His Glory.

My maiden name is Susan Denise Atkins. Some of you know me personally, some have read about me through the years, perhaps during the past two decades. Some of you know what brought me to where I have been for twenty-five years and that is all you know. Some have known that some twenty years ago I accepted Jesus Christ as my Lord and Savior. For those who do not fit any of the above, please allow my humble and brief explanation of who I am today and what Jesus Christ saved me from.

In 1969, I was involved with what the media and history have recorded as the "Manson Family Murders." In the 20th Century, I could echo the words of Paul, the Apostle, "This is a faithful saying, and worthy of all acceptation, that Christ Jesus came into the world to save sinners, of whom I am chief" (1Tim 1:15).

For my part in those heinous crimes, I was sentenced to death. In 1972, the United States Supreme Court abolished the death penalty and my sentence was commuted to the term of seven years to life imprisonment. On the night of September 27, 1974 God had mercy upon my sin-sick hell-bound soul and gave me one more invitation to accept the gift of eternal life and forgiveness of all my sins.

Today, more than twenty years later, I am still residing at the California Institution for Women. I still love God with all my heart, with all my soul, mind and strength and I love my neighbor. To date, the Board of Prison Terms has told me on no less than eight or nine separate occasions that "nothing you do will ever outweigh the evil and wrong you have done. You will spend the rest of your life in prison nobody in society wants you in their community it's good that you say you've found God, but we are not impressed with your jailhouse religion." I have stated to the Board of Prison Terms, to my friends and family, and God knows my heart, "Live or die, in or out of prison, I will forever follow Jesus Christ."

According to Linda Mann who works to provide information concerning Susan Atkins, Susan never stabbed anyone. Both Patty Tate (Sharon Tate's sister) and Steven Kay (the prosecutor) attend the parole request meetings whenever they occur, and, of course, object vigorously to Susan's ever being released. Susan's last request for parole was denied on June 25, 1996. She is not scheduled for another parole hearing until the year 2000.

1970

Leslie Van Houten: White; Commuted to life in 1972. Leslie Van Houten is considered a model prisoner at the California Institution for Women. In 1969 she was convicted of two counts of murder and one count of conspiracy to commit murder after inflicting post-mortem wounds on Rosemary La Bianca. A witness at the trial said Leslie had told her she'd stabbed a body after it was already dead.

In 1978 Leslie was granted a new trial because of ineffective counsel; however, her conviction stood. During her more than two decades in prison, she has earned a college degree, quit drugs and alcohol, received glowing reports from supervisors and psychiatrists, and renounced any affiliation with Charles Manson and his family. She has also helped inmates learn to read and write and started a project with other inmates to make quilts for the homeless. She is described by those who know her as a "gentle, kind woman who quietly waits."

Leslie, who is serving a life sentence, asked the parole board to judge her on her actions in the last 25 years and not just those of August 1969. She was convicted of first-degree murder in the slayings of Leno La Bianca and his wife Rosemary, and conspiracy in the deaths of Sharon Tate and the four other victims. The state opposed Leslie's parole, arguing that the Manson murders were among the worst in this country's history, and that society simply does not want anyone who was involved in them released from prison. In May 1998, the California Board of Prison Terms again denied parole for Leslie Van Houten citing concern over her eating disorder which, according to the board, may be caused by suppressed anger. Leslie has remained incarcerated at the California Institution for Women since 1969.

1970

Patricia Krenwinkle: White; Commuted to life in 1972. Patricia Krenwinkel — Katie, as she was known in The Family — was part of the death squad sent to Cielo Drive and the La Bianca house in Los Feliz. One of her fingerprints was found at the Tate home. Patricia admitted dragging Abigail Folger from the living room to the bedroom. After killing Leno and Rosemary La Bianca, Patricia carved the word "WAR" on Leno's stomach using a fork. When police discovered his body the next day, the fork was still protruding from him.

Patricia was ordered to give samples of her handwriting to the court during the trial but refused to do so and her refusal was entered as evidence against her. The court said that a refusal tends to show a consciousness of guilt. Patricia Krenwinkle remains incarcerated in California today.

OTHER WOMEN SENTENCED TO DEATH IN CALIFORNIA

Women sentenced to death in California are incarcerated at the Central California Women's Facility near Chowchilla, which was built in 1987 to take care of the overflow from the women's prison at Frontera.

Chowchilla is divided into five yard areas (A–E) each with a double-wing dormitory. Buildings 503 and 505 are each two-story. They are guarded from watchtowers and each has an enclosed cement exercise yard. Inside, Building 505 is the women's death row. This is a long corridor with nine cells. Individual cells have a metal cot and a stainless steel toilet. Ironically, the cement walk in front of the condemned unit is referred to as "The Freeway."

1975
Mabel Glenn: Black; Reversed in 1979. Mabel Glenn was sentenced to death in October 1975. She was on death row for four years before her sentence was reversed in 1979.

1989
Cynthia Coffman: White; Currently on death row. Cynthia Coffman was born Cynthia Haskins in 1962 and grew up in a Catholic family in St. Louis, Missouri. There were five children in the family and she was the second oldest. Cynthia remembered the absence of both her father and mother while she was growing up. Her father left before Cynthia was six years old and her mother was trying to pursue a singing career that often meant leaving her children with relatives.

After high school, at age 17, Cynthia married Ronald Coffman and had a son. According to Cynthia, Coffman physically abused her so she left him after five years of marriage with the intention of finding work to support her and her son. She worked for a while in various places and then decided she might find better work and a new life in Arizona.

After a month in Arizona, Cynthia met James Marlow who was incarcerated at the time. When Marlow got out of prison, Cynthia joined him. Together, the two led a vagabond-type life wandering around supporting themselves through petty thievery. They were doing drugs and picking up money here and there and eventually moved into a trailer in a small isolated town in California to set up housekeeping.

Cynthia was attracted to everything about Marlow and in 1986, the two were married on a Harley Davidson, after which Cynthia had the phrase "I belong to the Folsom Wolf" tattooed on her buttocks and two lightning bolts (a symbol of white supremacy) tatooed on her ring finger. "Folsom Wolf" was a nickname Marlow had been given by his buddies in prison.

By the time they were married, they had already killed one man. Marlow told Cynthia he had inherited some money in Kentucky, to get her to go there with him. The truth was he had been hired as a hitman to kill a man for $5,000. Cynthia participated in the murder by distracting the man so that Malrow could shoot him. At his trial, Marlow told the jury that the murder had been Cynthia's idea.

That first hit was the beginning of a cross-country crime spree during which Marlow became more and more abusive towards Cynthia. The next murder was a 20-year-old woman, Corinna Novis, an insurance agent who gave the couple a ride after Cynthia told her she was the cheerleading coach at the University of the Redlands. They took her to a friend's home and sodomized her, then drove to a vineyard where Marlow took her out of the car and returned to the car alone. He had strangled and buried her in a shallow grave. Cynthia said she never asked what happened to the woman because she didn't want to know. She thought he had tied her up and left her there alive. She also said she never questioned Marlow about anything because she was afraid he might kill her son.

After killing Novis, they went back to her apartment and stole her credit cards and other things they thought they could pawn. They used her car to find their next victim, a 19-year-old woman, five days later. Cynthia maintains that she did not assist in the actual killing although Marlow wanted her to help him.

The two were eventually arrested because they left a careless trail of evidence. After her arrest, Cynthia confessed to her role in the murders and took authorities to one of the bodies they had been unable to find.

When Cynthia was convicted she became the first woman to be sentenced to death in California after capital punishment was reinstated in 1977. Both Cynthia and James Marlow were given death sentences by Superior Court Judge Don A. Turner for the slaying of Corinna Novis on November 7, 1986.

Cynthia testified to the brutality of their crimes and her attorneys claimed she had been forced to participate arguing she was a victim of a classic battered-woman situation and afraid to leave her abusive husband. However, her demeanor in court, did not convince either the judge or the jury. According to reports during the trial she appeared to be flippant and showed no remorse whatsoever.

The judge upheld the jury's recommendation of death saying Cynthia was "in this thing up to the hilt and enjoyed it up to the last minute." At the time of

Cynthia's sentencing, Judge Turner remarked "It's still very difficult for judges and juries to vote death for an attractive young woman. But this jury got to know her well."

Cynthia, who had a nine-year-old son at the time, was incarcerated at the California Institution for Women at Frontera and in 1992 was sentenced to life without parole, for a second murder, that of a woman in Huntington Beach, California. She is now on death row in California with a death sentence for one murder and life without parole for the other.

1990

Maureen McDermott: White; Currently on death row. Maureen McDermott, a former Los Angeles nurse, was accused and convicted of hiring a hospital orderly at County-USC Medical Center to kill her roommate Stephen Eldridge who was 27 at the time. It was believed that Maureen wanted the $100,000 insurance policy on the Van Nuys home they co-owned.

James F. Luna, the orderly Maureen was accused of hiring, testified at her trial that she had wanted him to mutilate Eldridge's body in the hopes that police would wrongly conclude it was a homosexual crime of passion. Luna stabbed Elridge 44 times and cut off his penis. This was the second time Luna had attempted to kill Elridge. Elridge escaped the first time. Luna testified that Maureen had previously hired him to attack a co-worker so that she could have his job.

During her trial, Maureen, who was 42 at the time, tearfully swore she was innocent, but the jury found her guilty and sentenced her to die in the California gas chamber. Before Maureen was sent to death row she spent almost five years at Sybil Brand Institute in East Los Angeles. There, it was said, she used her nurses training on at least one occasion to save the life of another prisoner who was choking on an apple. On another occasion she alerted deputies of an inmate's attempted suicide. Her lawyer tried very hard to use the fact that Maureen was considered a model inmate to prove she was no threat to society and to ask that her life be spared without success. Maureen McDermott is on death row in California today.

1992

Maria del Rosio Alfaro (Rosie): Latina; Currently on death row. Maria del Rosio Alfaro was sentenced to death for stabbing a 9-year-old Anaheim girl. The child was stabbed 57 times in the bathroom of her home during a 1990 residential robbery. Maria was 20 years old at the time of the murder and had four children of her own. At the penalty phase of her trial, Maria's attorneys argued she was a victim of drug use and was a "woman-child" whose lifestyle and actions had led to tragedy. The judge who sentenced her said that the murder of Autumn Wallace was the most "senseless, brutal, vicious, and callous killing" he had ever known.

1993

Catherine Thompson: Black; Currently on death row. Catherine Thompson was accused and sentenced to death for supposedly arranging the murder of her husband, Melvin Thompson, in Los Angeles. Although no evidence was presented or heard by the jury that Catherine knew of the murder or was involved in any way, her motive was assumed to be his life-insurance policy. Three other co-defendants who were involved in the murder were convicted and sentenced also. Although Catherine was sentenced to death, the actual murderer was given a life sentence after perjuring himself in testimony. A second person involved was given six years and fourteen months and has since been released. The third person was given eleven years and was supposed to do two and one half years, but after getting into some trouble in prison got another three years. Catherine is on death row in California today.

1994

Celeste Simone Carrington: Black; Currently on death row. A jury in San Mateo County, California convicted Celeste Simone Carrington, an East Palo Alto woman, and sentenced her to death for fatally shooting two people during two separate 1992 robberies. According to court records, in one robbery, she took the victim's ATM card and asked him for the PIN number before murdering him. Celeste Carrington is on death row in California today.

1994

Mary Ellen Samuels: White; Currently on death row. Mary Ellen Samuels was sent to death row in 1994 by a Van Nuys judge for paying her daughter's fiancé to kill her husband and then for hiring a hitman to kill her daughter's fiancé. Robert Samuels was shot in the head in 1988, and seven months later the hitman was found dead strangled, beaten, and dumped along a highway in Ventura County. According to court records Mary Ellen arranged to have her husband murdered when she found out he planned to divorce her. Prosecutors said she killed the hitman because she was afraid he would implicate her in her husband's death. The defense argued that Mary Ellen Samuels was a victim of domestic violence.

On July 21, 1994, a jury recommended that Mary Ellen be sent to the California gas chamber although her attorney pleaded for her life and asked the jury not to impose the death penalty. The police dubbed her the "Green Widow" because she spent the $500,000 she inherited from her slain husband almost immediately after his death on a new Porsche and a huge party for herself.

Ms. Samuels denied that she hired a hitman to kill her estranged husband, or that she had the hitman killed. She testified that she is a shy person with normal spending habits. Mary Ellen Samuels became the fifth woman sent to California's death row since the state resumed capital punishment. She is on death row in California today.

1995

Kerry Lynn Dalton: White; Currently on death row. Kerry Lynn Dalton was sentenced to death in 1995 in San Diego County for participating in the torture-killing of a woman who was beaten, electrocuted, and injected with battery acid before being fatally stabbed with a screwdriver.

Kerry had a long criminal record before this crime occurred and was one of three co-defendants who bragged about the crime. Police records say that Kerry had accused the victim of stealing her possessions before the attack. Kerry is on death row in California today.

1995

Caroline Young: Latina; Currently on death row. Caroline Young, the first woman ever given the death sentence in Alameda County, California, was a 51 year-old-grandmother who stabbed her two grandchildren to death because she said she was afraid of losing custody of them to their father.

Superior Court Judge Stanley Golden sentenced her to death on two counts of first-degree murder in the stabbing deaths of her 6-year-old grandson, Darin Torres, and her 4-year-old granddaughter, Dai-Zshia Torres. She slit Darin's throat and then stabbed herself in the abdomen a dozen times. When her daughter, Vanessa, frantically called police. Caroline slashed her granddaughter to death.

The children's mother, Vanessa, said she saw blood on her mother's kimono, then found her son in bed with his throat slit. She picked the boy up and called police, and while she was on the phone, her mother, Caroline, went in the other room and stabbed Dai-Zshia, her 4-year-old granddaughter, and herself, telling her daughter she did not want to live.

Caroline told investigators she had killed the children out of anger because she was about to lose custody of Darin to his father, a Marine recruiter who had arrived in the Bay Area the day of the killings. The father, who was unaware he had children until the state informed him he owed $12,000 in child support, requested and received custody of his children and was expecting to take his son to his home in Virginia.

The court papers indicate that Caroline wrote a letter to the children the day she killed them which said, in part, "I am a very angry and vengeful person. An unhappy spirit now on a rampage to get even with all that hurt me and mine." To the boy's father she wrote, "I'll be back to show you how it feels to lose someone you really love your daughter. I'm coming back for her. Every baby your wife has I will come back and get."

It took the jury only 2½ hours of deliberation to decide that Caroline Young should be given the death penalty. The judge said that Caroline's actions were "totally repulsive to society and the killing of children is, in effect, the death of all society." Caroline received custody of the children after their mother,

Vanessa Torres, was judged to be unfit when she was sent to jail for alleged involvement in prostitution and drugs.

Caroline's lawyer told the judge she had killed the children because of mental illness for which she had undergone psychiatric treatment while at Santa Rita jail. "What sits before you is a sick woman and we have reached the point in the late twentieth century where we don't execute sick people," he said. However, the judge said, "Caroline Young's emotional problems did not affect her ability to know what she was doing."

In 1995 Caroline Young was sentenced to death despite pleas from her daughter who made a last-minute appeal for mercy to save her mother's life. She is the oldest woman on California's death row.

6

Connecticut: Lethal Injection

The state of Connecticut has sentenced one woman to death since 1900. No woman has been legally executed in Connecticut, and there are no women on death row in Connecticut today.

In 1995, in a matter-of-fact decision, the Connecticut Supreme Court voted 4 – 3 to allow the execution of death row inmates in the state after a thirty-five year hiatus. The decision represented the first time the seven sitting justices had upheld the constitutionality of the death penalty in the state (Frisman, 1996). It affirmed the death sentence of a state inmate for the first time since the U.S. Supreme Court invalidated death sentences in 1972.

The new Connecticut law requires a jury to balance both aggravating and mitigating factors in each case. Previously, the death penalty could not be imposed if even a single mitigating factor was present.

Currently, in order to get a death sentence the state has to prove that a murder falls into one of nine categories required for a capital felony These include the murder of a police officer, a murder for hire, a murder during the course of a kidnapping or sexual assault, and a murder of two or more people at a time.

Michael Ross, who brutally raped and murdered at least six women from eastern Connecticut in the early 1980s, was the first person sentenced to death in Connecticut in over a quarter of a century. But in 1994 the Connecticut Supreme Court threw his sentence out. Later, in 1998 Ross wrote a 10-page document that was signed by the special prosecutor in which he agreed to forgo a death penalty hearing and accept a sentence of death by lethal injection. Judge Thomas Miano ruled the document was unconstitutional and that Connecticut law requires a 3-judge panel or a jury to decide whether or not someone should be executed. Ross, acting as his own attorney said he didn't feel he needed a jury and that the judge should just sentence him to death.

In 1998, attorneys for convicted killer Robert J. Breton challenged the method of execution in Connecticut, saying that lethal injection can be excruciatingly painful if not done correctly. However, Hartford Superior Court Judge Roland Fasano ruled that the evidence the state presented him on the execution protocol showed that lethal injection, in most cases, is about as painful as a pin prick and results in a virtually painless death.

Also in 1998 the Connecticut Bar Association passed a resolution calling for a national moratorium on executions. The association cited racial bias and the quality of legal counsel available to capital defendants as the reason.

According to the Connecticut Legal Aid and Defender Organization, blacks are four times more likely to get the death penalty for murder in Connecticut, and if the victim is white, it goes to eleven times more likely.

As in several other states, more than 90 percent of capital defendants in the state are represented by public defenders. A representative of the Connecticut Capital Defense and Trial Services Unit said recently that in capital cases involving multiple defendants, their office could only represent one of the clients.

WOMEN SENTENCED TO DEATH IN CONNECTICUT

1914

Bessie Wakefield: Commuted. Bessie Wakefield and James Plew were jointly indicted for first-degree murder in the killing of Bessie's husband, William Wakefield, by shooting, stabbing, and strangulation. Plew pleaded guilty.

William Wakefield's body was found in a wooded area in Chesire about 500 feet from the highway on June 28, 1913. There were several bullet and stab wounds in his head and body and two shoelaces had been tied together and drawn tight enough around his neck to kill him. One end of the laces had been tied in a slip noose around his neck and the other end was tied to the stump of a tree. A revolver and an open pocketknife were found beside his body.

The state claimed that Plew killed Wakefield under some type of an agreement with Bessie — and, if there was not an agreement, Bessie was at least aware of the fact that Plew was going to kill her husband and encouraged him to do so.

Apparently, Plew had tried to chloroform Wakefield while he was at home and Bessie was present. His intention was to take the body to the barn and hang it in order to make it look like a suicide. However, the plan failed, so Plew used an unrecorded excuse to get Wakefield to go with him to a site in Chesire about ten miles away, where he killed him.

The coroner who testified at the trial related a conversation he'd had with Bessie and Plew after the body had been discovered:

Coroner to Plew:	Didn't she (Bessie) tell you to take him away from the house and do it?
Plew:	She said to push him in the lake if I could.
Coroner to Bessie:	Is that true, Mrs. Wakefield?
Bessie:	I might have said something about the lake. I don't remember.
Coroner to Bessie:	You don't remember that
Bessie:	I can't remember—I might have said it—I want to say I didn't say it.

Ultimately, Bessie denied any participation in the murder and said she had not made any arrangements with Plew to get rid of her husband, nor had she encouraged him to do so. The state never claimed that Bessie actually killed her husband or that she was even present when it happened, but she was given the death penalty for conspiring in her husband's murder. Her sentence was eventually commuted.

7

Delaware: Lethal Injection/Hanging

The state of Delaware has given the death penalty to two women, Mary (May) H. Carey, who was executed in 1935 and Marilyn Dobrolenski in 1972. There are no women on death row in Delaware today.

In 1996 the state of Delaware carried out its first hanging in 50 years. Bill Bailey, a convicted double murderer, was only the third hanging in the country since 1965. Bailey, who was sentenced to die for murdering an elderly couple in 1979 on their farm, had the option of lethal injection but did not choose it. At midnight he was marched up the steps of a brightly lit 15-foot gallows. Executioners put a black hood over his head and bound his feet. A trap door was then opened and his body fell through. He was pronounced dead eleven minutes later. The son of the murdered couple witnessed the hanging.

William Flamer, 41, was executed the week after Bailey for the stabbing deaths of his uncle and aunt, 69-year-old Bayard Smith and his 68-year-old wife Alberta, at their Harrington, Delaware, home in 1979. The two were stabbed more than 150 times with a bayonet and knife after they refused to turn over their Social Security checks. Flamer was put to death by lethal injection at the Delaware Correctional Center in Smyrna, Delaware. Flamer's companion in the crime was executed by lethal injection for his part in the killings, in June 1994. The tiny state of Delaware, with a population of less than 700,00 has executed eight people since 1992.

Prisoners such as Bailey, who were sentenced to death prior to the legislation introducing lethal injection, are given the choice between the two methods. Michael Castle, former Governor of Delaware, who signed the law introducing lethal injection to the state, called hanging "Barbaric and inhumane." The minimum age for execution in Delaware is 16.

The average time on death row in Delaware is 4 years and in 1998 the state of Delaware used emergency funding to construct a new Execution Chamber. Of the fifteen men currently on death row the possibility still exists for one of them to choose hanging.

WOMEN SENTENCED TO DEATH IN DELAWARE

1935

May H. Carey: White; Executed, June 7, 1935. Mary (May) Carey was convicted and executed by hanging with her eldest son, Howard, for the murder of her brother, Robert Hitchens, a likable bachelor who worked in a grocery store in Omar, Delaware. After May made the decision to kill her brother sometime in 1927, she convinced her two eldest sons to help her by promising them a new car. Apparently her sole motive was to collect his insurance money.

On November 5, Robert told the grocery store owner's wife, Daisey, he felt ill and was going home. May and her sons were waiting for him at his house. They attacked him as he came in, bludgeoned him to death, and ransacked his house to make it look like a burglary. Finally they doused his body with alcohol, and then shot him in the head.

The next day when Robert did not show up for work, Daisey was concerned and notified his sister, May. Together they went to his house and knocked on his door. When there was no answer the women got a neighbor to jimmy a window and go in. The neighbor found Robert lying on the living room floor in a pool of blood where his sister and her sons had left him, shot and beaten. The presence of a whiskey bottle near his body led the police to conclude it was probably a gang of bootleggers. With no suspects, the case was entered into the police records as "unsolved" at the time.

The case was actually forgotten until December 1934, seven years later, when May's youngest son, who had liked his murdered uncle, was arrested on an unrelated burglary. When a detective asked him what he knew about his uncle's killing, he said, "Plenty." And said that he recalled overhearing conversations between his mother and his two older brothers when they were planning it. May and her sons were arrested soon after this information was received.

May and her son Howard, possibly the only mother and son given the death penalty and executed as co-conspirators in the same crime, were hanged on a specially built gallows behind a six-foot fence, to keep everyone except the official witnesses from seeing a woman hanged. May's second son was given a life sentence, and the youngest, who had testified against them, was sentenced to seven years for burglary. Howard left a wife and three young children, and in his last statement he put the blame for everything on his mother, saying, "What I did was against my will. I feel sure anyone in my shoes would have done the same thing." Nevertheless, he and his mother ate ice cream and cake together for their last meal, and he was said to have comforted her during an electric storm that preceded their execution.

1972

Marilyn Dobrolenski: White; Commuted to life. Marilyn Dobrolenski was a teenager from Ohio who went on a bank-robbing spree with a man she'd known for only a week. They called themselves Bonnie and Clyde and, in the course of events, they killed two Delaware State troopers. Marilyn's accomplice was also killed. Eventually, Marilyn was arrested and given two death penalties in the state of Delaware and another death sentence in the state of Pennsylvania. All three death sentences were changed to life as a result of the Supreme Court's decision in *Furman v. Georgia* in 1972. She is now serving a life sentence in Pennsylvania and has two life sentences pending in Delaware. (Also listed under Pennsylvania)

8

Federal Jurisdiction

Since the federal government reinstituted the death penalty in 1990 no federal inmate has been executed. However, between 1927 and 1963, the federal government executed 34 people. These included two women, Bonnie Brown Heady and Ethel Rosenberg, both in 1953 in double executions, with their companions. Ethel Rosenberg was executed with her husband Julius and Bonnie Brown Heady with Carl Austin her companion in crime. Although Bonnie and Carl had asked to be married before they were executed, their wish was not granted.

The last federal execution, the hanging of Victor Feguer, took place in 1963 in Iowa at the State Penitentiary in Fort Madison. When the U.S. Supreme Court ruled that all death penalty statutes were unconstitutional in 1972, the federal statutes were also affected. But, in 1988, a new federal death penalty law was enacted for murder. The statute was modeled after other state statutes that were approved by the 1972 rulings. Since that time 16 people have been sentenced to death under the federal statutes, but no one has been executed. There are no women on death row in a federal jurisdiction today.

In 1994, the federal death penalty was expanded to include some 60 different offenses. Among federal crimes for which people in any U.S. state or territory can receive a death sentence are: murder of certain government officials, kidnapping resulting in death, murder for hire, fatal drive-by shootings, sexual abuse crimes resulting in death, car jacking resulting in death, and certain crimes not resulting in death including being a drug-kingpin.

In seeking a federal death penalty the U.S. Attorney must make a recommendation to the U.S. Attorney General on the issue of whether or not to seek the death penalty in a specific instance. The Attorney General then refers it to a special committee to review and make a recommendation. Ultimately, however, the Attorney General of the United States makes the final decision.

According to rules drawn up by Attorney General Janet Reno in early 1995, the recommendation from the U.S. Attorney of a particular state for a death penalty must include certain things. Biographical and criminal record information of the defendants should be included. Data on aggravating and mitigating factors is also necessary as well as any justification for a federal prosecution instead of a state prosecution. Where the possible sentence is death, or there is an indication that the Justice Department might seek the death penalty, the defendant has the right to give mitigating in-formation at the outset to try and talk the government out of it.

The 1988 federal death penalty law did not specify any method of federal execution in the statute. In 1993 President Bush issued regulations authorizing lethal injection as the method of execution in the Federal Jurisdiction. The law, however, indicates that the method of execution will be that decided by the state in which the federal sentence is handed down. If that state does not allow the death penalty, the judge may choose another state for the carrying out of the execution. The Federal Bureau of Prisons recently constructed a lethal injection chamber in Terre Haute, Indiana, at a cost of approximately $500,000.

Since the Anti-Drug Abuse Act of 1988 and the expansion of the death penalty under Title 18 in 1994, the U.S. Attorney General's Office has authorized seeking the death penalty in 102 cases. According to Attorney Steven Bright, 80 percent were members of minority groups; fifty-six were black, defendants, eleven Hispanic, five Asian, and twenty Caucasian. Out of sixteen people currently under penalty of death by the federal government, only one is white. In 1997 Bright said, "There is a commonality between the state and federal systems in that you have to be a minority to be prosecuted."

Under Title 18 each federal defendant who faces the death penalty must be assigned two attorneys, at least one of which must have had death penalty experience. The federal government pays attorneys $125 an hour.

The use of the federal death penalty on Native American reservations has been left to the discretion of the tribal governments. Almost all the tribes have opted not to use the federal death penalty. As of July 31, 1996, there were 49 Native Americans on state death rows.

The U.S. Military has its own death penalty statute, utilizing lethal injection, though no military executions have been carried out in over thirty years. In June 1996, the Supreme Court ruled that the president, as commander-in-chief, has the authority to establish rules for capital punishment for military personnel.

WOMEN SENTENCED TO DEATH IN FEDERAL JURISDICTION

1953

Ethel Rosenberg: White; Executed, 1953. Ethel Rosenberg was executed with her husband, Julius, on June 19, 1953, at Sing Sing State Prison in Ossining,

New York. It was the first federal execution of a woman after 1865, when Mary Surrat was executed for her role in the assassination of Abraham Lincoln.

Tried in the era of McCarthyism and the Red Scare, the Rosenbergs, appeals for clemency were turned down first by President Truman, who was about to leave office at the time and who felt Eisenhower should decide the issue, and then by President Eisenhower, hours before their executions. The Rosenbergs were the second husband and wife to be executed for the same crime in this century.

Ethel, the only daughter of Barnet and Tessie Greenglass, was born in New York City on September 28, 1915. Her father made a bare subsistence for the family while she was growing up by running a sewing machine repair shop. She attended the Downtown Talmud Torah as a child and then Seward Park High School, from which she graduated at age 15.

Following high school she worked as a clerk in a shipping company for 4 years. She was forced to leave her job there after she organized a strike of 150 female workers. Because of her political activism she joined the Young Communist League as well as the American Communist Party. She met Julius Rosenberg at a New Years Eve benefit in New York City and they were married soon after in the summer of 1939.

Julius was born in 1918 and like his wife, attended the Downtown Talmud Torah and graduated from Seward Park High School. He came from a family of five and was the son of Polish immigrants. His father, Harry, worked in the New York garment industry. After high school Julius went to the City College of New York and studied electrical engineering while becoming politically active in several organizations.

After marrying Ethel, Julius was hired as a civilian employee of the U.S. Army Signal Corps, where he was promoted to the position of Inspector. It was during this time that both Julius and Ethel became full members of the American Communist Party. In 1945 Julius was fired from his job with the Signal Corps when it was found out he had been a member of the Communist Party. He was then with the Emerson Radio Corporation for a brief time until he joined his brother-in-law, David, in forming the G & R Engineering Company, which was never much of a success. During this time Ethel was at home raising their two young sons, Michael and Robert. The boys were 7 and 3 years old in 1950 when Ethel's younger brother, David Greenglass, led the FBI to arrest their father, Julius, and subsequently Ethel, as a spy.

David, whom Ethel called "Doovey," was seven years younger than his sister, but also politically minded. Both he and his wife, Ruth, had joined the Young Communist League in 1943 before David was inducted into the Army. As a machinist he was stationed in Oak Ridge, Tennessee and Los Alamos, New Mexico. In New Mexico he became part of the Manhattan Project, the group that developed the atomic bomb. David testified that he was not aware of the purpose of the Manhattan Project until his wife, Ruth told him after Julius Rosenberg informed her.

In 1943, in Arlington, Virginia, the U.S. Army set up a code-breaking program they called VENONA. The explicit purpose of the project was to break Soviet diplomatic and KGB codes. Early in World War II the allies had broken both the German and Japanese diplomatic and military codes; and the knowledge they gathered from this proved invaluable, so the United States decided it needed a similar program of its own.

FBI agent Robert Lamphere, who joined the VENONA project in 1948 as a project cryptographer, and Meredith Gardner, who was already with the project when Lamphere joined, were responsible for piecing together the cables that ultimately made the Rosenberg-espionage connection.

According to the FBI, a November 27, 1944 cable from the KGB chief in Washington specifically referred to Ethel Rosenberg by her first name. In a memo to Moscow, they said, he referred to "Liberal's [Julius Rosenberg's] wife — surname that of her husband, first name Ethel, 29 years old. Married five years. Finished secondary school." Seemingly, this one reference eventually led to the demise of Julius and Ethel Rosenberg. Their trial and subsequent convictions in 1951 ended with one of the most controversial sentences ever to be handed down in the United States.

When the FBI questioned Ethel's brother, David Greenglass, about spy activities, in what could be interpreted the ultimate betrayal, he led them to his brother-in-law. Julius was arrested soon after being questioned by the FBI, and on August 11, 1950, his wife, Ethel, was also arrested. Although Ethel's brother, David had accused Julius, it was Ruth Greenglass, who implicated her sister-in-law, Ethel.

Ruth had grown up in the same New York neighborhood as her husband. They married in 1942 before David was drafted into the Army in 1943. Both were interested in politics and had joined the Young Communist League together. In November 1944, when Ruth left New York and went to visit David in Los Alamos, New Mexico, she asked him to forward any information he could obtain on the Manhattan Project to his brother-in-law, Julius, in New York.

At the Rosenberg trial Ruth testified that Ethel typed the notes that David provided them, thus implicating Ethel in the spying. She also testified that it was Julius and Ethel who urged her to convince David to become involved in espionage.

When Ethel and Julius Rosenberg were arrested, they were charged with espionage against the United States on behalf of the Soviet Union. FBI Director, J. Edgar Hoover, dubbed it "the crime of the century."

David Greenglass became a prosecution witness against his sister and brother-in-law in exchange for immunity for Ruth, his wife. He received a 15-year sentence and remained with his wife after his release from prison. In 1990 a reporter from the *New York Times* interviewed David Greenglass. He was then 68 and living in Queens under an assumed name. Asked if he would have done anything differently, he said "No."

Both Ethel and Julius Rosenberg were sentenced to death for giving the "secret of the atomic bomb" to the Soviet Union. A double death sentence for a husband and wife was practically unprecedented and provoked a storm of protests from around the world. It meant, amongst other things, that their two sons, Michael and Robert, would grow up without either parent. Pope Pius XII as well as the heads of several countries of the world protested the sentence. Massive demonstrations were held in France to raise money for the Rosenberg defense fund and Pablo Picasso even printed portraits of Julius and Ethel forwarding the money to their defense fund.

The Rosenberg sons did not have a stable home environment for some time after their parents were arrested. For three months they lived with Ethel's mother, Tessie Greenglass, until she became ill and unable to care for them. They were then sent to the Hebrew Children's Home where they stayed until Sophie Rosenberg, Julius' mother, took them to live with her. During the time they were with their grandmother, Sophie, the boys visited their parents at Sing Sing. After about a year they went to live with some friends of the Rosenbergs in New Jersey.

In their will, the Rosenbergs named their attorney, Manny Bloch, guardian for their two sons. As their guardian, Bloch allowed the two boys to be adopted in 1957 by Abel and Anne Meeropol. Only then were the boys able to have some semblance of a normal life.

Ethel wrote to her sons while she was in prison (Meeropol & Meeropol, 1986). And in June 1953 the two brothers went to Washington, DC to plead for their parents' lives. Michael had sent a handwritten letter to President Eisenhower, appealing his parents' sentence, which read in part, "Please let my mommy and daddy go and do not let anything happen to them. If they come home Robby and I will be very happy and we will thank you very much" (Radosh, 1983).

Before her execution, Ethel Rosenberg sent one last letter to her two sons reminding them that, even though they would miss their parents, she hoped they would come to realize that life is worth living (Goldstein, 1975).

The Rosenbergs' attorneys, Emanuel and Alexander Bloch, fought the convictions for two years. They brought numerous motions before several judges to open a new trial, but all of them failed. Finally on June 19, 1953, after all of their avenues of appeal had been closed, the Rosenbergs were put to death in the electric chair at the Sing Sing death house in Ossining, NY.

In 1996, at a forum that was cosponsored by the FBI and the National Security Council to discuss the release of the VENONA papers, retired agent Robert Lamphere surprised everyone by stating that both he and J. Edgar Hoover opposed the execution of Ethel Rosenberg (Dobbs, 1997). He said that although the evidence supported her guilt, they felt she was not as deeply involved in spying as her husband. Aside from that, he said they both thought it unwise to execute the mother of two small children. He said, however, it was ultimately President Eisenhower who refused to interfere with the judicial process and commute her sentence. Thus he laid the blame directly on President Eisenhower for the execution of Ethel Rosenberg.

In a 1997 interview with the *Washington Post* (1997) Alexander Feklisov, the 82-year-old former Russian KGB agent, spoke out about his connection with Julius Rosenberg. Feklisov said he is the only Soviet intelligence officer still alive with intimate personal knowledge of the Rosenberg case. He further stated his decision to tell his side of the story was the result of years of personal agonizing and arguments with his superiors in the foreign intelligence arm of the KGB.

He characterized Julius as a great sympathizer with the Soviet Union who was a true revolutionary, willing to sacrifice himself for his beliefs. Feklisov said he met with Julius in New York at least 50 times between 1943–1946, during which time Julius helped organize an important industrial espionage ring for Moscow. According to Feklisov, Julius Rosenberg was never involved in stealing nuclear secrets for the U.S.S.R. He said that the claim of Judge Irving R. Kauffman, who sentenced the Rosenbergs, that they had "altered the course of human history" by putting the atomic bomb in the hands of the Soviets was absurd. He also insisted that Ethel Rosenberg never had any direct contact with Soviet intelligence, but conceded that she was probably aware of her husband's activities.

The Rosenberg sons, among others, have always argued that the VENONA papers are not authentic, but rather files created from FBI assumptions and misinformation. Whatever the truth, the documents, as such, show that Julius and Ethel Rosenberg provided relatively little atomic information to the Soviets. One of Rosenberg's major accomplishments, according to the intercepts, seems to have been recruiting his brother-in-law, David Greenglass, who delivered the detailed drawings of the Los Alamos research site where the bomb was developed.

In a statement released in July 1995, Robert and Michael Meeropol, the sons of Ethel and Julius Rosenberg, gave their initial reaction to the release of the 49 VENONA documents that purport to prove that their parents were spies. Their statement said, in effect, that they had tried to secure the release of these documents for the past 20 years, and that the documents contain no evidence to justify the execution of their parents.

In a booklet released with the documents to help explain them (Introductory History of VENONA and Guide to the Translation) the following statement is included: "These messages disclose some of the clandestine activities of Julius and Ethel Rosenberg." Regarding this and other such statements the sons responded: "Our mother is barely mentioned in the 49 documents the agencies claim are KGB transmissions...and nowhere in them is it stated that she engaged in clandestine activities. The major reference to her states, 'Knows about her husband's work and the role of METR and NIL. In view of delicate health does not work...is characterized positively and as a devoted person' " (Rosenberg Fund, 1995).

In a 1994 book Pavel Sudoplatov, one of the Soviet players in this drama spoke of the Rosenbergs thus:

The irony is that the Rosenbergs are portrayed by the American counterintelligence as the key figures in delivering atomic secrets to the Soviet Union, but actually they played a very minor role. They were a naive couple, overeager to co-operate, who worked for us because of their ideological motivations. Their contribution to atomic espionage was minor.

He goes on to say

It was clear from the very beginning that the case had acquired a political character far out of proportion to their actual role as spies. More important than spying activities was that the Rosenbergs served as a symbol in support of Communism and the Soviet Union. Their bravery to the end served our cause because they became the center of a worldwide (anti-US) Communist propaganda campaign.

1953

Bonnie B. Heady: White; Executed December 18, 1953. When Carl Austin Hall was released from prison on April 24, 1953, a woman he had never seen before, Bonnie Brown Heady met him. Bonnie had been a gun moll in 1935 married to a bank robber named Don Heady. After being imprisoned Don was shot to death by a sheriff's posse, while trying to escape to meet his 21-year-old red headed wife Bonnie. When Bonnie was told her husband was dead her only recorded comment was, "That's too bad."

Bonnie, for whatever reason, was addicted to criminal types, and she'd heard about Carl Austin Hall from some ex-prisoners who called him the "playboy crook." This characterization appealed to Bonnie and when she learned of his eminent release from prison she went to meet him and took him to her home at 1021 South 38th St. in St. Joseph, Missouri. She was already an alcoholic, so the two of them drank themselves into stupors while they main-lined heroin. When they were sober, they began working out the details for kidnapping the 6-year-old son of Robert Greenlease, a 71-year-old car dealer who was the wealthiest man in Kansas City at the time.

Carl was the one who had come up with the idea of the kidnapping. He felt it was a crime he'd only have to commit once because he could live off of the money from it for the rest of his life. He'd heard about Robert Greenlease's money, and through the newspapers he learned of his two young children who were living with him and his wife. Carl decided to kidnap one of them and demand a large ransom.

The idea of committing an atrocious shocking crime seemed to excite both Bonnie and Carl. The night before the kidnapping, in the midst of a downpour, they took shovels and dug a shallow grave in Bonnie's yard where they would bury the child they kidnapped. Carl said he convinced Bonnie they'd have to kill little Bobby because otherwise he might be able to identify both of them

The next morning, on September 28, 1952, by 7:30 a.m. Bonnie and Carl were headed south down Highway 71 toward Kansas City in her blue Plymouth station wagon. They drove straight to the French Institute of Notre Dame de Sion, an exclusive pre-grade school in Kansas City, where they parked close enough to observe the children arriving. A blue Cadillac pulled into the drive and six-year-old Bobby Greenlease emerged, waved to his father, and entered the school building. Bonnie and Carl then drove off, and Carl sat in the car in the Katz drugstore parking lot while Bonnie returned to the school to get Bobby.

A nun, Sister Morand, answered the door and Bonnie sobbed as she told her she was Bobby Greenlease's aunt and that his mother had suffered a heart attack and was in St. Mary's Hospital. She said that Mrs. Greenlease was calling for her son and that she had come to get him. The nun asked Bonnie to wait in the chapel while she got him, and in a few minutes she returned with a small, blond boy. Bonnie was kneeling in one of the pews and when she got up she told the nun, "I've been praying for my sister's quick recovery. I'm not a Catholic and I don't know whether or not God heard my prayers." This probably helped the nun trust her, as well as the fact that Bobby didn't react to Bonnie and went with her without a word, even though she was a total stranger to him.

They took the cab that was waiting for them at the curb and got out at Main and Fortieth, where they crossed the street and got into a 1947 Plymouth station wagon. Carl drove west across the state line into Kansas, then south to a less populated area. When he reached a wheat field near Overland Park, Kansas, he stopped the car. In his testimony to the FBI Hall said

Bobby had not offered any resistance nor made any outcries, but seemed interested in his ride and appeared to be enjoying himself during the trip. After stopping the car, I got out, went to the rear and let the tailgate down, then laid out a blue plastic sheet. I then went around to the passenger side of the car and entered. Bobby was still sitting in the front seat, but Bonnie had left the car and was walking along a hedgerow behind the car. I had a piece of rope, which was part of a clothesline I had obtained from Bonnie's home. I placed the rope around Bobby's neck and endeavored to strangle him.

The rope was too short, and Carl couldn't twist it tight enough to strangle the kicking, struggling boy, so he pulled out his .38-caliber revolver and fired two shots point blank at Bobby. The first shot went wild, but the second entered Bobby's head, causing massive bleeding, and after a few moments, death. During the struggle Carl had pushed Bobby down onto the floorboard of the Plymouth. He then dragged his limp body out of the car and wrapped it in the blue plastic sheet he'd brought for that purpose and laid it in the back of the station wagon.

They then drove back to Kansas City, with Bobby's body in the car. En route, they stopped at a tavern where Bonnie brought drinks out to the car because Carl was covered with blood and was afraid if he went in it might make people suspicious. Afterward they drove back to Bonnie's home in St. Joseph and buried Bobby's body in the shallow grave they had prepared the night before. While Bonnie shoveled the last few scoops of dirt, Carl used the garden hose to wash the dried blood and bloodstains out of the station wagon.

Meanwhile, the nun had called St. Mary's Hospital and found out that Mrs. Greenlease was not, in fact, a patient, then called the Greenlease's home to find Bobby's mother there. She told Mrs. Greenlease the story, and the Greenleases realized immediately that their son had been kidnapped. They received a ransom letter the next morning demanding $600,000 in ten and twenty-dollar bills; they were told to put an ad in the *Kansas City Star* when the money was ready. The note assured the parents that Bobby was "in good hands," which gave them reason to hope he was still alive. However, he was by then already dead and buried.

The next day Bonnie and Carl began a week long drunken spree across the state continually driving back and forth from St. Joseph to Kansas City, and eventually to St. Louis. During this time Carl made repeated phone calls to the Greenlease estate, assuring them that Bobby was alive.

This was the first major kidnapping in the United States since the 1930s and, according to the 1932 Lindbergh Kidnapping Law, the FBI could not enter the case for seven days. Because of the tragic outcome of this case the Lindbergh Law was changed to allow the FBI to act immediately. The kidnappers, however, dragged out negotiations for delivery of the ransom money for several weeks. Carl made more than a dozen calls to the Greenleases setting up arrangements, then changing plans. He mailed 16 ransom notes that were all contradictory and confusing. During all this time, the Greenleases always assumed their son was alive. Carl kept promising to deliver "Little Bobby" in various places in Kansas City "alive and well." The money, weighing 85 lbs., was at one point delivered, stuffed in a duffel bag and thrown into high grass off a country lane. When Hall arrived to retrieve the money, he was so drunk he couldn't find it — so he went home and called the Greenleases and told them to retrieve the money and take it to another location. On the phone he said, "You'll see him in 24 hours — we will be glad to send him back." Carl Austin Hall finally retrieved the money and split it up into two large metal suitcases, which everyone thought he buried somewhere in south St. Louis. He then took about $300,000 of the money and had a wild party. When they got a cheap motel room and Bonnie passed out, Carl left her $2,000 and went to continue his celebration at a more expensive hotel. He was flashing so much money around employees of the hotel became suspicious and alerted the police. When the police took Carl in for questioning he told them everything and soon after that they arrested Bonnie.

They found Bobby Greenlease's body in Bonnie's yard where she and Carl had buried it. Bonnie insisted, at first, that she thought Carl was Mrs. Greenlease's ex-husband, and she was just trying to help him get his son back. Both Bonnie and Carl admitted the kidnapping; but both denied they killed Bobby. Later, both admitted killing him.

Bertha Nann Carroll, the superintendent of the Women's Prison at the time, recalled Bonnie, on her way to her death row cell saying [of her trial], "Some people looked at me so horrible." Because Bonnie was shivering, the Superintendent placed a coat over her shoulders. On death row Carl was in Cell #18 and Bonnie was in Cell #25. They could not see each other, but they could talk.

At the penitentiary, Carl showed some signs of remorse, confessing to a Presbyterian minister. But, he blamed alcohol for his downfall from a young man with a $200,000 inheritance and a bright future to a condemned killer.

Before their trial Bonnie and Carl wrote letters to the Greenleases saying they were sorry for what they had done and they asked their forgiveness. After they received the death penalty, Bonnie reportedly said, "I'd rather be dead than poor." Bobby Greenlease's father said, "Execution is too good for them, but it's all the law provides."

Bonnie Brown Heady was the first woman sentenced to death in Missouri after 1834. She was allowed to visit Carl on the night of their execution, and they ate fried chicken together. Bonnie sat outside of Carl's cell as he nervously gripped the bars. She was clearly the stronger of the two. She stroked his hand and patted his head, telling him "Everything is going to be all right." Carl had been kept in a separate holding cell from the general population for fear that other prisoners might kill him. About half an hour before they were to die the warden allowed the two to be alone together in a cell without supervision. Reportedly, they asked to be married before they were executed, but that request was denied. Carl was apparently covered with lipstick after the visit.

Since the two were being executed side by side at the same time, the warden had originally told reporters they would be wearing bathing suits, Carl trunks and Bonnie a two-piece suit. But when word of this got out, there were protests from women's groups, who said it was indecent. Therefore, Carl wore green denim slacks and Bonnie wore a green denim dress. Blindfolds were placed on both as they were led to the gas chamber.

One of Bonnie's main concerns was how she would look, so she had put her hair in curlers that morning and spent several hours combing it and putting on make-up for the occasion. She was led trembling to the chair next to Carl's in the gas chamber. She turned her blindfolded face to the warden and said, "Thanks for everything. You've been very kind." Then she turned to Carl and said, "Are you all right, honey?" To which Carl replied in a dull resigned voice "Yes, Momma." A U.S. Marshall leaned in and asked the two of them if they had anything to tell him, since half of the money provided by the Greenleases was never found — but both remained silent. After the doors were closed

Bonnie and Carl were seen talking to each other, but none of their words were heard. Reporters said Bonnie had told Carl, "Take it like a man." After the pellets were dropped Carl breathed once, sighed, and was dead immediately. Bonnie held her breath until she could do so no longer.

Bonnie Heady was buried in St. Joseph, Missouri. She had asked that Carl be buried next to her, but the people of St. Joseph would not allow it.

9

Florida: Electrocution

The state of Florida has given the death penalty to fifteen women since 1900. In 1998 Judi Buenoano became the first woman executed by electrocution in the state of Florida. There are four women on death row in Florida today.

Prior to 1923 the method of execution in Florida was hanging, carried out in the counties where the crime had been committed. In 1923 the state legislature declared electrocution the official mode of capital punishment; and the first inmate to be electrocuted in Florida was Frank Johnson, on October 7, 1924 (Driggs,1993). Between 1930 and 1990 there were a total of 195 executions by electrocution in Florida.

In June 1972 the U.S. Supreme Court declared capital punishment unconstitutional, and 95 men and one woman in Florida had their death sentences commuted to life. By December of that same year the Florida statutes were revised, and by July 1976 the Supreme Court approved the new statutes and found them to be constitutional. After a fifteen-year hiatus, executions resumed in Florida with the death by electrocution of John Spinkelink on May 25, 1979. Since 1976, Florida has executed 43 people.

The state's 75-year-old electric chair, located at the Florida State Prison in Starke, is made of oak and was constructed by inmates in 1923. Originally it was located at Union Correctional Institution, but was moved to Starke in 1962 when Florida's death row was transferred.

CAPITAL SENTENCING IN FLORIDA

Before *Furman v. Georgia* in 1972, when the U.S. Supreme Court invalidated existing death penalty statutes, Florida had what was known as the "mercy statute" in its capital sentencing scheme [(FLA.STAT. § 755.082 (1)(1971)]. Under the "mercy statute," a death sentence was mandatory when a defendant was convicted of a capital felony unless the jury voted for mercy, in which case, the defendant would be sentenced to life in prison (Lafferty, 1995). The defendant had the right to appeal to the Florida Supreme Court, but the court's review was limited to the question of guilt or innocence and not to the question of punishment. Therefore, unless a defendant chose to waive a jury trial, the decision of what punishment to impose belonged to the jury.

After *Furman,* Florida adopted its current capital sentencing scheme which consists of the bifurcated trial (guilt or innocence phase and sentencing phase), with the final sentencing decision made by a judge. After a defendant's guilt is determined, in the sentencing phase, both judge and jury listen to relevant information about the nature of the crime and the defendant's character (aggravating and mitigating circumstances), after which the jury deliberates and recommends a sentence to the judge. Regardless of the jury recommendation, the judge makes the final decision according to what he/she feels to be an appropriate sentence. In this last part, judges in Florida are allowed to exercise the jury override provision. Although this provision was originally intended to allow a judge to override a jury's recommendation of death and impose a sentence of life, most cases have involved judges overriding juries' recommendations of life and imposing a sentence of death. In every state where this provision exists, there has been overwhelming evidence in case after case that judges have set themselves up as the final arbiters of justice and sentenced people to death in the face of juries who, ideally representing the community, have recommended life.

In a 1988 article in the *Miami Herald,* Von Drehle noted that in more than 20 percent of the state's death sentences (544 at the time) judges had sentenced defendants to death for whom juries had recommended life. He said then that in 7 out of 10 "judicial overrides" higher courts reversed the trial judges' decisions. By law, every death sentence in Florida is automatically reviewed by the state Supreme Court.

DEATH WARRANTS AND CLEMENCY

In Florida, clemency lies in the hands of the governor. Between 1925 and 1965 Florida governors granted clemency in 57 out of 268 cases (Von Drehle, 1988). However, after Governor Bob Graham granted six clemencies during his first term of office, he received a lot of political backlash and began avoiding the whole clemency issue by not signing death warrants in cases where he felt uncertain.

Governor Lawton Chiles signed 31 death warrants, including one for Judi Buenoano in December 1997. Every two weeks or so the governor's assistant general counsel goes by the Florida Supreme Court and picks up a roster of the state's death penalty cases and reviews them to see where they are in the court process. Any cases that have been upheld on appeal are then referred to the governor. When such a case comes up the governor is required to review the case. According to Tom Crapps, Governor Lawton Chiles's assistant general counsel in 1998, Governor Chiles looks at the facts of the murder, what the courts have ruled, the legal issues involved, and the background of the victims. If the governor sees there is no reason for a person not to be executed he tells his assistant to draw up a death warrant.

By signing death warrants, governors appear tough on crime. Critics say governors use death warrants as vote getters. The more warrants signed, the more votes. Usually, a death warrant is signed shortly after a clemency hearing, and a date of execution is set for anywhere from 30 to 60 days later. But death warrants don't necessarily mean execution. It is not unusual to have as many as 10 death warrants before an actual execution.

After a death warrant is signed, Florida Supreme Court Justice Gerald Kogan noted "We get hit with appeals that are a foot high as much as 1,200 pages each." Governor Bob Graham signed more death warrants during his terms of office than any Florida governor before him, but he was always careful never to have more than four death warrants in effect at a time because he felt the system couldn't handle any more. In contrast, Governor Bob Martinez had as many as nine death warrants out at the same time because he felt that death warrants were necessary to move cases along. He said that without death warrants cases don't go anywhere, they just sit in the system.

When warrants are signed, costs go up. Courts issue "stays of execution" to give them time to go over the appeals. According to Von Drehle (1988), instead of mailing documents, lawyers use couriers, judges call emergency meetings, everything else on the docket is put on hold. The signing of death warrants, and the frenzy it sets off, is one of many unresolved issues in the death penalty process. The larger the death row population, the bigger the problems tend to be.

After the governor signs a death warrant the state Department of Corrections is notified and the governor's office and prison officials decide on a day and time for the execution In Florida, most executions are held at 7:00 a.m. According to the governor's office, there is no particular reason for this except it is the time when the guard shift changes and, therefore, the best time for a lockdown, which is done whenever there is an execution.

Andrea Jackson, a woman on death row in Florida today, described her reactions to hearing her death warrant had been signed by the governor:

Even when I heard that they had signed my warrant, I wasn't scared. Christ told me that I won't die here, and I have faith in Him. They let me call my mother, and that was hard. Then they took all my property and guarded me twenty-four hours a day. They stripped me down and put me by myself in the deathwatch room. (Allen, 1998)

DEATH ROW

A death row cell in Florida measures 6′ by 10′ by 10′. The cinderblock walls at Broward Correctional Institution's death row for women are painted a pastel blush. One woman on death row in Florida described it this way:

Florida houses the five of us in a segregation unit marked "X" for 'Xecution.' We are locked down 24 hours a day. The only human contact is the brief nod or hello from the officer who places the food tray through the slot at 6 a.m., 11 a.m., and 4 p.m. The health officer makes rounds once a week. All mail is read incoming and outgoing. Even though our contact is minimal, our cells are searched daily. We are allowed no personal items. Packages from home were discontinued January 1, 1997. Each woman on death row is issued the following:

- 2 pair of pajamas
- 2 towels
- 2 washcloths
- 1 pair state tennis shoes
- 4 state uniform dresses
- 1 pair state pants
- 2 state shirts
- 1 housecoat
- 4 pair state underwear
- 1 bras
- 1 jacket
- 1 mattress
- 2 sheets
- 1 pillow
- 1 pillowcase
- 1 13-inch black/white TV

Once a week all hygiene items are purchased from the canteen marked up 50 to 300 percent. Books must come from the publisher, no hardcover. We are only allowed 4 books in our cell, 1 Bible. We pay $3.00 co-payment for medical or dental visits. Even though we are cell searched daily and we see no one, there is a mass shakedown once a month. We are handcuffed for showers, walks, anytime the cell door is open. We are allowed four hours per week in the walk yard. No church services are allowed and no law library visits. We are not allowed to participate in any activities that require us to leave our cell. We are cuffed/shackled to go to medical, the compound is cleared and "DEATH ROW WALKING" announced. Our overhead light stays on 24-hours a day. There is no privacy at all. Male officers watch us when we bathe.

Florida's death row for women lies in the farthest reaches of Pembroke Pines, Florida. Only the squawk of birds, and occasionally the whine of mosquitoes, breaks the silence. It is at the edge of the Everglades, with pine trees and scraggly vegetation stretching for miles around it in all directions.

EXECUTIONS IN FLORIDA

On October 20, 1997 the Florida Supreme Court upheld the constitutionality of the state's use of the electric chair which had been under question due to failures in its mechanism in two executions.

The week prior to his/her execution, an inmate on Florida's death row begins what is called "Phase II" of their death sentence. Phase I is the time they actually spend on death row after their sentencing, before they are executed.

When Phase II begins, inmates, whether male or female, are moved to a cell in the Florida State prison at Starke. It is located in the X-Wing (X for Execution) down the hall from the death chamber. Andrea Jackson, who has had two death warrants signed recalled her experience of being moved five days before her scheduled execution in an article in *Grand Street* (Allen, 1998):

They took me to Starke five days early for security reasons. I had this motorcade with two armed officers inside with me, and two cars in front of me. They were really mad when they had to turn around that death caravan and bring me all the way back. Coming down, they were laughing and joking. They said I'd fit just right in the chair. I was riding with an officer, and she was angry about turning around. She said to me "It might not be today, and it might not be tomorrow. But we're gonna fry your black ass."

During Phase II condemned prisoners are kept on a suicide watch in case they try to kill themselves before the state does. They are allowed a small black and white TV, cigarettes, and some magazines. But, most of the week prior to their execution inmates spend with their attorneys.

Execution equipment is tested during Phase II also. In all it is tested three times before the actual execution. The first time is right after a person's death warrant is signed, the second time, a week before the execution, and finally it is tested the day before the death sentence is carried out.

One woman, who worked at the state prison in Starke, reported that when the electricity is tested prior to an electrocution there is a tremendous rumble of machinery and the lights throughout the prison dim. In protest inmates hang out of windows and cells and yell and bang on the bars with anything they can get their hands on.

The night before they are executed, prisoners in Florida are allowed a final meal of whatever they request not to exceed the cost of $20. Later that same night, prisoners are allowed a final visit with their family in a contact setting where they can embrace although they are not alone.

The superintendent of the prison is in charge of the execution team made up of administrative personnel, maintenance people, security, and medical staff. Serving on the execution team is voluntary except for the superintendent and the medical executive director.

The condemned are awakened (if they are able to sleep) one hour before their execution. Their heads and lower right leg are shaved. They are then allowed to shower after which they are issued clean clothes to be executed in. These include underwear, a pair of trousers, a dress shirt or blouse, and socks. They do not wear shoes. They are shackled at the wrists and ankles as they are led to the death chamber where the executioner is already waiting. If the condemned requests it, the chaplain may accompany them to the execution chamber. As the condemned enters the chamber, the time is recorded.

Official witnesses and media witnesses are locked in the witness room by two designated Department of Corrections' escort staff. Witnesses may include twelve family members (including members of victims families) and twelve media representatives who see a part of the execution process, but not all.

In 1998, Mike Vasilinda, owner of *Capitol News Service* contested a 1977 rule of the Florida Department of Corrections banning all forms of video cameras and audio equipment from the witness area. Vasilinda claimed "The public has a right to have the light of day shown upon the exercise of this very awesome ultimate power of the state"(Noack, 1998).

The executioner is an anonymous private citizen who is paid $150 per death and is recruited by advertising in various Florida newspapers. A 1998 report by the Committee on Criminal Justice in Florida stated that the executioner must "exhibit a willingness to participate and must uphold the confidentiality of the execution proceedings." Applicants for the job are interviewed, but who conducts the interviews or makes the final decision is a secret of the Florida Department of Corrections.

In his book *Among the Lowest of the Dead* (1996) David Von Drehle described how the executioner was chosen for John Spinkelink:

The executioner, whose job was to trip the circuit breaker, had been chosen from several hundred applicants who had answered a classified ad. His identity was painstakingly concealed: He was picked up on a lonely road and driven to the prison by a circuitous back route; his $150 fee was paid in cash so no record would appear on any checking account. (99–100)

Once an inmate is seated in the chair eight leather straps are used to secure lap, arms, legs, chest, and waist. A leg piece is laced to the inmate's right calf and a sponge and electrode are attached. The sponge covers all areas of the electrode to prevent contact with the skin. Just prior to the execution, the superintendent reads the death warrant aloud to the offender and the inmate can make a final statement if he/she chooses to do so.

The headpiece, consisting of a piece of metal and a leather hood, is then used to conceal the offender's face. The metal part of the piece is a copper wire mesh screen to which an electrode is secured. A wet sponge is placed between the inmate's scalp and the electrode.

Two Department of Corrections staff are posted in the execution chamber during the execution to ensure that the condemned remains seated and that the equipment is functioning properly. The signal that an execution should begin, which is only known by the warden and the executioner, is given. The executioner engages the circuit breaker. The cycle is 2,300 volts for eight seconds, followed by 1,000 volts for twenty-two seconds, followed by 2,300 volts for eight seconds.

William F. Hamilton, medical examiner for the state of Florida, who has done more than twenty-five autopsies on executed inmates has said once the electricity enters the head it scrambles the normal electric signals in the brain and the inmate loses consciousness and all feeling. According to Hamilton, it travels through the inmate's body quickly causing muscle spasms in the legs, arms, and wrists so that heart and lung activity ceases almost immediately.

When the cycle is finished the electrician indicates that the current is off. The equipment is then disconnected, the manual circuit behind the chair is disengaged, the safety switch is opened, and the time is recorded.

Two minutes after the current is shut down a physician examines the body for vital signs. If the offender is not dead, the execution cycle is repeated. If the physician pronounces the offender dead the time of death is recorded and the death certificate is signed.

When Pedro Medina was executed in 1997, as thousands of volts of electricity coursed through his body, flames burst out from under the facemask. A similar problem happened in 1990 during the execution of Jesse Tafero and, although there were sixteen executions between Tafero and Medina, no changes were made in the design or the material used in the electric chair apparatus between the two executions.

In the days following Medina's execution, Florida Attorney General Bob Butterworth proposed that the state require lethal injection for new death row inmates and allow the 380 inmates on death row then to choose between lethal injection or electrocution. However, leading lawmakers in Florida said they were afraid a change would lead to more appeals and more delays. Governor Chiles said he was satisfied that the electric chair is as humane a method of execution as any and "If the legislature wants to change it, they can."

A court challenge in 1997 temporarily suspended the use of the electric chair in Florida and the state started looking for experts in the execution process to certify the efficiency of the chair. John Fuller, executive director of the Corrections Commission said they scoured the country for experts, but since there is really no science of execution, people rely heavily on the experiences of others.

After receiving the Commission's final report, in October 1997, the Florida Supreme Court ruled that use of the electric chair does not violate state or federal constitutions. Two justices who upheld the legality of the electric chair at the time called upon state officials to find another method of execution.

THE DEATH PENALTY IN FLORIDA

In the spring of 1996, Michael Medina, then head of the state's Office of the Capital Collateral Representative, resigned his position on ethical grounds. One of his reasons was he did not believe his office had the resources to handle the case of death row inmate Gerald Stano, which they had been ordered to take on. Medina said the resources in his office were so restricted that attorneys at one point were not allowed to make out-of-state calls. It was this office that challenged the state's use of the electric chair after it malfunctioned during the execution of Pedro Medina in April 1997.

During the summer of 1997 Florida did away with the Office of the Capital Collateral Representative (OCCR), completely. The main focus of the office had been the representation of death row inmates. To replace the defunct office three different offices were established in Tampa, Miami, and Tallahassee. Governor Lawton Chiles appointed three lawyers to head the offices who had no experience filing appeals for death row inmates. One lawyer had worked as an assistant statewide prosecutor and had run for state attorney in Hillsborough County, Florida. A second wrote the state's brief against Ted Bundy twelve years earlier, and the third had extensive defense experience in several murder trials but not one capital appeal.

Senator Locke Burt (R-Ormond Beach), who is on the CCRC oversight commission was in favor of the change. He justified it by saying what made this division necessary was a group of attorneys in Florida who are fundamentally opposed to the death penalty. According to the Senator, these attorneys are trying to make cases so time consuming and expensive that the death penalty would, in effect, be abolished in the state.

After the three offices were established, however, expenses tripled, offices were understaffed, bills unpaid, and there was little or no money for expert witnesses. Many experienced attorneys quit after the change. When Judi Buenoano's death warrant was signed in December 1997, an inexperienced team was quickly assembled to try to save her from execution. The most qualified person on the team was not even qualified to work in federal courts.

Elisabeth Semel, Director of the American Bar Association's death penalty representation project said no area of the law is "more complicated, arcane and ever-changing than capital appeals . . . you're talking about the brain surgeons of the legal profession," she said.

In Florida, a citizen's right to due process does not guarantee a lawyer in death sentence appeals. In March 1998, a group of private attorneys in Florida sued the state to halt executions until the right to counsel is made a constitutional guarantee in that state.

Ryan Banfill, a spokesman for Governor Chiles, said his new appointments were all outstanding lawyers with high ethical standards who are well-versed in criminal law and "The governor is confident in their competence and feels that they will master this area of criminal law."

In 1997 only twenty-two people were sentenced to death in Florida. This was the lowest number in twenty-five years. Professor Michael Radelet of the University of Florida attributed this change to a law enacted in 1994 that gave juries and judges in Florida the option of giving a sentence of life without parole instead of death, in first-degree murder cases. "Given the alternative of life, support for the death penalty drops like a brick," said Radelet, who had testified in the penalty phase of Judi Buenoano's trial in favor of life in prison.

A 1998 poll of 813 Florida voters found that the 63 percent still favor the death penalty. If they could be assured that those who murder would remain in jail for life, only 50 percent were in favor of death. The poll had a margin of error of plus or minus 3.5 percent.

WOMEN SENTENCED TO DEATH IN FLORIDA

1926

Bertha Hall: Black; Commuted in 1929. Twenty-three-year-old Bertha Hall and her accomplice, 22-year-old Gordon Denmark, were sentenced to death in Florida's electric chair for killing Bertha's husband, a grocer. Their sentences were both commuted in 1929, and Bertha was released in 1934 or 1935.

1927

Billie Jackson: White; Commuted. Billie Jackson was a white woman in Duval County, Florida sentenced to die in the electric chair for the stabbing death of her husband, who was a musician. Governor Martin commuted her sentence after seven months and she was released in 1935.

1953

Ruby McCollum: Black; Overturned and committed to a state hospital. In 1952, Ruby McCollum was the 37-year-old wife of a wealthy black gambler in Live Oak, Florida. She was convicted of shooting Dr. Clifford LeRoy Adams, a prominent local white politician. At her trial she said that she and Dr. Adams had had "more than a doctor-patient relationship," and that Adams was the father of her daughter. She also said she was pregnant with another child of his at the time of the murder. A jury found her guilty and sentenced her to death in August 1952.

She spent two years in jail awaiting her execution until the Florida Supreme Court reversed her death sentence. She was sent to the Florida State Mental Hospital in Chattahoochee before retrial and remained there 20 years before she was released to her family in 1974.

The story of Ruby's case was told in the 1957 book *Ruby McCollum: Woman in the Suwannee Jail* by William Bradford Huie. The book was controversial, and Huie was charged with contempt of court for claiming in it that Circuit Judge Hal Adams was a gambler and racially biased. For this travesty Huie was fined $750.

1962

Irene Laverne Jackson: Black; Re-sentenced to life in 1964. Irene Laverne Jackson was sentenced to death with her son and another man in Pasco County, Florida, on April 24, 1962, for murdering her husband for his insurance money. In 1964, she was retried, convicted, and re-sentenced to life for second-degree murder. She was paroled on January 17, 1972, and discharged from parole status in 1980.

1968

Maria Dean Arrington: Black; Commuted to life on August 28, 1972. Maria Dean Arrington was born August 8, 1933. In 1968 she was sentenced to twenty years in Volusia County, Florida, on charges of manslaughter in the death of her husband. While out of prison on an appeal bond, for reasons that were undetermined, she murdered the secretary of the Lake County public defender, Robert Pierce, who had unsuccessfully defended her teen-aged son and daughter when they stood trial for armed robbery and forgery in 1968. It is believed that Marie took a cab to the public defender's office with the intention of killing him. However, he wasn't there so she forced his 37-year-old secretary, Vivian Ritter, to leave the building with her. Though police were alerted the same day, the shotgunned remains of Ritter were not found until six days later. There was evidence that she had been tortured before her death.

Marie Dean Arrington was picked up shortly after the body was found. She was convicted of first-degree murder in the death of Vivian Ritter and, on December 6, 1968, she was sentenced to die in the electric chair.

In 1970, Marie escaped from the Florida Correctional Institute by cutting through a heavy window screen and became only the second woman ever to be named to the FBI's Ten Most Wanted List. She was captured two years later, in New Orleans, by FBI agents and sentenced to ten more years for her escape. Her death sentence was commuted to life on August 28, 1972, when the U.S. Supreme Court declared capital punishment unconstitutional. She is currently in prison at Broward Correctional Institution in Pembroke Pines, Florida.

1976

Sonia Jacobs aka Sonia Linder: White; Released for time served in October, 1992. Sonia (Sunny) Jacobs and her companion, Jesse Tafero, were sentenced to death for the murder of two officers, a Florida highway patrol trooper and his friend, a Canadian constable on vacation, at a highway rest stop in 1976. A third co-defendant received a life sentence after pleading guilty and testifying against Sunny and Tafero. The jury recommended a life sentence for Sonia, but the judge overruled the jury and imposed death. She began serving her sentence at the Broward County Correctional Institution on August 20, 1976. Her sentence was overturned by the Supreme Court on March 26, 1981, and Sonia Jacobs was re-sentenced to life with a 25-year minimum mandatory term.

In May of 1977 while she was confined on death row, Sonia filed a civil rights suit in the U.S. District Court charging discrimination because, unlike the men on death row at the time, she was kept in solitary confinement. The court ruled in her favor stating that "such confinement afforded the plaintiff solely because she is a female sentenced to death, constitutes cruel and unusual punishment."

Sunny was on death row for five years before her sentence was reduced to life. A childhood friend of Sunny's discovered the chief prosecution witness had failed a lie-detector test and that this had been concealed in Sunny's trial. To cover his tracks, the prosecutor accepted a plea to second-degree murder in which Sonia did not admit guilt, and she was remanded to time served and immediately released. Her companion, Jesse Tafero, whose conviction rested on much of the same evidence, had been executed in 1990, two years before the evidence of innocence had been uncovered. His execution was one in which flames shot out from underneath the headpiece. A particularly cruel death for an innocent man. Their story was told in a made-for-TV film directed by Sunny's friend Micki Dickoff, "In the Blink of an Eye."

1984

Andrea Hicks Jackson (aka Felice): Black; Reversed, 1997. Andrea Hicks Jackson was accused, convicted, and sentenced to death for shooting a Jacksonville police officer six times when he tried to arrest her on April 17, A19 for filing a false report about a vandali ed car her own . or Andrea the incident is ha y. She had been drinking and doing drugs before it happened. She also had a history of abuse and domestic violence. In her testimony, she said she thought the police officer was trying to rape her. She only remembered struggling with a "man in black." Her explanation was totally disregarded in trial because the police officer she shot had such a good reputation; everyone thought it unlikely that he would have tried to assault her. She was found guilty of first-degree murder with two aggravating circumstances, first, that she killed in a cold, calculated, and premeditated manner and second, that she killed to avoid arrest.

Andrea was born in Jacksonville, lorida on ebruary 26, 195 , and has two sons of whom she says she is very proud. During her childhood, her stepfather sexually molested her on an ongoing basis. This began when she was years old. It was then that her stepfather called her into the bedroom, put a towel on the bed under her, placed a pillow over her face, and brutally raped her. By age ten or eleven Andrea had begun to numb the emotional trauma and pain by drinking and taking drugs. During this time in her childhood, she also suffered from various illnesses that were related to what was happening to her such as vaginal infections and migraine headaches. This continued until she was 16-years-old and ran away from home. It was then she married a man who continued to abuse her physically, sexually, and psychologically. In trial, however, her attorneys did not recognize her as a battered woman and did not seek information from hospital records or neighbors on her history of abuse. Had they done this it would have been proven that she was a victim of domestic violence. Of her trial, Andrea said:

My lawyer didn't have a defense for me. At first they thought I was going to be charged with second-degree murder. When they found out it was murder in the first, he only had two months to prepare my case. He told the judge that I was competent to stand trial, that I understood the facts in my case. But I didn't. (Allen, 1998)

When Andrea was put on death row in Florida, there was no other woman with her until Judi Buenoano was given the death penalty two years later. Four years down the line, when Andrea could speak more lucidly about her past, her attorney had her evaluated by a psychiatrist who specialized in using hypnosis to recover memories repressed due to trauma. This evaluation showed that Andrea suffered from drug and alcohol blackouts, incest and childhood sexual abuse, battered woman's syndrome, post-traumatic stress syndrome, and rape trauma syndrome at the time she committed the crime. The evaluation also indicated that Andrea was under extreme emotional distress and impairment, which impacted her ability to function at the time of the shooting.

On March 7, 1989 Andrea became the first woman on death row in Florida (at the time) to have her death warrant signed. However, the Florida Supreme Court granted her a stay on May 4, 1989.

In 1996, her attorney argued that Andrea's crime was not premeditated because she had been repeatedly raped as a child and was suffering a flashback at the time of the incident with the Jacksonville police officer. At this hearing Andrea asked for forgiveness for her "uncontrollable actions" after which a jury sentenced her to death for the third time.

Andrea says it is her faith that has given her the strength to face each day on death row. She said she dealt with it better when her sons were small because she kept telling herself that she would still have time to spend with them because she would be free before they grew up. But now she says it is painful knowing all the time and precious moments have been missed and they have grown up without her. This gives her a great sense of urgency, all those years lost.

Of her days on death row Andrea says she spends a lot of time just standing in her cell looking out of the peephole. She gets up at 5:00 a.m., prays, reads her bible, and eats breakfast at 6:30. Meals are served through a slot in the 32-inch steel door of her cell. After breakfast Andrea washes up, gets dressed, and reads the bible some more, or, if she has a good Christian book, she reads that. She is allowed to shower three times a week and she cleans her cell on those days. She is allowed fresh air for one hour, four times a week but says that sometimes she doesn't come out of her cell or talk to people for weeks. She says she's gotten used to being locked inside and mostly likes to keep to herself. She says that life on death row is all about punishment. But, the highlight of her day is getting mail since she has about sixty-five pen pals. She said she hates when there is no mail.

Audrey Kaufman, a personal friend of Andrea's from Ireland visited Andrea and her two sons in the summer of 1997 and wrote this:

Andrea is a very spiritual person. She smiles and looks radiant despite her past and present conditions. She will tell you that it is her faith in God who gives her unconditional love that keeps her going from day to day. She does not fear death because of this strong belief neither does she bear malice or grudges against anyone. Despite the 14 years of separation from her sons she has always maintained a deep and consistent relationship with them; they have reciprocated this in a very loving and respectful way. Her son told me that he goes to her for advice. Andrea's day is full of prayer and God and is a very important factor in her life. When she finally leaves prison, she hopes to work with women of similar misfortunes. (1998)

Andrea's sentence was overturned again in November, 1997, and she now awaits re-sentencing at Broward Correctional Institute in Pembroke Pines, Florida.

1985

Judias Buenoano aka Judy Ann Goodyear: Latina; Executed, 1998. Judi Buenoano was executed by the state of Florida on March 30, 1998 at 7:01 a.m. She was pronounced dead at 7:13 a.m. Judi was the first woman to be executed in Florida since 1848 when a woman who was a freed slave was hanged for killing her master. She was the third woman executed in the United States after the death penalty resumed in 1976. The other two were Velma Barfield in 1984 in North Carolina and Karla Faye Tucker in 1998 in Texas.

Judi Buenoano was born in 1943 in Quanah, Texas, a little town about 200 miles northwest of Dallas. Her mother died when she was 4-years-old and she spent her early years between relatives and foster homes in Texas and Oklahoma.

At a hearing in 1990 she said she was sexually abused in some of the homes and physically abused in others. At age ten she was living in Roswell, New Mexico, with her father and his wife who, she said, beat her. By age seventeen she became pregnant and gave birth to a son Michael in 1961. She met and married James Goodyear a few months later.

In 1971 James Goodyear, a former Air Force pilot, was poisoned and died just three months after completing a tour of duty in Vietnam. In 1985, Judi was accused of his murder. After deliberating for 10½ hours, a jury found her guilty of poisoning him with arsenic.

Her motive for the murder was said to have been his insurance benefits. During her trial Judi referred to the case against her as a "witch-hunt" and said she had no idea why arsenic was found in the exhumed bodies of James Goodyear and an ex-husband.

Judi's daughter, 18-year-old Kimberly Goodyear, surprised everyone at her mother's trial by testifying that she had seen her older brother poison her stepfather seven years earlier. However, the last man who lived with Judi, John Gentry, testified that she had given him poisoned vitamins after taking a $500,000 life insurance policy out on him. He said that when the vitamins made him sick, Judi suggested that he double the dosage.

A former friend of Judi's testified that when the two of them had gone shopping, just a few months after James Goodyear's death, Judi had confided to her that she had fatally poisoned her husband. Another woman who said that she and Judi were "as close as sisters" testified that Judi had told her they could end their unhappy marriages by lacing their husbands' food with arsenic. Beverly Owen, who knew Judi when she had lived in Pensacola and ran a beauty shop called "Faces and Fingers," said that Judi had told her it would be easier to kill her husband with arsenic than to divorce him.

Assistant State Attorney Belvin Perry told the court that in talking to her friend, Judi had said that if she gave her husband arsenic she would "have to have a strong stomach because it was a slow painful process" (*Sun-Sentinel*, 1985). Defense witnesses raised the possibility that the arsenic found in James Goodyear's body may have come from chemical defoliants he was exposed to in Vietnam.

During her trial Judi was nicknamed the "Black Widow" by Prosecutor Russell Edgar, who told the trial judge, "She's like a black widow. She feeds off her mates and her young." This statement was partly in reference to the life sentence Judi was already serving for the May 13, 1980, drowning murder of her paralyzed son in Santa Rosa County, Florida.

Her defense attorney, James Johnston, argued before the court that his client was convicted on "nothing stronger than suspicion." He said they had built their cases on circumstantial evidence and failed to rule out every reasonable theory of innocence as required by law. Nevertheless, Orange County Circuit Judge Emerson Thompson, Jr., announced the death sentence to Judi moments after she begged him for mercy. She was also found guilty of attempted murder for masterminding a car bombing outside a downtown Pensacola restaurant of her then-fiancé's car.

Judi had three death warrants signed before her execution in 1998. In an appeal in 1990 she claimed that Florida's 66-year-old electric chair wasn't working and that the state hid evidence of its need for repairs. Her lawyers said the chair might malfunction and "burn her at the stake." A federal judge refused to halt her execution, rejecting those arguments.

In 1990, less than 20 hours before she was scheduled to die, the Florida Supreme Court stayed her execution; then in 1996, Judi lost another appeal. Judi's last appeals before the Florida Supreme Court, which were not successful, argued that prosecutors withheld confidential documents about the investigation by an FBI chemist whose testimony helped convict her.

Florida Department of Corrections officials described Judi as a "Very well-behaved inmate, very accommodating and pleasant to deal with." Her daughter Kimberly Hawkins said before her mother's execution, "She goes one day at a time you never give up hope, but my mother would rather die than spend the rest of her life in prison. She's not afraid because it's like she said, she goes to a better place." In describing her mother she said, "Little has changed about my mother since she went to prison more than a decade ago even now she's the same. I love her letters. They cheer me up."

Judi Buenoano was a Roman Catholic and Department of Corrections officials said that before her execution she asked for a rosary. She spent her last years knitting baby blankets which her daughter sold and her story has been told in a 1991 book by Chris Anderson and Sharon McGehee, *Bodies of Evidence: The True Story of Judias Buenoano Florida's Serial Murderess.*

Regarding her execution, one Florida Department of Corrections official said he had witnessed 13 executions and that Judi's created the most interest of any he'd ever seen. He said they received more than 100 requests to interview her and were contacted by media from Germany, Italy, and Poland, who either wanted to interview her or witness her execution.

Prior to her execution, Judi told a Florida television station "Seeing the face of Jesus that's what I think about. I'm ready to go home."

1987

Carla Callier: White; Reversed in 1988, re-sentenced to life. Carla Callier was born in 1963 and was sentenced to death on March 19, 1978, in Hillsborough County, Florida, for having her lover kill her husband in Tampa on November 20, 1986. She was re-sentenced to life with a mandatory minimum of 25 years on July 26, 1988.

In a related matter, in 1992, Gilbert F. Hadas, 52, a prison chaplain who was in love with Carla, was convicted of trying to help her escape from the Broward Correctional Institution. Carla pleaded guilty of attempting to escape, and she is currently serving her sentence.

1987

Dee Dyne Casteel: White; Vacated in 1990, re-sentenced to life. Dee Casteel was born on June 5, 1938, and worked as a waitress at the International House of Pancakes in Naranja, Florida. She was sentenced to death in Dade County, Florida, on September 16, 1987, after being found guilty of the 1983 murders of her boss, Arthur Venecia, and his 84-year-old mother. Dee and James Alan Bryant, another employee who was also Venecia's lover, had Venecia killed. About a month later when his mother, Bessie Fischer, began asking about him they paid two auto mechanics $7,500 to kill her, too. Dee was the first woman sentenced to death in Dade County, Florida. The two auto mechanics were also sentenced to death.

After Dee was found guilty, Circuit Judge Ralph Person agreed with the jury's unanimous death penalty recommendation. Her death sentence was vacated on December 6, 1990. She was re-sentenced to life on December 19, 1991, and is currently at Broward County Correctional Institution in Pembroke Pines, Florida.

1987

Kaysie Dudley: White; Reversed in 1989. Kaysie Dudley was born on July 24, 1963, and was sentenced to death in Pinellas County, Florida, on January 27, 1987, for the 1985 murder of her mother's employer, a 77-year-old wealthy Redington Beach widow. She was re-sentenced to life with 25 years mandatory minimum on October 2, 1989, and is currently at Broward County Correctional Institution in Pembroke Pines, Florida.

1990

Deidre M. Hunt: White; Re-sentenced to 8 life terms, 1998. Deidre Hunt was born on February 9, 1969 and was formerly of Manchester, NH. She was sentenced to die in Volusia County, Florida, on September 13, 1990, for the 1989 shooting murders of two men. She was the youngest woman on death row in the United States at the time. Mark Ramsey, 19, and Bryan Chase, 18, were two drifters hired by Deidre's boyfriend to commit a murder for him.

Deidre had a criminal record before she left New Hampshire for Florida in the late 1980s due to her involvement in the robbery shooting of a woman in Manchester. She pleaded guilty to being an accomplice to armed robbery at the time, and an attempted-murder charge was dropped.

At her trial for the Florida murders, Deidre's mother took the stand in her defense and said she did not want her daughter to be executed; she asked the court to consider that her daughter had suffered years of physical and sexual abuse. She said Deidre had a violent relationship with her fiancé, Mr. Fotopoulos, who was also involved. An ex-boyfriend testified that Deidre had bragged to him about the killing, but Deidre said her boyfriend forced her to do the killing by threatening to kill her if she did not.

Fotopoulos videotaped the shooting of one of the men, Mark Ramsey. The 57-second videotape was shown in Deidre Hunt's six-day sentencing hearing. It showed Deidre in the woods west of Daytona Beach, shooting Ramsey, who was bound to a tree, three times, in the chest, with a .22-caliber pistol. She then grabbed him by the hair and delivered a final shot to his head. Deidre pleaded guilty, saying she should not be given the death penalty because she lived up to her end of the bargain with the prosecutors, which was testifying against her former lover, Konstantinos Fotopoulos.

When she was given the death penalty, Deidre said the state reneged on a deal to give her life in prison. Deidre wept and bowed her head as Circuit Judge S. James Foxman imposed the death sentence in Daytona Beach.

In 1995 the Florida Supreme Court granted Deidre a new trial after a judge ruled she was the victim of her attorney's deal with a tabloid television show. Peter Niles, a former court-appointed attorney sold Deidre's story to a tabloid TV show for $5,000. Circuit Judge Edwin Sanders allowed her to withdraw her guilty plea and stated that the deposition she had given before her first trial could not be used against her in the second trial, as her attorney had requested.

The prosecutor in her second trial was State Attorney Brad King of Ocala instead of a Volusia County prosecutor. The trial itself was moved to St. Augustine, because too many people in Volusia County knew about the previous trial. Deidre's defense attorney asked that she be examined by a psychiatrist for any mental disorders and that experts on battered woman's syndrome be brought in to her second trial.

Carol Hunt, Deidre's mother told the *New Hampshire Sunday News* that her daughter would go for the insanity defense, saying she was suffering from battered woman's syndrome at the time and that she believed she would have been killed had she not done what her boyfriend asked. Her boyfriend also shot the victim with a rifle, her mother pointed out.

Mrs. Hunt said her daughter had wanted to leave Konstantinos Fotopoulos, but he went to New Hampshire and found out about her family and threatened to kill them all and everyone she knew if she left him.

In her 1998 trial Deidre chose to forego sentencing by the jury that had convicted her and instead asked the trial judge to determine her sentence. Circuit Judge Edwin P.B. Sanders imposed 8 life sentences on Deidre saying, "This is a sentence that requires you to die in prison." Aside from two consecutive life terms with no chance for parole for 50 years, Deidre received six other life sentences for attempted murder, conspiracy to commit murder, and armed burglary.

In determining Deidre's sentence, Judge Sanders said that her abusive childhood, her age at the time of the crime, her mentally ill mother, her rape as a child, her remorse, and her cooperation with law enforcement after the crime were all reasons to spare her life. He also determined that Deidre was acting under the domination of Fotopoulos and that her comprehension of the criminality of her acts at the time they took place was impaired.

1992

Ana Cardona: Latina; Currently on death row. Ana Cardona, a Cuban immigrant from Miami, was born November 26, 1961. She had four children in 1990 when she was addicted to cocaine and was convicted of killing her three-year-old son.

Lazaro Figueroa's body was found in Miami Beach but remained unidentified for several weeks. The child was beaten with a baseball bat and dumped in the bushes of a Miami Beach neighborhood. After he was found, the local press pushed the story strongly and dubbed the unknown child "baby lollipops" because of the shirt he was wearing when he was found. The child appeared undernourished and had been beaten savagely over most of his body, apparently dying from repeated blows to the head. Ana Cardona has always denied abusing her child. Ana, who neither speaks nor reads English had this to say of her trial:

Yo misma no sabia ni lo que decian en mi juicio. El traductor me decia que no era importante lo que decian — y los abogados que tenian no hablaban espanol. (I did not understand what was said in my trial. The translator told me it was not important and the lawyers I had did not speak Spanish.)

El juez nunca permitio que se presentaran prueba a mi favor. Por ultimo el juez me dijo que si me veia llorando me iba sacar de la sala de juicio. (The judge never allowed evidence in my favor. Ultimately he told me that if he saw me crying I would be taken out of the courtroom.)

Ana's primary defense was that her lover, Olivia Gonzalez, had repeatedly beaten her child and Ana did not have the courage to protect him. She said she took cocaine to escape from the horror of the abuse that was happening in her life.

Olivia, testified for four hours against Ana in exchange for a forty-year sentence for second-degree murder and child abuse. Although Olivia admitted beating Lazaro and dumping his body in Miami Beach, she placed the primary blame for the homicide on Ana. Of Olivia's testimony Ana said:

Olivia tenia abogado privado. Aunque ella confeso que si que mato a mi hijto Lazarito, su abogado hizo un areglo con la mia que ella testificara en contra mi y eso es lo que ella queria. Desgraciadamente en este pais el dinero es todo y la familia de ella le pudieron ponder abogado privado. Pero yo no tengo ni donde caeme muerta. No tengo familia en este pais y no tengo ningun tipo de contacto con mi familia. Estoy sola ya no tengo ni fuerza para seguir adelante. (Olivia had a private attorney. And even though she confessed to killing my son, Lazaro, her lawyer made a deal with mine that she would testify against me and that was what she wanted to do. Unfortunately in this country money is everything and her family had money to get her a good lawyer. I can't even afford a place to die. I don't have family in this country nor do I have any contact with family elsewhere. I am alone without strength or courage to do anything.)

Ana's defense attorney said, "As the case unfolded, it became clear that Ana was going to be held up to our community as a monster." The trial judge concluded that "the long period of time over which this baby was subjected to torture, abuse, pain, and suffering separates this crime from all other crimes seen in the Dade County Courthouse within the memory of anyone working in this building." Press reports suggested that Ana was responsible because she was the child's mother.

Ana stood in front of the judge after her conviction and begged for her life. "Please have pity on me I'm asking for mercy," she said, "I'm not a monster and I'm not my son's murderer." She said her cocaine habit blinded her to her lover's abuse of Lazaro. The jury recommended 8–4 in favor of the death penalty and Circuit Judge David L. Tobin ordered Ana to die in the electric chair. From death row in Florida Ana wrote:

Lo unico que yo pido es justicia, justicia. Estoy pagando un crimen que yo no hice y no soy ninguna criminal. Vivo momento a momento. Estoy viviendo momentos muy duros. Mis hijos y yo hemos sufrido mucho y estoy sufriendo sin familia en este pais y sin saber que hacer. Dia tras dia vivo la peor angustia que pueda vivir un ser humano. Por favor comprenda mi desperacion. (The only thing I ask for is justice, justice. I am paying for a crime I did not commit. I live from moment to moment. This is a very difficult time for me. My children and I have suffered much and I am suffering without any family in this country and not knowing what to do. Day after day the pain is beyond what a human being can suffer. Please understand my desperation.)

Ana went on to say that she wants to prove her innocence, but without money there is not much hope. "Justice" she said, "is all I ask."

1989

Aileen Wuornos: White; Currently on death row. Aileen Wuornos was born on February 29, 1956, and is, perhaps, the most notorious death row inmate, male or female, of this century. Her story has been broadcast in one form or another in both national and international media as well as in several books and TV movies. Aileen was ultimately accused of seven murders, which caused her to be labeled a female serial killer.

She has received six murder convictions and six death sentences, so far, having pleaded guilty and asked for the death sentences in the last three instances. The state of Florida characterized her as an alcoholic and drug-addicted prostitute who murdered and robbed her customers and who was finally arrested outside a biker bar as she was sleeping off a drinking binge. Aileen explained the murders as acts of prostitution during which her customers became violent and/or raped her, so that she ultimately had to shoot them in self-defense.

Although Aileen was apparently alone with her victims when each of the crimes occurred, she was living with a woman named Tyria Moore at the time. She stated several times that she and Tyria originally had a sexual relationship that later developed into a non-sexual long-term relationship which involved living together and sharing expenses.

Born in Colorado to teenage parents, who separated before she was born, Aileen "Lee" Wuornos never experienced much security in life. Her father was incarcerated for sodomizing a 7-year-old girl and committed suicide in prison. Her mother abandoned her in infancy and left her in the care of her sister and her grandfather. People said she had an explosive temper as a child, and from her early teens on she experienced violence and abuse. By age 13 she was pregnant and gave her baby up for adoption. By age 14 she turned to prostitution. Aileen recalled being raped at least six times before the age of 18. Then, in her twenties she married a 70-year-old man, but later divorced him. Both claimed the other had physically abused them.

Aileen carried her childhood temper into adulthood, and it may have been the combination of an explosive temper and a history of abuse by men, that caused her to have such violent reactions toward customers who were abusive to her.

In 1986 Aileen met Tyria Moore. Together they lived in a series of rented rooms paid for by Aileen turning tricks. Tyria ended the relationship in January 1991 and after that, with Tyria gone, Aileen's life changed dramatically. She started drinking heavily and sleeping in her car when she ran out of money. She was often broke and homeless.

Eventually, seven bodies were found, all men, all shot in the upper and lower torso. Ocala police Sergeant Bruce Munster thought it was significant that the victims were shot in the body, as opposed to the head. He believed that male killers usually went for head shots and that women aimed lower. With this information, investigators released a composite sketch of a possible female suspect. Aileen Wuornos was arrested outside The Last Resort, a biker bar in Daytona Beach.

Aileen admitted killing Richard Mallory because, she said, he had raped and tortured her. But her explanations of why and how she apparently shot and killed at least four and perhaps seven other men under similar circumstances made it difficult for judges and juries to believe she acted in self-defense.

The prosecution had strong evidence against her, including fingerprints, cigarette butts in victim's cars, pawnshop tickets from selling the victims' belongings, and a storage bin she'd rented that held some of the dead men's possessions. Despite all this, the most damaging evidence was the testimony of Tyria Moore, who described how Aileen had told her she'd just shot a man and how she had at first refused to believe her. She said Aileen had never said anything about it being self-defense, nor did she ever show any remorse. The court also allowed the judge and jury to listen to the taped phone conversations between Aileen and Tyria

Aileen did little to help herself during her trials. She frequently used profanity and she not only showed no remorse but also threatened the judge and prosecutor and their families. The prosecution called Aileen a "lesbian whose hatred of men caused her to murder again and again." The press dubbed her "the nation's first lesbian serial killer" and lesbianism was brought up as an "aggravating circumstance" during the sentencing phase of her trial.

The jury that convicted Aileen deliberated for only two hours before reaching a 12–0 agreement that she should be sentenced to death. Since Florida has a jury override their recommendation was not binding on Circuit Judge Uriel Blount, but he took the opinion of the jury and on January 31, 1992 pronounced the first death sentence for Aileen Wuornos. She has since received five more. Aileen Wuornos is on death row in Florida today.

1993

Virginia Larzelere: White; Currently on death row. Virginia Larzelere was born on December 27, 1952, and was sentenced to death on May 11, 1993, after having been found guilty of arranging the murder of her husband, an Edgewater dentist. Her presumed motive was the money from his life insurance policies. Dr. Larzelere, who was 39 at the time of his death, was killed by a masked gunman who entered his office and shot him in the back. Virginia has consistently said she did not have anything to do with it. She tells her story this way:

My husband, Norman, was shot and killed in our dental office on March 8, 1991. He was shot through a closed solid door leading to the waiting room. I tried to stop the intruder as he was leaving and scraped his arm leaving skin and blood under several of my broken fingernails. Even though I was able to get a partial tag number at the time it was not pursued. The Edgewater Police Department was not interested in the skin and blood samples under my nails or my information about the license plate. Although the police said the door to the office safe was open, they never acknowledged that coins, cash, and narcotics had been taken from the safe; there was an inventory logbook in the office detailing the contents of the safe.

Two months after the murder, in exchange for immunity from his own criminal charges, a friend of my sons (Steven Heidle) led police to a shotgun and handgun in a river basin claiming that those were the murder weapons he had dumped in the river on March 10, 1991. My son Jason and I were arrested May 5, 1991. Ultimately, my son was acquitted — he had been in Orlando recuperating from a car accident at the time his father was shot. The police were never able to identify the shotgun as the murder weapon because it was totally inoperable and FDLE crime lab reports stated that the shotgun had not been discharged in years. Another crime lab report stated that the guns had not been in the river basin for long, maybe a few days. In addition, three people testified that the blue 45 Argentine handgun retrieved from the river had been in Heidle's possession since March 10, and not in the river bed as he had claimed.

No motive was ever established for charging me with my husband's murder. Insurance agents testified that my husband, Dr. Larzelere, personally purchased the life insurance policies on each family member, as well as himself, over the years. Norman signed the applications, took the physical exams, and paid the premiums himself. The insurance companies paid the life insurance amounts in trust for the children.

Steve Heidle testified that Virginia had said that anyone who came between her and her husband's life insurance money would "end up like Norman." It was later shown that there were many discrepancies in Heidle's testimony and in one instance he told the court he had seen a $200,000 insurance policy on

Norman in November, despite the fact that the policy was not drawn up until December. Virginia says:

My attorney, Jack Wilkins, did not provide effective assistance. He made no effort to provide a defense of innocence. He constantly assured me that lack of evidence and Heidle's lies could not convict me and I, of course, believed him. During the course of the trial I learned that he (Wilkins) was "tampering" with the family's cash monies and property. I tried to bring this to the attention of the court, but was unsuccessful. The judge, Judge Watson, ruled that I could not dismiss my attorney, Jack Wilkins.

I was found guilty and a few days afterward one of the jurors, a woman named Joyce Kelly, approached the state saying she was uncomfortable with the verdict because so much newspaper coverage was used during the trial. After that a motion for a new trial was filed for me.

At the same time I filed a *pro se* motion to dismiss Jack Wilkins because of his illegal activities. However, Judge Watson denied my oral motion for a continuance in order to produce witnesses and evidence and then denied my *pro se* motion because it was not signed by my counsel and, according to the judge, to find new counsel would involve a delay and impede justice.

Fifteen months later, after all the jurors had been questioned, the motion for a new trial was denied and Judge Watson sentenced me to death. A public defender, Chris Quarles filed a direct appeal that said Jack Wilkins made no motions during my trial that could be raised on appeal. My attorney, Jack Wilkins, pled guilty and was sentenced to 54 months in federal prison for criminal activities dating back to 1989 through 1994.

At this moment (1998) I have no attorney. Although, an eyewitness from the neighborhood has come forward with a deposition confirming the description of the assailant and of the car as I gave the police, I have no one to present the evidence for me. A satellite photo of the area banks confirms the details of the automobile leaving the dental office and there is a taped confession from Heidle saying he lied to the police.

There was no hired gunman, no gun, and no motive for me to murder my husband. But without legal counsel, without an attorney, I have NO VOICE to prove I am innocent. The time limit for me to produce new evidence of innocence expires June 1, 1998. But time cannot alter the fact that I had nothing to do with my husband's death. I lost my husband, my children and my own life. I was convicted by perjured testimony, which Heidle admits. I have no faith in the legal system, and only go through the motions of being alive.

Virginia Larzelere's sister asked a judge for temporary custody of her two nephews, Virginia's youngest sons, while their mother was under arrest. However, the judge placed the two boys in the custody of their paternal grandparents.

The jury deliberated for 6 hours before finding Virginia guilty of planning the murder of her husband, but the judge refused to sentence Virginia until after her son's trial. A jury acquitted Jason of the murder after two days of deliberation. Four days after his acquittal, Jason told a judge he wanted to take on the responsibility of raising his siblings. He said he wanted custody of his sister, Jessica, and his two half-brothers David, 3, and Benjamin, 6, and he would use the money from the insurance policies to provide for them. The court did not grant him custody.

Ultimately, a circuit judge said each of the three minor children would get one fourth of his $800,000 in life insurance benefits. The share belonging to Jason was held by the court pending his civil suit. Later, when the amount had shrunk to $600,000, a judge gave an equal share to each of the four children who were by then 21 (Jason), 17 (Jessica), 7 (Benjamin), and 4 (David).

In 1996 Virginia lost an appeal of her conviction and sentence when the Florida Supreme Court ruled unanimously against her despite evidence and affidavits available to the court that the case against Virginia and her son was totally fabricated by the state. There is ample evidence that Virginia's defense lawyer (who is now in prison) used none of the evidence that was made available to him to prove her innocence.

Since her trial, eyewitnesses have come forth with testimony that supports Virginia's testimony and with descriptions of the assailant who was seen leaving the scene of the crime. Virginia is unable to present this evidence without a lawyer. The offices set up by Governor Chiles for the defense of capital defendants are currently under investigation for wrongdoing.

Virginia is currently at Broward Correctional Center in Pembroke Pines, Florida. The day of the execution of Judi Buenoano, March 30, 1998, Virginia wrote

My emotions remain on a roller coaster today as I say good-bye to Judi in my heart. I don't judge her past but accept the person I have known for almost 5 years. A friend who helped me adjust to "living" on death row, someone that eased the daily pain with laughter. I continue in the legal battle to prove my innocence but remain without the needed voice.

10

Georgia: Electrocution

The state of Georgia has sentenced seven women to death since 1900, and one, Lena Baker, was executed. There are no women on death row in Georgia today.

Between 1930 and 1967 the state of Georgia performed 366 executions. This was the highest number of executions of any state during that period. Since the death penalty was reinstated in 1977, there have been 23 executions in Georgia, all men. The first man executed under Georgia's new laws was John Eldon Smith who was executed in December 1983. In June 1998 David Cargill became the twenty-third inmate executed in Georgia since 1983.

The average age of the men on death row in Georgia is 38. The racial distribution is 58 percent white and 42 percent black (1998).

Known as the buckle of the Death Belt several important rulings on the death penalty by the U.S. Supreme Court have been on cases from the state of Georgia. Three of these were *Furman v. Georgia* [408 US 238, 92 S.Ct. 2726 (1972)], *Gregg v. Georgia* [428 US 153, 96 S.Ct. 2909 (1976)], and *McCleskey v. Kemp* [481 US 279, 107 S.Ct. 1756 (1987)].

In *Furman v. Georgia,* the Court declared the death penalty unconstitutional. In *Gregg v. Georgia,* the revised death penalty statutes of Georgia, Texas, and Florida were declared constitutional and validated by the Supreme Court. This allowed, executions to resume in the United States; and in *McCleskey v. Kemp,* the Court rejected a comprehensive statistical study pointing to racial discrimination in the application of the death penalty in Georgia.

FURMAN V. GEORGIA

William Henry Furman was a black man convicted and sentenced to death in Georgia for the murder of a white man during an attempted robbery. Evidence that he was mentally deficient was presented at his trial. He appealed his death sentence on the grounds that his Fourteenth Amendment rights were violated because a disproportionate number of blacks were receiving the death penalty. The Supreme Court set Furman's death sentence aside by a 5–4 vote, saying that the racially discriminatory way in which the death penalty was being administered in Georgia constituted cruel and unusual punishment in violation of the Eighth and Fourteenth Amendments to the U.S. Constitution.

The Eighth Amendment prohibits the infliction of "cruel and unusual punishments," and under the Fourteenth Amendment a state may not deprive a person of "life, liberty or property, without due process of law, nor deny to any person within its jurisdiction the equal protection of the law." This ruling was primarily in response to the "arbitrary and capricious" manner in which the death penalty was applied. Because of the unlimited discretion given to the sentencing authorities, that is, prosecutors, judges and juries in capital trials, the death penalty was unfair throughout the United States. Despite years of legislation, it undoubtedly remains so today.

Of the nine Supreme Court judges seated at the time, two of the five who upheld the appeal (Brennan and Marshall) ruled that the death penalty was inherently "cruel and unusual." The other three (Douglas, Stewart, and White) based their opinions on the uneven manner in which the death penalty was applied. In separate opinions, the three justices concluded that unguided discretionary sentencing violated the Eighth Amendment because it allowed the death penalty to be imposed "wantonly" and "freakishly" (Stewart). It was "pregnant with discrimination" (Douglas). And there was no meaningful basis for distinguishing the few cases in which it was imposed from the many cases in which it was not (White). In finding the death penalty discriminatory. Justice Douglas wrote:

The discretion of judges and juries in imposing the death penalty enables the penalty to be selectively applied, feeding prejudices against the accused if he/she is poor and despised and lacking political clout, or if he/she is a member of a suspect or unpopular minority, and saving those who, by social position, may be in a more protected position.

In his concurrence, Justice Brennan wrote:

Death is a unique punishment in the United States. In a society that so strongly affirms the sanctity of life, not surprisingly the common view is that death is the ultimate sanction. There has been no national debate about punishment, in general by imprisonment, comparable to the debate about the punishment of death.

Justice Brennan went on to say:

Death is truly an awesome punishment. The calculated killing of a human being by the State involves, by its very nature, a denial of the executed person's humanity.

Although this decision referred specifically to *Furman v. Georgia* and its two companion cases, it effectively invalidated all existing death penalty laws in the rest of the states, most of which contained provisions similar to Georgia's statute. This ruling led to the commutation of death sentences of over 600 prisoners then on death row throughout the U.S.

Following *Furman,* fourteen states and the District of Columbia abolished their death penalty laws. Thirty-five states reviewed and revised their death penalty statutes to limit the discretion of judges and juries in capital trials and focused on the issue of racial bias in the administration of the death penalty. But the situation remained uncertain until the new laws could be tested in the Supreme Court.

William Henry Furman was paroled in April 1984, and in 1976 the first major test case involving appeals by prisoners sentenced to death under the new laws enacted in Georgia, Texas, and Florida was considered.

GREGG V. GEORGIA

Troy Gregg was sentenced to death for the murders of Fred Simmons and Bob Moore during the course of a robbery. Using his case, the U.S. Supreme Court ruled by a 7–2 vote that the death penalty was constitutional, under the revised statutes of Georgia, Texas, and Florida.

The statutes of these states stipulated that in trials for which the death penalty may be imposed, the guilt or innocence of the defendant must be decided separately from the sentencing phase of the trial (bifurcated). If a defendant is found guilty of a capital offense, the trial court must conduct a hearing specifically to determine whether the defendant will be sentenced to death or life in prison. Further, when deciding the appropriate sentence, the court must consider aggravating and mitigating circumstances in relation to both the crime and the offender. The statutes also provide for an automatic review of death sentences by the highest state court of appeal to ensure that the death penalty was imposed proportionately to the gravity of the offense. Although Gregg appealed his death sentence, the Supreme Court upheld it saying that the procedures Georgia had instituted for applying the death penalty were constitutional and were not in violation of either the Eighth or Fourteenth Amendments.

Troy Leon Gregg escaped from prison with four other death row inmates on July 28, 1980, and was killed later that same night during a fight in a biker bar in North Carolina.

McCLESKY V. KEMP

Warren McCleskey was the 155th person put to death in the United States after capital punishment was restored in 1976. He was convicted as one of four people charged with killing a policeman in 1978.

In *McClesky v. Kemp* the U.S. Supreme Court rejected his challenge, alleging racial discrimination in the administration of sentencing based on a statistical study by Professor David Baldus of Iowa State University. The Baldus study was a comprehensive academic study that looked at every murder conviction in Georgia between 1973 and 1978. This amounted to more than 600 cases. In this study, Baldus was able to show black defendants and defendants who kill white victims were between four and eleven times more likely to receive the death penalty than other defendants in Georgia. Disparities were found to be a result of prosecutorial decisions on whether or not to seek the death penalty.

In reviewing the case, the Supreme Court actually accepted the findings of the Baldus study but stated that "Apparent disparities in sentencing are an inevitable part of our criminal justice system." McCleskey's appeal was denied because the Supreme Court felt he had failed to prove that the decision-makers in his case had discriminated against him. The result of a ruling in McCleskey's favor would have produced the same results as the *Furman* decision in 1972.

The four judges who upheld the McCleskey appeal spoke out strongly against the majority in their dissents. Justice William Brennan wrote: "The statistical evidence in this case . . . documents the risk that McCleskey's sentence was influenced by racial considerations. The way in which we choose who will die reveals the depth of moral commitment among the living."

Ramifications of the McCleskey case are still seen today. In 1995, the Georgia Supreme Court ruled that there was a *prima facie* case that gross disparities existed in sentencing for some drug offenses showing that 98.4 percent of those serving sentences for certain drug offenses were black. Discretion to pursue life sentences for these offenses is entrusted to the District Attorneys, and all of the District Attorneys in Georgia are white.

RACIAL BIAS AND THE DEATH PENALTY IN GEORGIA

According to a 1996 Amnesty International Report, the death penalty in Georgia continues to be racist, arbitrary, and unfair. Georgia has a long history of racism, and the use of the death penalty in the early part of the twentieth century was closely related to the issue of lynching. Between 1880 and 1930, 460 blacks were lynched in Georgia. The fact that the lynching of blacks was one crime that was never investigated made it socially acceptable. During the same period, only 49 whites were lynched in Georgia. Prior to the Civil War there were different punishments for certain crimes based on the race of the defendant or victim. The rape of white women by black men was a capital offense, but the rape of white women by white men carried a sentence of 2–20 years. The rape of a black woman was punishable by a "fine and imprisonment, at the discretion of the court." Georgia lynch mobs were often led by the "finest citizens" of the community. Eventually, as lynching became more and more socially unacceptable, public demand for the execution of criminals could only be satisfied by the use of the death penalty. Between 1924 and 1972, 337 blacks were executed in Georgia, as opposed to seventy-eight whites. Of the sixty-six men who were executed for rape during that time, sixty-three were black.

In 1972 Georgia's death penalty statutes were rewritten following the *Furman* decision. The new death penalty statute specified 10 aggravating factors that would allow a district attorney to classify a murder as a capital offense. Nevertheless, today in Georgia the death penalty is primarily sought against anyone accused of murdering people who are deemed valuable by society by virtue of their economic, social, or racial standing.

A study of the capital cases in the judicial district of Chattahoochee, Georgia, between 1973 and 1990 showed that 85 percent of the defendants were accused of the murder of a white person while only 6 percent involved a black-on-black murder. During the 27 years covered by the study the death penalty was never sought for the murder of a black person by a white person.

Another study in Flint, Georgia, showed that the death penalty is sought six times more often if the victim is white. In the same study, the death penalty was sought in six out of thirteen cases involving the murder of a white woman, but never in 11 cases involving the murder of a black woman. Nevertheless, in July 1995 the Assistant Attorney General of Georgia stated, "I don't think we have a racist problem statewide. We're all human. People are not perfect."

In a 1997 study by *The Augusta Chronicle* (Hodson, 1997) ninety-one out of 115 inmates on Georgia's death row killed white victims while only two white inmates killed black victims. Of the 115, fifty-one were black, sixty-three white and one American Indian.

The 1990 Georgia census indicated that blacks comprise only 27 percent of the state's population, and of the 20 inmates executed since 1983, 19 murdered whites. But no white person has ever been executed in Georgia for the murder of a black victim.

JURY SELECTION IN GEORGIA

Six of the 12 blacks executed in Georgia since 1983 were convicted and sentenced by all-white juries. Although the U.S. Supreme Court ruled in *Batson v. Kentucky* [47 U.S.79, 106 S.Ct. 1712 (1986)] that it is unconstitutional for prosecutors to remove potential jurors from a jury on the basis of race, it is still a common practice in Georgia.

The case of Rebecca Machetti, a white woman who was given the death sentence in Bibb County, Georgia, was challenged by her lawyers on the grounds that the jury composition was unconstitutional under the U.S. Supreme Court ruling prohibiting gender bias in juries. Rebecca was granted a new trial by the federal court of appeals and received a sentence of life.

In 1996 the Georgia Supreme Court upheld a death penalty imposed by a jury from which the trial judge excluded five people who had doubts about capital punishment. In their decision the justices held that even if there were "ambiguities" during jury selection, the trial judge's decisions could not be overturned.

CLEMENCY IN GEORGIA

In Georgia the State Board of Pardons and Paroles has the right to grant or deny clemency in all death penalty cases and a defendant whose death sentence has been commuted to life must serve 25 years before being considered for either pardon or parole.

The board is made up of five members appointed by the governor and approved by the Georgia Senate. There must be a majority vote to commute a death sentence to life imprisonment. The board is required to ask for relevant information concerning an applicant, and all hearings are held in public. The Georgia Board of Pardons has commuted four death sentences in the post-*Furman* era.

THE ELECTRIC CHAIR IN GEORGIA

Before 1924 hanging was the legal method of execution in Georgia. In 1924 the state changed to electrocution which has been used as the sole means of execution since then. The state's first electric chair was built by an inmate, who was later executed in it and was set up at the Georgia State Prison Farm, near Milledgeville. In 1937 executions were changed to Reidsville and the chair was moved to the Georgia Diagnostic and Classification Prison in June 1980. Since 1924, a total of 436 men and one woman have been put to death in Georgia's electric chair. The chair itself is constructed of wood and is mounted on a platform. There are four 10,000-volt insulators between the chair and the platform. Two electrical control panels are in a small room adjacent to the execution chamber, but only one is used during an electrocution. The use of the panels is rotated for executions so that both panels are in working condition at all time.

The execution team consists of six special escort officers and three executioners. The team is selected by the warden and confirmed by the commissioner of the Georgia Department of Corrections. The executioners must be full-time correctional employees and cannot be employees who are assigned to security posts where they interact with death row inmates. Executioners are given a stipend and are paid for any overtime accrued by participating in an execution.

During an execution the three executioners press buttons on the control panel simultaneously. Three cycles of electricity are administered: 2,000 volts for four seconds; 1,000 volts for seven seconds; 208 volts for one minute and forty-nine seconds. The control panels have timers and contractors that adjust the voltage and the levels of current automatically during an execution. The total length of the cycles is three minutes. The estimated average length of time that elapses from the time the prisoner is restrained to the time of death is eight to nine minutes.

Like other states using the electric chair, Georgia has had its problems. In 1984 Alpha Otis Stephens struggled for 8 minutes after receiving and surviving the first jolt of electricity. Prison officials had to wait six minutes for his body to cool down before the doctors could examine him to see if her was dead. According to witnesses, during that six minutes Stephens took 23 breaths. When the doctors finally said he was still alive, another round of electricity, which he did not survive, was administered.

In 1997 two Supreme Court Justices in Georgia, Chief Justice Robert Benham and Justice Norman Fletcher, began to urge the state legislature to come up with another method of executing inmates, since Georgia is one of only seven states not to offer lethal injection. In their special opinion the judges said, "Neither our concept of what is humane nor our concept of what is cruel and unusual punishment must remain in a vacuum." The justices also expressed concern that electrocution may at some point be declared unconstitutional and the state would then be left without a method of execution.

Corrections Commissioner Wayne Garner supported the idea of lethal injection as a viable option. In 1997 the Georgia Department of Corrections developed a feasibility study and cost analyses on lethal injection to submit to the Georgia General Assembly. According to their study, costs for the implementation of lethal injection as a method of execution are minimal. Garner wanted Georgia law to be changed so that all current and future death row inmates can choose between the two methods of execution.

Georgia law designates the witnesses at an execution as the superintendent or his/her designee; at least three executioners; two physicians to determine death; an electrician; other correctional officers, and assistants and witnesses determined by the commissioner. The offender may request the presence of his/her counsel, a clergy person, and a reasonable number of relatives and friends.

POLITICS AND THE DEATH PENALTY IN GEORGIA

According to Amnesty International (1996), 71 percent of the population of Georgia favors the use of capital punishment. Georgia elects its key judicial figures, and many of the state judges were previously District Attorneys. In seeking re-election, District Attorneys frequently quote the number of trials at which they have sought the death penalty.

In the Chattahoochee judicial district, which is responsible for more death sentences than any other judicial circuit in Georgia, three of the four superior court judges are former prosecutors. The largest contributor to the election fund of the District Attorney of Chattahoochee in 1985 was the father of a murder victim. When the accused, John Davis, came to trial the District Attorney asked the victim's father if he wanted him to seek the death penalty. When the father said "yes" the District Attorney replied "That's all I need to know."

The Flint Judicial Circuit, comprised of four rural counties, is where the Georgia Diagnostic and Classification Center (death row) is located. The prison is a major employer of the area. In the past ten years, the two local judges have never once granted *habeas* relief to an inmate sentenced to death.

In another death-penalty development, Georgia State Representative Ray Holland introduced a bill to lower from 17 to 16 the age at which the death penalty could be imposed on offenders in Georgia.

To date, the state of Georgia has handed down death sentences for six offenders who were 17 years old at the time of their crime. Three sentences, one of them a woman, Janice Buttrum, were overturned on appeal. Two juvenile offenders are still on death row in Georgia, and one was executed in 1993. There are eleven other states with teenagers on death row, with Texas having the most, 17.

In 1996, the Georgia state Attorney General Michael Bowers went on record as saying he believed there were no innocent prisoners on death row in Georgia. Bowers said "There is rarely any question about the guilt of these people, virtually none. The idea of them being innocent is a myth, these guys on death row are the pits" (Amnesty International, 1996).

The state of Georgia makes no guarantees that indigent defendants will be represented beyond the direct appeal of their convictions. In Georgia, if you can afford a lawyer, you are entitled to his or her services. If you cannot, you are essentially on your own. Recently, however, Chief Justice Robert Benham of the Georgia Supreme Court has started recruiting lawyers to represent the condemned in post-trial appeals. As the state's highest-ranking judge, Benham said, "This is a crisis," and he asked several of the state's largest law firms to provide free legal representation to persons sentenced to death. His efforts have created a stir among some Georgia prosecutors, who believe they are already overmatched and outmanned by defense attorneys. According to Susan V. Boleyn, a senior assistant state attorney general, Georgia only has three lawyers assigned to death row appeals for the 73 currently active cases.

Wilburn Wiley Dobbs spent 24 years on Georgia's death row. He was sentenced to death in 1974 after his attorney offered no witnesses and no evidence to support sparing his life. In 1998 the Eleventh Circuit Court of Appeals granted Mr. Dobbs a new sentencing hearing.

In 1987 both the U.S. and Georgia Supreme Courts held that convicted murderers have no constitutional rights to legal counsel during post-conviction procedures, and no state guarantees appellate counsel for convicted felons.

Former state Attorney General Michael Bowers said he quit trying to enlist defense teams for convicted killers because he was convinced the Georgia appellate practice is only interested in delaying the implementation of the death penalty in whatever way they can. Convicted murderers in Georgia spend an average of 10½ years on death row.

GENDER BIAS IN GEORGIA

In April 1998, in Clayton County Georgia attorneys for David Aaron Perkins used gender bias as the reason for appealing his death sentence. Perkins was convicted and sentenced to death in 1997 for stabbing a man eleven times to steal his wallet. According to Perkins' attorneys he would have been less likely to receive the death penalty had he been a woman. They based this claim on the fact that eleven of the 84 people indicted for murder in Clayton County between 1985 and 1996 were women, but in the 12 cases where the death penalty was sought, all were men.

At least two of the women indicted for murder, during that period met the criteria for seeking the death penalty, they said, and they believe the reason the District Attorney did not seek the death penalty was because the defendants were female.

In response, then District Attorney Brandon Hornsby said a number of factors are involved in deciding whether or not to seek the death penalty in a particular case. Nevertheless, for the defense to say that a woman did not receive the death penalty because of her gender does not mean the opposite is also true — that the death penalty is sought against a man because of his gender.

WOMEN SENTENCED TO DEATH IN GEORGIA

1945

Lena Baker: Black; Executed, March 5, 1945. Lena Baker was convicted of killing a white man for whom she worked and with whom she had a long-term relationship. She said that he attacked her with an iron bar, and that she killed him in self-defense, but she was found guilty of first-degree murder and executed. She had children who distanced themselves from her after her conviction because of the stigma of her crime. After she was sentenced to death, they never communicated with her again. She was the only woman ever to be legally executed in Georgia.

1958

Anjette Lyles: White; Sent to a mental institution. Anjette Lyles was a housewife, mother, and restaurant proprietor in Macon, Georgia, when her youngest daughter, Marcia, became ill in the spring of 1958. Her two previous husbands and one mother-in-law had all died under mysterious circumstances. The police were alerted that Anjette might be a poisoner by an anonymous letter that turned out to be from the Lyles family cook.

When Marcia died and arsenic was found in her body, the police exhumed the bodies of Anjette's two husbands, who were also found to be full of arsenic. Anjette suggested her daughter might have ingested poison while playing doctor. Prosecutors maintained that Anjette committed the murders for the insurance money. Anjette Lyles was found guilty of the murder of her daughter and sentenced to death; but after an insanity hearing, she was ruled insane and sent to the Central State Hospital in Midgeville, Georgia, where she remained until she died of natural causes in December 1977.

1975

Rebecca Smith aka Rebecca Akins Smith; aka, Rebecca Machetti: White; Reversed in 1983. Ron Akins and his wife, Juanita, had only been married twenty days when they were murdered in Macon, Georgia. And Rebecca Machetti, Ron's former wife, had only been married to Tony Machetti a month when she was accused of the murders. The state never claimed Rebecca was present at the scene of the crime, but eventually found her guilty of conspiracy to commit murder. When she was sentenced to death Rebecca Machetti was the only woman on death row in Georgia.

She was the mother of three children, a member of MENSA, and a college graduate. She said she was innocent because she was in Miami when the murders took place.

Rebecca grew up in Athens, Georgia, and lived a happy life until her senior year in high school, when her father whom she adored killed her 3½-year-old brother and committed suicide as the result of an undiagnosed brain tumor. Because of the suicide, the family was denied any claim on her father's insurance. Rebecca got the idea that if she married she would be able to help her mother repay the loan she had taken out for the two funerals.

With this in mind, she married Ron Akins in Macon the Saturday after she graduated from high school. They had three children, all daughters, and, although there were the normal amount of problems, she remained married to him for sixteen years. After divorcing him she moved to Miami where she found employment as a nurse.

In Miami she married Tony Machetti. Four weeks after their wedding the murders took place. It was generally believed that Rebecca paid someone, namely her new husband, to kill Ron and his wife. Because of her training as a nurse, it was alleged that she prepared a poison drug in a syringe for her husband, Eldon Smith, aka Anthony Machetti, to use in the murders. Because Machetti was unable to administer the drug he shot the Akins couple instead. Tony denied having anything to do with the murders, but an associate of his,

John Maree, who admitted doing the shooting, plea-bargained for two consecutive life terms and fingered Machetti.

In a prison interview (Magee, 1980), Rebecca said the district attorney claimed the murders of her former husband and his wife were revenge killings for the way she had been treated in her sixteen years of marriage. The state also believed her motive was the life insurance policy her husband held and other money that would be given to her and her three daughters when her husband died. There was also some suggestion that the murders would somehow help Tony Machetti establish Mafia ties. It was assumed that the intention was to murder Ron Atkins and that his new wife was killed because she had the misfortune of being there.

A judge sentenced Rebecca Machetti to die at 1:00 a.m. in the morning and at the moment of sentencing he told her how many people could attend her execution and exactly how the invitations were to be sent out. Rebecca recalled that moment, saying she cried until about 4:00 a.m. or 5:00 a.m. while one of the prison matrons held her.

In prison Rebecca Machetti developed various physical problems such as migraine headaches, depression, skin rashes, and a stroke that left her with impaired vision. In 1978 Rebecca claimed a black chaplain who was employed at the prison sexually assaulted her. She said at the time she feared revenge from some black inmates because she told authorities.

In summing up her life Rebecca said, "I'm not too hot on being in the bosom of Abraham . . . but I'm not ashamed to read the book of life on me." Her death sentence was reversed in 1983 and she is now serving a life sentence.

1979

Emma Cunningham: Black; Reversed in 1983. Emma Ruth Cunningham received a double death-sentence at the age of 27 for the armed robbery and the murder of a sixty-three year old white man from Lincolnton, Georgia. She was convicted on the basis of "vicarious liability" even though she did not actually participate in the beating death of the victim.

As a teenager, Emma wanted to be a rhythm and blues singer, and made some attempts to do so, though she never became famous. After dropping out of high school at age 18 she married, she said, to escape overprotective parents.

In 1979 she accompanied her husband, James, to see a man, William B. Crawford, on business. She waited across the street while her husband went in. Later Crawford was found murdered, and Emma and James were both arrested for his murder on their way to New York. Police had received an anonymous tip about where they could be found.

James confessed to the murder and said that he panicked when he was caught burglarizing the home. Emma signed a statement that she had peeked into Crawford's window before her husband went in. She also stated she had received money from the burglary. Later, Mrs. Cunningham said she was pressured by the police to make the statements she made and was told that if she did not make them, her children would be taken away from her and she would never see them again.

In the trial, James refused to testify on Emma's behalf and implicated her in the murder by saying she had planned the whole thing. Her death sentence was reversed in 1983. Emma Cunningham served eleven years and is home afte doing a year at a half-way house.

1979

Shirley Tyler: Black; Reversed in 1985. The Georgia Supreme Court affirmed the death sentence given to Shirley Tyler on February 13, 1981, for the murder of her husband, James Wilson Tyler. In a 6–0 decision, the court found that the aggravating circumstances of "inhuman torture" supported the death sentence.

Two weeks after her husband's death, Shirley, who was 34 at the time, went to see the sheriff and somehow ended up signing a confession that she had murdered her husband. There was no attorney present, and Mrs. Tyler did not see her court-appointed lawyer until two weeks before her trial.

According to the state, Shirley wanted her husband's insurance money and had put rat poison, parathion, in her husband's chili twice after her first attempt to kill him failed. Shirley said she did not have anything to do with his death. Her husband, she said, was suicidal and in their twelve years of marriage she had to have him locked up several times because he drank and beat her and her children. She said that because of depression, he frequently threatened suicide. An all-white jury found her guilty of first-degree murder.

Shirley Tyler was not housed with the other two women on Georgia's death row at the time (Cunningham and Machetti), but was sent to the Pike County jail. For the most part, she was the only woman there. She was allowed visits twice a month from her son and daughter, but the years of incarceration affected her physically. She lost weight and suffered periodic ear infections. In 1981 after losing an appeal to the Georgia Supreme Court to overturn her death sentence, she joined the other two women on death row at the Hardwick Center.

The contention was made, on appeal, that Shirley did not make her confession of her own free will to a Georgia Bureau of Investigations agent. The Georgia Supreme Court, however, ruled that "for an officer to advise the accused that it is always best to tell the truth does not render the subsequent confession inadmissible."

In January 1982 Shirley Tyler was moved to the State Diagnostic and Classification Center at Jackson, Georgia, and was then transferred to the Women's Correctional Institute. Her death sentence was reversed in 1985. Shirley did seventeen years in prison and went to a half-way house in 1997. After six months of working she went home and now lives at home with her family.

1981

Janice Buttrum: White; Reversed in 1989. Janice Buttrum had a history of abuse. She had been born to an alcoholic unwed mother who gave her away as a baby to be raised by foster parents who were also alcoholics and sexually abused her. She married Danny Buttrum at age fifteen, who although he was eleven years older, was borderline retarded, and abused drugs.

After being married for two years Danny and Janice decided to move from Adairsville, Georgia, to Dalton, Georgia, and were living temporarily in a small motel with their 19-month-old baby, Marlena. Janice was pregnant at the time with a second daughter, Marie, who was born while she awaited trial. At the motel they became friendly with Demetra Faye Parker, a pretty, white, 19-year-old who had moved to Dalton from Kenton, Tennessee, and was also living temporarily at the motel. Demetra seemed to be fond of the Buttrums' daughter, Marlena.

In her confession, Janice Buttrum said she was jealous of Demetra because she was prettier and she was afraid of losing her husband. Pretending the baby was sick, Janice and her husband went to Demetra's room and while the baby crawled around on the floor, they beat, raped, and sodomized her. After the initial attack, it was alleged that Janice sexually abused Demetra herself and then stabbed her 97 times with a small pocketknife. Although there was no evidence that Janice Buttrum had molested the victim, rumors of lesbianism on Janice's part fueled the shocking fires and brought about the charge that she had "aided and abetted rape."

They then took Demetra's car and some of her rings and clothing and left the motel that night. The motel manager found Demetra Parker's body at about 11:00 a.m the next morning and called the sheriff.

Suspicions focused immediately on the Buttrums, and they were arrested the next day in a restaurant in Pensacola, Florida. Both were indicted for the murder of Demetra Parker.

Both Janice and her husband were sentenced to death at separate trials. The Georgia Supreme Court described the murder as "butchery and barbarism." Her husband committed suicide by hanging himself, a week after being sentenced to death. After human rights groups intervened on the grounds that Janice Buttrum was a minor, her sentence was commuted to life in 1989.

In 1991 prosecutors in Whitfield County, Georgia, decided not to seek the death penalty again in the case of Janice Buttrum. Her lawyers successfully argued that the death penalty should be rejected in this case since Georgia has never executed a female juvenile offender in its history. The state agreed to accept a guilty plea and a sentence of life imprisonment without possibility of parole.

1982

Teresa Faye Whittington: White: Reversed, 1984. Teresa Faye Whittington was nineteen-years-old when she was sentenced to die in the Georgia electric chair for shooting her lover's wife, Cheryl Marie Soto, who was three months pregnant at the time.

Richard Soto, the victim's husband, was sentenced to life for his part in the same crime even though it was revealed at his trial that he had purchased a gun and taken out an insurance policy on his wife several months before meeting Teresa.

According to court records, on January 26, 1982, Teresa went with Soto to his home. Her emotional state at the time was not good because she had just ended an abusive relationship with a man she was supposed to marry.

After arriving at the house, Soto gave Teresa a gun and told her to go in and shoot his wife. His apparent motive was to avoid the consequences of a love triangle. At his bidding, Teresa went in and shot Cheryl. She had never used a gun before and inflicted only a flesh wound. Teresa then ran out. Realizing his wife was still alive Soto sent her back to shoot Cheryl again. This time it was fatal. Teresa has no memory of the second shot which killed Cheryl.

Teresa turned herself in to the police the next day. She was told to take the blame for Richard Soto so that he would not receive the death penalty. Her trial lasted two days. Her public defender presented no defense and she was not allowed to testify. She was convicted of murder with malice aforethought, of being an agent of torture, and of seeking insurance money. Teresa was given the death penalty and was on death row in Georgia for three years even though the Georgia Supreme Court had reversed her death sentence in 1984. Teresa is now serving a life sentence. She was given an eight year denial in June, 1998.

Teresa gave her life to God after going to prison and actively participates in Christian services and counseling programs. Those who know her say she is a caring, conscientious woman who deeply regrets the pain she caused others and is not the cold-blooded killer she was made out to be at the time of the trial.

A close friend recently said that when Teresa took part in the crime that ended another person's life she was young, insecure, naive, and wanted to be loved. Today, she is a determined, self-directed woman and a living testimony to the fact that people can grow and change even in prison.

11

Idaho: Lethal Injection/Firing Squad

The state of Idaho has sentenced two women to death since 1900. No women have been executed and there is one woman on death row in Idaho today. Idaho allows the death penalty as an option in cases of first-degree murder and aggravated kidnapping. The sentence is death by lethal injection or the firing squad.

In 1994 Keith Eugene Wells dropped all his appeals and became the first person executed in Idaho in 35 years. He was sentenced to death in 1990 for the unprovoked beating deaths of two people. He told police he attacked the two people with a baseball bat because he "knew it was time for them to die. I was a predator on the prowl for prey," he said. Idaho's last execution before Wells was the hanging of Raymond Allen Snowden on October 18, 1957, for the murder/mutilation of a woman he picked up in a bar. That was before Idaho gave death row inmates the option of lethal injection. As Snowden's execution took place, inmates at the maximum-security prison pounded on walls, shook cell doors, and stomped on floors in protest.

Death-row inmates in Idaho are only allowed non-contact visits from their immediate family. They speak through telephones and face-to-face interviews are not allowed.

For death by lethal injection, the state of Idaho employs a team to perform the execution. The team is responsible for inserting the IV line and administering the drugs. The sequence of drugs administered is:

- 5g. with dilutent of sodium pentothal
- 10 mg of Pavulon (generic name for pancuronium bromide)
- 2mEq/ml of potassium chloride

Each drug takes 45 seconds to administer and it takes 45 seconds for each saline flush after each drug is administered. The average length of time that elapses from the moment the prisoner is restrained to the time of death is approximately 12 minutes.

The witnesses authorized by the state to attend an execution are the coroner, the sheriff and prosecuting attorney from the county of conviction; the offenders spiritual advisor, the sentencing judge, a representative from the governor's office, the attorney general, a representative from the Board of Corrections, seven members of the news media, the director of the Idaho Department of Corrections, and the warden.

WOMEN SENTENCED TO DEATH IN IDAHO

1984

Karla Windsor: White; Reversed in 1985. On September 10, 1983, Karla Windsor and Donald Fetterly were apprehended driving a vehicle registered to Sterling Grammer, who was found stabbed to death in his home on September 7. The two were charged with first-degree murder, burglary, grand theft, and the use of a deadly weapon in connection with Grammer's death.

According to statements made at the time, Karla and Don had become acquainted with Grammer several weeks before his death. Apparently, Grammer was dating Don's ex-mother-in-law, Viola Hogan, and Karla and Don met Sterling through her.

On Monday, September 5, Karla and Don, who had been living together for approximately six months, went to Sterling's house around dinnertime. Both were unemployed at the time and had sold most of their possessions in order to have money to travel to other states looking for work. As a result, they were without money, a vehicle, or a place to stay. Sterling invited them to stay for dinner and to spend the night in an extra room he had. Grammer, Karla, and Don all left the house together the next morning.

Karla and Don found out there were several warrants out for their arrest and spent September 6 trying to figure out how they could get out of the state. While at Grammer's house the previous night, they had seen he owned two cars, a large TV, and a diamond ring, among other things. According to Karla's testimony, they decided to ask Grammer to loan them one of the vehicles and if he refused they would tie him up and steal it. With this in mind, they went back to Sterling's house and waited for him to come home from work. He didn't come back that night, and Viola Hogan testified he had spent the night with her. Karla and Don entered the house through a window and spent the night.

When Grammer arrived home at 6:30 the next morning they explained their situation to him, and when he refused to help them, they tied him up using duct tape to bind his hands and feet. Karla testified that Grammer did not offer any resistance and agreed to let them tie him up. This point was disputed, however, in the trial because the autopsy report showed that Grammer had sustained a bruise on the back of his head sufficiently severe enough to knock him out. Grammer's mouth and face were covered with enough duct-tape to cut off his air supply, but Karla testified that she had taped his face and that he was still able to breathe after she finished.

According to Karla, Grammer was taped up and left lying on his bed while she and Fetterly decided what they wanted to steal. When Grammer began making a lot of noise Karla and Fetterly became alarmed because they thought the neighbors would hear him so they went into the bedroom to see what was happening. Grammer was thrashing around on the bed so Karla lay across his legs to try to hold him still. At that point, Fetterly grabbed the knife they had used to cut the duct-tape off the headboard and held it to Grammer's chest. When he continued to struggle, Fetterly stabbed him several times in the chest and killed him. Karla said it all happened so quickly she couldn't do anything about it.

They dumped Grammer's body in the Snake River where fishermen discovered it on September 9. A police officer saw Karla and Don driving Grammer's pick-up and stopped them, then took them in for questioning. Karla was interrogated without being read her Miranda rights. One of the detectives who questioned her told her if she was involved in anything it would be best for her to tell the truth. Karla responded that she did not want to say anything without Fetterly in the room. They brought Fetterly in and after the two had a conversation, they agreed to make a statement. At that point they were read their Miranda rights. Both Karla and Don signed statements waiving those rights and gave detailed confessions of what had happened.

On the basis of their confessions, they were indicted on charges of first-degree murder, burglary, grand theft, and the use of a deadly weapon in the commission of a felony. In separate jury trials, Karla was found guilty of the charges of first-degree murder (the first-degree premeditated verdict was returned unsigned), second-degree burglary, and Grand Theft. Although no longer on death row, Karla remains in prison in Idaho today. Of her case Karla writes:

My case involved two people, my fall partner and myself. My fall partner (a man with an extensive history of violence) is currently on death row and I was sentenced to indeterminate life. In the eyes of the law, I am guilty of "Felony murder in the First Degree." My sentence of indeterminate life made me eligible for parole in 1993. At that time the Parole Board denied me parole and asked that I come back in four (4) years. I saw them again in August 1997 and again they denied me parole and asked that I come back in seven (7) years. I feel strongly that if I were a man with the excellent record that I have in prison, I would have been released. I have done fourteen (14) years and I have used the time to look at myself and my culpability in the murder. I recognize the defects and events that led up to the murder. This was important because without understanding how I can be a part of something like that I cannot prevent myself from allowing it to happen again. Both times the institution has recommended release for me, but the parole board seems more intent on further punishment. Since you know that I was on death row, I will assume that you know I did not actually kill the man, but was truly an accessory, before, during, and after.

Of her time on death row, she writes:

The prison where I am now is located on a hill, in a desert, outside of the city. When I was on death row my surroundings were some mountains and trees, a 12-foot high fence, some grass and occasional wildlife could be seen from a 36 by 64 inch window. I could see the rec yard and the other inmates (men and women) when they went back and forth to the rec yard. My cell was located at the back of the building. The building was an old red brick, mental hospital that had been condemned. My cell was 5 feet wide and 12 feet long. There was a twin-size bed, metal frame; stainless steel toilet/sink setup — a small table/bench (metal) bolted to the wall, a shelf for my TV (I purchased with my own funds) also bolted to the wall. I had a small wooden box for underwear and other items. There was a big circular mirror above the bed, in the corner so that the officers could see all areas of the cell including the toilet, without opening the door and only looking through the window of the steel door. An average day started around 6 a.m. when breakfast was brought to the cell. Then about 20 minutes later they would come back for the tray. Before I had my TV I listened to my radio and did Bible Studies, prayed, wrote letters and read books. This usually took me to lunchtime. Most often I was taken out to rec in the mornings. I had to remain handcuffed and shackled (at first) until about 3–4 months when they changed it because the men in Boise weren't handcuffed and shackled. I'd read and pray until 4 p.m. count — then dinner — lights out at 9 p.m.— a security light stayed on all night so the officers could see me. The only privacy was between the hourly checks. Otherwise, an officer watched me shower and I was never alone outside my cell. In the cell, they came in at any time and did a daily shakedown of my pencils and other possibly dangerous items. I was pat-searched leaving and entering my cell.

The hardest to do was to accept the court's decision as truth. You see, I believed in the justice system before I was sentenced to death — therefore if a judge decided I was a bad person and was of no value then it must be true, and if it was true, I deserved to die. I had to convince myself in the bottom of my heart that I was absolutely worthless! That was hard to do, but it was the only way I could accept my circumstances, my position. Even though I knew there was a mandatory appeal that meant nothing because it had not happened yet. I couldn't afford to hope, because hope hurt and it still does. I have not yet been able to erase that particular scar. It has been 12 years and I still have a hard time believing that I am a worthwhile human being just because I live.

Right now I am OK. My faith in God has gone thru many tests. But, in general, I am dealing with my incarceration okay. I have a lot of scars — emotional and mental but through God's grace and lots of good programs — I am healing — slowly.

The thing I would like people to know is that I am human. I was ready to die but God granted me a new sentence. Indeterminate life is bearable, but only because there is still hope no matter how small. But the system can be very cruel. For those who have life without the possibility of parole, it can be much crueler, but also maybe much easier. There are pluses and minuses on all sides. I think it is important for people to be realistic about the majority of violent criminal offenders (women):

• Usually it is only a one-time offense.

- There are often extenuating circumstances/conditions that influence the thoughts and actions at the time of the crime.
- Even one-time violent crime offenders are capable of re-entering society and becoming productive citizens if they are given a chance. Especially when social workers and everyone who works with them recommends release saying they are no longer a threat to society. Instead of continuing to cost the taxpayers money, these offenders should be allowed to pay back society in a positive, constructive, way.

In the state of Idaho, Karla was technically charted under first-degree murder, subsection "Felony Murder." This means that anyone who is present during the commission of a crime in which someone dies can be charged with first-degree murder as a principal. When the jury retired to deliberate they had 4 pieces of paper on which to write their verdicts, but they only returned with 3 signed verdicts: First-degree murder, Second-degree burglary (which was dismissed on appeal), and Grand Theft. The paper for first-degree premeditated murder was left unsigned. Karla noted this is important to her because it means that the jury did not believe she deliberately planned to commit murder.

1993

Robin Lee Row: White; Currently on death row. Robin Lee Row was found guilty of the arson/murder of her husband Randy and their two children in Boise in 1992. She was sentenced to death in Idaho in December 1993.

In the early morning hours of February 10, 1992, a fire broke out at the duplex apartment in Boise, Idaho, where Randy Row and Robin's two children Joshua (age 10) and Tabitha (age 8) were living.

Robin was not there at the time. Because of problems in their marriage she was living with a friend. After the fire was under control the firemen entered the apartment and found the bodies of Randy and the two children. All had died from carbon monoxide poisoning as a result of the fire. Firemen found that one fire had been started in an area where the apartment joined the garage and a second fire had been started in a pile of clothes in the living room. In both places a flammable liquid was used to ignite the fires, and the smoke detectors had been disabled before the fire started by turning off the power at the circuit breaker. It was, therefore, determined that the three victims died because they had not been properly alerted by the smoke alarms.

This is what initiated a police investigation. After police learned that Robin had lost a daughter to SIDS in 1977 and another son, Keith, in a house fire in California in 1980, they got a warrant to search the burned apartment as well as the residence where Robin was staying. They also searched Robin's car and a storage unit, which Robin kept in Meridian, Idaho. During the search, police discovered six insurance policies carried by Robin and naming her as the beneficiary on those who had died in her family. They totaled approximately

$276,500 in death benefits. The most recent policy had been obtained seventeen days before the fatal fire.

In the same search, the police claimed to have discovered evidence that Robin had been stealing from a bingo operation run by the YWCA where she worked. As a result, Robin was arrested for grand theft by unauthorized control of funds belonging to the YWCA and was placed in the Ada County jail with bail set at $100,000.

With Robin in jail, the arson and multiple-death investigation continued, and police asked Robin's friend, whom she had been staying with, to put a tape recorder on her telephone to record any conversations between herself and Robin if Robin happened to call. On the afternoon of March 20, 1992, Robin called from the jail when she found out that charges were going to be filed against her. As detectives had instructed Joan, her friend, she told Robin she had awakened during the night of the fire and gone downstairs, but had not found Robin there. Robin told her she had left the house and was outside talking to her psychiatrist at the time. After the first taped conversation, Robin called Joan again on the same day reiterating that she had been talking to her psychiatrist until about 4:30 a.m. on the night of the fire.

The following Monday, on March 23, 1992, a Detective Raney went to the Ada County jail and advised Robin she was under arrest for three counts of murder and read the arrest warrant to her. Later, the charge of arson was added. Following a jury trial, Robin was sentenced to death on December 16, 1993, for three first-degree murders that the jury found to be willful, deliberate, and premeditated. In its conclusions, the court further stated that "two additional statutory aggravating circumstances have been proved beyond a reasonable doubt." These were, according to the court, that Robin's anticipation of the insurance proceeds established that the murders were committed for remuneration or the promise of remuneration, and that the nature of the murders established that Robin exhibited utter disregard for human life.

Robin is on death row in Idaho today, and in March 1998 the Idaho Supreme Court upheld her sentence. Of her life on death row Robin writes:

When I look out my window, which doesn't open, my view is a large lot and the foothills in the distance. From the window in my door I see the day room which I pass through to go to the shower, outside or to use the telephone.

I believe my room is 8 by 10. I have a cabinet, a table attached to the wall, no stool or chair, and my bed frame. All are painted a light blue. There is a foam mattress, a toilet and sink and the walls are cinderblock, painted ivory.

I have access to the Law Library and when I go down there, I'm put in a secure study booth. The best way to describe it is it reminds me of a movie ticket booth, the same size and the same kind of speaker. I speak through a glass pane. This is also the regular library. If I need legal materials a law clerk assists me by getting books for me. The library is small and I love to read. The librarian teases me about reading all the books available. I'm re-reading books now.

I have access to medical and they have always been good to me. If I put in a request to be seen, I am seen within two days. I've had to go outside of the prison for medical care and it was done promptly. Medical is like a mini-clinic. I've seen an OB-Gyn, dentist, physical therapist, eye doctor, who all contract with medical. Also, a psychiatrist and psychologist are available.

I have access to religious counseling in a non-contact setting and I have Bible study once a week. The woman I see comes from a local church. I've been seeing her for about three and a half years and I feel I'm finally ready and will be baptized in January.

When I leave my room, I must be in restraints and the halls must be cleared before I am escorted to my destination. On a typical day lights are on at 6:00 a.m. and off at 10:00 p.m. This doesn't mean I have to go to bed. I can stay up all night if I want, being isolated and alone I can't disturb anyone, so no one cares.

Breakfast is at 6:30 a.m., lunch at 11:30 a.m., and dinner at 4:45 p.m. It's on a tray that is brought to me. I get a beverage with breakfast only. The food is usually cold, but not always. There is pill call at 6:00 a.m. and 6:00 p.m. — medication is dispensed and medical requests are picked up. A nurse comes to my room for that.

There is no privacy and I can be patted or strip-searched on demand. At first the hardest thing for me was what other people thought of me. Now, it's the lack of contact visits with friends and family. If visits weren't immediate family only, I'd have visits. I don't know what's worse, the loneliness or the boredom. I'd like people to know I have feelings. I laugh and cry just like they do. I'd also like people not to believe everything the media says and don't judge me until you walk a while in my shoes.

Since the state of Idaho does not have a women's death row. Robin is housed at the Women's Prison in the section for solitary confinement and isolation. In prison jargon this area is known as "the hole." Robin reports she can hear the inmates in solitary confinement when they yell to each other, but she cannot communicate with them in any way.

As the only woman on death row in Idaho today the state allows Robin one envelope and eight sheets of paper per week, with a limit of four envelopes per month. All indigent supplies are purchased through a special fund established through commissary sales (10 percent) and monies made from copy machines used by inmates. This fund pays the salaries of two inmate commissary workers and all equipment that inmates are allowed to use such as Zerox machine and supplies, typewriters, and so on. It is also used to purchase gym equipment, videos, basketballs and the like for the General Population. Robin received a death warrant on June 3, 1998 with the date of execution set for June 18, 1998. She is now pursuing federal appeals.

12

Illinois: Lethal Injection

The state of Illinois has sentenced seven women to death since 1900. One woman, Marie Porter, was executed, and there are three women on death row in Illinois today.

Since the death penalty was re-enacted June 21, 1977, there have been 251 death sentences in Illinois. The Illinois Department of Corrections received its first female inmate with a death sentence in 1991. Women on death row are held at the Dwight Correctional Center, located approximately 75 miles south of Chicago. This facility was opened in November 1930 as the Oakdale Reformatory for Women. Later it was named the Illinois State Reformatory for Women and in, August 1973, it was renamed the Dwight Correctional Center.

Between 1928 and 1962 there were 98 executions in Illinois. Thirteen of these took place at the Stateville Correctional Center. Old Sparky, the electric chair, was designed to deliver an initial 15-second jolt of electricity at 600 volts followed by a second charge of 2,400 volts. The last man executed in the chair, died in relative obscurity on August 24, 1962 at the Cook County jail in Chicago. His name was James Dukes. Dukes, a former Post Office employee, was arrested in 1956 for the fatal shooting of a police detective. Dukes, who was black, was convicted by an all-white jury. A few months after the execution of Dukes executions were stopped in Illinois.

The Illinois death penalty law was 12 years old and had never been used, in 1989, when it was ruled unconstitutional by U.S. District Judge, Harold A. Baker of Danville, Illinois. The ruling came as a result of the case of a man who had murdered two sisters in Danville in 1980. At the time Baker said the death penalty in Illinois was exercised in an "arbitrary and capricious" manner because it granted too much discretion to state prosecutors. In addition, the judge said, the law was constitutionally defective because it did not require prosecutors to disclose whether they planned to seek the death penalty until after a defendant was convicted.

This order granted a new sentencing hearing in the case it pertained to, and it granted the 120 inmates on Illinois death row reprieves. Incorporated in the argument was part of an opinion written by Illinois Justice Howard Ryan. In 1979 he wrote "Our statute contains no directions or guidelines to minimize the risk of wholly arbitrary and capricious action by the prosecutor in requesting or not requesting a sentencing hearing."

In September 1990 the state of Illinois resumed executions after a 28-year hiatus, with the death by lethal injection of Charles Walker, a 50-year-old man convicted of shooting a young engaged couple in the course of a $40 robbery. Walker dropped all of his appeals about five years prior to his execution. He confessed to the crime and said he would rather be executed than have to spend the rest of his life in prison. Walker's execution was hailed in the papers as "A dignified, professional, uneventful killing."

Recently (1998) the Illinois state Senate approved a bill by Senator Walter Dudycz (R-Chicago) calling for the death penalty for people who deliberately kill community activists engaged in working against street-gang activity. The measure was inspired by the murder of Arnold Mireles, who worked in a South Chicago neighborhood.

One ad that ran in Governor Jim Edgar's campaign promoted his support of the death penalty. "In death penalty cases in Illinois, the last appeal comes to this desk. Who do you want sitting here?"

ILLINOIS DOCTORS AND EXECUTION

In 1991, the Illinois State Medical Society was the first group of doctors in the nation to declare it unethical for physicians to pronounce executed inmates dead. In its statement, the society promised to seek an amendment to the Illinois law that requires physicians to make the formal declaration of death in capital punishment cases.

The policy was adopted after society members learned that in several executions involving lethal injections, physicians assigned to declare the inmate dead found that the inmate's heart was still beating. The president of the Medical Society said, "The physicians had to say this man isn't dead and in effect, you've got to do more to kill him. This is diametrically opposed to what our profession is all about."

Guidelines were prompted by the execution of Charles Walker (1990). Reportedly, several unidentified physicians participated. Prison officials indicated they felt Walker's death by lethal injection was about as clinical and routine as such an event can be. Scott Mansfield, chief assistant state's attorney of St. Clair County, who was one of the observers, said the execution was "uneventful." The chief spokesman for the Illinois Department of Corrections, said, "It appeared to come off without a hitch." The execution took about 11 minutes.

In 1994, in the execution of convicted serial killer John Wayne Gacy, an intravenous tube leading from the machine to the inmate became clogged, delaying his death by about 10 minutes. After that, Illinois scrapped its $24,900 lethal injection machine and in March 1995 for its first double execution in more than four decades, employed an executioner. James Free and Hernando Williams were put to death an hour apart at the Stateville Correctional Center near Joliet by a mixture of toxic chemicals administered manually.

In 1996 Illinois lawmakers passed a bill that would prohibit a third party from appealing on behalf of a death row inmate without the inmate's consent. The House voted overwhelmingly to require that a death row inmate's signature be included in any appeal for a hearing before the Prisoner Review Board. Representative Flora Ciarlo, a co-sponsor of the bill, said, "If an inmate is of sound mind, they ought to be able to determine what happens to them. Someone else shouldn't be able to come along and say otherwise." This bill was proposed as a direct response to the case of Guinevere Garcia, who specifically requested execution but was granted clemency and sentenced to life because of requests by national and international organizations.

WRONGFUL SENTENCING

In 1997 a coalition of prominent legal figures and religious organizations asked the Illinois Supreme Court to halt all executions in Illinois until an investigation is made of the state's extraordinarily high rate of defendants wrongfully sentenced to die.

The petition asked justices to establish a blue-ribbon committee to study "a problem of extraordinary magnitude that has plagued the Illinois capital punishment process in recent years." It also requested that justices defer setting execution dates in all cases until the commission's work is done and evaluated.

Since capital punishment was reinstated Illinois has released nine men from death row after it was determined they never should have been convicted. Four of the men were freed on the basis of DNA evidence; six were men of color. No other jurisdiction comes close to Illinois's record for imposing the death sentence on people who were later exonerated.

In reviewing the nine cases of wrongful capital convictions, the special commission found three general trends:

Inadequate Representation. Most of the defendants were without funds to hire competent counsel and were therefore poorly represented. One of the lawyers representing a capital defendant was defending himself in disbarment proceedings at the same time, and one had a record of disciplinary problems. Frequently the defense was not given funds to hire experts. Nationally, poor representation was one of the reasons the ABA called for a moratorium on executions.

Prosecutorial Misconduct. In Illinois most of the wrongful capital convictions involve questions of possible police or prosecutorial misconduct. The case of Rolando Cruz and Alejandro Hernandez resulted in the indictments of seven prosecutors and sheriff's officers on charges of perjury and official misconduct. Gary Gauger, who was wrongfully convicted of the murder of his parents, testified that he was interrogated by authorities for 20 hours, deprived of sleep and food, and lied to by investigators, who told him falsely that they could prove he committed the crimes. They also told him falsely that he had flunked a polygraph examination.

Racial Bias. Six out of the nine cases involved a defendant of color and a victim who was white. There are many studies that show nationwide more death sentences are given when the perpetrator is believed to be a person of color and the victim is white (Baldus, 1990). Discrimination in capital sentencing was another reason the ABA called for a moratorium on executions.

Illinois leads the nation in acknowledging mistakes in capital cases, according to Richard C. Dieter, executive director of the Death Penalty Information Center in Washington, DC, but this does not necessarily mean that Illinois courts are more diligent than those of other states in correcting it. All but one of the nine men in Illinois were released only after outside sources developed evidence of their innocence. The evidence included the confession of the real perpetrators, DNA testing, and/or witness recantation.

Richard Cunningham, a defense lawyer in Illinois, said, "The chilling rate of wrongful death sentences in Illinois shows something is terribly wrong. It raises enormous questions about our system of justice in Illinois." And, Locke Bowman, legal director of the MacArthur Justice Center of the University of Chicago Law School, stated that "The court's leadership is urgently required to dispel the cynical perception among some members of the public that the capital process is flawed and unreliable."

In July 1996, four black men were released in Illinois because they were proven innocent of murders of which they were convicted 18 years ago. Two of the men had been given the death penalty. These men gained their release because they were represented by lawyers who had been working for their freedom since 1990.

Students of journalism from Northwestern University had studied their cases as a possible miscarriage of justice, and in their study they unearthed police notes that implicated other suspects in the crime. The students also located the main prosecution witness, who admitted she had been coerced by the police into falsely implicating the four men.

The Illinois legislature passed a bill that would enable some prison inmates to establish their innocence by allowing genetic testing of old evidence — only on evidence from the original trial, and only if DNA technology was not available at the time. Attorneys have to prove the evidence has not been tampered with or altered in any way, and the tests have to prove a defendant's "factual innocence" rather than creating a "reasonable doubt" of guilt. An inmate can lose six months or more of good-time credit for filing frivolous DNA testing requests. Currently Illinois inmates have only two years post-conviction time to request DNA testing. DNA tests are very expensive; analysis of a single sample can cost as much as $600, and expert testimony costs about $1200 per day.

WOMEN SENTENCED TO DEATH IN ILLINOIS

1938

Marie Porter: White; Executed. Marie Porter was executed by electrocution on January 28, 1938, at the age of 38, for arranging the murder of her brother on his wedding day. Reportedly, Marie thought that if her brother got married she would no longer be the beneficiary on his $3,300 insurance policy. So she hired two young men, one of them her lover, Anthony Giancola, to kidnap her brother from his rooming house and drive him around for a couple of hours, to try to convince him not to take her name off his policy. When Marie saw that this was not working she allegedly ordered the two men to kill him. Afterward, they dropped his body in a field of poison ivy, and the rash on their arms was what helped to incriminate them.

Governor Henry Horner in office, at the time, had vowed that no woman would be executed during his term, but he turned down Marie Porter's appeal for clemency because he felt he couldn't pardon her without pardoning her accomplice, who was the actual triggerman.

Marie Porter and Anthony Giancola were electrocuted, and Anthony's younger brother was sentenced to life. Marie had four daughters; the eldest at the time of her execution was 21. She was the first woman executed in Illinois after 1845, and none has been executed since.

1991

Geraldine Smith: Black; Sentence vacated in 1997. Geraldine Smith was given the death penalty for paying $500 for the contract killing of her boyfriend's wife, Valerie McDonald. She had been having an affair with Valerie's husband for some time when she allegedly asked a woman named Marva Golden to find a hit man for her. Golden put her in touch with Eddie Williams, who agreed to do the hit. Valerie was gunned down outside her home on her way back from church with her two young daughters and husband at her side. Geraldine Smith became the first woman to be sentenced to death in Illinois for many years.

The Illinois Supreme Court vacated her death sentence in 1997. In his opinion Justice John Nickels wrote "We see here an individual with no past criminal record who would in all probability be leading a life acceptable to our society had not her unfortunate affair triggered this tragic sequence of events."

1991

Dorothy Williams: Black; Currently on death row. Dorothy Williams, the mother of two children, was sentenced to death at the age of 37 for the strangulation murder of Mary Harris, a 97-year-old woman, during a drug-related robbery. Dorothy stole a stereo from her to sell for drugs. In his argument, the prosecutor said, "The defendant selected a 97-year-old 99-pound helpless senior citizen to kill. She set the value of Mary Harris's life on a small stereo." Dorothy had allegedly panhandled door-to-door at the Chicago Housing Authority senior citizens' homes, and the people there knew her. Witnesses said she had terrorized people in the Washington Park Home for years. In imposing the death sentence, Judge Singer said Dorothy had preyed on the elderly. Dorothy pleaded guilty to two additional murders, both elderly men, for which she received two life terms.

1992

Guinevere Garcia: Latina; Commuted in 1996. Born in 1958, Guinevere Garcia was abandoned as a toddler by her father after her mother committed suicide. She was raised by her grandparents. At age six she was raped by an uncle who continued to sexually abuse her for years. By age eleven, she was an alcoholic. She was gang-raped at fifteen by five teen-aged boys at a birthday party. Shortly after that, her grandfather arranged for her to be married to an illegal alien to prevent his deportation, for which her grandfather received $1,500.

By age seventeen, she was working as a stripper and a prostitute. She then became pregnant and gave birth to a daughter she named Sara. Her grandmother wanted custody of baby Sara because she felt Guinevere was not a suitable mother due to her heavy drinking and prostitution. After an argument with her grandmother about the baby's custody, Guinevere went home and drank herself into a blackout. When she regained consciousness her 11-month old daughter was dead in her arms, having been suffocated. In a television interview she stated, "I was not going to have my daughter in that house with my grandparents or my uncle. In my mind I was protecting her." The baby's death was originally ruled as accidental suffocation. However, after a series of fires that coincided with the anniversaries of Sara's birth and death, the police questioned Guinevere again and she confessed to killing her daughter and committing arson. In 1983, four years after the death of her daughter, she pleaded guilty and was convicted of her daughter's murder and four charges of arson. She was then sentenced to 20 years in prison.

While she was incarcerated Guinevere married George Garcia, a former client of hers from her days of prostitution. They divorced but remarried when she was released in 1991. By then she had spent ten years in prison. Shortly after her release, she shot and killed her husband in a drunken argument. He had broken a bottle and used the glass to slash a 2-inch wound in Guinevere's genitalia. Guinevere said her husband was abusive and continually beat her. Sixty-year-old George Garcia was shot in the front seat of his pickup truck in the parking lot of their condominium

Guinevere waived her right to a jury at the sentencing phase of her trial and was sentenced to death by three judges in October 1992. The judges decided that the mitigating factors of Guinevere Garcia's life did not outweigh the aggravating factors of her criminal history and the crime, even though the judges were aware of the sexual abuse in Guinevere's childhood. Of this case, Linda Thurston, director of the Program to Abolish the Death Penalty at Amnesty International said, "Mitigating circumstances in her case were very strong and were not brought up adequately at trial."

Court hearings determined that Guinevere was mentally competent to drop her appeals and consent to her own execution. She told a judge, "I don't want to die, your honor, but my life is miserable." She added, "I made my peace with God and myself. I am sitting in prison while my victims are dead. My life has no purpose, no meaningful existence." Describing her time in prison, she stated, "My life is over. This is not living. I don't want to exist in Room Six of the condemned unit waiting until someone decides to put that needle in my arm."

A spokesperson for the Illinois Coalition Against the Death Penalty said, "We believe in Guinevere's case the state will be killing a battered woman and an abused child, and this is opposed to any sense of justice. It's a step in a direction the state hasn't taken before."

Hours before she was to be given a lethal injection, Governor Jim Edgar stayed her execution and commuted her sentence to natural life without parole because, he said, her crime did not justify the punishment. He cited evidence that she apparently had not planned to kill her husband and said, "It is not the state's responsibility to carry out the wishes of a defendant." This was the first time Edgar had granted such a request to a convicted murderer who rejected all attempts to save his/her life. Edgar, who refused clemency to all six men who were executed after he took office in 1991, denied suggestions that he made an exception because Guinevere Garcia was a battered woman. "Some who have sought clemency on her behalf have raised the possibility that she was a victim herself, a victim of battered woman syndrome," Edgar said. "However," he added, " the evidence does not support that assertion."

Of Bianca Jagger, who intervened on her behalf against her wishes, Guinevere said, "This must be her cause of the week rather than the Screen Actors Guild or cruelty to animals." She told the review board, "I killed George Garcia, and only I know why. Do not generically label, package, and attempt to justify my actions as that of an abused woman." In 1997 Guinevere slashed her left wrist with a broken light bulb from her cell at Dwight Correctional Center in an apparent suicide attempt.

1993

Marilyn Mulero: Latina; Reversed, discharged, 1998. Marilyn Mulero was the mother of two children when she was sentenced to death for the murders of Hector Reyes and Jimmy Cruz, two members of the Latin Kings gang on the night of May 12, 1992. Reyes and Cruz had thought they were going to a party when they met the three female members of an opposing gang, Marilyn Mulero, Madeline Mendoza and Jacqueline Montanez, in Humboldt Park in Chicago.

Hector Reyes was shot first when he went into one of the park restrooms with Madeline Mendoza and kissed her. Just outside the restroom, Marilyn Mulero shot Jimmy Cruz next and kicked him while he was on the ground. The motive for the murders was believed to have been to avenge the murder of a friend.

The three women were arrested within 24 hours. A witness testified she thought she was watching three girls and two boys in search of romance when she saw a gun flash and one of the men dropped. Marilyn pleaded guilty to two counts of first-degree murder and was given the death penalty. Her sentence was reversed in 1997. Madeline Mendoza who was sixteen at the time received a 35-year sentence for her part in the murders and Jacqueline Montanez, who was 15, received a sentence of "natural life."

1994

Latasha Pulliam: Black; Currently on death row. Latasha Pulliam was sentenced to death for the brutal kidnapping, rape, and murder of a 6-year-old South Side Chicago girl. Latasha received the death sentence for sexually attacking and killing Shenosha Richard on March 21, 1993, after luring the child to an apartment she shared with Dwight Jordan, 50. Before she was beaten and strangled, 6-year-old Shenosha Richard pleaded with her attackers to stop hurting her and promised not to tell anyone—except her parents—of her rape. Her body was discovered on the back porch of an abandoned building, authorities said. A court psychologist described Latasha as a "female John Gacy" who derived sexual gratification from hurting someone weaker than herself. Jordan, convicted of the same crime, was sentenced to life in prison.

At the time of her death, Shenosha Richard was a kindergarten pupil at Sexton Elementary School. She was considered a treasure in her family, school and South Side Chicago neighborhood.

1998

Jacqueline Annette Williams; Black; Currently on death row. On March 28, 1998, a jury in DuPage County, Illinois, sentenced Jacqueline Annette Williams, 31, of Schaumburg, IL, to death for the 1995 triple murders of Debra Evans, her 10-year-old daughter, Samantha, and her 7-year-old son, Joshua. Debra's one-and-a-half-year-old-son survived, as did the full-term baby boy cut from her womb in the attack. A week earlier, after deliberating only two hours, the same jury had convicted Jacqui of the murders as well as the kidnappings of Joshua and the newborn infant. One prosecutor described the case as one that would "give nightmares to Stephen King."

In closing arguments of the trial, prosecutors said they would seek the death penalty for Jacqui. They said that her motive in the killings was "her desire to take from the womb what she couldn't have," because, although she was the mother of three children, she was unable to have any more because of a tubal ligation after her third child. According to prosecutors, Jacqui had faked a pregnancy before masterminding the murders. She held a baby shower for herself in August 1995 and even had a false birth certificate made out for the baby. Her sister testified that Jacqui called her the day after Debra Evans was killed to tell her she had good news, her baby had just been born. A DuPage County employee who knew Jacqui also testified that Jacqui had told her the same week in which Debra Evans was murdered that she'd just given birth to a baby boy she was going to name Elijah.

When Jacqueline Williams and Fedell Caffey arrived at their Schaumburg home just before midnight the night of the murders, they were carrying a newborn baby in a baby carrier. Police were there waiting and Jacqui told them "That's my child."

Patrice Scott, a friend, who testified against Jacqui, said that Jacqui arrived at her apartment the night of the murders with 7-year-old Joshua Evans, saying that his mother had been shot in a botched drug deal and asked Patrice to watch him for a while. Jacqui, who had blood on her sweater at the time, also told her she had just had a baby and that she would be back for Joshua later.

Patrice said she made a bed for Joshua in her living room, but he kept crying and eventually told her that his mom and his sister were dead and that they had been cut up. She said Josh named Jacqui and the other two defendants, Laverne Ward and Fedell Caffey, and implicated an unidentified fourth person as the ones responsible. She said he kept saying, "I've got to get back to my brother." When Jacqui returned, Patrice said she yelled at Joshua for talking too much. She told him she had brought him some medicine which she forced him to drink and he ran out of the room gagging. The bottle was later found and identified as iodine. Patrice took her own baby and went back to the apartment that Jacqui shared with Caffey. While she was there, Caffey and Jacqui tried to strangle Joshua with a cable cord. Patrice intervened, and then the three of them left in a car with Joshua. Patrice said she was in the front seat of the car with her baby and saw Jacqui hold Joshua down in the back seat while Caffey stabbed him. The county medical examiner said Joshua died of strangulation and two deep stab wounds to the neck. Patrice said they had threatened they would kill her and her family if she said anything.

Prosecutors said the murder of Debra Evans and two of her children were probably the most brutal murders ever committed in Illinois. Debra, the mother of three, was found shot in the head on the floor of her living room, her stomach bloody and ripped open from someone extracting the full-term baby from her womb. A Dr. Christopher Jordan testified that Debra Evans was alive when the baby was taken from her. Samantha, her 10-year-old daughter, was found in her bedroom in Pocahontas pajamas. Her forearms were riddled with knife wounds and her throat was slashed so deeply it cut into her back muscles. Joshua, her 7-year-old, was kidnapped and killed later.

Prosecutor John Kinsella said in the courtroom, "If you want to know what a crazy killer looks like just look over there; she's earned the title" and he pointed to Jacqui. In response, Jacqui muttered, "So have you," which caused a hush in the room.

Her defense took only one hour to present its case and portrayed Ms. Williams as an abused and frightened woman who would do anything to please her boyfriend and co-defendant, Fedell Caffey. Her attorney said she was not an evil person and that as a person caught up in a relationship of dependency and fear, she was an unwilling participant.

Jacqui Williams said she thought Ward, the father of the baby Debra Evans was carrying, had set up an arrangement with Debra to take custody of the baby. She claimed she was in the bathroom when Debra Evans and her children were killed and that she came into the living room just as her two co-defendants were removing the baby from Debra — who lay bleeding to death from a gunshot wound to the head. Her attorney, Jeanine Tobin, said, "She stepped into violence beyond any control she had." She also said that Jacqui had resuscitated the baby after it was delivered not breathing and that she had stopped the bleeding from the baby's umbilical cord.

In rebuttal, the prosecution said the most telling evidence was that Jacqui changed her story to the police several times, and a gynecologist testified that it would have taken at least two people to extract the baby by crude cesarean without the proper tools.

During the penalty phase of the trial several police officers said they had seen Jacqueline Williams bruised and battered by Caffey and other boyfriends. A psychologist also said she had a dependent personality and was vulnerable to predatory men. But the same psychologist said that during several jailhouse-counseling sessions Jacqui never showed any remorse for the killings and denied any involvement in them.

Jacqui's mother, Martha Martin, described her as a good student who went to church every Sunday. She said she was a Girl Scout in grade school and a flag girl at Wheaton Central High, and that she got along well with both of her parents. She said Jacqui's behavior began to change in high school when she stopped going to church regularly and then dropped out of school in her sophomore year after getting pregnant. Her mother, who now has custody of her three children, said, "She was a better mama than I ever would be." But Mrs. Martin also testified that Jacqui is a person who likes to do what other people do and others can easily influence her. Her sister agreed with the mother and said that Jacqui was too trusting of people.

DuPage County Judge Peter Dockery confirmed Jacqueline Williams' death sentence on Monday, May 11, 1998. The date of her execution was set for June 22, 1998, although this will most likely not be carried out in view of the appeals process.

Given the opportunity to speak, Jacqueline said she was not guilty of the three murders she was accused of and that her friend, Patrice Scott, who testified against her was the guilty one. She also commented on the fact that there were no blacks on the jury and objected to the fact that the public defender did not allow her to testify on her own behalf.

Besides her death sentence Jacqueline was given two consecutive 15-year prison terms for the kidnappings of Joshua and Elijah. One of Jacqui's co-defendant, the father of Elijah, Ward, has been tried and received a life sentence.

13

Indiana: Lethal Injection

The state of Indiana has sentenced four women to death since 1900. One woman, Paula Cooper, was a 15-year-old juvenile when she was sentenced to death. No woman has been executed in Indiana and there is one woman with a death sentence in Indiana today.

Indiana allows the death penalty as an option in murder cases that are accompanied by at least one of 15 aggravating circumstances. The current minimum age for the death penalty is 16, and Indiana forbids the execution of the mentally retarded. Between 1930 and 1976 there were forty-three executions, by electrocution and since 1977 there have been three.

In October 1985 the state's 72-year-old electric chair required five jolts of electricity and 17 minutes to execute William Vandiver. After the first jolt of 2300 volts, physicians found Vandiver was still breathing, and the executioner, had to apply the current four more times before he died. The Department of Corrections commented on the event, saying the execution "did not go according to plan." The physician who pronounced William Vandiver dead said, "This is very rare."

Indiana resumed capital punishment in 1994, and on July 18, 1996, Tommie Smith became the first prisoner to be executed by lethal injection. The execution team could not locate a suitable vein in Smith and had to get a doctor to help. According to press reports it took over an hour to find a suitable vein, during which time Smith was strapped to the execution gurney fully conscious. An attempt by the doctor to insert the needle into his neck failed and the injection was finally administered through his foot. Witnesses to the execution were permitted to view Smith only after the needle was inserted.

On January 29, 1998 Robert Smith, a lifetime criminal who stabbed another inmate to death at the Wabash Valley Correctional Institution, became the sixth person to be executed in Indiana since the death penalty was reinstituted in

1976. Smith said he couldn't bear the thought of growing old behind bars and turned down a 50-year prison sentence and asked to be executed instead. Without a trial, a jury, or lawyers, the judge granted Smith his wish. A spokesperson for Amnesty International said, "It would appear that his death sentence is a result of the state of Indiana complying with his wish to die, thereby making it a case of state-assisted suicide."

Retired Judge Alred W. Moellering, who sentenced five people to death in Indiana, said he never found it difficult to do (*News Sentinel*, 1997). He said that a jury recommended it and he did not feel it was his place to say a jury was wrong. He said his job was to "go over the case and ensure that all the requirements of the law have been met." But, he said, he could never conceive going against what a jury has recommended.

His successor, Judge Kenneth Scheibenberger, who has sentenced one person to death, sees it a little differently. Judge Scheibenberger said, "There's no question there is some emotion attached to it. You're dealing with a person's life. It's not the easiest thing to do, but the fact that a jury's recommended it makes it a little easier."

INDIANA DOCTORS AND EXECUTION

A debate currently raging in Indiana, as in other states, has to do with the participation of medical doctors in executions. State Representative Charlie Brown (D-Gary) vowed to reintroduce a bill that would prohibit physicians from taking a direct role in an execution. Brown said he was appalled that a physician assisted in the execution of Tommie Smith.

LEGAL REPRESENTATION IN INDIANA

The state of Indiana requires the court to appoint two attorneys to represent a defendant facing the death penalty if he or she can't hire private counsel. The lead attorney must have five years' experience in trying criminal cases and must have defended clients in at least five felony jury trials before taking a death penalty case.

The primary attorney is also required to have completed a minimum of 12 hours of training in a course approved by the Public Defender Commission on capital cases. The co-counsel is required to have at least two years experience in criminal trials and must have served on the defense in at least three felony trials. Co-counsel must also complete the required training. Defense attorneys that are appointed by the court get $70 an hour.

Robert Gevers, a county prosecutor in Indiana, said a number of things go into the decision as to whether or not to seek the death penalty. These include the nature of the crime, the aggravating and mitigating circumstances, the strength of the case, legal issues surrounding the case, and last but not least, the potential cost of the trial and its appeals.

The number of death sentences in Indiana was reduced when jurors were allowed the option of life without parole several years ago, and recently state Representative Brent Steele announced he would introduce legislation allowing the death penalty for people who sell large amounts of illegal drugs. He said such measures were needed to stem an increasing drug-use problem.

FEDERAL DEATH ROW INMATES IN INDIANA

The Bureau of Prisons is constructing a federal death row and execution chamber inside the U.S. Penitentiary at Terre Haute, Indiana. This facility was selected in an effort to minimize costs. Federal prisoners held and executed in Terre Haute's D block will be escorted through a tunnel to a death chamber outside the cellblock. The chamber will include a witness area and the gurney. The warden at Terre Haute said that he considers this special death row a way of protecting federal prisoners from substandard conditions in other states.

WOMEN SENTENCED TO DEATH IN INDIANA

1985
Lois Thacker: White; Reversed in 1990. At age 27, Lois Thacker of Paoli, Indiana, was convicted of recruiting six friends and family members in a plot to kill her husband. Dubois Circuit Judge Chad Songer said it was a "sad, sad duty" to pass judgment on Lois, who tearfully testified in her own behalf before sentencing. Mrs. Thacker broke down while telling the judge how her husband John had abused her and her three children. Lois was the second woman in Indiana history ever to receive the death penalty. Her sentence was reversed in 1990.

1986
Debra Denise Brown: Black; Serving a life sentence in Ohio. In 1986 Debra Brown was sentenced to death for the murder of a 7-year-old girl and the attempted murder and sexual assault of a 9-year-old girl in Indiana. In a six-state crime spree with her common-law husband, Alton Coleman, eight people were killed. Debra was also sentenced to die in Ohio's electric chair for the strangulation rape slaying of Tonnie Storey, 15 whose decomposed body was found in a vacant apartment building in Cincinnati. In that sentencing Judge William Morissey told her, "You showed your victim no mercy so this court will show you no mercy." Debra Brown, 22 at the time, wept when a jury recommended death. It was her third murder conviction.

Debra was born in 1963, one of eleven children. She was a high school dropout and engaged to be married when she met Alton Coleman in 1984. She was so struck by him that she broke off her engagement and moved in with him, soon becoming a target of his sexual and physical abuse. Coleman had done time in prison for several different crimes before they met.

As a couple they began their mutual crime spree in the summer of 1984. Travelling through several states over a period of two months, they murdered at least eight people. Their first victim was nine-year-old Vernita Wheat. Three weeks later they attacked two young girls, ages seven and nine. All of their victims were beaten, raped, and strangled. From the second attack, one victim survived and was able to identify the couple. Victims throughout Indiana, Ohio, Illinois, and Michigan were all beaten, raped, and sexually molested often by both Debra and Coleman. The two were finally arrested in Evanston, Illinois.

Debra testified at Alton Coleman's sentencing hearing for the murder of Marlene Walters, and said that she, not Coleman, bludgeoned Marlene to death during a crime rampage. In a chilling statement she said, "I killed the bitch, and I don't give a damn. I had fun." Debra Brown and her companion, Coleman both received two death sentences. Alton Coleman was executed and although Debra is incarcerated in Ohio serving a life sentence her death sentence still stands in Indiana.

1986

Paula Cooper: Black; Reversed in 1989. Paula Cooper was sentenced to death on July 11, 1986. She was 15-years-old at the time. This made her the youngest woman in nearly a century to be given the death penalty in the United States. Her three companions in the crime were given long prison terms. In an interview at the Indiana Women's Prison Paula described the moment she was sentenced to death as "a night-mare." She said she was affected by it more than she might have been because the judge spent so much time talking about how he didn't believe in the death penalty before giving it to her.

By the age of 15 Paula had attended nine different high schools in the Gary, Indiana, area and had suffered beatings and violence in her family environment. Her father would frequently strip Paula and her sister in order to beat them with an electrical cord. He also beat their mother and forced them to watch while he raped her.

Paula was in and out of juvenile detention centers from the time she was 11, and when she was old enough, she ran away from home. She remembered juvenile detention as a nightmare, but said it was better than living at home with her father. She found detention a safer place.

Paula's mother, who divorced her father, was so frustrated and terrorized by her husband's abuse that she tried to commit suicide and kill Paula and her sister by locking them and herself in a car with the motor running. Despite this childhood of "just surviving, just living day to day," Paula had no history of serious criminal conduct and had completed her sophomore year of high school before she was sentenced to death.

On May 14, 1985 Paula, then 15, and three friends cut their afternoon classes to drink and run around. They needed money and thought about robbing Ruth Pelke, a 78-year-old widow who lived in the neighborhood and gave Bible classes. They went to her house pretending to have an interest in Bible classes and knocked twice soliciting money. Both times they were sent away. The third time they went about 3:00 p.m. in the afternoon and asked Ruth to give them an address for Bible lessons. With this, she let them in.

As soon as they got inside the house they hit her with a vase and knocked her down. Paula then stabbed her 33 times with a knife she had brought with her. After the attack, they left the house with $10 in cash and Ruth Pelke's car, and bragged to several friends about what they had done. Ruth Pelke's body was discovered by her step-grandson, Robert Pelke, at 2:25 p.m. the following day. Paula Cooper and the other three girls were arrested almost immediately. They still had Ruth's car.

The Indiana prosecutor said without hesitation that he would seek the death penalty even though Paula admitted to inflicting the majority of the wounds and planning and leading the other three girls to the slaying and robbery. Capital charges were filed against Paula alone on June 28, 1985, with amendments ten days later. After considerable legal maneuvering on April 21, 1986, Paula pleaded guilty to capital murder, waiving her right to a trial by jury and her right to present any defense.

Paula's brief sentencing was held on July 11, 1986, and she was sentenced to death. At the sentencing hearing, Robert Pelke testified and read into evidence a letter expressing his outrage at the crime and asking that the court impose the death penalty. Later he changed his mind and worked aggressively to have Paula's death sentence reversed. Post-sentencing legal procedures were halted for a time by the death of the trial judge in a traffic accident on May 1, 1987.

Paula Cooper went from being a struggling child in Gary's black ghetto to an international cause celebre. In Europe the political effort on her behalf was intense: "In Italy, the young murderer has attained celebrity bordering on saint-hood," the papers said. Even Pope John Paul II intervened on her behalf, urging the Indiana governor to commute her sentence. Cardinal Ugo Poletti, vicar general for the diocese of Rome and president of the Italian bishop's conference, wrote Paula, saying, "Italians are thinking of you; they would like to hold your hand to give you courage."

In a videotaped interview from her cell at the Indiana Women's Prison in Indianapolis, Paula expressed shock that thousands of Italians and Pope John Paul II were concerned about her. She said, "All my life nobody cared for me." She also said that if she ever regained her freedom, she would like to start a family and "do something for young people."

Governor Robert Orr, the governor of Indiana at the time, said he could appreciate the humanitarian instincts of the pope and thousands of Italians, but he said their pleas for clemency ignored the brutal nature of Paula's crime.

Staff at the Indiana Women's prison told reporters in 1987 that the way Paula Cooper was portrayed in the media was different from the way they knew her. They indicated that during the first year and a half she was there, she had been difficult and had even physically assaulted the guards.

For her part, Paula said she had only found a reason to live after she was sentenced to die, and that she learned the value of life in her beige-colored cell at the Indiana Women's Prison.

In 1987 an Italian friar, Friar Vito Bracone, who worked with Rome's Commission for Peace and Justice, visited then 17-year-old Paula Cooper on death row for two hours at the Indiana Women's Prison. He spoke to her on behalf of thousands of Europeans who were appalled that she was given the death penalty and could have died in the electric chair.

Italian public television devoted half an hour to appeals on behalf of Paula, including an interview with William Pelke, the grandson of 78-year-old Ruth Pelke who Paula murdered. William appealed for forgiveness for Paula and at least 10,000 students from Florence, Italy signed a petition urging clemency.

After four months on death row, Indiana's youngest condemned prisoner said she felt as if she had been on death row all her life. "My life has always been on death row," Paula Cooper said in a telephone interview with the *Gary Post-Tribune*.

Two guards and a recreational therapist were charged with having sex on seven occasions with Paula while she was in jail awaiting sentencing, which seems to have historical precedent in Indiana. According to Estelle Freedman (1981) in her book *Their Sisters Keepers: Women's Prison Reform in America, 1830-1930* "Sexual abuse of female prisoners by prison guards was apparently so acceptable (in Indiana) that the Indiana state prison actually ran a prostitution service for male guards using female prisoners."

However, in 1987, Governor Robert Orr signed a bill into law that made it illegal for jail employees to have sex with inmates. He also signed a bill that raised the age that someone can be executed for murder in Indiana from 10–16 (House Bill 1222). Both bills came directly out of Paula Cooper's case.

On July 13, 1989, Paula's death sentence was vacated and replaced with a sentence of sixty years. The Supreme Court of Indiana reached this decision because of the extraordinary uniqueness of Paula's sentence under Indiana law and because of the impact of the United States Supreme Court in *Thompson v. Oklahoma*. It was Paula's exceptionally young age, only fifteen at the time of her crime, which forced the Indiana court to void her death sentence. According to the Justice Department's "Capital Punishment 1995" in 16 states the eligible age for the death penalty is between 14 and 17. Thirteen states and the federal government require a minimum age of 18. One state requires 19.

Paula Cooper will be seventy-five years old when she is released from prison if she serves her full sentence. But, she says, "The future is tomorrow. You do your time, one day at a time." She says she is still haunted by the memories of that day. "I think about it all the time," Paula said, "It's something that's always going to be there. I'm more or less at peace with it now."

1989

Cindy Landress: White; Reversed in 1992. Cindy Lou Landress was convicted of stabbing her former boyfriend (Leonard Fowler) to death in his home in Hammond, Indiana, in 1988 during a robbery at his residence. He was stabbed 22 times. Cindy and her co-defendant William Lewellen were apprehended in San Diego, California.

The jury deliberated four hours before deciding to impose the death penalty. In part because it was felt that Cindy had carried out the crime with willful determination by going to bed with Fowler to give Lewellen time. Cindy claimed she was an alcoholic and did not plan to have Fowler killed. She wept when Judge Richard Conroy accepted the death recommendation made by a jury. William Lewellen, 39, her co-defendant who had pleaded guilty to the murder was sentenced to sixty years in prison. Cindy's lawyer questioned the fairness of the judge's decision. Cindy's sentence was reversed in 1992.

14

Kentucky: Electrocution

The state of Kentucky has sentenced two women to death since 1900. No women have been legally executed in Kentucky and there are no women on death row in Kentucky today.

Although the electric chair was installed in Eddyville in 1911, it wasn't until 1936 that 15,000 people crowded around the gallows in Owensboro, Kentucky, and witnessed the last public hanging.

On July 7, 1911 Jim Buckner became the first man ever executed in Kentucky's electric chair. During his execution, according to written accounts, the prison doctor, a Dr. Moss, who was in attendance, was almost electrocuted himself until someone warned him not to touch the inmate's body while the electricity was still on. Newspapers of the day say that Buckner did not die immediately and had to be given a second jolt of electricity.

Forty-five days after Buckner's execution, Oliver Locks was put in the chair and when the first volt of electricity hit him, his body response broke both the arm and leg clamps "as if they were paper." When the prison doctor checked, Locks was found to be still alive and was also given a second jolt. Both men were black.

In the 1920s and 1930s at least eighteen botched executions by electrocution were documented in Kentucky and there were three in the 1940s. In the 1950s James Robinson needed four shocks of 2,300 volts to die in six minutes. The Tarrence brothers, Roy and Leonard, each required two rounds of 2,000 volts one taking six and the other eight minutes to die. And Earl Brichman had to have 2,300 volts for two minutes before he was pronounced dead. All in all the electric chair in Kentucky never functioned very well, although 162 inmates were executed in it.

In 1984 the chair, a three-legged one made of oak, was overhauled by Fred Leuchter whose execution equipment had been noted in other states for causing undue pain and agony to the condemned. At the same time the overhaul was taking place, Leuchter apparently advised the state on their execution protocol.

Fred Leuchter is currently under indictment in the Federal Republic of Germany for "hate crimes" specifically, organizing and abetting neo-Nazi organizations.

As far as improvements on the chair itself, over the years straps have been replaced and for Kentucky's last execution, a new headpiece and leg piece were designed. The head electrode is secured to the headpiece and the leg electrode is secured to a bracket that fits on the offender's right calf. A natural sponge soaked in a salt solution is also used in the headpiece. A larger exhaust fan was also recently installed in the execution chamber.

In 1997 the Kentucky Department of Corrections announced that it would have to move the state's execution chamber if the Kentucky General Assembly changes the method of execution to lethal injection. The current death chamber is at the Kentucky State Penitentiary in Eddyville in the basement of the penitentiary's Cellhouse 3. The area is too small to accommodate both an electric chair and a lethal injection chamber and there is no space for official witnesses and family members to be in separate rooms, the Department said.

Corrections' spokesperson Michael Bradley said the site for the new execution chamber would be the Green River Correctional Complex, a medium security prison in Muhlenberg County. Though the chamber has not yet been designed, the agency has asked the state for $643,000 for it. It was included in the major-projects list submitted to the planning board that makes recommendations to the General Assembly.

THE DEATH PENALTY IN KENTUCKY

Since the reinstatement of the death penalty by the Kentucky General Assembly in 1976, Kentucky's Supreme Court has upheld the constitutionality of Kentucky's death statutes, KRS 507.020, 509.040, 532.025, and 532.075 [*White v. Commonwealth*, 671 S.W.2d 241 (1984)]. These statutes are modeled after Georgia's death penalty scheme and it is at the prosecutor's discretion to decide whether the facts in any particular criminal case warrant seeking the death penalty. In Kentucky, the prosecutor must give notice that he will seek the death penalty before the trial.

According to a 1989 study conducted by the University of Louisville's Urban Research Institute, 70 percent of the people polled in Kentucky favored the death penalty. When offered the option of life without parole, only 36 percent of those surveyed favored it.

Since July 13, 1990, Kentucky has prohibited the execution of persons who are "seriously mentally retarded" which is defined as "someone who has significantly sub-average intellectual functioning (an IQ of 70 or below) with substantial deficits in adaptive behavior." The minimum age for execution in Kentucky is 16.

In the midst of a debate on whether or not to abolish the death penalty, in June 1997, a committee of lawmakers in Kentucky approved lethal injection as the official form of execution. At the time, Reprensentative Mike Bowling filed a bill that would give prisoners on death row the option of lethal injection or the electric chair, saying he supported the death penalty but believed prisoners should be able to choose lethal injection, which, he said, is more humane.

A Republican Representative from Louisville, Representative Bob Heleringer, said he does not believe judges, correction officials, or legislators should have the authority to decide when to end a human life. He said, "I think it is wrong to take a life regardless of what that person has done." He said he would attach an amendment to Bowling's bill to abolish the death penalty. Heleringer also commented that lethal injections are nothing more than a way for society to sanitize legal executions.

Representative Katie Stine and Representative Kathy Hogan Camp said that if Kentucky allows lethal injections, physicians should not be required to give the fatal shots. Senator David Karma, a Democrat from Louisville said such concerns and a ban on videotaping executions suggest that Kentuckians may not be as supportive of the death penalty as advocates say they are.

Other proposed changes in the Kentucky death penalty scheme would make murder of anyone under 12 or over 60 a capital offense since people of those ages are often the most victimized.

The most recent measure regarding the death penalty in Kentucky was sponsored by Senator Gerald Neal (D) in 1998. This measure would allow defendants in death penalty cases to ask judges to decide whether or not prosecutors were motivated by racial concerns in deciding to seek the death penalty in any particular case.

Governor Martha Layne Collins was the first governor to sign a death warrant after 1976. She signed it in July 1986 for the execution of Eugene Gall. The next death warrant in Kentucky was not signed until July 1994 by Governor Brereton Jones for the execution of Kevin Stanford.

Governor Patton signed five death warrants in January 1996 and the death warrant for Harold McQueen, which was signed on June 11, 1997. Mr. McQueen had a brief reprieve when U.S. District Judge, Thomas Russell, granted a stay of execution saying the court should consider whether electrocution is cruel and unusual punishment. But, a three-judge panel of the U.S. Sixth Circuit Court of Appeals in Cincinnati dissolved the stay, saying McQueen had effectively used up his appeals and Judge Russell lacked jurisdiction to hear the appeal that led to the stay.

JUVENILES AND THE DEATH PENALTY IN KENTUCKY

Kentucky is one of fourteen states that allow the death penalty for juveniles. Under Kentucky law, offenders sixteen and over are eligible for the death penalty if they commit a capital offense with at least one aggravating circumstance. State Public Advocate Ernie Lewis, who opposes the death penalty for juveniles, says it is illogical to say 16–17 year-olds are responsible enough for their actions that they can be killed for a crime, but at the same time be considered too young to drink. Ray Franklin, the state secretary of the Fraternal Order of Police, said eliminating the death penalty for juveniles would be a signal for gang leaders in urban areas to have juveniles do the shooting.

Commonwealth Attorney Tom Handy said he could not give a victim's family a good reason why he should not seek the death penalty against a 17-year-old accused of a brutal capital offense. He said, "My experience has been 17-year-olds have committed the most brutal murders."

MEDICAL DOCTORS AND EXECUTION IN KENTUCKY

Recently, the Kentucky Medical Association's delegates voted for a measure stating "it is unethical for a physician to participate in an execution, except to certify cause of death." This would mean that a doctor would not have any role in the actual execution, such as administering the lethal injection. Currently, the method of execution in Kentucky is still electrocution, but the measure was proposed in light of pending legislation to change the method to lethal injection.

EXECUTIONS IN KENTUCKY

On July 1, 1997, Harold McQueen, became the first inmate executed in the state of Kentucky in 35 years, and his execution in the 87-year-old-electric chair once again opened discussions about the use of that method of execution. McQueen was executed for putting a gun to the back of Becky O'Hearn's head and shooting her to death while robbing a convenience store in Richmond, KY, in January, 1980.

Before an execution there is a "dress rehearsal" with the key staff from all the agencies involved in the execution process. There is also a quarterly testing of equipment where the electrodes are attached to a bank of resistors and a voltage and amp meter are attached to the resistors and monitored. This quarterly check keeps everything in good working order so that it can be used at a moment's notice, if need be. The equipment also has a built-in testing device that monitors the output of the voltage and the length of the cycles. This test is documented on graph paper.

Three executioners, who are Kentucky Department of Corrections employees, are used for each execution. Members of the execution team are volunteers and they may or may not serve on more than one execution. The entire execution team is made up of 12 security staff selected from Kentucky adult correctional institutions other than the Kentucky State Penitentiary, where death row is located and where executions take place. Members of the team are selected by interview. A team of administrative staff, the warden and a mental health professional does the interviewing. Once the team is assembled, a captain is named who is in charge.

During an execution, a leather veil is placed over the condemned person's head. The execution apparatus is activated by one of three buttons on a console. Each of the three executioners pushes a button, but only one of the buttons is active. In Kentucky, two cycles of electricity are administered: 2,100 volts for 15 seconds (7.5 amps); 250 volts for 105 seconds (1 amp). The estimated average length of time that elapses from the time the inmate is restrained to the time of death is approximately 15 minutes.

Witnesses authorized to attend an execution by the state of Kentucky are the electrician, the warden of the penitentiary and his deputies and guards; the sheriff of the county in which the condemned was convicted; the commissioner of the Department of Corrections and representatives of the department designated by him; the doctor and chaplain of the prison; a clergyman and three other individuals selected by the offender. Nine representatives of the media are allowed. Media representatives include one from the United Press International, one from the Associated Press, one from Kentucky Network, Inc., three representatives from Kentucky radio and television media, and three representatives from Kentucky newspapers.

WOMEN SENTENCED TO DEATH IN KENTUCKY

1980

La Verne O'Bryan: White; Reversed in 1982. On October 5, 1979, La Verne O'Bryan was indicted by the Jefferson County Grand Jury for the murder of Harold Sadler, which took place on or about December 23, 1967, and for the murder of John O'Bryan which took place on or about July 5, 1979. In March of 1980, the state decided to seek the death penalty for the murder of John O'Bryan based on evidence that the murder was for monetary gain. On May 2, 1980 La Verne O'Bryan was again indicted for the attempted murder of Le Anne O'Bryan. This indictment was combined with the murder of John O'Bryan for the trial.

La Verne O'Bryan ultimately became the first woman sentenced to death in Kentucky and the first person in over a hundred years to be charged with murder by poisoning in the state. She was sentenced on September 12, 1980, at the age of 43 for the arsenic poisoning of her ex-husband, John O'Bryan, who died in July 1979.

According to reports, John O'Bryan was admitted to the hospital on June 28, 1979, suffering from abdominal pain, vomiting, weakness, dizziness, kidney malfunction, and deteriorating mental capacity. He died on July 5, 1979, and an autopsy revealed the cause of death to be acute arsenic poisoning. For the investigation, police interviewed John's brother, Donnie O'Bryan, and his wife Le Anne.

Information also surfaced about the death of Harold Sadler, a former husband of La Verne's, indicating that he had died in December 1967 of unknown causes. Sadler's body was exhumed and an autopsy showed that he, too, had died of chronic arsenic poisoning.

Added to this, Le Anne O'Bryan told police that while John was in the hospital, she had told La Verne that if he died she'd see to it that there'd be "one hell of an investigation." After this conversation La Verne apparently gave Le Anne numerous cups of coffee that made her feel ill and she vomited for two days. Eleven days later a urine sample revealed that Le Anne had traces of arsenic in her system. A subsequent search of La Verne's home turned up some arsenic in a bottle of horse medicine.

Based on available evidence, La Verne was charged with the 1967 murder of Harold Sadler. La Verne had met Harold while both were working at the P. Lorillard Corporation in the 1960s. She left her job there to work as a book-keeper at Sadler's auto salvage company in Louisville, a place where Harold kept certain substances containing arsenic for use in salvaging cars. Although she and Sadler lived together for several years, they were not married, but presented themselves to the public as if they were. It appeared Sadler had dated another woman and had put La Verne off whenever the issue of marriage came up.

Between August 1967 and December 1967 Sadler was in and out of three different hospitals and treated by several doctors. When he died, La Verne got his life insurance and inherited the business. She also got seven pieces of real estate he owned by filing a false affidavit identifying herself as his widow and co-heir with his mother.

Not long after Sadler's death, La Verne began dating John O'Bryan who was married to someone else at the time. After O'Bryan's divorce, in 1970, he married La Verne. They were divorced in 1972, but continued to live together and John operated the salvage business La Verne had inherited from Sadler. When La Verne decided to move she and John signed a contract indicating that he would buy part of the "inherited" real estate from her.

Although La Verne moved back in with John after a year, between 1976 and 1979 their relationship continued to deteriorate, and the final blow seemed to be when John began to make plans to sell the property he had purchased from her and buy a horse farm in Brandenbury, Kentucky. It was shortly after John decided to move in 1979 that he became ill.

In trial the state made a point of emphasizing the similarities between La Verne's relationship with Sadler and with O'Bryan, and the similarities in the manner in which the two men had died. Ultimately, the state claimed that in both cases La Verne cared for the men and that she was with both men almost constantly before they died. The state further claimed that La Verne was an insecure person who needed money, and that in both cases her financial security was threatened and she did not tell anyone about her husbands' illnesses until it was too late.

La Verne O'Bryan said she did not think she committed the crimes she was accused of and she believed that both men had died of "a rare form of cancer." But the state said the motive in both cases appeared to be money. Sadler left her the business that he and O'Bryan operated even after they were divorced in 1972; and for seven years after their divorce until his death, the O'Bryans lived together. It was brought out in the trial that Mrs. O'Bryan had agreed to sell the home and the business to her ex-husband for $52,000, but as the time to close the deal got nearer, Mrs. O'Bryan was afraid of being left penniless. Psychologists found her to be suffering from an extreme form of neurosis called hysterical amnesia, which they believed would take as long as four or five years to treat. When she was in the Jefferson County Jail during her trial, Mrs. O'Bryan herself complained of symptoms that resembled arsenic poisoning.

At the time of La Verne O'Bryan's conviction, the state of Kentucky did not have a women's prison, so she was held in "death row conditions" at the medium-security state reformatory for women. Her cell was 10 by 6 feet, with a metal bed attached to the wall, a sink, and a toilet. She had a twenty-four hour guard, no contact with other inmates, and she exercised alone in an unused prison courtyard five days a week. She was allowed to leave her cell to take showers.

In March 1982, the Kentucky Supreme Court reversed La Verne's sentence, stating, in part, that the admission of evidence of Sadler's death did not show the commission of a crime and that the only connection that could possibly be made was that La Verne O'Bryan was living with Sadler when he died and that he died of arsenic poisoning. Evidence such as "Sadler looked as if he had been poisoned" was totally rejected. The court further stated it would take a "quantum leap of fact and logic" to say that the evidence was of such a nature as to show a connection between the two deaths which occurred twelve years apart.

1987

LaFonda Fay Foster: White; Reversed in 1991. LaFonda Fay Foster was sentenced to death on April 24, 1987. In her trial she was portrayed as a drug-addicted prostitute who had a lesbian relationship with a woman named Tina Powell. Over the course of several hours one evening, LaFonda Fay and Tina killed five adults by shooting them in the head, stabbing them, cutting their throats, running over them with a car, and (in one case) burning them up. The five victims were found scattered in a suburban neighborhood outside the city of Lexington.

After a four-week-trial in which the two women were tried together, the jury recommended that Tina Powell be sentenced to life imprisonment without the benefit of probation or parole and that LaFonda Fay Foster be sentenced to death on each of the five murder convictions.

The first victim, 59-year-old Trudy Harrell, was found in the parking lot of a Lexington shopping center at 9:00 p.m. April 23, 1986. She had been shot in the back of the head, stabbed five times, run over, and dragged around by a car. Next, police found 45-year-old Virginia Kearns, who was also shot in the back of the head, had numerous stab wounds including sixteen on her neck, and had been run over by a car. Roger Keene's partially burned body was found under a car, shot twice, stabbed five times in the chest and twelve times in the back. He had also been run over. Theodore Sweet, 52, had been stabbed several times in the face, chest, and back, and shot twice in the head, one shot in each ear. Seventy-three-year-old Carlos Kearns, Virginia's husband, was found inside a car with burns all over his body, shot twice in the head, twice in the neck, stabbed in the neck, and run over. After being run over, Carlos's body was placed back in the car and the car was then set on fire. Despite all this he was still alive when he was found, but died later.

All of the victims except Theodore Sweet lived in the same apartment building in Lexington, and both Virginia and Carlos Kearns had been arrested several times each for various infractions of the law including drunkenness, theft, and carrying a concealed weapon. Neighbors said they made an interesting couple, although some said Carlos had married Virginia only because he felt sorry for her. Roger Keene had been an alcoholic most of his life and was unable to hold a steady job. He had numerous convictions. Trudy Harrell lived with the Kearnses and did their cooking and cleaning as well as driving. She too was an alcoholic and had numerous convictions for public intoxication. Some said she was a street person that Carlos had taken in.

On the afternoon of the day the murders took place, Mrs. Kearns had called the police to file a complaint against Tina and LaFonda Fay, saying they were at the Kearns' apartment intoxicated and refused to leave. When the police arrived, according to a filed report, they found the two women were not intoxicated, but rather Mrs. Kearns, who had called the police, was the one who was intoxicated. Since she was in her own home and not endangering anyone, the police left.

LaFonda Fay and Tina started drinking after they left the Kearns apartment, and Tina tried to sell a knife she had on her to raise some money to buy more alcohol. When Mrs. Kearns left the apartment to go to a nearby drugstore, LaFonda Fay and Tina apparently followed her and a witness claimed to see LaFonda Fay grab and shake her, after which the three women returned to the apartment together.

At the apartment Mrs. Kearns asked her semi-disabled husband to give the women some money. At first he refused, but then he agreed to write a check which, he said, he would have to drive somewhere to cash. While this exchange was going on, Roger Keene and Theodore Sweet dropped by the apartment. Eventually, all of them — LaFonda Fay, Tina, and the five friends— piled into the Kearns car with LaFonda Fay driving. Tina later stated that they were trying to raise enough money to purchase a gram of cocaine. At a local bait shop, the manager cashed a $25 check for Mr. Kearns.

Between 8:00 p.m. and 9:00 p.m. the carload of people drove around, eventually ending up in a field off Mont Tabor Road. There, according to Tina Powell, LaFonda Fay forced the five victims out of the car and told them to lie face down in the grass. She then shot and stabbed Ms. Harrell and Mr. and Mrs. Kearns. The Kearnses, although wounded, were directed to get back in the car with Mr. Keene and Mr. Sweet, who were not wounded at the time.

Ms. Harrell's body was lodged under the car as they left, and it was dragged for a considerable distance in a parking lot before becoming dislodged. Her body was found some 225 feet from the field in the parking lot of the Berke Plaza.

Tina Powell then drove the car to a tavern where, a customer testified, she went in looking for bullets, specifying ".22s or .38s," which she said she needed to "shoot some rats." The manager gave Tina four .22-caliber bullets, and as she was leaving he said he observed that the car had blood on it. The carload of people, now minus Ms. Harrell, drove to a loading area behind a paint store in Lexington where they killed Mrs. Kearns. Her body was also dragged under the car. She died of multiple stab wounds and from being run over. A sweatshirt, later identified as Roger Keene's, was found at the accident scene with blood smears that seemed to indicate the murderers had wiped the knife they used for the stabbings clean. The blood on the sweatshirt was Virginia Kearns's.

An hour later Tina and LaFonda Fay returned to the tavern asking for more bullets. This time LaFonda Fay was driving and the blood had been wiped off the car. They were not able to get any more bullets from the manager of the tavern, so they went to see LaFonda Fay's father. Tina said that while LaFonda Fay was in her father's trailer, the three men who were in the car begged her to help them get away. She said she was not able to help them because LaFonda Fay had the keys to the car. Instead, she honked the car horn for LaFonda Fay to hurry up.

Another witness at the trial, Ms. Cross, stated she was sitting in a car outside the bar that evening when LaFonda Fay approached her and asked her for some money because she "needed a fix." When she asked LaFonda Fay what was wrong, LaFonda replied "I just shot a man" and "told the old man if he bled in the car I'd shoot the old son-of-a-bitch again." She said LaFonda Fay appeared to be calm and had no problems such as walking or standing that might indicate she was intoxicated.

The three men were then driven to another field and killed in the same way the women had been. Each was shot in the head, stabbed repeatedly, throat cut, and run over by the car. The car itself was then doused with gasoline and set on fire. Roger Keene, who was shot twice in the back of the head and once in the ear, was pinned under the car while it burned. Theodore Sweet was found face down on the ground near the car.

After setting the car on fire LaFonda Fay Foster and Tina Hickey, aka Tina Powell, walked to Humana Hospital, which was nearby, looking for a phone. Tina found a phone and called a cab while LaFonda Fay went to clean up in the bathroom. An emergency room nurse reported the women to hospital security and they were arrested for drunkenness. They told the police they had been in a fight.

They were taken to the Fayette County Detention Center where LaFonda Fay managed to flush her bloody socks and shoestrings down the toilet and trade her bloody sweatpants with another inmate for clean ones. Tina still had the bloodstained knife on her, and between them they had three .22-caliber bullets.

In jail, LaFonda Fay told another inmate she'd shot the women first and made the men watch. When asked why she had killed them all she said the women were "bitches" and the men had seen too much. Of one of the men, she said, "The son-of-a-bitch wouldn't die. He was the hardest man I ever killed." She told another cellmate she planned to plead insanity.

LaFonda Fay Foster was born in 1963 in Indiana. She started using drugs at age 9 and attempted suicide three different times at ages twelve, fourteen, and nineteen. She was often out of school and quit school completely after the ninth grade. Much of her childhood was spent with various relatives and in foster homes. She was sexually abused by a great-uncle at one point and had her feet put in a fire when she objected. She was sexually active as a teenager and engaged in prostitution.

At thirteen LaFonda Fay was arrested for shoplifting, and after that was sent to at least five different youth facilities. As an adult, after her first conviction for robbery she was sentenced to ten years and released within a month on five year's probation. By this time she was using drugs, including LSD, daily. Her next arrest, for a parole violation led to her acquaintance with a Lexington businessman who offered her a job and an apartment. Although he committed suicide, through him LaFonda Fay met Carlos Kearns. She apparently lived with Kearns for a time, then stole money from him and left.

Tina Marie Hickey Powell admitted that she had helped kill the five people, but because she wouldn't admit that she intended to kill them, Circuit Judge James Keller refused to accept her guilty plea. She was born in 1958 in Youngstown, Ohio, but lived in Lexington most of her life. Tina left high school before graduation. She was married for a brief time, and by 1980 she had been arrested several times, mostly for public intoxication. She mixed drugs and alcohol frequently and seemed to be on the road to self-destruction. In jail, Tina staged hunger strikes and was so depressed that jail officials had her on a suicide watch. Exactly when Tina Powell and LaFonda Fay Foster became friends is uncertain, but both of them went to the same Lexington bars, and by 1986 they had been friends for some time.

LaFonda Fay had a long history of being battered by men, being extremely emotionally disturbed, being drug-addicted, and being violent toward others. Her attorney's strategy for avoiding the death sentence was to portray her as a victim of battering, violence, and drugs. Although LaFonda Fay had clearly been the perpetrator of the violence, she might have been spared if she could have been seen as a victim of violence.

However this was not to be. LaFonda Fay's sentencing hearing was joined with that of Tina's and Tina's defense strategy was to portray LaFonda Fay as a violent lesbian who battered her into submission. Tina Powell used the battered woman syndrome to demonstrate the degree to which she was dominated and controlled by LaFonda Fay. Judge James Keller, a Circuit Court judge, allowed Tina to plead guilty to avoid the death penalty and to allow a jury to determine her sentence.

These conflicting defense strategies played into the hands of the prosecutor's efforts to defeminize LaFonda Fay and portray her as a brutal, "manly" murderer. Since LaFonda Fay and Tina were co-defendants in a joint trial for all the murders, it was inevitable that the judge and jury would learn of their lesbian relationship. Nevertheless, the sexual nature of their relationship seemed irrelevant until the sentencing phase, at which time Tina used the battering defense.

Although the prosecutors portrayed LaFonda Fay Foster as a ruthless killer, a friend of LaFonda Fay described her in the trial as a caring woman who once took money she had earned as a prostitute to buy food and clothes for two small children. Twenty-two prosecution witnesses in the second day of the trial provided a nearly hour-by-hour account of what happened on the day of the murders.

Quietly in an even voice, Judge James E. Keller said he had sympathy for the abuse LaFonda Fay Foster had received as a child and as a young woman, but he said he also had to consider the aggravating factors. As she was sentenced to death LaFonda Fay bowed her head and cried.

In 1991 LaFonda Fay's sentence was reversed and her attorneys, Russ Baldani and Kevin McNally, who had represented her as public defenders in 1987, were re-appointed to handle her trial, although both attorneys are now in private practice and are working pro-bono on LaFonda Fay's case. They had at first indicated they would seek a change of venue and a different judge for her re-sentencing, but Circuit Judge James Keller who had sentenced her to death in 1987 removed himself from the re-sentencing trial. Circuit Judge Lewis Paisley was chosen randomly by a computer to replace him. LaFonda Fay's sentence is currently pending and Tina Powell is serving a life sentence.

15

Louisiana: Lethal Injection

The state of Louisiana has sentenced five women to death since 1900. Three of these women, Ada LeBoeuf, Julia Moore, and Toni Jo Henry, were executed, and there is one woman on death row in Louisiana today.

There were 152 executions in Louisiana between 1930–1977 and there have been nineteen since 1977. Antonio James who was the subject of the TV documentary *Final Judgment* and an ABC-TV *Prime Time Live* episode, was the only prisoner executed in Louisiana in 1996.

Louisiana's electric chair, "Old Sparky," once located at Angola, was retired after the state changed to lethal injection in 1991. It is presently being stored by the state museum system at the old U.S. Mint in the New Orleans French Quarter, where the museum director has said, "We have no plans to exhibit it in the foreseeable future."

In 1991 when Louisiana switched its method of execution to lethal injection, about 400 inmates at the Louisiana State Penitentiary at Angola laid down their tools in protest after they were given an order to help build the table that would be used for executions. The warden intervened and said it had been a mistake to ask prisoners to participate in the venture, and an outside contractor built it.

Andrew Lee Jones, executed July 22, 1991, was the last person to die in Louisiana's electric chair, and Robert Wayne Sawyer was the first person to die in the state by lethal injection. Sawyer was Louisiana's 21st and the nation's 194th person to be executed since 1976.

A 1993 study (Klemm) showed that whether or not a person is sentenced to death in Louisiana largely depends on three factors — the race of the victim, the victim-offender relationship, and the geographical location of the crime. According to Klemm's study, in Louisiana one is more likely to receive a sentence of death if one kills a white victim and the crime is committed in the southern part of the state.

Like other death penalty states, Louisiana has a review board (the Pardon Board) that conducts hearings and forwards favorable recommendations for clemency to the governor. The state constitution says the governor has final responsibility for life and death decisions and may commute a sentence if the Pardon Board recommends it. One woman, Catherine "Kitty" Dodds, had her sentence commuted in Louisiana.

Of the 21 men executed at Angola, Governor David Treen (1980–1984) sent three to the electric chair, Governor Buddy Roemer (1988–1992) sent four, and Governor Edwin Edwards (1984–1988, 1992–1997) was responsible for the execution of fourteen. Speaking of the power to grant clemency Governor Edwards said, "I act as responsibly as I can. No reasonable person would want to make life or death decisions. I think having that responsibility — deciding whether or not a prisoner should be executed — is awesome."

Louisiana's clemency process has not been free of corruption. A former Pardon Board chairman, Howard Marsellus, pleaded guilty in 1987 and served 20 months in federal prison for his role in a pardons-for-sale scheme. Marsellus said that under his chairmanship the pardon system was "corrupt, unfair, and unjust." He said he lacked the courage to vote on the basis of what he felt or believed. Instead he gave in to the prestige and power that went with his job. He said he knew what the Governor wanted most of the time and since he was the man who appointed him to his office, he usually followed the governor's wishes.

Marsellus described his first day on the job when he was handed a "cheat list" with the names of prisoners and those interested in their cases. "Everyone involved — inmates, families of inmates, attorneys, ministers, friends, and elected officials — participated in the process of influencing and lobbying those in positions of power who could change the outcome of a case," he said.

Of death penalty decisions, Marsellus said, "Morally, from day one, I knew it was wrong yet I continued to participate in this ugly process. It was only after the Baldwin case that I woke up." Marsellus had grave misgivings about Timothy Baldwin's guilt. Baldwin was convicted of the murder of an elderly woman in 1978. After the trial his lawyers found a hotel receipt that proved he was hundreds of miles away in another state on the night of the murder. But the prosecution claimed he had driven to the hotel to establish an alibi and then returned to Louisiana to commit the murder.

The prosecution's main witness against Baldwin was his girlfriend, who received a life sentence for her part in the murder in exchange for her testimony. The prosecution claimed that Marilyn Hampton, Baldwin's girlfriend, waited outside in a car while Baldwin committed the murder. The governor of Louisiana visited Marilyn in prison before signing the death warrant for Baldwin's execution. Marsellus said he thought the purpose of the visit was to make sure Marilyn had not changed her mind about her testimony. Timothy Baldwin was executed a short time later and two months after that

Marilyn Hampton was released from prison. She had served seven years of a life sentence.

Marsellus witnessed Timothy Baldwin's execution and said that Baldwin looked him right in the eye and said, "You are murdering an innocent man" and Marsellus believes till this day that that was true.

"I was part of the system," he said. "The overriding factor surrounding the death penalty is the politics involved." Marsellus said that most governors who commute death sentences do so when they are leaving office. If they're not leaving, they look at the public's attitudes toward the death penalty and do not usually extend any mercy to the defendant.

In most cases, Marsellus said, by the time there's a public hearing in a case, the decision (to execute) has already been made. He said he believes "The deck is stacked against the condemned," from the prosecutor on down. "In the strongly religious Deep South," he said "death-penalty supporters reconcile themselves spiritually with their role in state killing by utilizing the Bible to support their way of thinking. Amid their compassion and concern for the poor and hungry, when it comes down to killing a person, they justify it by saying: 'This is what God would have us do.' Every time there's an execution, I relive my past involvement from beginning to end. I can never forget. I think they need to fall on their knees and ask for forgiveness, I did."

In 1996, the Supreme Court of Louisiana determined that death is a just and constitutional punishment for the rape of a child under 12 in the case of *Louisiana v. Wilson* [WL 718217]. The bill became a law in June 1996. Bills are also being introduced in Louisiana on giving the death penalty for the rape of a victim over 65.

WOMEN SENTENCED TO DEATH IN LOUISIANA

1929

Ada LeBoeuf: White; Executed, 1929. Ada LeBoeuf, "Miss Ada," was executed in Louisiana on February 1, 1929, for the contract killing of her husband. She was the wife of James LeBoeuf, a power plant superintendent in Morgan City, LA. Dr. Thomas Dreher, the family doctor, had apparently been flirting with Ada, and James, her husband, reportedly threatened to kill him. Ada and Dr. Dreher hired a trapper to shoot James one night while he was aboard his boat in a Louisiana swamp. After the shooting, the trapper slit James's body open and put lead in it to weigh it down, then dumped it overboard.

Ada and Dr. Dreher were both arrested for the murder and both were given the death penalty. The trapper they had hired to do the killing was given life. Mrs. LeBoeuf had to be carried to her final hearing on a stretcher. She was unable to have a last visit with her crippled mother and was led to the gallows saying, "My mother, my mother. Oh my God, isn't this a terrible thing?"

Ada had four children, her lover three. After the execution her 9-year-old daughter, Liberty, wept at her casket as she had been denied permission to have a last visit with her mother.

1935

Julia Moore: Executed, 1935. Julia Moore, aka Julia Powers, aka Julia Williams, was convicted of the murder of a man named Elliot Wilson, and, although she pleaded not guilty, she was hanged for the crime on February 8, 1935.

1942

Toni Jo Henry aka Annie Beatrice McQuiston aka Annie Henry: White; Executed. Toni Jo Henry, the only woman executed in Louisiana's electric chair, was executed the Saturday after Thanksgiving at the Lake Charles courthouse. She was 26 years old and was executed for the murder of a Houston salesman, Joseph P. Calloway, on St. Valentine's Day in 1940.

She was born in Shreveport, Louisiana, on January 3, 1916, as Annie Beatrice McQuiston, the third of five children. Growing up she lived for a time with her grandmother while her mother was ill. Then when she was six her mother died of tuberculosis and her father remarried. Annie's aunt testified at her trial that Annie had begged her many times to take her away from her father and her stepmother between the ages of six and thirteen, but she never did.

At age thirteen Annie was fired from a part-time job in a macaroni factory when the manager found out there had been tuberculosis in her family. After her father gave her a severe beating, Annie left home for good and as a teenager was arrested six times between the ages of seventeen and twenty-one, once for beating a man and snipping his ears.

After leaving home, Annie became a street hustler and prostitute, and changed her name to Toni Jo Hood. According to her aunt, she was smoking pot and drinking alcohol by then so she, Mrs. Holt, arranged for Toni Jo to marry someone in hopes that she would settle down. However, this did not go exactly as her aunt had planned, and both Toni Jo and her husband ended up living with the aunt.

Toni Jo (Annie) then went to live in a bordello in Shreveport's red-light district and began working full-time as a prostitute. She was addicted to cocaine at the time and worked the Louisiana and South Texas areas, including Lake Charles, Beaumont, Houston, and San Antonio.

It was in Texas that she met Claude D. "Cowboy" Henry. Claude was one of Toni's customers before he married her in the fall of 1939 in Calcasieu Parish, Louisiana. He already had a criminal record when they met, and both he and Toni Jo became a part of the criminal underworld of South Texas. At the time they were married, Cowboy had homicide charges pending over the shooting of a former San Antonio police officer for which he was eventually tried and found guilty. A judge sentenced him to 50 years in the Texas penitentiary, and after the sentencing Toni Jo vowed to get him out of prison as quickly as possible.

With this as her only goal, Toni Jo recruited an ex-con nicknamed "Arkie," for Arkansas, to help her. Her idea was to get Cowboy out of prison any way she could. After hooking up with Arkie, she got a couple of teenagers to break into a store to steal guns for her. They stole 16 guns, mostly .32 − .38-caliber revolvers, and ammunition. Guns in hand, Toni and Arkie started hitchhiking along a Louisiana highway looking for a car to drive to Texas.

At some point, Joseph P. Calloway, a 43-year-old Louisiana tire salesman picked them up. He was driving a new car that he was supposed to deliver to some friends who ran a trucking business in Jennings, Louisiana. It was raining and after they drove through St. Charles, Toni Jo pulled a gun on him. Calloway offered them all of his money, but Toni said they wanted his car. She made him pull off the road and stop the car where she took his watch and money and made him get into the trunk. She then told Arkie to drive south toward the Gulf of Mexico.

In a desolate area southeast of Lake Charles called Plateau Petit Bois they found a small trail that led to a rice field. Toni made Arkie stop there and she got Calloway out of the trunk, then led him at gunpoint into the field and told him to strip and say his prayers. He did as he was told and Toni Jo shot him directly between the eyes with a .32-caliber revolver with him kneeling on the ground in front of her. She left his naked body there and took all of his clothes with her so Cowboy would have a change of clothes when they got him out of prison.

After seeing what Toni Jo had done, Arkie realized she wasn't kidding around and he got a little scared, so he left her when they reached Camden, Louisiana. Toni Jo, finding herself alone, returned to her Aunt Emma's house and told her she had shot and killed a man somewhere around Lake Charles. Her aunt contacted her brother, who was with the Louisiana State police, and they picked Toni Jo up.

When she was questioned she confessed immediately to killing Calloway. At first the police didn't believe her and thought she was making it up because when she tried to lead them to his body she couldn't find it. But after showing them Calloway's wallet and drivers license, they began to believe her, and about three days later she was able to lead them to the spot where they had left Calloway. After the body was found, Toni Jo refused to help the police any more because she was angry at the newspapers for the way they portrayed her.

The newspapers said Toni Jo took full responsibility for Calloway's murder although she admitted having an accomplice. She refused to make any further statements at the coroner's inquest about the murder or why she committed it.

During the investigation people were appalled to learn that Calloway's body showed signs of torture. There were marks on his penis that led investigators to believe that Toni Jo had clamped pliers around Calloway's penis and led him to the spot where he was executed. For this reason, Toni Jo became known as the torturer-murderer.

In separate trials Toni Jo and Arkie were both convicted of Calloway's murder and sentenced to the electric chair. When the governor of the state upheld the conviction, Toni Jo admitted that she alone had done the killing. When Toni Jo's impending execution was announced, her husband, Cowboy, broke out of the prison farm in Texas hoping to somehow free her, as she had tried to do for him. There were rumors that Cowboy planned to kill the judge, but a number of heavily armed guards picked him up in a motel and he never had the chance.

Toni Jo and her husband were never allowed to see each other again, but they did get to have a long distance phone call before her execution and Toni Jo reportedly begged her husband to give up his life of crime.

1975

Catherine Dodds: White; Reversed in 1978. In 1975, Catherine "Kitty" Dodds was convicted and sentenced to death along with Rodney Blackwell for the murder of her husband, a New Orleans police officer who had retired and was on disability pension. The prosecution contended that Kitty had hired Blackwell to do the killing. Kitty always said that she was a battered woman and that continued physical abuse led her to want to have her husband killed.

She told interviewers, "It was either him or me." Rodney agreed with Kitty's account and said he also believed that her husband would kill her if something wasn't done.

When a 1976 Supreme Court ruling found Louisiana's capital punishment statute unconstitutional both Kitty and Blackwell had their sentences commuted to life. Blackwell is still in prison serving a life sentence.

Kitty Dodds escaped from prison in 1980 during a trip to the hospital and went to Missouri, where she changed her name to Linda D. Winter and got married. The FBI arrested her two years later and brought her back to Louisiana to serve her life sentence. She was granted clemency four years later and is a free woman now. A TV movie was made of Dodd's account of the murder.

1995

Antoinette Frank: Black; Currently on death row. Antoinette Frank is the only woman on death row in Louisiana today and the only woman police officer on death row in the country. The scene of her crime, three murders and a robbery was a Vietnamese family restaurant called Kim Anh, in New Orleans where a former police partner of Antoinette's, Ronald Williams, and Antoinette herself often moonlighted as security guards.

The night of the murders Antoinette had been in the restaurant three times and had called there several times. Her strange behavior made Chau Vu, the cook and the adult daughter of the restaurant owners, uneasy, so she took the cash that was on hand, approximately $10,000, from the restaurant safe and hid it in the microwave.

After eating a steak dinner with Roger Lacaze, according to trial records, Antoinette and Roger pulled out their guns and forced Ronald Williams to kneel on the floor where Antoinette shot him, execution style, in the head. Chau Vu was hiding in a walk-in freezer during the murder-robbery rampage, and after Antoinette left Chau found the security guard and her siblings, Cuong Vu, 18, and Ha Vu, 24, all dead and the money from the microwave missing.

She called the police and when they arrived, Antoinette Frank was one of the officers. Antoinette asked Chau Vu what had happened, to which Chau Vu responded, "You were here, why ask me?" After Vu's accusation, and under questioning, Antoinette broke down and confessed, but in a taped statement she blamed all the killings on 18-year-old Roger Lacaze. In a second statement, she changed her story and said Lacaze had killed Williams and had then forced her to kill the other two while they were praying on their knees. Both Antoinette and her accomplice, Lacaze, were indicted the next day for first-degree murder, and the prosecution did not hesitate to seek the death penalty. Antoinette was twenty-four at the time.

At first Lacaze denied even being in the restaurant, but later changed his story, saying that Antoinette had done all the killing. At his trial, which was before Antoinette's, Lacaze blamed his confession on police brutality. But the jury found him guilty and sentenced him to die.

At Antoinette's trial, her attorney did not offer a defense, although they had thirty-nine witnesses lined up. Instead, her lawyer told the jury that it was not the defendant's obligation to prove her innocence, but rather the state's duty to prove her guilt.

Prosecutors played the tape of Antoinette admitting she had shot the two workers. The prosecution's two key witnesses were the siblings of the deceased, Chau Vu and her brother, Quoc, who described how they survived the murders by hiding in a walk-in cooler. An hour into her trial Antoinette rose from her seat and demanded a new attorney. This was met by a threat from the trial judge to bind and gag her for the rest of the trial.

The jury took only twenty-two minutes to find her guilty and thirty-five minutes to sentence her to death. She is on Louisiana's death row today. Antoinette is the first New Orleans police officer to be convicted of murdering another officer.

In a strange turn of events, in searching for evidence, police found bones buried beneath Antoinette's former residence and began questioning whether or not they were the remains of her father whom she had reported missing in 1994.

In response to a lawsuit filed in federal court by the Vu family seeking 10 million dollars in damages, the city of New Orleans, tried to avoid financial responsibility for the murders of three citizens by one of its officers. The city shifted the blame for the murders on the restaurant for hiring Antoinette as a part-time security guard. The family said police administrators ignored clear signs that Antoinette was unfit for duty and needed better supervision.

Apparently, at the time Antoinette was hired, police had a missing-persons report on her filed by her father who was later missing himself. Included in the file was a note in which Antoinette said she had been "doomed" since the day she was born.

The wife of the officer who was killed also filed a $10 million lawsuit against the New Orleans Police Department for hiring Antoinette Frank. Her suit contended that she and her two young sons, one only a week old when his father was killed, were entitled to damages from the city for the murder of her husband.

16

Maryland: Gas/Lethal Injection

The state of Maryland has sentenced two women to death since 1900. No woman has been legally executed in Maryland, and there are no women on death row in Maryland today.

The history of the death penalty in Maryland is long. In fact, as a common law state, in keeping with the common laws of England Maryland has always had the death penalty as a punishment for murder. However, in 1809 the Maryland state legislature divided murder into varying degrees and decided on the death penalty as the punishment for first-degree murder only. This was sufficient until 1908 when the legislature again considered the question and decided to eliminate mandatory imposition of the death penalty for first-degree murder and give the seated judge at a murder trial the option of imposing the sentence of death or incarceration for life. Eight years later, in 1816, the legislature gave juries the power to return a verdict of guilty "without capital punishment" which, when used, would prevent a judge from imposing a sentence of death.

Until 1922 those found guilty of first degree murder and sentenced to death in Maryland were hanged, in the county where they were tried. In 1922 the state legislature decided that hangings were too much of a public spectacle and ordered executions to take place at the Maryland State Penitentiary. Between 1923 and 1961 there were eighty executions in the state of Maryland. Fifty-three were for murder and twenty-seven for rape. There were twelve double and two triple hangings.

The first indoor hanging was in the Baltimore City Jail in 1913. George Chelton was hanged inside the Maryland State Penitentiary on June 8, 1923. He was executed for rape. Hangings continued in Maryland until 1955 when the state legislature replaced that method of execution with the gas chamber.

One of the unusual hangings still remembered in Maryland was that of Jack Johnson on January 30, 1920. Johnson was 56-years-old and had been convicted of a double murder. When his body dropped through the trap door of the gallows, the rope broke and he fell through. He was injured but still alive. Prison attendants quickly ran down and retrieved his body and put it on a stretcher. Then they carried it back up the scaffold where the noose was again placed around his neck, while he was still on the stretcher, and he was hanged a second time. The rope did not break again and he died. The last man to be hanged in Maryland was William C. Thomas on June 10, 1955.

A man named Mr. A. Bennett Brown designed the Maryland gas chamber, which was installed in June 1956 at the Maryland State Penitentiary at the cost of $20,000. It is hexagonal steel and glass vault about 8 feet high and 6½ feet in diameter. Five sides of the gray steel chamber have windows. The remaining side is a heavy steel door. Inside the chamber is one metal chair with a mesh bottom. Four men were executed in Maryland's gas chamber, the last on June 9, 1961.

In 1994 changes were enacted in the Maryland Death Penalty statute and House Bill #498 made lethal injection the official method of execution in Maryland. However, any persons sentenced to death before the bill was enacted are given the option of choosing gas or lethal injection.

RACIAL DISCRIMINATION IN MARYLAND

In December (1996) the Governor's Task Force on the Fair Implementation of the Death Penalty found evidence of racial disparity in the outcome of death penalty sentencing in Maryland, citing it as "a cause for concern" warranting remedial action. As a result, two bills that would establish and fund a committee to more rigorously investigate racial disparities in Maryland capital prosecutions and sentencing were considered.

Today (1998) in Maryland, 87 percent of the inmates on death row are African-American (Dieter, 1996). The first prisoner put to death in Maryland after June, 1961 was John F. Thanos. He waived his appeals and asked the state to execute him as soon as possible. His execution raised concerns among capital punishment foes that as the death penalty is being revived in Maryland it will be used disproportionately against blacks.

RECENT DEATH PENALTY LEGISLATION IN MARYLAND

In 1995 the Maryland State Legislature again looked at the death penalty and made the following changes:

- The right of a defendant to file a second post-conviction petition was eliminated. However, the court may reopen a death penalty proceeding if it is "in the interest of justice."

- The period for filing a post-conviction proceeding in a death penalty case was shortened from 340 to 210 days.

- Defendants now have the right to waive the automatic stay of a warrant of execution that is in place for the 210 days after a direct review by the U.S. Supreme Court.

- A date for a hearing on a post-conviction petition must be set within 30 days after the day on which the petition is filed and held no later than 90 days after the date on which the petition is filed unless a party requests a change of the date and shows good cause. In addition, the court is required to issue a decision on the petition within 90 days after the hearing.

In 1997 a bill was introduced in Maryland to lower the minimum age of the death penalty to 16 and the state remains a leader in taking measures to limit court challenges by inmates.

Public defenders continue to argue that Maryland is not entitled to invoke the new federal deadlines it is seeking to impose because it does not meet the condition that the federal law requires, which is, assurance that death row inmates have competent lawyers to pursue their cases. The state of Maryland disputes this argument, according to Assistant Attorney General Gwynn Kisey, Jr. "Maryland's position is that it complies with the statutory requirements for application of the new federal law."

In the only ruling so far, Chief U.S. District Judge J. Frederick Motz of Baltimore sided with inmates saying the state's system for assigning lawyers to death row inmates is inadequate. His ruling said, in effect, that Maryland has not established any standards of competency for lawyers who represent death row inmates. It noted too that the existing system of selecting and paying court-appointed lawyers does not ensure that there will be competent lawyers for death row inmates who cannot afford their own attorneys. However, the Fourth U.S. Circuit Court of Appeals in Richmond, Virginia overturned Motz's ruling on a procedural ground six months after it was issued.

Judges and juries in Maryland have shown a clear preference over the years for the option of life without the possibility of parole over both death and life with the possibility of parole.

WOMEN SENTENCED TO DEATH IN MARYLAND

1981

Annette Stebbing: White; Reversed in 1985. At the time of her conviction, Annette Stebbing was the ninth woman on death row in the United States and one of the youngest, at age twenty. She was sentenced to the gas chamber in Maryland for a murder that involved the strangulation of her step-niece. In separate trials Annette and her husband, Bernard Lee, were found guilty of the murder-rape of their step-niece, 19-year-old Dena Marie Polis in April 1980. Annette's husband received a life sentence in a bench trial, while Annette, then nineteen, opted for a jury trial and was sentenced to death.

When the Stebbings were driving Dena to Baltimore to visit her boyfriend they made a stop in Hartford County, Maryland. In her trial, Annette testified that after returning from the woods, where she had gone to relieve herself, she found her husband having sex with Dena in the back of their van and strangled her. Earlier, however, Annette had confessed to the Baltimore police that she "held Dena down in the back of the van and strangled her while her husband raped her." The latter version is the one the jury believed. Before announcing the death sentence, the judge described the crime as "the most heinous and despicable of activities ever to come before the court," adding "your crime involved rape and murder, the act of sodomy when the victim was dead and the theft of the victims ring." The sentence of death was reversed in 1985.

1982

Doris Foster: Native American; Commuted in 1987. Doris Raven Dark Wing Foster, also known as Nuketa Leah Ansara, also known as Doris Ann Foster, a Native American woman, was given the death penalty in Maryland on February 8, 1982. She was convicted of the murder of her landlady, seventy-one-year-old Josephine Dietrich. Ms. Dietrich was stabbed to death on January 28, 1981, at the Maryland Manor Motel where she lived and worked as the motel manager. Doris, her husband Tommy Foster, and a stepdaughter, Elizabeth Phillips, all lived at the motel at the time.

During the trial in Cecil County, MD, Doris's husband, Tommy, testified against her, as did her teenage stepdaughter, Elizabeth, who received immunity from prosecution in exchange for her cooperation. Elizabeth testified that she was with her stepmother when Doris plunged a screwdriver into Ms. Dietrich during an attempted robbery. According to Elizabeth, after the assault, the two of them went to the back of the motel, where Doris threw the screwdriver into the woods. The defense was not allowed to present the testimony of a friend of Ms. Dietrich who said that the victim had told her that Tommy Foster, not Doris, had threatened her. Cecil County Circuit Judge Donaldson C. Cole heard the testimony of Helen Douglass in his chambers and said the testimony was merely "hearsay" and, therefore, not reliable enough to be presented to the jury. In chambers, Ms. Douglass, who managed another nearby motel, told Judge Cole that Ms. Dietrich had called her a few days before the murder and warned her about the Fosters. She said Mr. Foster had refused to pay the rent they owed her and that they were "Bad news." Ms. Douglass said, "She told me she was afraid for her life and she was crying. I told her, you do not have to put up with this. Why don't you call the police?" To which Ms. Dietrich replied, "They won't help me unless I'm dead." Ms. Douglass went on to say that Mr. Foster had "Threatened to kill her (Ms. Dietrich) these were the words she used . . . he had threatened to kill her."

After drinking some beer, Elizabeth testified, her stepmother decided to go back and make sure Ms. Dietrich was dead. She retrieved the screwdriver from where she had thrown it, went back inside, and returned later saying she had stabbed Ms. Dietrich in the heart. Both Doris's husband and Elizabeth testified they'd all tried to cover up the murder by cleaning everything and dumping the body in the Chesapeake & Delaware Canal.

At her trial, Doris gave a different version of the story. According to Doris, she was asleep when the murder took place and she had two letters from her husband admitting he'd committed the murder. Since the stories of what happened that night were vastly different, the credibility of everyone was a major issue in the trial.

Doris was ultimately given the death penalty, and Governor Harry Hughes commuted her sentence in 1987 after considering the large number of mitigating circumstances and the fact that her husband confessed to the crime.

17

Massachusetts: No Death Penalty

The state of Massachusetts, which executed a number of women in the 1600s, 1700s, and 1800s, condemned one woman to death in 1912, and none after that. Despite the fact that it is debated every year in the state legislature, Massachusetts has no death penalty today.

In the state Acts of 1898 it was specified that executions would be carried out in Massachusetts by electrocution. To accommodate this, the state's electric chair was installed at the State Prison in Charleston, Massachusetts on January 1, 1900. Between that date and May 1, 1947, 65 executions took place in the state.

The most famous of persons executed during that time were two Italian immigrants, Nicola Sacco and Bartolomeo Vanzetti, whose murder trial lasted from 1920–1927. The two men, who had arrived in the United States in 1908, were charged with the murders of a paymaster and a guard and the theft of more than $15,000 from a shoe factory in South Braintree, MA.

The trial took place in Dedham in the summer of 1921, and the state based its case on two facts: Sacco possessed a pistol of the type used in the murders, and when the two of them were arrested they were at a garage trying to claim a car that had been connected with the crimes. Many people thought the evidence was inadequate and that much of the testimony from witnesses was contradictory. Furthermore, the trial judge, Judge Webster Thayer, and the jurors were all accused of bias. Nevertheless, the jury found the defendants guilty. Immediately there were protests and cries of outrage from socialists, radicals, and many prominent intellectuals throughout the world, who said the men were found guilty because they were immigrants and outspoken anarchists.

For 6 years after the trial all motions to submit new evidence and appeals were denied, and in 1925 another man who was already condemned to death confessed to having been one of a gang who had committed the crimes. Despite this confession, Sacco and Vanzetti were given the death penalty in 1927. So many appeals were made to Governor Alvan Tufts Fuller on their behalf that he appointed a committee of intellectuals to investigate the trial and the verdict. After receiving the committee's final report in August 1927 the governor announced he would uphold the death sentences, and Sacco and Vanzetti were electrocuted in the electric chair at Charlestown State Prison on August 23, 1927.

It was widely maintained that Sacco and Vanzetti were innocent, and they came to be regarded as martyrs of the system. In a strange turn of events, in August 1977 Governor Michael Dukakis of Massachusetts signed a proclamation that recognized the faults of the trial and cleared the names of Sacco and Vanzetti. Then, in 1997, the mayor of Boston, Thomas Menino, accepted a sculpture dedicated to their memory and stated at the time, "This case was a watershed in the U.S. justice system."

Massachusetts conducted its last execution 50 years ago in May 1947 when it electrocuted two men who committed murder during the course of a burglary. The state Supreme Judicial Court threw out the death penalty law in the 1970s, when the Justices of the Massachusetts Supreme Judicial Court were asked to express their opinions on the constitutionality of a death penalty bill. They stated that, in their opinion, Act 26 of the Declaration of Rights of the Massachusetts Constitution forbids the imposition of a death penalty: "In the absence of a showing on the part of the Commonwealth that the availability of that penalty contributes more to the achievement of a legitimate state purpose, i.e. deterring criminal conduct, than does the penalty of life imprisonment."

In 1979 Chapter 488 was passed by the Massachusetts Legislature providing for the death penalty in the case of murder-one; in 1982 the issue was placed on the General Ballot and voters approved a Constitutional Amendment providing for capital punishment in the state. This lasted until 1984 when, in a decision in *Commonwealth v. Colon-Cruz,* the Massachusetts Supreme Court declared the death penalty Amendment unconstitutional. Now, every year since the election of former Governor Weld a new death penalty bill has been filed and defeated in Massachusetts.

The most recent measures in the state call for death by lethal injection in instances of first-degree murder. They also include the bifurcated trial system to ensure that precautions will be taken against executing the innocent. In 1994 a bill passed in the Senate but failed in the House by an 86–70 vote. In 1995 the Senate passed it again but it again failed in the House by a vote of 83–73. In 1996, the Senate again approved the bill, however it never emerged from committee for a House vote.

In 1997, the Massachusetts Senate voted to bring back the death penalty again, but only for cases in which public safety officers are slain in the line of duty. By limiting the circumstances under which a death sentence could be imposed, proponents hoped to gain more support in the House.

Senate Minority Leader Brian P. Lees offered a narrower death penalty proposal as an amendment to another bill. The Senate approved the amendment by a vote of 23–4. It was then added onto a bill that would increase from 15 to 25 years the minimum time a person convicted of second degree murder must serve in prison before becoming eligible for parole.

House Speaker Thomas Finneran said he believes a state law calling for life in prison without parole for first-degree murderers is a "credible alternative" to capital punishment. He recalled the debate in 1994 that took place after a state trooper was shot and killed by an ex-convict. He said that as much as your heart goes out to the widow, the children, and anybody else, it doesn't resolve the issue of possibly executing an innocent person when you have a credible alternative.

The governor of the state, however, said that people in Massachusetts are ready for the death penalty and want it now. Nevertheless, abolitionists in Massachusetts have a well-organized grassroots and lobbying campaign, which has the support of religious organizations, lawyers (the ABA and the National Lawyers Guild), the Massachusetts criminal defense lawyers, sociologists, and medical doctors.

This coalition has developed excellent lobbying materials, including an abolitionist booklet prepared by Chief Justice Hennessey. They have also made use of polls directed by Northeastern University on death penalty views in Massachusetts. One such poll found that few legislators or citizens knew that the state has a provision for a sentence of life in prison without possibility of parole (LWOP).

Abolitionists successfully targeted newly elected legislators and those who were uncommitted and addressed the specific concerns of each (*Boston Globe*, 1997). Nevertheless, according to Governor Paul Celluci, debate over the death penalty is a staple in the Massachusetts legislature.

WOMEN SENTENCED TO DEATH IN MASSACHUSETTS

1912

Lena Cusumano: White; Commuted. Lena Cusumano, a white woman was given the death penalty in Massachusetts in 1912 for the murder of her husband. Her sentence was later commuted. No further information was found about her or her crime.

18

Mississippi: Gas/Lethal Injection

The state of Mississippi has sentenced eleven women to death since 1900. Five of these women, Carrie McCarty, Pattie Perdue, Mary Holmes, Mildred Johnson, and Ann Knight, were executed. One woman is on death row in Mississippi today.

Execution in Mississippi, previously by gas, is now by lethal injection and the minimum age for the death penalty is 16. Between 1930 and 1976 there were 158 legal executions in Mississippi and since 1977 there have been four.

According to the NAACP (1997), African Americans make up half the death row population in Mississippi, despite the fact that African Americans make up only 40 percent of the state population. In Mississippi, killers of whites are five times more likely to receive the death penalty than killers of blacks.

In his recent book (1996) *Worse than Slavery: Parchman Farm and the Ordeal of Jim Crow Justice,* Rutgers University history professor David Oshinsky looks at Mississippi's penal system from the early 1900's to the present and notes that among the thirteen southern states, Mississippi led the South in every imaginable kind of mob atrocity:

the most lynchings, most multiple lynchings, most lynchings of women, most lynchings without arrest, most lynchings of victims in police custody, and most public support for the process itself. Mob violence was directed at burglars, arsonists, horse thieves, grave robbers, peeping toms, and troublemakers — virtually all of them black.

Despite this fact, the Mississippi State Textbook Board rejected the use of a revisionist state history textbook entitled *Mississippi: Conflict and Change* because it had a picture of a lynch-mob posing for a camera with the body of someone they'd just hanged. At the book trial a committee member said that material like that would make it hard for a teacher to control her students, especially a "white lady teacher" in a predominantly black class. The presiding judge asked, "Didn't lynchings happen in Mississippi?" To which a committee member responded yes, but it was all so long ago, why dwell on it now? The judge ruled in favor of the book.

Mississippi has a vigilante tradition of white supremacy, Jim Crow laws, lynchings, and KKK terrorism. It was Mississippi that gave birth to white Citizens Councils, and Mississippi was where several of the civil rights era's most notorious racist murders occurred. Among these were the 1954 lynching of Emmett Till, the 1963 assassination of Medgar Evers, and the 1964 murders of freedom riders James Chaney, Michael Schwerner, and Andrew Goodman (Dennis, 1996).

In 1993, the U.S. Department of Justice, under the supervision of Attorney General Janet Reno, investigated 46 hanging deaths in Mississippi jails since 1987 (Johnston, 1993). These deaths came to national attention after the hanging death of 18-year-old Andre Jones in a jail in Simpson County in south central Mississippi. Mr. Jones was the son of the president of the Jackson Chapter of the NAACP. The federal officials contended that Mr. Jones had taken his own life, but a pathologist hired by his family said the death was a homicide. In reviewing the cases, Ms. Reno asked, "How can that many people die?" She asked the Civil Rights Division of the Department of Justice to launch a thorough investigation.

In 1988, a BBC producer-director, Paul Hamann, produced a documentary film about the last fourteen days in the life of Mississippi death row inmate Edward Earl Johnson. Johnson was a 26-year-old black man, who was executed on May 20, 1987, for the murder of a white town marshal in Walnut Grove, Mississippi, in 1979.

In the film, which was shown on HBO and appears to be a straightforward report of events leading up to an execution, prison warden Don Cabana, is depicted as a sensitive, competent professional who says he has reluctantly come to believe that some sort of ultimate punishment is necessary in society.

In recent years, however, Don Cabana authored the book *Death at Midnight: The Confession of an Executioner* and has become an opponent of the death penalty. In various press interviews he has described his experiences of being involved in six executions, including two in which he was the executioner. He is quoted as saying, "I was just an instrument of the legal system. God wanted me to do it. He wanted a humane killer. I was humane. I was compassionate." Today he uses his personal experiences to campaign against the death penalty, particularly the horror of execution in the gas chamber.

In speaking of executions, he said the audience of twenty or so was always kept seated so that they never saw the contortions, the rolling eyes, the gritted teeth, the saliva, the seizures, and the clenched fists. He said doctors and prison staff were given the full frontal view and he would have his eyes glued to the inmate's face, and would be thinking "I know him. That man was in my care and just minutes before he would be a living being and then he was someone I was killing. If I live to be 80," Cabana said, "I will recall every wrinkle, every crease of the face — the style of the haircut, every reaction in the chamber."

On September 2, 1983, Jimmy Lee Gray was sent to the Mississippi gas chamber. Officials had to clear the room eight minutes after the gas was released, when Gray's desperate gasps for air repulsed witnesses. His attorney, Dennis Baiske of Montgomery, Alabama, criticized state officials for clearing the room while the inmate was still alive. Jimmy Lee Gray died banging his head against a steel pole in the gas chamber while reporters counted his moans.

Cabana has described the legal system in Mississippi as being "imperfect" and says he is haunted by the suspicion that one of the men he executed, Edward Earl Johnson (May 20, 1987) was innocent. Cabana believes that prison staff should not be expected to take part in executions, but that the job should be given to the foreman of the jury or the prosecuting attorney.

In 1997 the Washington, DC office of Chicago's Jenner & Block filed a federal civil rights suit challenging Mississippi's failure to provide lawyers to indigent death row inmates during state post-conviction appeals. The suit was filed on behalf of Willie Russell, a mentally retarded man incapable of representing himself. He has been on death row since 1990 for killing a prison guard. But the suit faces a 1989 U.S. Supreme Court decision that held that neither the Eighth Amendment nor the due process clause requires states to appoint counsel to indigent death row prisoners seeking state post-conviction relief.

This case has been helped by a study by the Southern Poverty Law Center of Mississippi and Jenner & Block jointly, which included extensive testing of Mississippi death row inmates by two psychologists. Conclusions of the study showed the inmates have an average verbal IQ of 81 which is two points above the range of borderline retarded; 52 percent of the death row inmates could read only below the fourth grade level and 70 percent, at or below the sixth grade level.

Amnesty International (1997) has said it is alarmed at the crisis on Mississippi's death row where poor prisoners have "no access to post-conviction relief, and after first appeal are on their own to find legal representation." Amnesty International also pointed out that new prison regulations have made access to legal materials difficult for those who attempt to represent themselves.

In 1997 a new bill was introduced to the Mississippi legislature to impose mandatory death penalty for rape of a child.

WOMEN SENTENCED TO DEATH IN MISSISSIPPI

1920

Carrie McCarty: Black; Executed, early 1920s. Carrie McCarty was executed for murder in Mississippi in the early 1920s. The date of her execution, April 23, 1920, is unconfirmed (Streib, 1988).

1922

Pattie Perdue; Black; Executed, 1922. Pattie Perdue was executed for murder in Mississippi in 1922. The date of her execution was January 13, 1922 (Streib, 1988).

1922

Ann Knight; Executed, 1922. Ann Knight (race unknown) was executed for murder in Mississippi in 1922. The date of her execution, August 11, 1922, is unconfirmed (Streib, 1988).

1937

Mary Holmes: Black; Executed, April 29, 1937. Mary Holmes was a black woman who worked as a plantation cook in Mississippi. She and another worker were convicted and sentenced to die for the murder of their employer, the plantation owner. They were accused of going in and beating him to death while he was alone preparing the plantation payroll. They partially scalped him and ultimately dismembered his body. Later they returned and set fire to his body to conceal the crime.

At first the victim's wife refused to believe Mary could have been involved in such an act because she had worked for them for such a long time, but as the trial went on, the wife became more and more convinced that it was Mary who had done it.

1944

Mildred Louise Johnson aka James: Black; Executed, May 19, 1944. Before her trial, Mildred Louise Johnson, aka Mildred Louise James, confessed to murdering Annie Laura Conklin, an elderly lady who lived alone and who was apparently her landlady. In a confession she implicated her common-law husband, Jessie James and her father-in-law, Charles H. Bartley. Annie Conklin had been beaten to death with a stick, a fire poker, and a pair of tongs in her home and because of the violence and brutality of the murder it was believed that Mildred had accomplices. But, when she was arraigned under indictment in court, she told the judge that she alone had committed the crime and, in fact, had no accomplices. She asked the judge to let the two men she had implicated go free.

On the afternoon of the murder, Mildred had been seen on two different occasions in Annie's yard, and the second time, a witness remembered seeing her carrying a suitcase or a large handbag of some sort.

The police later collected the bag from a cab driver who had held onto it because Annie had been arrested and put in jail before she could pay the cab driver for his services. The next day, Mildred acknowledged that the handbag and its contents belonged to her. According to police, it contained a blouse with bloodstains on it and a rent receipt for Mildred, signed by Annie. When

Mildred was arrested, she was wearing a skirt and shoes that were covered with blood and she told the police that the blood had come from the wounds she had inflicted on Annie Conklin.

Mildred had also taken a receipt book from Annie's house which she later threw away, and after her arrest took the police to the spot where she had tossed it.

The court concluded that "the confession of the accused is consistent with the physical facts, and having been freely and voluntarily made, guilt is proven beyond any reasonable doubt therefore, the sentence of death should be carried out. Date of execution will be Friday, May 19, 1944."

Mildred Johnson died insisting that she alone had committed the crime. Witnesses were amazed at her calm facing death. She was black and her victim was white.

1982

Attina Cannaday: White; Reversed in 1984. Although chronologically a child when she committed her murder at age sixteen, Attina Cannaday had endured a life far more demanding than that of most adult women. Her mother had been a stripper in Mobile, Alabama, thus providing a prophetic role model for Attina's childhood. Attina was borderline retarded, with an IQ of 71 and the mental age of nine. At the age of nine, Attina was raped by her father. Her mother and father divorced, but Attina was still not safe — she was raped again by her stepfather at the age of thirteen. At age fourteen, Attina welcomed the opportunity to marry her boyfriend and leave home. Eight months later, still only 14, the age of her friends in the ninth grade, Attina was a divorced stripper in Biloxi, Mississippi. During the next two years she progressed to prostitution and a series of short-term affairs.

Early in 1982, sixteen-year-old Attina met Air Force Sergeant Roland Wojcik, a twenty-nine-year old divorced father of two children. They lived together for some time, but he forced her to leave when his military superiors learned he was living with a 16-year-old girl. Although Wojcik moved on to a new lover, Attina continued her affection for Wojcik and became quite jealous of the new woman in his life.

Late in the evening of June 2, 1982, Attina went to Wojcik's Biloxi apartment with two of her friends, 28-year-old David Gray and 15-year-old Dawn Bushart. The three drove off with Wojcik and his lover, Sandra Sowash, in Wojcik's van leaving his children asleep in his apartment.

During the early morning hours, Attina drove along rural Mississippi roads as Gray raped Sowash at knifepoint in the back of the van. When Attina stopped in a secluded wooded area near Gulfport, Sowash escaped. After being beaten by Gray, Wojcik was stabbed nineteen times in the upper body by Attina.

Attina, Gray, and Bushart then drove away in Wojcik's van, while Sowash, unbeknownst to them, alerted a nearby farmer who called the sheriff. When the van reached Slidell, LA, Bushart left and began hitchhiking back to Biloxi, where she was arrested later that afternoon. Attina and Gray stayed with friends in Slidell and were arrested there at about noon, June 3, 1982.

At first Attina told police that Gray killed Wojcik but later told a jailer about her own participation. Attina, Gray, and Bushart were all indicted for capital murder, and all pleaded not guilty. Bushart, the 15-year-old girl who was only peripherally involved, pleaded guilty to manslaughter and received a ten-year prison sentence. Gray was convicted and sentenced to death in August 1982.

Attina Cannaday's trial began on September 20, 1982. During jury selection, two prospective members were rejected because of their admissions that they would automatically vote against the death penalty for a 16-year-old. In response to the trial testimony against her from Sowash and Gray, Attina testified that Gray was solely responsible for the kidnapping, the rape, and the murder. The jury chose not to believe her and returned a verdict of guilty on September 23, 1982, after only one hour of deliberation. In a brief sentencing hearing it took less than an hour for the jury to return a recommendation for the death penalty. Attina cried as the judge sentenced her to die in the Mississippi gas chamber.

Attina spent less than two years on death row. On May 16, 1984, the Mississippi Supreme Court reversed her death sentence but left her murder conviction intact. The court found that her age alone was not a sufficient grounds for reversal of the death sentence, but that the misuse of Attina's statement to the jailer was a constitutional violation that should result in a different sentence. Attina is currently serving a life sentence in prison.

1984

Cecilia Williamson: White; Reversed, 1987. Celia Williamson was given the death penalty for capital murder in March 1984 and her death sentence was reversed in 1987.

1985

Judy Houston: White; Reversed, 1988. At age 37, Judy Houston confessed to killing her 11-year-old daughter, whose body was found in a trash dump with evidence that she had been strangled with a belt. Paula Houston was described as a very bright student who would have received top honors at her junior high graduation.

School officials criticized the county welfare department for not acting on their reports of frequent abuse. The school first reported that Judy beat her daughter nine years before her death. Judy's sentence was reversed in 1988 and she is serving a life sentence.

1989

Susie Balfour: Black; Reversed, 1992. Susie Balfour was given the death penalty for murder in Mississippi in October 1989 and her sentence was reversed in 1992.

1990

Sabrina Butler: Black; Reversed in 1992. 19-year-old Sabrina Butler was sentenced to death for the murder of her nine-month-old son. She said she found her baby not breathing, performed CPR, and then took him to the hospital. But when the police interrogated her, she was arrested and later prosecuted for her son's murder. The Mississippi Supreme Court overturned her conviction in 1992. Upon re-trial she was acquitted on December 17, 1995, after a very brief deliberation and released from custody. It is now believed that the baby may have died either of cystic kidney disease or from sudden infant death syndrome (SIDS).

Sabrina Butler's case is one of many cited in *Innocence and the Death Penalty: The Increasing Danger of Executing the Innocent,* a 1997 report prepared by the Death Penalty Information Center in Washington, DC.

1993

Vernice Ballenger: White; Currently on death row. Vernice Ballenger planned to just rob her elderly aunt, but something happened and she ended up killing her instead. In 1995 the Mississippi Supreme Court upheld Vernice's capital murder conviction and death sentence and set her date of execution for October 25 of that year. She is currently on death row at the State Penitentiary in Parchman.

19

Missouri: Lethal Injection

The state of Missouri has sentenced five women to death since 1900. One, a federal prisoner, Bonnie Brown Heady, was executed. One woman is on death row in Missouri today.

In 1991 the state of Missouri made history by becoming the first state to sentence two married couples to death in separate trials and for separate crimes in the same year. Not since the era of the Rosenbergs had the U.S. courts dealt such a lethal blow.

Faye Copeland, who was 69 at the time, and Ray Copeland, who was 76, were tried separately for the same crime, the murders of five transient men on their farm in Missouri. Faye's trial was first. She was found guilty and the jury recommended the death penalty. When Ray was sentenced to die in April 1991, the couple had been married over fifty years. They became the oldest couple on death row in the United States, and, quite possibly, the oldest couple ever sentenced to death.

The same year, 1991, Zein and Maria Isa, married for thirty years, were both given the death penalty for the murder of their 16-year-old daughter, a murder recorded on tape by the FBI, who had their apartment bugged.

Each wife was given the death penalty as an accomplice to her husband's crimes. Both husbands died while on death row, leaving their wives to awaiting execution.

THE DEATH PENALTY IN MISSOURI

The local sheriff, as elsewhere, handled Early executions in Missouri. Most were public hangings carried out in the county where a murder occurred. In September 1937, Missouri Governor, Lloyd Crow Stark, signed into law a bill calling for executions by lethal gas. The state officially took over capital punishments in 1938 and built a gas chamber at the penitentiary in Jefferson City, Missouri, in a brown brick building next to the baseball diamond on the prison's East Side. Prison records of executions began in 1938 when Missouri executed four people in the month of March (Shelley, 1997). Once, in the 1880s, the state executed five prisoners in one month (Shelley, 1997).

The first executions by gas in Missouri were in March 1938, when William Wright and John Brown were put to death together for murder during a bank holdup in Kansas City. One of the most publicized early executions in Missouri was that of a woman, federal prisoner Bonnie Brown Heady in 1953. In a double execution, which was somewhat of a record in modern times in that it took place only 81 days after the crime itself, Bonnie and her lover, Carl Austin, were executed for the kidnapping and murder of 6-year-old Bobby Greenlease (see Chapter 8).

Missouri prison records show that a total of 39 people were executed in the gas chamber. Of the 39, twenty-three were black sixteen white. Thirty of the executions were for first-degree murder, six were for rape, and three were for kidnapping (Mosley & Ganey, 1989).

The door through which a prisoner entered the Missouri gas chamber, nicknamed "the tank," was an old submarine hatch, which prison officials were constantly checking, concerned about its security. They were never quite sure it wouldn't leak a little gas during an execution. Once those in charge knew an execution was a "go," the condemned prisoner was brought in and strapped into a white perforated metal chair that had an earthen jar filled with sulfuric acid underneath. At a signal from the warden, the executioner would pull a lever releasing pellets of sodium cyanide into the acid, which would mix to form cyanide gas. After inhaling this, the prisoner was supposed to die within minutes.

In 1965, Lloyd Leo Anderson, the last person to die in Missouri's gas chamber, went to his death on February 26 cursing Governor Warren Hearnes who refused to pardon him for a hold-up murder in St. Louis in 1961.

In 1988, when "the tank" was undergoing a $25,000 renovation, to get geared up for a new spate of executions, Missouri state legislator Bob Ward (R) introduced a measure to do away with the gas chamber and use lethal injection as the form of execution. In proposing it, Ward said, "The gas chamber is a hideous form of death your eyes bulge, your tongue tries to jump out of your mouth, you convulse and your bowels give out" (*Post-Dispatch,* 1988). He said safety was also a consideration because if a leak occurred during an execution, witnesses would be in danger of inhaling gas.

A bill to change the state's official method of execution from gas to lethal injection which included relocating executions to the state's new maximum security facility in Potosi, was approved by the Missouri legislature and signed by Governor John Ashcroft in 1988. Ashcroft said it would be a "safer and more humane way to carry out the orders of the court" (*Post-Dispatch,* 1988).

In Missouri, as elsewhere, when a person is sentenced to death, the case is automatically appealed to the Missouri Supreme Court. If the court upholds the conviction, the prisoner then appeals through the state court system, and then the case goes to the federal courts. The time this takes depends on each individual case. The average length of time in Missouri is more than ten years (Bryant, 1997).

EXECUTIONS IN MISSOURI

The pace of executions started to speed up again in 1989, and Missouri has executed thirty-five men since then, beginning with George C. "Tiny" Mercer, the first man executed in Missouri by lethal injection. In a journal interview (McGuire, 1996), Mercer's wife, who married him while he was in prison and who attended his execution, said the "bloodthirstiness" of the witnesses continues to haunt her.

Tiny Mercer, a former bike-ganger from Belton, Missoui, was convicted of raping and murdering Karen Ann Keeton, of Lake Lotawana, on August 31, 1978, Mercer's 34th birthday. Mercer reportedly said that members of his gang gave him 22-year-old Karen as a "present" that day. Before her death she was raped by three men, including Mercer, in his home. When it was over, Mercer straddled her and choked her to death. When told that Keeton was still alive and had a pulse Mercer began hitting her on the side of her head, yelling, "Die, you bitch, die." During this assault and murder, Mercer's 11-year-old daughter was in the house. Tiny later took Karen Keeton's body, which was not found for a month, and dumped it in a rural area of Johnson County, Kansas. When Mercer committed this murder he was free on bond for raping a 17-year-old.

Terry Ganey, Bureau Chief for the *St. Louis Post-Dispatch*, who was one of the official witnesses at Mercer's execution, reported that the first execution in Missouri in 24 years was carried out with swift, clinical precision (Ganey, 1989). Mercer, who wore a dark blue hooded sweatshirt and a black head band and was covered up to his neck with a white sheet, shook hands with the warden before he died and kept his eyes on his wife until, in Ganey's words, his eyes "stared lifelessly at the ceiling."

Since this was the first time the state had used its new lethal injection machine, the execution took place in the old gas chamber with the steel chair replaced by a gurney. Mercer was strapped to the table at 11:42 p.m. He had requested and been given a mild sedative. His execution began at 12:01 a.m. As Warden Delo points out in Stephen Trombley's documentary "The Execution Protocol," death warrants are dated and the earliest you can execute anyone on a given day is 12:01 a.m.

Two employees of the Missouri Department of Corrections (DOC) activated the machine designed to inject the lethal dose of the drugs Pavulon, sodium pentothal, and potassium chloride; and by 12:05 a.m. Mercer had lost consciousness. He was declared dead at 12:09 a.m. Nineteen people witnessed the execution, including Fred Leuchter, the inventor of the lethal injection machine who described himself at the time as an "expert in execution technology." Of Mercer's execution, Leuchter said it was an "interesting first," adding "to be happening in Mid-America, the Bible belt." Over the years Leuchter's technology has been called into question and some states have reported that condemned inmates have suffered excruciating pain during execution.

THE MISSOURI PROTOCOL

After Tiny Mercer's execution the Missouri Department of Corrections began working on what has become known as the *Missouri Protocol,* a set of written procedures for carrying out executions. This protocol is now used in many states that have lethal injection as the method of execution. According to Warden Paul Delo, his execution team has revised the protocol 13 times, constantly striving to perfect it, to become more efficient "as we age in the business of executing."

The *Missouri Protocol* choreographs the movements of the execution team in their dance of death. Its main purpose is to diffuse responsibility, so that no one person is dancing alone. It is ritualistic and purposeful—which can be seen, perhaps, in the explanation by one of the execution team about why a prison like Potosi (where the inmates are, for the most part, destined to be executed) is good for the local economy. Besides providing jobs, it is "non-consumptive and non-pollutive," he remarked.

The protocol itself begins 48 hours before an execution, when the execution team has what is called a mock-execution to make sure everyone knows what to do and to see that everything is working correctly. They even go so far as to strap someone about the same size as the inmate to be executed on the gurney.

On the actual day of an execution around 6:00 p.m. things start to get tense, according to Warden Delo. At 7:00 p.m., the inmate to be executed is given a sedative if he/she requests it. Although it is supposed to be optional, Doyle Williams, an inmate who has since been executed, said in Trombley's documentary that when he refused it the first time he was supposed to be executed, they insisted he needed it.

The tranquilizer they use, Versed, is 5 times as potent as Valium. A second dose is given an hour after the first, and then another 15 minutes before the execution. According to Warden Delo, they also give inmates antihistamines to prevent a reaction to the chemicals used in the execution.

At 8:00 p.m., four hours before the execution, the execution team reports and the Operations Office makes a ledger entry that reads, "All people are at their post." At this time assigned nurses bring the drugs from the pharmacy to the execution chambers, and an anesthesiologist fills the syringes in their proper sequence. One of the members of the Potosi execution team said in the documentary that the last thirty minutes are the most difficult for the team. That is when a person has to keep telling him/herself, this individual has killed someone and been convicted by the state. I am an instrument of the state — a mantra repeated over and over again. Thirty minutes before the execution, six officers bring the accused in and strap him/her to the gurney. A doctor then comes in and inserts a catheter and a rectal plug. The doctor, working with the anesthesiologist, also finds a vein and inserts the IV from which the lethal chemicals will flow.

In Missouri, the condemned is strapped on the gurney facing away from the windows where the witnesses are, so that in order to see the witnesses, the condemned person has to look back over his/her forehead. At 12:00 midnight an order is given to commence the execution. The warden then reads the death warrant to the condemned and asks, "Do you have anything to say?" If the condemned person wishes to say something he/she does. The warden then leaves, and the person is executed by three separate injections. After the inmate is pronounced dead, a member of the team takes his fingerprints to make sure no mistake was made and to close the person's FBI files. An order to "stand down" is given and everyone goes home.

Mercer had been on death row for more than nine years and was the first of 70 inmates on Missouri's death row to have exhausted all his appeals. One woman, Virginia Twenter, was among Missouri's walking dead at the time.

In Stephen Trombley's documentary, the inmates at Potosi tell how they were affected by this execution. During the actual execution the DOC played "girlie movies" on the televisions to distract the inmates. But, according to the inmates, no one was distracted. Tiny Mercer's execution was a wake-up call for everyone — they said it was a sign that it was happening and it could happen to you.

Governor John Ashcroft turned down requests that he delay Mercer's execution or commute his sentence to life, saying, "After more than 10 years of judicial proceedings, all the available evidence shows that the judicial process has functioned properly (in this case). Accordingly, I do not intend to interfere with that process" (Mosley & Ganey, 1989). When Mercer's execution was over, Governor Ashcroft said, "This painful event is necessary to reaffirm the value the state of Missouri places on innocent human life."

Although Missouri's first execution by lethal injection was, in Warden Delo's words, a "good one" not all executions by lethal injection in Missouri have been. On May 3, 1995, Emmitt Foster was strapped to the gurney at Potosi to be executed by lethal injection and ten minutes into the execution a worker closed the blinds of the windows of the execution chamber. They did not open them for approximately 20 minutes. Witnesses could not see what was going on at the time and ultimately one witness refused to sign the statement that she had witnessed the execution. Foster was not pronounced dead until 30 minutes after the executioner began the flow of chemicals into his arm. According to the coroner, the heart monitor attached to Foster had been showing a "dying heartbeat," but it seemed to be taking a long time, so he entered the chamber to see what was happening. The problem seemed to be that the leather strap that bound Foster to the execution gurney was too tight to let the flow of chemicals into his veins. Several minutes after a prison worker loosened the straps, Foster was pronounced dead.

LEGAL REPRESENTATION IN MISSOURI

The Federal Anti-terrorism and Effective Death Penalty Act (1996) limited *habeas corpus* appeals. In a *habeas* the court is asked to overturn a conviction and sentence because certain constitutional rights have not been upheld, such as a person's right to effective counsel. For death row inmates the time limit is now a year. If a state can show that it is providing competent legal representation to death row inmates, the delay can be as short as six months.

Missouri's plan, approved by the state Supreme Court in 1997, allows a lawyer with three years' experience to handle a death-penalty appeal, if the lawyer has worked on at least five appeals of felony convictions. The plan states that lawyers should get "reasonable" compensation from the public defenders office. Sean O'Brien, executive director of the Public Interest Litigation Clinic, a not-for-profit law firm in Kansas City, said the money amounts to between $5,000 and $10,000, which is simply not enough.

Attorney General Jay Nixon has said that he believes Missouri has plenty of competent lawyers and that the state is interested in good defense counsel, since a poor defense leads to more appeals. He said he is not interested in cases where prisoners can get appeals by showing that their court-appointed lawyers or the public defenders were ineffective.

In a related incident, the criminal law committee of the Missouri Bar passed a resolution in May 1997 asking Governor Mel Carnahan to halt the use of the death penalty until procedural changes can be made that will ensure fairness in sentencing (Bradford, 1997). Elizabeth Unger Carlyle of the Missouri Bar said, "The steps are in place, but there are a lot of questions about whether they are functioning." Once a case is heard and appealed, according to Carlyle, a person who is sentenced to death should have the opportunity to say, "This is what went wrong with my case." The resolution stated that several studies have shown evidence of racial bias in Missouri's death penalty practices. It was felt that attorneys should spend more time trying to uncover racial biases among potential jurors.

There are currently seventeen lawyers — nine in St. Louis — at the Missouri Public Defender's Capital Litigation Division, commonly referred to as the "death squad." They work long hours for modest pay and are the least popular members of the Missouri criminal justice system. They range in age from early thirties to mid forties and work out of three offices, one in St. Louis, one in

Columbia, MO, and one in Kansas City. There are also nine "mitigation assistants" and a small support staff that is kept busy preparing defendants' life histories. In 1995 the Public Defenders Office completed 68 death penalty cases; and in 1996, they completed 54. Each attorney usually works on at least five death penalty cases at once, averaging 12–14-hour workdays. They are the ones who handle cases no one else will take. Karen Kraft, the division director, says lawyers stay with them for about three or four years. The emotional stress in capital cases is intense and, according to Kraft, "some do better than others."

Two lawyers are assigned to each death penalty case. One lawyer usually handles the guilt phase and the other the penalty phase. In the guilt phase, the defense is often put in the position of proving that a murder wasn't pre-meditated, because many defendants on their own have already made multiple confessions or there have been witnesses to the murder. Part of the annual $2 million budget is spent on expert witnesses that fall into two categories: experts on scientific evidence, or psychiatrists and psychologists. Experts on scientific evidence are used to rebut the prosecution's evidence, and psychiatrists and psychologists are used to profile the backgrounds of the accused.

If the defense loses its case and the client is given the death penalty, then the case moves to the appellate stage, where it is automatically appealed to the Missouri Supreme Court. In the appellate stage, it is very likely that the lawyers who first handled the case will be accused of being incompetent, because the appellate team will need to fuel their case for an appeal, and incompetent counsel is excellent grounds.

According to an article in the *St. Louis Post-Dispatch* (Lhotka, 1997), only a handful of private practitioners still take death penalty cases in the St. Louis area, and few people on death row can afford their services. The people who can afford their services usually pay anywhere from $50,000 to $150,000 in legal fees, which include hiring experts and private investigators as well as taking sworn statements and spending numerous hours in preparation and trial time.

Reverend Larry Rice of the New Life Evangelistic Center in St. Louis held a press conference in March 1996 in which he called Governor Mel Carnahan and the Missouri Attorney General Jay Nixon "the biggest premeditated murderers in the world" (Lindecke, 1996). He accused them of indiscriminate use of the death penalty against the poor, the retarded, those without adequate defense, and those who are victims of false testimonies. Although Rice acknowledged that in the polls Missourians consistently favor the death penalty, he said the public is not adequately informed.

In 1997 Missouri executed four men — each a week apart. According to Attorney General Jay Nixon all four men had been on death row for more than ten years and had exhausted their appeals. So far, in 1998, Missouri has executed three. The minimum age for the death penalty in Missouri is 16.

ORGAN DONATION IN MISSOURI

In 1998 a bill was proposed in the Missouri legislature that would allow condemned prisoners to trade organs for transplant in exchange for life sentences. The bill would require prospective donors to take physicals and agree to donate a kidney or bone marrow upon request and to give up the right to appeal their convictions. The measure, called "Life for a Life," is being hotly debated. Opponents say it violates medical ethics, while proponents say the inmates would be giving something back to the community.

Dr. Jeffrey Lowell of Washington University in St. Louis said the measure violates the concept that transplant donations should be voluntary acts. He said the bill amounts to coercion. "Organ donation must be a purely altruistic gift and organ donors are heroes" (*St. Louis Post-Dispatch*, 1998).

WOMEN SENTENCED TO DEATH IN MISSOURI

1988

Nila Wacaser: White; Reversed; Committed suicide awaiting sentencing. In January 1989, Nila Jeanne Wacaser, at the age of 40, became the first woman condemned to death in Missouri after the state reinstated capital punishment in 1977. After the court ordered her to give her two sons to her first husband in a custody battle, she took them to a motel in Platte County, north of Kansas City, and stabbed them to death. Jeremy, the eldest, was 11 and was stabbed a total of 39 times. Eric, his brother, who was 8, was stabbed 15 times. After admitting she killed her sons, Nila said her former husband would not be able to "take anything else from me."

Nila was only tried for the murder of her youngest son, Eric. Her public defender, Dan Miller, said the trial was as much about the life of Nila Wacaser as it was about the death of her son. He said she was in a "disassociative state" at the time of the murders — a state of unreality brought on by stress. He said the police had found Nila "dazed and confused" when they tried to question her the night of the slayings.

There was some discussion after her arrest about where she would be held if she was sentenced to death, since the Missouri State Penitentiary, where the 59 condemned men were held at the time, was not set up to house a woman. Warden Bill Armontrout said it would have been difficult to find a place for her at the prison because there would have been a lot of "management problems," such as "recreation, showers, lots of privacy-type things." Ultimately Nila was sent to Fulton, where other high-risk women prisoners were held.

Circuit Judge John M. Yeaman gave Nila Wacaser the death penalty because the seated jury was unable to agree on a sentence after her conviction. The judge said that the murder of her son Eric was "outrageously or wantonly vile, horrible and inhuman." George Wacaser, her husband at the time, told the jury he loved his wife "more than anything" and sobbed after she was sentenced.

Defense Attorney Susan Chapman told the jury that Nila had had a disruptive childhood, but did not abuse alcohol or drugs and had strong religious convictions. She had been a model prisoner, and had no criminal record before her arrest.

Her conviction for Eric's death was ultimately overturned because of a legal question about a prospective juror. The Missouri Supreme Court reversed the first-degree murder conviction and death sentence in a 5–2 decision, saying the judge in Nila's trial should have removed a juror because his answers indicated he might be prejudiced. In response to a defense attorney's question, the juror said he could be fair on the question of guilt or innocence, but that he was "not sure about" the matter of punishment. The man said he would "lean toward the death penalty" since the case involved a child's murder. The trial judge should have honored the defense lawyer's request that the juror be removed, the Supreme Court ruled. With that decision, the court ordered a new trial for Nila.

In a second trial for the death of her son Jeremy, she was again convicted of capital murder. Her attorney argued unsuccessfully for mitigating circumstances based on the fact that she was using the drug Halcion, which had been identified as a factor in a number of otherwise inexplicable homicides in the U.S. The morning the jury was to deliberate the penalty phase (death, or life without possibility of parole) — a Saturday morning, May 9 — Nila was found dead in her cell, an apparent suicide.

Her attorneys were devastated when they were told she was dead the morning they went to argue her case at the courthouse. They had invested over 2,000 hours of pro bono work on her case. Her death was an embarrassment to the court. Ultimately, she had the last word. The jurors told the judge that they planned to return a sentence of life without possibility of parole. Nila had said she did not remember killing her children.

1989

Virginia Twenter: White; Reversed in 1991. Virginia Twenter, a woman from Sedalia, Missouri was sentenced to death by a Circuit Judge Donald Barnes. The jury recommended death for Virginia for the murder of her stepmother, Marilyn K. Wells, who was shot once in the chest. She was sentenced to life without parole in the shooting death of her father, John D. Wells. Prosecutors charged that after shooting her father twice in the back in a dispute over money, Virginia took her stepmother to a field about eight miles away from their Missouri home and shot her too.

Judge Donald Barnes denied a motion for a new trial and rejected Virginia's contention that she had poor legal counsel saying no death row inmates feel their representation is adequate.

On January 10, 1989, three days after Virginia was sentenced to death the superintendent of the Fulton Diagnostic Center where she was held reported that she had apparently attempted to commit suicide. He said that since inmates are expected to keep their living quarters clean, they have access to cleaning fluids and Virginia had apparently swallowed an unknown substance that made her ill.

In September, 1990, Circuit Judge, Judge Kenton Askren of Cooper County ruled that Virginia should be given another trial. According to the judge the state's case against her was built largely on circumstantial evidence tied to the fact that Virginia needed money to pay her bills. The fact that she cashed thousands of dollars in checks drawn on her parent's bank account the day after the murders was used as evidence.

Judge Askren ruled that Virginia's attorneys failed to interview key witnesses who might have established an alibi for her and cast doubt on the state's case. He also held that her attorneys did not hire experts to analyze the evidence, a pair of tennis shoes and bloody footprints, that was used to link Virginia to the crime. Virginia consistently denied any involvement in the incidents.

Judge Askren ultimately said that Virginia had been treated poorly by the public defender because she did not have money to hire her own attorney and that the public defenders office had not even prepared for the penalty phase of her trial. The judge wrote that because Virginia looked to the state to provide effective representation what she received in actual fact, was a general air of disinterest.

From death row, Virginia expressed bitterness about sitting on death row for two years for something she did not do and for not being allowed to see her children during that time (Young, 1990).

The lawyers who represented Virginia originally said they felt "satisfied" with what they had done in the six-day trial. One lawyer said he had asked for $1,200 to hire experts to evaluate the footprints but that the court and the public defenders office had refused to pay for the request.

The public defender in 1990 said "I don't know if she's guilty or not, but I do know she didn't get a fair trial and she's entitled to that."

In September 1991, the Missouri Supreme Court upheld Virginia Twenters two convictions for first-degree murder, but set aside her death sentence. She is currently incarcerated in Missouri.

1991

Faye Copeland: White; Currently on death row. In 1991, Faye Copeland and her husband, Ray were accused and convicted of murdering five farmhands who had worked for them in the 1980s. According to prosecutors in the case, the Copelands had their victims buy cattle for them using bad checks, and then they resold them for a profit. They promised $50 a day plus room and board to drifters willing to open checking accounts in their own names to buy cattle at livestock auctions. It was assumed the men were then killed to cover up the scheme. Part of the evidence brought against Faye was that she had apparently marked the names of each victim in the farm's record books with an "X." It was estimated the Copelands pocketed $32,000 in cash from 1986 to 1989 reselling cattle.

The victims' bodies were found buried in Livingston County in northwestern Missouri. The first three in a barn twelve miles south of the Copeland farm, a fourth body in another barn, and a fifth body was found at the bottom of a 28-foot-deep well, weighted with a cement block. Each victim had a bullet in the head. The Assistant Attorney General, at the time, Kenny C. Hulshof said, "There has never been a more callous disregard for human life." At Faye's trial her attorney presented a motion asking that Judge Richard Webber disqualify himself from the case alleging that the judge was predisposed to the death penalty and that he had had dinner with the sequestered jury during the trial. However, the judge stayed. On November 13, 1990 a jury recommended that Faye, 69 at the time, be sentenced to death for participating in the murders. Prosecutor Doug Roberts said Faye had "aided, abetted and profited from the deaths of five innocent men."

In January, 1991, before Ray's trial began, prosecuting Attorney Doug Roberts announced that they had reached an agreement with Ray Copeland that he would plead guilty, and accept a life sentence without parole on the condition that a death sentence for his wife be waived. Judge E. Richard Webber, who would sentence Faye, refused to accept the deal. To emphasize his displeasure, he threw the Prosecuting Attorney, Doug Roberts, off the case and ordered the Attorney general's office to prosecute instead.

Ken Hulshof, the Assistant Attorney General who prosecuted Faye, said he had a conflict because although he was bound to uphold the plea-bargain the prosecutor had made, the jury's verdict against Faye would force him to seek the death penalty for her husband. At the same time the defense again motioned for Webber to disqualify himself from the case since his actions seemed to indicate that "the court had a predisposition in this case," based on his refusal, and the fact that Judge Webber had also presided over the trial of Faye Copeland.

The Missouri Court of Appeals denied the defense motion to disqualify Webber in a one-page order. Webber told reporters later that "Plea-bargaining is inappropriate in some cases" and, he said that in any case, he would sentence Faye Copeland to death (Poor, 1991). There was a lot of discussion at the time about how the death penalty, which usually takes anywhere form eight to ten years to carry out could possibly serve justice in the case of a 69-year-old woman and a 76-year-old man.

In a 1991 interview (Smith, 1991) at the Fulton State Hospital before his trial, Ray Copeland, looking frail and weak said he and his wife were innocent. Of the whole ordeal, Ray said "I never killed anybody in my life . . . me and my wife lived together for 50 years. We never killed nobody, we never hurt nobody and we never talked about hurting nobody." He said there were no witnesses that saw him shoot anybody or bury anybody and they were being accused of the murders because some of the victims had left personal belongings at their farm and because they found a list in the house with the victims names on it. Copeland said he had seen somebody dump a body in the well and had told the police about it. As for the guy who had testified at his wife's trial that he had threatened him with a gun, Copeland said it was a lie.

Ray Copeland was sent to the Fulton State Hospital to see if he was competent to stand trial, which the judge said he was. In the interview Copeland said he'd worked hard all his life, often getting up at 4:30 a.m. to milk the cows and he'd sent the farmhands to buy cattle for him because he was hard of hearing and couldn't always hear the bids at the auction. He said that being accused of the murders and incarcerated as he was was "The worst thing that could ever happen to anybody." He said, "I'm not going to be able to hold up much longer ... I feel like I'm going to completely lose my mind."

It took eleven days to select a jury for Ray Copeland's trial. Once it got underway two men who had worked for Copeland told of obtaining post office boxes and opening checking accounts with $200 provided by Copeland. One man said that Copeland had told him to buy a carload of cattle, but because of the small amount of money Copeland gave him, he only bought two or three which made Copeland mad and Copeland threatened him with a gun. Some of the victims' family members also testified.

The trial lasted for ten days. The jury deliberated for 2½ hours. Ray Copeland showed no emotion as the judge asked jurors to confirm the guilty verdict on each of five charges. Hulshof, the assistant state attorney general said afterwards, the jury came through and gave them what they wanted.

The estimated cost of the two trials was $200,000. This included transportation, motels and meals for jurors because they came from a distance plus $400 a month in medical costs for the couple. There were also trial transcripts, bringing in out-of-state witnesses, and public defender costs. Juries in both cases recommended that the Copelands be put to death.

Later, when Judge Webber read his sentence Ray Copeland wiped his eyes with a handkerchief and cupped his hand over his ear to better hear what the judge, who was only about 3 feet away from him, was saying. He shook the judge's hand before being led from the courtroom.

Although the jury found Faye guilty in November 1990, Judge E. Richard Webber did not impose the sentence of death until five months later, in April 1991, after her husband's trial was over. After hearing motions for a new trial or a lighter sentence, Judge Webber sentenced Faye to death in the Livingston County Circuit Court on four counts of first-degree murder and life without parole on a fifth count. At the hearing, Faye testified "I am not guilty of these charges, and I want you to know it." She cried when Webber pronounced her sentence. Ray Copeland died of a stroke at age 78 in prison, awaiting execution at Potosi Correctional Center.

In 1994, attorney Cheryl Rafert sought a new trial for Faye on the grounds that she had suffered years of abuse from her husband. Psychologist Lenore Walker, who is responsible for the concept of the "battered spouse syndrome," testified at a hearing on Faye's behalf at Boone County Circuit Court, saying that among other abuses, her husband had "thrown her halfway across the room." Faye herself testified that she had been pushed, shoved, slapped, kicked, and beaten on numerous occasions by her husband and that her husband had also forced her to have sex with some of the transient men while he watched.

The couple's daughter described a childhood of wearing "hand-me-down clothes" and a stern father who always got his way at home. "From the time I was little, you did as you were told, and that was it," she testified. She said she had never seen her father physically abuse her mother, but recalled "He would say things like 'shut up' and 'you're stupid.' "

A daughter-in-law, when asked if Ray Copeland had ever physically abused his wife said "He'd tell her to hush up and be quiet," but she testified she'd never seen Copeland physically abuse his wife.

In August 1996, Faye's claim of abuse was rejected. The Missouri Supreme Court said the battered woman syndrome could only be used to support a claim of mental illness and that Copeland's attorney had made it clear it wasn't being used for that purpose.

In a newspaper interview Faye blamed her husband for the murders. She said, "He has done me great damage. I begged him time and time again to please stay out of trouble. We had our home and everything paid for. So, why would he turn around and mess all that up just like he has?"

In 1996 Faye filed a request for the U.S. Supreme Court to hear her case. Her attorney, Janet Thompson of Columbia asked the court to hear the case hoping to get a new trial, after an execution date of January 3, 1997 was set. Three issues were raised in Faye's petition, the battered woman's syndrome, the courts refusal to accept her husband's plea bargain, and the fact that the Missouri Supreme Court did not review the case to see whether her sentence was proportional to the crime as the law requires. By filing this petition, Faye's execution date was automatically stayed.

The Supreme Court refused, without comment, to hear Copeland's appeal of the Missouri Supreme Court's ruling upholding her 1990 conviction. Sean O'Brien her attorney said he would file an appeal in federal court and continue seeking a new trial for having her conviction set aside.

Faye Copeland, now 80, spends her days at the Chillicothe state prison for women. "She reminds me of my grandmother," her lawyer says. Her attorneys say Faye deserves a new trial, largely because she was not allowed to present battered spouse syndrome as a defense at her trial in 1990.

1991

Maria Isa: Brazilian; Reversed in 1993. In December, 1991 Maria Isa and her husband of 30 years, Zein, were given the death penalty for the murder of their youngest daughter Tina, a high school honor student whom they named Palestina in honor of her father's homeland, Palestine. On gruesome tapes recorded secretly by the FBI, Zein's voice can be heard in Arabic saying, "Die quickly, my daughter, die" as he stabs his daughter while his wife, the prosecution contended, held her down.

The FBI had begun monitoring the "St. Louis cell" of the Abu Nidal, a terrorist group, in late 1986 by taping the happenings in the Isa apartment. The followers of this fanatical Palestinian group were responsible for more than 90 attacks in 20 countries since their formation in 1974. The stated purpose of the organization was to kill Jews anywhere and everywhere, an FBI agent said. A 1993 indictment specifically accused Zein Isa and three other men of planning terrorism, conspiring to kill Jews and discussing blowing up the Israeli Embassy in Washington, DC. The FBI suspected that 16 year-old Tina was killed to keep her from revealing the connection her parents had with the Abu Nidal terrorists.

In 1990 Senior U.S. District Judge John F. Nangle ruled that the electronic bugs at the Isas' apartment, at 3750 Delor Street, were lawfully authorized by the Foreign Intelligence Surveillance Act. So, it was these FBI tapes of the stabbing of Tina Isa on November 6, 1989 that were the state's main evidence in convicting Zein and Maria of the first-degree murder of their daughter.

"Where were you, bitch?" were the first words those in the courtroom heard translated from the FBI tapes, as Tina returns home from her first night working at Wendy's. These words, supposedly hissed at Tina by her mother, Maria, on November 6, 1989, were the state's most damning evidence against Maria Isa.

Maria's attorney objected to the use of the tapes, which were given to the prosecutors soon after the stabbing, indicating that jurors had reacted emotionally to the sounds since at least two jurors wept while it was being played. Although screaming, gasping, and moaning from the dying daughter could all be heard (Bryant, 1993), it was doubtful that an audio tape could prove or show in any way that Maria had held her daughter down so her husband could kill her.

Nevertheless, the chief counsel for the attorney general's office said that the tapes indeed clarified Maria's role in the murders and that she had "held the victim around the neck from behind for some seven minutes while she was being stabbed to death" (Young, 1993). This idea, apparently deduced by the prosecutor from the audio-tape, stuck in everyone's mind. Nothing could be more horrendous than the image of a mother holding her dying daughter so a father can stab her to death.

The prosecutor also contended that the tapes proved Maria Isa had fabricated a story with her husband after the murder of their daughter about it being in self-defense when she (Tina) had pulled a knife on her father and demanded $5,000. Since there were 700 reels of tape in Arabic that had to be translated, one can imagine a lot was lost in the translation. However, playing the tapes aloud coupled with the prosecutors' interpretation was enough to send chills through every decent human being present that day. Despite all this, Maria's attorney felt that the greatest travesty to justice was that the Isas were tried together and Maria's fate depended entirely on what happened to her husband.

It should be noted too, that although the FBI tapes were used to prosecute Zein and Maria Isa, none of the attorneys knew why the tapes were made in the first place. This was only revealed in 1993 when the FBI handed down its indictments for international terrorism on Zein Isa and his fellow Palestinians, a full two years after the Isas had been sentenced to die.

Of the FBI revelations Assistant Circuit Attorney Robert Craddick said, "The tapes we had indicated a family conflict. We didn't have any evidence what they were being bugged for" (Bryant, 1993). Prosecutors were only given the tapes they needed to try the Isas for murdering Tina. Lawyer Daniel P. Reardon said, "I just thought the FBI was eavesdropping on Palestinians" and admitted being stunned that the FBI might think killing Tina Isa was part of a terrorist plot.

Once FBI motives were known, agents said that family problems were among the reasons Tina was killed, but additional evidence indicated that her death was to silence her. She had turned her back on Palestinian ways and had become too Americanized which was a threat to their terrorist activities. The FBI said they recorded two conversations in which plans to kill Tina were discussed. Since the FBI were not monitoring the tapes daily, they said they were not aware of the plot to kill Tina until later and thus were unable to prevent it, which one of the Isas' other daughters later contested.

Trial testimony shows that Tina had an unhappy home life. Her sisters were always criticizing her and considered her disrespectful of their father's authority. Tina's relationship with a black youth, whom her father had offered $5,000 to marry her, was also discussed at the trial. According to Maria Isa's attorney she was completely controlled by her husband as is customary in his culture, and thus had no foreseeable way to act differently than she had. Attorneys also felt that Zein was goaded to kill his youngest daughter by the bitter criticisms of her older sisters recorded in phone conversations to their father.

According to Ellen Harris, author of *Guarding the Secrets: Palestinian Terrorism and a Father's Murder of his Too-American Daughter*, Tina's father was a small-time operative in the Abu Nidal movement. He was used as a messenger, carrying money from one country to another and as a money-launderer through his small grocery store. He resented not being trusted to do more in the organization. Talking with representatives of Palestinian organizations in Israel Harris found that the family had been involved in such things as food stamp fraud, grocery coupon fraud, and other such activities to raise money for the organization (Pollack, 1995). Harris also said that in much of the Palestinian world wives and daughters are subservient to husbands and fathers and appearance is everything. In light of this, Tina's Americanized behavior was unacceptable. Harris said that in the Palestinian culture a man may punish, even kill, a female relative for disobeying or disgracing the family. Such a killing is called an "honor killing."

The jury needed only four hours to deliberate before reaching their verdict. Both parents were found guilty and the death penalty was recommended. Neither Maria nor Zein showed emotion as translators relayed the jury's verdict to them in their native languages. One of Tina's older sisters said her parents did not get a fair trial because her father is Palestinian.

Judge Charles A. Shaw rejected the notion that culture played any part in Maria's guilt saying, "This is a country of laws, not men. The court does not believe culture can be used as an excuse for murder. The rule of law is the thread that binds this country together" (Bryant, 1991).

Zein, a native Palestinian, was a naturalized U.S. citizen and operated a small grocery store in the Dutchtown South neighborhood of St. Louis. Ultimately people were shocked to find a Palestinian Terrorist Organization committed to the elimination of Jews, being monitored by the FBI and operating out of a neighborhood in St. Louis.

Before the judge pronounced her sentence Maria Isa said through an interpreter that she and her husband Zein should not be punished. When she left the courtroom she waved and blew kisses to her surviving daughters. One daughter, said her parents trial was unfair and that her father had acted to "defend his honor" (Bryant, 1991).

In 1993, the Missouri Supreme Court reversed Maria Isa's death sentence while upholding her guilty verdict. The court ruled that the jury had received flawed instructions that linked Maria Isa's punishment to the actions of her husband. This ruling sent the case back to the St. Louis Circuit Court for a new sentencing phase. In testifying at her re-sentencing trial, Maria Isa, then 53, tearfully told a jury that she remembered little of the night her husband murdered her daughter eight years ago. She said she touched her daughter with love that night and had nothing in her heart against her. She said she remembered trying to pull Tina away from her father. Speaking in her native Portuguese Maria said that she had no idea her husband was going to kill her daughter and that she had tried to separate the two of them.

Attorney Robert Craddick told jurors that actually Zein Isa had attacked his daughter with a knife and his wife had wrestled her to the floor and held her there. Again reiterating the idea that this was somehow indicated on the audiotapes, he emphasized that Tina had cried out three times on the tapes for her mother's help and her mother had responded by telling her to shut up.

The jury of seven men and five women returned a recommendation of life without parole. The Isas have three other daughters. A son-in-law said, "This family has hurt so much already. She is a victim of her husband and the society here. I'm sure she hurts as much as anyone" (O'Neil, 1997). Zein Isa, in poor health, died while on death row awaiting execution.

Defense attorney Charles Shaw indicated that he might at some point appeal Maria's conviction. He has always contended that Maria is also a victim. "I don't think she is guilty of anything," Shaw said, "She was reduced from being a woman to being a beast of burden. She didn't stab anybody, she didn't help stab anybody" (Bryant, 1997).

1992

Shirley Jo Phillips: White; Overturned, 1997. Shirley Jo Phillips aka Jo Ann Phillips was 55 and living in Springfield, Missouri when she was arrested for forging a check for $4,000 on Wilma Plaster's bank account. She was then charged with the first-degree murder of Wilma whose body was found on a rural road in October of 1989.

Wilma Plaster, who was sixty-six, was the wife of an elderly minister. Her dismembered body was found on October 6 by the side of a busy farm road in rural Greene County. She had been shot in the head. Her body, was cut in four sections, beheaded, and wrapped in several plastic bags where it was dumped near Willard in southwestern Missouri. A kitchen knife and garden shears were found with the body, but her arms were never found.

Wilma was last seen alive on October 3rd. Her car was discovered in a motel parking lot in northern Springfield, Missouri. Both Shirley and Wilma were country music groupies and had spent time together in a bar the night Wilma Plaster was murdered. Prosecutor's believed Shirley tried to rob Wilma and then killed her. Autopsy reports showed she died of a gunshot wound to the back of the head.

Shirley was convicted and sentenced to death in February 1992 by a Jasper County jury and was the fourth woman on Missouri's death row at the time. Shirley professed her innocence to Circuit Judge Don Bonacker before she was sentenced and led handcuffed from the courtroom.

Because the state, despite numerous requests, withheld exculpatory evidence, the state Supreme Court ordered a new penalty phase trial for Shirley Jo Phillips at age 60, in 1997 (ACLU Abolitionist, April 1997). The evidence excluded was an audiotape given by a witness who said Phillips' son told her that he and his mother killed Plaster but that he dismembered her. Shirley Phillips was sentenced to life in 1997.

20

Nevada: Lethal Injection

The state of Nevada has sentenced two women to death since 1900, neither of these was executed and one woman is on death row in Nevada today.

In 1890, a woman, Elizabeth Potts was hanged with her husband on a double gallows in Elko, Nevada for murdering and dismembering Miles Faucett in Carlin, Nevada. Beginning in 1903, hangings were carried out at the Nevada state prison. Ten men were hanged between 1903 and 1912, including four in one day in 1905 using a double gallows. Then in 1913 the state of Nevada came up with a new execution device that was only used once to execute Andriza Mircovich. It was an automated firing squad that consisted of three rifles mounted on an iron frame that fired simultaneously.

In 1924 Nevada started using the gas chamber, and thirty-two men were executed by gas. Although Nevada now uses lethal injection, the old gas chamber at the Nevada state prison is still used as the execution room. Nevada has executed six inmates since the death penalty was reinstated in 1977. The latest execution, Richard Allen Moran, took place on March 30, 1996.

THE DEATH PENALTY IN NEVADA

As one of ten non-jury-sentencing states Nevada has a unique system for capital conviction. If the jury cannot unanimously find at least one aggravating circumstance, or cannot unanimously agree to a death sentence, the decision passes to a three-judge panel. The panel can only impose a death sentence if it unanimously finds at least one aggravating circumstance and unanimously agrees to impose a sentence of death. If these criteria cannot be met the sentence defaults to life in prison.

In Nevada when someone is sentenced to die, the first appeal is to the state Supreme Court. A second round of appeals to test the quality of legal representation follows this. The case goes first to the district court and then back to the Supreme Court if the death penalty is upheld. If it is upheld it moves to the federal system.

LEGAL REPRESENTATION IN NEVADA

There is a policy in the state Nevada of not paying lawyers in death penalty litigation until a case is finished at the state level. This greatly reduces the number of lawyers willing to take on appeals. Nevada state law sets aside $750 for legal fees for appeals. Any additional cost is considered excessive and lawyers must ask the court to be paid.

One Reno attorney said the amount set by the court is minimal. He said he finds himself in a process that is set up to ensure he will not get paid for up to three years and he does not have the personal financial resources to work that way.

Assistant Public Defender Michael Pescetta has said that one result of such a system is that "Lawyers who are trying to do good work" are deterred from taking death penalty cases (*Reno Gazette-Journal*, 1997), which lowers the quality of state post-conviction proceedings.

In September 1996, Roberto Miranda was released from Nevada's death row where he had been under sentence of death for 14 years. A Cuban national, Miranda was sentenced to death for the murder of Manuel Rodriguez Torres. He always maintained he was innocent and that the main prosecution witness against him had committed perjury because he was having an affair with the girlfriend of the witness.

The attorneys who represented Miranda in his appeals process located the girlfriend and other witnesses his original lawyer had failed to find. He was granted a new trial on appeal and the case was dismissed after the prosecution refused to pursue it further.

WOMEN SENTENCED TO DEATH IN NEVADA

1982
Priscilla Ford: Black; Currently on death row. Priscilla Ford or "Miss Priscilla" as she is affectionately referred to in prison, was born in 1929 in Berrien Springs, Michigan and grew up in a family of nine girls and two boys. She and her siblings were raised in the Seventh-Day Adventist Church where her parents were devout members. She had two sons by her first marriage and after a divorce she remarried and had one daughter whom she named Wynter.

Priscilla earned both a degree and a teaching certificate and taught school in Cass County, Michigan, from 1957 to 1964. She also ran successfully for a position on the Board of Trustees of a local junior college. People there remembered her as a very pleasant person and a good teacher. An incident in

1957 between Priscilla and her husband ended in both of them suffering gunshot wounds. Investigating police in Niles, Michigan said they thought Priscilla wounded her husband and then shot herself, but charges were never filed.

Around 1966, Priscilla left Michigan with Wynter and for a number of years drifted around the country, never staying long in any one place or state. She supported Wynter and herself by working at a number of low-paying, unskilled jobs and by 1971 was using marijuana heavily. During that time she felt she was receiving revelations from Ellen G. White, a Seventh-Day Adventist prophet from the previous century. It was then that she began calling herself Reverend Dr. Priscilla Ford.

On one occasion, she and Wynter spent time with her son Frank, and in 1972 she went to Miami thinking she had been invited to the Republican Convention to speak on White's prophecies. When she got there, however, the security officers threw her out of the convention center. By this time her letters to friends were beginning to sound like endless ramblings.

In 1973 Priscilla moved to Reno where she had a few minor scrapes with the law that resulted in Wynter being taken away from her more than once. One of her jobs during this time was as a cook at a rest home. She exchanged this for room and board. She was eventually fired from this job and arrested when she returned and tried to physically assault the owner.

After the attempted assault, Wynter was taken away from her again and the authorities refused to return her until Priscilla proved she could support her by getting a job. This made Priscilla angry and she wrote a letter to Nevada authorities saying she would murder the caseworker if Wynter was not returned to her immediately. After that letter, the welfare people never heard from Priscilla again and she never tried to contact her daughter until 1980 when she wrote her a letter and asked her how she was doing. When her mother finally contacted her, Wynter was living with one of her half-brothers in Los Angeles.

Priscilla went to Boise, Idaho in 1978 again as the Reverend Dr. Priscilla Ford. In Idaho she launched a lawsuit against the Mormon Church and the Secretary of the Department of Health, Education and Welfare demanding $500 million in damages for having suffered mental distress at the loss of her daughter.

In Buffalo, NY, there were eight charges against Priscilla in 1979 for bad checks and possession of marijuana, and in Buffalo she was first diagnosed as a paranoid schizophrenic.

In 1980 Priscilla showed up in Jackman, Maine, a small town of about 900 people near the Canadian border. No one knew why she was there, since it is a town frequented mostly by hunters and fishermen. The reason she gave for being there was that she was a writer. The owner of one of the motels she stayed in remembered her as being depressed and spending most of her time in her room writing. She confided in some of the town women that her daughter had been kidnapped. Then she suddenly moved to Bangor, Maine. In Bangor she allowed one woman to read a manuscript she had of 200–300 pages which seemed to be her autobiography. In Maine, Priscilla again tried to bring civil and criminal suits against the people she said kidnapped her daughter seven years before. At one point she threatened to drive her car from Jackman to Portland and run over everyone on the road if she didn't get some action.

After that, Priscilla left Maine and returned to Reno, where a man let her have an apartment he was remodeling rent-free when she told him she was living in her car.

She got a job at Macy's in Reno as a gift wrapper for a couple of weeks. People who worked with her there said she was pleasant and told them she was a retired teacher and writer. She also told them her daughter had been kidnapped in 1973 and that she had returned to Reno to try to find her.

On Thanksgiving Day, 1980, around 3:00 p.m., Priscilla drove her blue Lincoln Continental at approximately 50 m.p.h. onto a crowded sidewalk in downtown Reno for two blocks, killing six people and injuring 23. According to eyewitnesses, bodies were everywhere and the scene resembled a battlefield. Priscilla was arrested at the site without incident. She reportedly told investigators that she deliberately planned to get as many people as possible — the more dead the better."I deserve vengeance...Vengeance is mine," she said. She also told the police she was upset because the welfare people had taken her daughter away from her in 1973 and placed her in a juvenile facility.

After her arrest Priscilla was taken to the Lakes Crossing mental hospital for prison inmates. She was certified as competent to stand trial by three psychiatrists. There the doctors prescribed anti-psychotic drugs for her and said she needed to take them to stay competent during her trial (Ryan, 1998).

Priscilla was tried in 1981 on six counts of murder and 23 counts of attempted murder. Her trial, the longest in Nevada history, lasted six months. Her lawyer entered a plea of not guilty by reason of insanity. Three psychiatrists testified that Priscilla was a paranoid schizophrenic with delusions and that she didn't know it was wrong to kill at the time of the murders. A psychiatrist for the state said she did know it was wrong and still maintains his opinion today.

Priscilla took the stand on her own behalf and claimed she had no memory of running anyone down with her car. She was adamant that her doctors were wrong and that she was not mentally ill. After 13 hours, the jury found her guilty on all counts. She was condemned to death during the penalty phase of her trial after five days of deliberation. Upon hearing the verdict she said she wanted to be left alone to die in peace and tried to give up her automatic appeal to the Nevada Supreme Court.

In April 1986 when the state Supreme Court considered her case they upheld her death sentence saying, in essence, that despite Priscilla's weird behavior she has above average intelligence.

In 1996 the U.S. Supreme Court ruled against an appeal from Priscilla without comment. The appeal was filed after Priscilla lost her lower federal courts appeals. She has continued to file appeals in Nevada Courts for the past

17 years, including one in 1995 which asked the Nevada Supreme Court to change her sentence to life without parole based on her belief she did not have a fair trial. Michael Pescetta, executive director of the Nevada Appellate and Post-conviction Project maintains there were many constitutional errors in Priscilla's six-month trial caused mainly by inadequate counsel. Pescetta says Priscilla slips in and out of mental competency, which is really the crux of the problem because in Nevada the law prohibits the execution of persons who are mentally incompetent. "It comes and it goes," said Pescetta who continues to pursue her appeals in the Nevada Courts. Ultimately, however, Pescetta feels if there is ever any justice in Priscilla's case it will have to be in the federal courts. According to Pescetta, any judge who ruled in favor of Priscilla in Nevada would be writing his own ticket out of town.

Today, Priscilla lives in a single cell at the Southern Nevada Women's Correctional Facility located in North Las Vegas (Ryan, 1998). It is a private prison run by the Corrections Corporation of America. Because of her status she is isolated from the general population. She is allowed one hour a day of exercise in a yard adjoining her cell. Her meals are brought to her and she has access to the library and a television. A spokesperson for the prison said she is a model prisoner.

1983

Sheila Summers: White; Reversed, 1986. Sheila Summers was convicted of murder and given the death penalty in Nevada in 1983. Her death penalty was reversed in 1986 after she had been on death row for three years.

21

New Jersey: Lethal Injection

The state of New Jersey has given four women the death penalty since 1900. No woman has been legally executed in New Jersey and there is one woman on death row in New Jersey today.

New Jersey is one of ten states that have death penalty laws where there has been no execution since the death penalty was reinstated. The last execution in New Jersey took place in 1963.

Since capital punishment was reinstated in 1982, forty-nine defendants have been sentenced to death in New Jersey. Two died while on death row. The state Supreme Court reversed the death sentences of 30 for reasons such as trial error and prosecutorial misconduct and upheld the sentences of nine others. Of the nine upheld, one defendant died.

The others are currently at various stages in the appeals process. Only one convicted murderer, Richard Marshall, who was the subject of a best-selling book and the made-for-TV movie "Blind Faith" has exhausted all his state court appeals. He was convicted of hiring someone to kill his wife, Maria, in order to collect her $1.5 million insurance policy and is appealing his death sentence in the federal courts, a process that could take several more years.

THE DEATH PENALTY IN NEW JERSEY

In July, 1996, the New Jersey Supreme Court reluctantly upheld a statute allowing relatives to testify during the sentencing phase of a capital trial, making families of murder victims parties in capital cases for the first time in the state. In upholding the constitutionality of this statute the Court reversed its previous position of rejecting the use of victim-impact statements. In the majority opinion, Justice Marie Garibaldi noted that the change was necessary because of the Victim's Rights Amendment. The ruling is subject to a number of procedural safeguards. Among these are:

- Testimony may be given only in cases in which the jury finds that the state has proven at least one aggravating factor beyond a reasonable doubt and in which the jury finds the existence of a mitigating factor.

- Only one victim-impact witness can be called, and that witness must be an adult. No minors will be allowed to testify unless there is no adult survivor.

- The family member testimony must be in writing and must be pre-approved by the trial judge. The family member must stick to the statement and not introduce additional testimony.

- The impact statement may not include any testimony regarding the family member's opinions about the defendant, the crime or the appropriate sentence.

- A Rule 104 hearing must be conducted outside the presence of the jury before any statement may be made. The trial judge must use the hearing to make a preliminary determination as to the admissibility of the statement.

- The state must notify the defendant before the penalty phase that the state plans to introduce a victim-impact statement if the defendant asserts the catchall provision. The state must also provide the name of any witness who may be called so the defendant can interview that witness prior to the testimony given.

Due to the slow movement of death penalty cases through the New Jersey system, in August 1997 Governor Christine Todd Whitman announced she would set up a 15-member commission to make recommendations on how to speed up the death penalty process.

Among other things, Governor Whitman wanted the commission to look at why it takes more than a decade for defendants in death-penalty cases in New Jersey to exhaust their state and federal appeals. She also asked the commission to make suggestions as to how the process can be expedited. Governor Whitman said "For every prisoner stalling execution with interminable appeals, there's a family member who has spent all those years of appeals waiting for justice to be done . . . we owe these families something. We owe the victims something."

An assistant public defender, Dale Jones, who oversees the capital crimes division in New Jersey's Office of the Public Defender said he believes the wait in New Jersey is no longer than in any of the other states. He said the lengthy process ensures "we are not executing the innocent, we are not executing the mentally incompetent, and we are not executing people because they were selected to be prosecuted due to racial or gender bias."

Besides the above, the governors commission, headed by former Representative Dick Zimmer, also looked for ways to fill the empty death row cells in their state. In their process, the commission visited death row and held public hearings throughout New Jersey to take the public pulse on death penalty issues. As a result of their study, final proposals approved by the committee and presented to the state in 1998 included the following

- Allowing prosecutors to repeat the sentencing phase of a death penalty trial with a new jury where the previous jury could not reach a unanimous decision. Currently opposition by even one juror means no death penalty.

- Making prior violent crimes a condition for the death penalty. Currently only prior murders may be considered. Requires legislation.

- Making the murder of a mentally or physically disabled person a condition for the death penalty. Requires legislation.

- Allowing adult family members of the victim to attend the execution. Requires legislation.

- Allowing death row inmates to end their appeals and hurry their execution dates if they so desire. The first appeal following conviction would be retained. The change would require voter approval of an amendment to the constitution.

- Using special judges to handle all death penalty cases. Requires order by the Chief Justice of the Supreme Court.

- Ordering convicted murderers to refrain from emotional outbursts while speaking to the jury during the sentencing phase of a death penalty trial. The same restraint now placed on the victim's family. Requires legislation.

- Requiring defense lawyers to disclose the mitigating factors they intend to use before jury selection and trial. Juries must weigh aggravating and mitigating factors in deciding death. This would require a constitutional amendment to enforce, but the commission opted to recommend it.

- Allowing the defense to remove without cause only 8 jurors during jury selection. Currently the defense can remove 20 and prosecutors can remove 12. Requires legislation.

- Tightening deadlines for trial transcripts and filing of appeals. Requires new rules from the Supreme Court.

In 1997, The New Jersey Assembly approved a state constitutional amendment giving death row inmates the right to waive repeated appeals of their sentence. The action was prompted by the case of John Martini, a convicted murderer, who did not want to continue to challenge his death sentence.

However, in July, 1998 the New Jersey state Supreme Court ruled that persons convicted of capital crimes cannot automatically waive a motion for post-conviction relief (*New Jersey v. John Martini, Sr.*). The justices were divided in their decision about this. Justice James Coleman Jr. said he would have upheld Martini's decision to waive the right to file post-conviction relief because Martini was of sound mind and competent to make that decision. The majority ruled that since a defendant cannot waive a sentencing hearing, a presentation of mitigating evidence or an appeal from sentence, then he/she cannot waive a motion for post-conviction relief either.

Acknowledging the public interest in seeing the execution process streamlined, the Court issued a set of guidelines to be followed in situations where a defendant does not wish to pursue appeals:

- There should only be one proceeding in which defense lawyers are allowed to raise common appeal issues as well as issues which normally would not be allowed such as new evidence of innocence or the unconstitutionality or illegality of a sentence.

- There will be a requirement of accelerated disposition "in the interest of the public that seeks to know that justice is done."

- When counsel learns that the defendant does not want to pursue post-conviction relief claims, the application must be filed in 30 days and standby counsel will be appointed to represent the defendant.

- Cases should be assigned to judges who can handle matters on an expedited basis.

- A trial judge can issue either an oral or written opinion, but must immediately certify to the Supreme Court the transcribed record and copies of all exhibits and briefs.

- The party that loses at the trial level must file a notice of appeal with the Court within 15 days of the trial judge's ruling. The Court will then issue its ruling within 45 days of the receipt of the notice of appeal and any supplemental briefs, or within 30 days of any oral argument.

THE COST OF THE DEATH PENALTY IN NEW JERSEY

In New Jersey, the public defenders office represents death row inmates and it has been estimated that it costs the state over 1 million dollars per case. To house and feed an inmate on death row is about 20 percent higher than housing and feeding an inmate in the general population. This is primarily due to the special requirements for security. In dollars and cents it is about $33,000 a year.

In a twenty-four-hour day, nine guards spend the day with the inmates on New Jersey's death row, three guards per shift, 8 hours a shift. The guards say they try not to think of the possibility of an inmate being executed, although, if it happens, they will not be required to participate.

One guard noted that depression is common among the inmates on New Jersey's death row due partly to the monotony of their daily routines. There is a bookshelf with some old romance novels and a few magazines in one corner of the unit. Occasionally the inmates may read something and after breakfast each day they are allowed two hours of recreation in an area called "the cage" where they can spar with each other in a game of checkers. But, according to the guards, death-row inmates in New Jersey spend a lot of their time each day in bed.

WOMEN SENTENCED TO DEATH IN NEW JERSEY

1913
Madeline Ciccone: White; Commuted. Madeline Ciccone was sentenced to death in New Jersey in 1913 for the 1910 murder of her husband at the request of her lover. Her sentence was eventually commuted.

1935
Marguerite Dolbrow: White; Commuted, 1936. At age 28 Marguerite Dolbrow was found guilty of murdering her husband for his insurance money and for the purpose of being "rid of him" and given the death penalty. She had an accomplice in the crime, a white, 39-year-old male. In 1936 her sentence was commuted to life.

1984
Marie Moore: White; Reversed in 1988. In 1984 Marie Moore was found guilty of the murder of Belinda Weeks, a teenager she and a young man, Tony Rogers, starved and tortured to death in Marie's home over a period of weeks. In a pre-trial psychiatric evaluation it was discovered that Marie had at least two personalities (Lewis, 1998). Aside from the face she presented to most, a young punk named Billy also lived inside her psyche. Tony seemed to be able to get Billy to come out and it was the three of them — Tony, Marie, and Billy — who were responsible for Belinda's slow tortuous death. Nevertheless, Marie was the one sentenced to death. Tony was tried as a juvenile, served his time and was released. Marie was on death row in New Jersey for four years before her sentence was reversed in 1988.

1995
Leslie Ann Nelson: White; Currently on death row. Leslie Ann Nelson, a transsexual who was formerly Glen Nelson, is the only woman on death row in

New Jersey today. She can be found in an 8 by 10-foot cell at the far end of the lower deck of the 21-cell death block at the New Jersey State Prison in Trenton.

In May 1997 she was given the death penalty for killing one police officer and a life sentence for the murder of a second. A third police officer, a woman, who was also shot five times by Leslie, escaped. The second and third police officers were brother and sister. The brother was killed. Leslie pleaded guilty to two counts of capital murder and one count of aggravated assault and a trial was held to determine her sentence.

The officers went to Leslie's house on April 20, 1995 to serve a search warrant. The defense contended that Leslie was mentally and emotionally distraught at the time the officers arrived due to a sexual identity crisis brought on by her sex change in 1993. The result was she shot and killed two of the officers and injured another.

After the shootings, Leslie, who was 38 at the time, barricaded herself inside the house for 14 hours with a cache of weapons. Eventually police pumped tear gas into the house and Leslie emerged wearing a bulletproof vest and a gas mask.

In appeals, the public defender, Stephen W. Kirsch argued that the trial judge should have allowed the jury to consider an alternative to a death sentence. "It tilts the scales in favor or death" Krisch said. "They (the jury) ought to be deliberating with full knowledge of the consequences. Juries should not operate in a vacuum."

Leslie, who is the only woman in the United States held on death row with men, like the men, is allowed to shower every other day and when she does, the guards put a hospital screen between her and the other inmates. Roy Hendricks, the prison's associate administrator said "The screen gives her a little privacy."

22

New York: Lethal Injection

The state of New York has sentenced seven women to death since 1900 and all of them were executed in the electric chair at Sing Sing. Ethel Rosenberg was also executed at Sing Sing, although her death sentence was from the federal government rather than the state of New York. Between 1819 and 1963 there were 614 inmates executed in the electric chair at Sing Sing. There are no women currently on death row in New York and in June 1998, Darrel K. Harris, a former prison guard, became the first person to receive a death penalty since capital punishment was reinstated in New York.

In 1995 New York Governor George Pataki signed a bill restoring the death penalty to the state of New York. After 1977 a death penalty bill was passed in every legislative session by both houses of the New York state legislature only to be vetoed first by Governor Hugh Carey and then by Governor Mario Cuomo. Deterrence was the focus of those who supported the bill as captured in the words of Joseph Bruno, the Senate majority leader, who said, "This bill is a direct response to the people of New York who are fed up with senseless, barbaric killings and with soft-on-crime attitudes."

The new death penalty law allows prosecutors to seek the death penalty for murder in the act of another felony, such as rape, serial killing, torture killing, contract killing, killing a witness, killing while on escape from prison, and killing while serving a life sentence. The law applies to those convicted of murdering a police officer, a prison guard or judge, as well as serial killers, and terrorists. Persons under 18 and women who are pregnant (until the child is born) are exempt. The mentally retarded are also exempt unless they kill while incarcerated.

On December 14, 1995, newspapers reported that the Attorney General of the state of New York proposed an addition to the death penalty law. He would like to have the law changed to include the possibility of death for anyone caught with the raw materials for making a nuclear bomb although what the ingredients are were not delineated.

New York's last execution was on August 15, 1963, at Ossining State Prison, when Eddie Lee Mays was electrocuted for killing someone during a robbery.

THE ELECTRIC CHAIR

In 1881, Dr. Albert Southwick, a dentist and former steamboat engineer, saw an elderly drunk electrocute himself by touching the terminals of an electrical generator in Buffalo, New York. He was amazed at how quickly the man was killed and reported the episode to his friend, New York State Senator David McMillan. Due to some horrific stories of gruesome hangings, by 1886 the New York state legislature enacted Chapter 352 of the Laws of 1886 entitled "An Act to Authorize the Appointment of a Commission to Investigate and Report to the Legislature the Most Humane and Approved Method of Carrying into Effect the Sentence of Death in Capital Cases."

Elbridge Gerry, whose grandfather signed the Declaration of Independence, Dr. Southwick, and Matthew Hale, a judge from Albany, were appointed to the commission which eventually produced a report detailing and analyzing methods of execution.

On June 4, 1888, the New York legislature passed Chapter 489 of the Laws of New York State establishing electrocution as the state's official method of execution. The Medico-Legal Society of New York was designated to recommend how to implement this new law. The Society appointed Dr. Fred Peterson of Columbia University to carry out the research.

Inventor Harold P. Brown and Dr. Peterson presented their first experiments to the School of Mines at Columbia University on July 30, 1888. They applied a series of direct current (DC) shocks to a large dog. At 1,000 volts the dog was in agony, but not dead. It took 330 volts alternating current (AC) to finally do the dog in. Over the course of a few months, Dr. Peterson and Mr. Brown executed about two dozen dogs, two calves, and a 1,230 pound horse. Ultimately, Dr. Peterson recommended the use of a chair.

On January 1, 1889, the world's first "Electrical Execution Law" went into effect. The Westinghouse Company refused to sell AC generators to prisons to power electric chairs but three generators were purchased from somewhere for around $8,000.

In the spring of 1889, Joseph Chapeau was convicted of poisoning a neighbor's cows and became the first man sentenced to death under the new law, but his sentence was eventually commuted to life in prison. In March of the same year William Kemler murdered his lover Matilda (Tillie) Ziegler with an axe in Buffalo, New York. Kemler was found guilty and sentenced to death in May of 1889. After his conviction, the Westinghouse Corporation funded a series of appeals for Kemler, stating that electrocution is cruel and unusual punishment, but all the appeals were denied.

In 1890 Edwin R. Davis, an Auburn electrician, designed an electric chair and developed elaborate testing procedures that included applying electrical voltage to large slabs of meat. On August 6, 1890, Kemler was executed in the new electric chair at Auburn Prison. First a current of about 700 volts was delivered for almost seventeen seconds. Some witnesses said they smelled burnt flesh and clothing. After the first current it was noted that Kemler was still alive. The second jolt was 1030 volts after which smoke was observed rising from Kemler's head and he was pronounced dead. William Kemler thus became the first person ever executed by electrocution. An autopsy of his body showed that the portion of his brain below the headpiece had hardened and the flesh under the electrode on his back had burned through to the spine.

Over the years, three different chairs were built in New York State. The original one was at Auburn, then there was one at Sing Sing and the third, was at Dannemora state prison. The chair at Dannemora was eventually moved to the state prison guard training facility at Albany and is still there today.

By the late 1970s LeMuel Smith was New York's only death row inmate. He had murdered a female guard while in solitary confinement, which made him eligible for the death penalty. His sentence, however, was overturned in July 1985 when the New York State Supreme Court declared the death penalty in New York unconstitutional.

THE DEATH PENALTY IN NEW YORK TODAY

New York Governor Pataki campaigned on a promise to restore the death penalty, and in one of his first acts as governor, he signed the bill only seven hours after it was passed by the New York General Assembly. Republican State Senator Dale Volker, who is a former policeman and a chief sponsor of the bill, said, "We are sending out a message across the country."

The Act established a "Capital Defender Office" (CDO) funded at $3.2 million, which conducts capital murder defenses in primary trials and state court appeals. By the end of October 1995, the CDO had been notified of 102 murder cases that potentially qualified for death sentences. Of these, it took on eight cases, and seven were referred to outside lawyers.

Since New York's capital punishment law took effect two years ago, prosecutors have considered seeking it in 191 cases, and announced they would do so in 13. In two of these cases they changed their mind, and one person committed suicide before indictment. The director of the New York Prosecutor's Training Institute said the law has had an effect, because "murderers are plea bargaining to take life in prison." However, in August 1997, in New York City's first death penalty case, a judge rejected a plea bargain agreement, saying the plea bargain provisions of the state's death penalty law are unconstitutional.

According to Justice Albert Tomie of the state Supreme Court of Brooklyn, allowing a defendant to avoid the death penalty by pleading guilty penalizes a defendant who exercises his right under the U.S. Constitution to a jury trial. He also suggested that the plea provisions of the death penalty law allow prosecutors to coerce guilty pleas from capital defendants and win their acceptance of harsh sentences like life in prison without parole. In New York, if a prosecutor does not ask for the death penalty, a first-degree murderer must receive Life Without Parole (ACLU Abolitionist, April 1997).

Due to judicial review of the thirty-one-page statute with numerous provisions and their application to particular cases, it is doubtful that there will be an execution in New York for some time to come.

LETHAL INJECTION IN NEW YORK

The new law, making New York the 38th state to restore the death penalty calls for execution in the state by lethal injection. When Darrel Harris was given the death penalty in 1998, the state prison system said, "We are ready. Death row and the death house have been ready since September 1, 1995 when the death penalty went into effect." Harris' arrival at Clinton state prison in Dannemora opened death row, which had been closed since 1981. Prison officials reported spending $375,000 to convert a 12-unit cellblock into death row. Dannemora is approximately 200 miles north of Green Haven state prison where executions take place. Now, instead of the electric chair the execution room is equipped with a gurney and other supplies needed for death by lethal injection.

A spokesperson for the New York Department of Correctional Services said they do not have an executioner, nor have they begun to look for one, since they have not decided what a candidates qualifications must be for the job. They have not needed an executioner since 1963 when Eddie Lee Mays was electrocuted. But, even before the death penalty was reinstated the Department of Correctional Services was receiving letters from people volunteering to be executioners.

The executioners job description is available now and has been spelled out in the "Procedures for the Operation of the Capital Punishment Unit" guidelines which New York State Correctional Officials wrote the summer before capital punishment was reinstated in 1995. Among other things, the manual indicates that eight prison guards will be necessary to strap the condemned inmate to a gurney, wheel him/her into the death chamber, and lock the gurney in place. Once there, two people who are legally qualified to administer intravenous fluids will connect an empty tube to each of the prisoner's forearms, and release a flow of saline solution to carry the lethal chemicals through the inmate. They will then connect a heart monitor to the condemned and open the curtains for witnesses to see.

Once the curtains are open, the executioner will enter the death chamber. In front of 14 witnesses, four of whom may be relatives of the condemned, he/she will inject one syringe of sodium pentathol into one of the tubes and he/she will follow this with a syringe of saline solution to flush the line. Then two syringes of Pavulon will be administered and after this he/she will again flush the line with saline. Finally, the executioner will inject two syringes of potassium chloride and then observe the inmate for five minutes. Once the inmate has stopped breathing, the curtains will be closed and a physician will certify that he/she is dead. If the inmate is not dead, the curtain will be opened and the process repeated.

Employees of the Department of Corrections, including prison staff, are not allowed to participate in executions; and a senior official at the Green Haven prison said prison physicians have refused to participate on the grounds that executions violate the Hippocratic Oath which stipulates that doctors will do no harm. The DOC has said they are considering using a different person for each execution and may place an ad in the paper when the need arises.

WOMEN SENTENCED TO DEATH IN NEW YORK

1909

Mary Farmer: White; Executed. At age 29, Mary Farmer, an Irish immigrant, was convicted of killing her neighbor in order to fraudulently acquire her land and leave it as an inheritance to her son. She hit her neighbor in the head with an axe from behind and then hacked her to death, ultimately trying to hide the body in a trunk. Her husband was also convicted in the murder but his sentence was later commuted. Before being executed, on March 29, 1909 Mary cared for her infant son in her cell and arranged for him to live with his father's brother. She left a letter to be given to him by her attorney when he was old enough to understand it. In it she urged him to lead a good life.

1928

Ruth Snyder: White; Executed. At age 33, Ruth Snyder, dubbed the "Marble Woman" was executed for the murder of her husband, Albert, who was killed while lying in bed at home in Queens Village near Jamaica, New York. Ruth and their young daughter were in the house at the time. A physical description of Ruth in the *World Encyclopedia of 20th Century Murder*, described her as: "A tall, overage flapper with bobbed blond hair, a voluptuous body, and a ravenous appetite for men of all kinds and sizes."

The Snyders lived in a large three-story house in Long Island. Albert Snyder, who had his office in Manhattan, was the art editor of a boating magazine and spent much of his free time hunting, fishing, and boating. He apparently enjoyed antagonizing Ruth by constantly reminding her of his former lover and fiancé, Jessie Guishard, although she had been dead for ten years. He even placed a picture of her above their bed and referred to her as "The finest woman I've ever known."

Ruth had grown up in a poor family and by age thirteen she quit school to work as a night telephone operator. She studied shorthand and bookkeeping during the day and later became a secretary. She met and married Albert in 1915. Soon afterward, dressed as a flapper, wearing short skirts and high heels, Ruth began having a number of brief affairs with other men.

In 1925, at a lunch in Manhattan, a friend of Ruth's introduced her to Henry Judd Gray. Gray, who was thirty-three at the time, wore thick glasses and stylish clothes, including hand-made gloves, fitted three-piece suits, and spats. He lived in Orange, New Jersey, and sold corsets. At their first meeting Ruth told him she was in Manhattan to buy a corset and asked him to show her his merchandise, and that was the beginning of their affair. Over the next two years they met frequently in Manhattan hotels, usually the Waldorf Astoria. Lorraine, Ruth's 9-year-old daughter, would sometimes accompany her mother only to be left in the lobby to read while her mother was upstairs with Judd.

Sometime in 1926 Ruth took out a $100,000 life insurance policy on Albert and started to think about how she could kill him. According to later testimony, Ruth unsuccessfully tried to kill her husband seven times in 1926 by gas, poison, and even one attempted drowning. Finally, she told Gray he would have to help her. By all accounts Gray was not a very willing accomplice and the more Ruth pressed him to get rid of Albert, the heavier he drank. Nevertheless, on the appointed night, the two of them did kill Albert. Gray apparently hit him in the head with a heavy weight and then Ruth strangled him with the wire from the back of the picture of his former fiancé.

Ruth told police that she woke up a few hours after her husband was killed and found herself tied hand and foot by robbers, who had knocked her out, or since she wasn't sure, she thought she might have lost consciousness from fright.

The house was in such a mess that it appeared robbery might have been the motive. The police, however, were suspicious of Ruth's story, and after finding a tie clasp in the bedroom with the initials "JG" on it and a canceled check in Ruth's desk made out to "Judd Gray," they arrested Gray. They told Ruth that Gray had confessed and she broke down and said that Gray had killed her husband by bludgeoning him to death, and that after the murder she had let him tie her up to make it look like a robbery.

Henry Judd Gray confessed too. But according to him, Ruth played a much bigger role in the murder than she admitted. It was believed that her motive was a desire to be rid of her husband, but not through divorce since she was afraid of losing her daughter.

Although Ruth asked to be tried separately from Henry, the state denied her request and they were tried together. In the trial each of them placed most of the blame on the other. Ruth testified that her confession had not been voluntary and that, because of her nervousness, she had confessed under pressure. She also said that she had tried to stop Henry from carrying out his plan to murder her husband, and she had even tried to stop him during the actual murder. When she could not stop him, she said she decided to help him make it look like a robbery. Henry, for his part, testified that because he was drunk, he was very weak and found it impossible to resist Ruth's suggestion that they murder her husband.

After only 98 minutes of deliberation, both Ruth and Gray were found guilty of premeditated murder and both were sentenced to death. While waiting to be executed both Ruth Snyder and Judd Gray wrote their autobiographies in which each portrayed the other as evil and themselves as good. Ruth also wrote a poem that attacked the press for making her out to be such a villain.

After her conviction, although she often cried for her daughter, Lorraine, Ruth would not let her come to see her until the end because she did not want her child to have a memory of her being incarcerated. Lorraine Snyder and her grandmother visited Ruth right before she was executed. Reporters took a picture of Lorraine kneeling in an attitude of prayer on behalf of her mother.

On January 12, 1928, a cold wintry night, Judd Gray and Ruth Snyder were both executed. Gray was electrocuted first. Ruth's last words were, "God has forgiven me and I hope the world will." A black hood was placed over Ruth's head, and although all cameras were banned, Thomas Howard, a reporter from the *New York Daily News* strapped a small one to his leg. At the moment Ruth was executed, he took a picture which is the only one known to have ever been taken of a female execution. The picture resurfaced on the Net last year.

1934

Ana Antonio: White; Executed. Ana Antonio, nicknamed "Little Ana" was twenty-seven at the time of her execution. She was an Italian immigrant and had been married for many years to a man who earned his living by selling drugs and participating in other underworld activities. When her husband was found beaten and stabbed along a deserted highway Ana was charged with his murder. She was convicted of hiring two men to kill him by offering to pay them with his insurance money.

Eventually she was exonerated of the killing because one of the murderers was a person who had been burned in a drug deal by her husband, but she was executed anyway, even though she had three small children — a boy three, and girls seven and nine years of age. She spent her days on death row writing to her children, and she begged her brother to adopt them into his family. He took her three-year-old son, Frank, but her daughters were sent to an orphanage.

She spent her last days making a birthday dress for her seven-year-old daughter and when the little girl received the dress, she said she hoped she would also receive her mother's stay of execution as a present. However, in a cruel twist of fate, Ana was executed precisely on her daughter's birthday. She weighed only 82 pounds at the time of her execution and was described as looking like a small child in the electric chair.

1935

Eva Coo: White; Executed. At forty-one, Eva Coo was convicted and sentenced to death. She murdered Harry Wright, the crippled alcoholic son of an old friend, at her bordello outside Cooperstown, New York. Canadian born "Little Eva" ran a combination brothel, roadhouse, and gas station where Wright had lived for four years prior to June 1934 when his body was found in a ditch not far from the establishment.

Eva was sentenced to death on the testimony of Martha Clift, one of her "hostesses" who admitted she had run over Wright after Eva had clubbed him with a mallet. The motive was supposed to have been Wright's insurance policy which, when it turned up, showed Eva as the sole beneficiary. In exchange for her testimony, Martha Clift was sentenced to 20 years. Eva was executed on June 27, 1935. Warden Lewis Lawes told of how Eva's friends took her belongings after she was incarcerated and often wore them to visit her.

1936

Mary Frances Creighton: White; Executed. At 36, Mary Frances Creighton was accused of poisoning a woman she and her family were boarding with, a Mrs. Applegate. To save money, Mary, her husband, and their two children, a son Jackie who was 12 and a daughter Ruth who was 15, shared a two-bedroom apartment with Everett Applegate, his wife, and their 12-year-old daughter, Agnes.

In 1923 Mary had been tried for murder in connection with the death of her brother, Raymond Avery, who had died of arsenic poisoning. Raymond had named his sister, Mary, the sole beneficiary on his insurance policy. Since there were no witnesses to the murder, Mary was acquitted of all charges. However, when it was discovered that Mrs. Applegate had died of poisoning also, Mary and Mr. Applegate were the immediate suspects.

Under questioning, Mr. Applegate said he knew nothing of the murder and disclosed that he was having an intimate relationship with 15-year-old Ruth Creighton with the approval and knowledge of her mother, Mary Frances.

Mary Frances Creighton confessed to the murder of Mrs. Applegate and also to the murder of her brother, who she said, was an invalid and a pervert. Her motives for the murder of Mrs. Applegate were never clear. Possible motives mentioned were anger because Mrs. Applegate gossiped about her or a desire to free Mr. Applegate so he could have her daughter, or jealousy.

Before she was executed, Mary Frances refused to see her children and lapsed into an unconsciousness from which she never awakened. She had to be lifted and placed in the electric chair and died without ever opening her eyes.

1944

Helen Fowler: Black; Executed. By age 37, Helen Fowler was supporting herself, her four children, and a nephew, by prostitution in an area near Niagra Falls, New York known for its gin mills, gambling, and run down bawdy houses. The body of a local garage owner, a 62-year-old white man, who frequented the houses of prostitution and who was last seen chasing Helen down the street, was found in a nearby river, badly decomposed. He had apparently been robbed and murdered. Helen was arrested for the murder along with George Knight, a 27 year-old man. Local tensions ran high during the trial because both Helen and Knight were black, and the victim was white. It was the first trial in New York, where women were allowed to sit on the jury.

Knight, Helen Fowler's teenage daughter, and Helen herself presented three different versions of what had happened to the garage owner during the trial, and the prosecution made attempts to gloss over the reason the victim was in the seedy area in the first place. Nevertheless, both Helen and Knight were found guilty and eventually executed. Their executions drew almost no media attention.

1951

Martha Jule Beck: White; Executed. Martha Jule Beck developed early physically and was a heavy child, which caused her to be constantly ridiculed. During her childhood an older brother repeatedly raped her, and when she told her mother, her mother said she was lying and put her in isolation for long periods of time making her feel guilty about what had happened.

Martha eventually put herself through nursing school but couldn't find any work except with an undertaker. She traveled from one coast to the other, marrying at least once. She had two children and a number of affairs, but she never really found the romance she read about in romance novels.

While running a home for crippled children in Pensacola, Florida, Martha met Raymond Fernandez through a lonely-hearts club. At the time Fernandez was involved in a scheme stealing the life savings of lonely widows, and he was suspected of having killed, at least one of them. He was not interested in a long-term relationship, possibly because of what he was doing, but Martha convinced him they were meant to be together, and she gave her two children to the state so she could be with him.

After they got together Raymond and Martha continued to take advantage of widows for their income. Fernandez would introduce Martha as his sister, who, after the wedding, would move in with the newlyweds. But sometimes Martha was so jealous of the women Fernandez picked out that she would insist on sleeping in the same bed with them.

Martha and Fernandez were finally caught in 1949 after the murder of twenty-eight-year-old Delphine Dowling and her two-year-old daughter. Fernandez shot Delphine and Martha drowned her daughter, Rainelle in the bathtub, then they buried the two bodies in the basement of the house. Neighbors who became suspicious when Delphine and her daughter suddenly disappeared and the strange couple began living in their home turned them in. When police came to investigate, Martha let them in and when she was unable to answer some of their questions, they searched the house and eventually discovered the two bodies.

Known as the "Lonely Heart Killers" because of their method of finding their victims, the two were tried in New York specifically to make them eligible for the death penalty. Though both were tried on an insanity defense, they were found guilty of multiple counts of murder and sentenced to death.

Four people were executed the same night as Martha and Raymond. Martha was executed last apparently because they thought she could hold up better than the men. It was said that she died happy because Fernandez had told her he loved her again just before being executed.

23

North Carolina: Gas/Lethal Injection

The state of North Carolina has sentenced fifteen women to death since 1900. Three women, Rosanna Phillips, Bessie Mae Smith, and Velma Barfield were executed and there are three women on death row in North Carolina today. The Governor has the power to grant a reprieve, commute the death sentence, or even pardon the offender.

THE DEATH PENALTY IN NORTH CAROLINA

Legislation enacted by North Carolina's Colonial Assembly first governed the administration of capital punishment in the state. Statutes passed in 1836–1837 mandated the death penalty for murder, highway robbery, burglary, arson, dueling, rape, sodomy, bestiality, and stealing or hiding a slave. A person could also be sentenced to death for taking a free Negro out of state for sale into slavery, escaping while under a capital charge, horse stealing, bigamy, and for inciting slaves to insurrection or circulating pamphlets that did so (Nakell & Hardy, 1987). After 1837 capital punishment statutes were enacted in 1872–1873 that mandated the death penalty for willful murder, rape, arson, and burglary, all crimes that remained punishable by death in North Carolina until 1976. In 1910 the power to execute criminals was assumed by the state

The electric chair, the gas chamber, and lethal injection have all been used as methods of execution in North Carolina and all executions have taken place at the Central Prison in Raleigh.

North Carolina first used the electric chair on March 28, 1910 when Walter Morrison, a black laborer from Robeson, County, was convicted of rape and executed. There were 171 prisoners electrocuted after him during a period span of 28 years.

Although the electric chair was still in use as late as 1938, the state began using the gas chamber in 1936. Allen Foster, sentenced to death in Durham Superior Court for murder, was the first person put to death in the state's gas chamber on January 24, 1936. From 1936 to 1961 the gas chamber was used in the execution of 190 people.

In 1983, the North Carolina General Assembly gave death row inmates the option of choosing between gas or lethal injection. Since that time, seven inmates have chosen lethal injection. Most recently, in January 1998 Ricky Lee Sanderson, sentenced to death for the stabbing death of a 16-year-old girl chose to be executed by lethal gas.

In 1997, the North Carolina Department Of Corrections (DOC) did a study and showed the difference in cost between executing a prisoner by gas and executing a prisoner by lethal injection amounted to $24.52.

Between 1910 and 1961, two women, Rosanna Phillips and Bessie Mae Smith, were among those who were executed. Their executions accounted for 7 percent of the total number of executions during that time. There have been nine executions, in North Carolina since 1977 — two in 1984, one in 1986, 1991, 1992, and 1994, two in 1995, and one in 1998.

In 1972 (*Furman v. Georgia*), when the U.S. Supreme Court ruled the death penalty unconstitutional where juries were permitted to exercise unbridled discretion in imposing it, the North Carolina Supreme Court ruled that the death penalty would be mandatory for certain crimes. But, in 1976, with 120 inmates on death row, the U.S. Supreme Court overturned North Carolina's mandatory death penalty in *Woodsen v. North Carolina* (428 US 280, 1976), and the inmates on death row at the time had their sentences vacated. Many received new trials and most were re-sentenced to life.

On June 1, 1977 a new death penalty law went into effect modeled after the statutes in Florida and Georgia. This law provided for the 2-step (bifurcated) jury process in all first-degree murder trials and required a unanimous jury vote to impose the death penalty. A jury's recommendation of life is binding and there is an automatic direct appeal to the state Supreme Court. In North Carolina, as elsewhere, the decision whether or not to seek the death penalty is left completely in the hands of the prosecutor and nothing in the law requires prosecutors to give any reason for his/her choice.

All inmates currently on death row in North Carolina were convicted and sentenced under the state's revised capital punishment law which restored the death penalty for first-degree murder, defined as the willful, deliberate, and premeditated killing of another or the killing of someone during the commission of another felony.

Kermit Smith Jr., who was executed in North Carolina, was only the second white person in the country executed for killing a black person after the death penalty was reinstated. The minimum age for the death penalty in North Carolina is seventeen.

After 20 years on the bench, North Carolina Superior Court Judge Gordon Battle expressed his thoughts about the death penalty when he retired. He said, "We'd be better off if we didn't have the death penalty. Our Superior Court spends over half its time hearing death penalty cases. It doesn't seem worth it" (*The News & Observer*, 1997). Judge Battle noted that life in prison without parole would be a better option. "Doing away with the death penalty would take a tremendous load off the criminal justice system and free up a whole lot of time to do other things." Justice Battle joins a growing number of judges who have spoken out against the death penalty.

In North Carolina, the total cost of a capital case is $2.16 million per execution over the cost of a non-death penalty murder case with the sentence of life imprisonment (Duke University, May 1995).

THE NORTH CAROLINA GAS CHAMBER

The gas chamber at the North Carolina Central Prison is an airtight compartment that has a wooden chair with a high back, armrests and a footrest mounted to the chamber's back wall. There is a steel door to the left of the chair (as viewed from the witness chamber), and the control room is to the right. The chair is equipped with a metal container under the seat where cyanide is placed. There is another metal canister on the floor filled with sulfuric acid solution. When the executioners turn the keys in the control room, an electric switch causes the bottom of the cyanide container to open allowing the cyanide to fall into the solution and produce lethal gas. Inhalation of the gas is supposed to render the inmate unconscious and death is supposed to occur within six to eighteen minutes.

Before an execution three tests are conducted of the chamber using the same chemicals that will be used for the execution. There are three executioners who are staff members chosen by the warden of the Central Prison. They are not given a psychological evaluation unless one is requested. The execution team consists of the warden, deputy warden the three executioners, a trained medical team (three people), the chaplain, the escort team (four people), and the security coordinator. No team members are compensated beyond their regular salary. Being a member of the execution team is voluntary except for the warden and the deputy warden. The warden selects the members of the execution team and is in charge of the team.

When an inmate enters the gas chamber and sits in the chair he/she is restrained at the chest, waist, arms, and ankles. A mask is placed over the inmate's face and a staff member attaches a heart monitor to the inmate that can be read in the control room.

After the warden pronounces an inmate dead, ammonia is pumped into the execution chamber to neutralize the gas; exhaust fans pump the fumes from the chamber into two scrubbers containing water that serves as a neutralizing agent. Members of the prison staff then enter the chamber and remove the body for release to the county medical examiner. The execution team is debriefed after an execution and counseling is available to team members.

In 1994, David Lawson, a murderer who wanted his execution televised by Phil Donahue, did not request lethal injection and became the first person in 30 years to die by lethal gas. Lawson was strapped into the chair wearing only boxer shorts, socks, and a diaper. Witnesses said he screamed for nearly five minutes while the deadly fumes filled his lungs. The chamber's double-paneled windows made it difficult to hear him, but as he thrashed against the leather straps that tied him to the chair, he appeared to be bellowing through a leather mask, "I'm human, I'm human."

Although both the Phil Donahue show and Lawson had petitioned the Supreme Court to film his execution, the court refused the request without comment. Because Lawson refused to choose his method of execution, the state chose the gas chamber.

In May 1998 the North Carolina House Judiciary Committee approved a bill that would no longer allow inmates to choose between gas and lethal injection. According to Representative Larry Justus (Rep.) it is a matter of safety for the Department of Corrections because in past executions by gas some of the gas has escaped into the prison area. In the last execution by gas, Justus said, when they were carrying out the deceased some gas escaped and the equipment supplying oxygen malfunctioned.

Under present North Carolina law a condemned inmate has up until five days before his/her execution to choose lethal injection. If he/she does not choose then they are executed with gas.

Justus said he believes lethal injection is more humane. He added that only five inmates have been executed since 1985 so "In essence, we don't have a death penalty anyway."

Representative Mickey Michaux (Dem.) suggested that instead of making it safer for people to be executed, the state should just do away with the death penalty all together.

In North Carolina, killers of whites are four times more likely to receive the death penalty than killers of blacks (NCADP, 1996) and African Americans make up half of the North Carolina death row population.

DEATH ROW IN NORTH CAROLINA

According to a 1997 report by the North Carolina DOC more than 1,000 inmates have been sent to death row in the state since 1910. Male death row inmates are at the Central Prison and female death row inmates are at the North Carolina Correctional Institution for Women near Raleigh. The women are housed in a cellblock of the maximum-security building. Each of the single cells has a bed, a sink, and a toilet. There are seven cells for women, which are side by side down a single corridor. The women eat their meals in a dayroom that also serves as a visiting area. The correctional staff supervises all visits. As a group, the women on death row are given at least an hour of daily exercise and showers. Volunteers provide Sunday worship services, and chaplains are available for counseling.

When a death row inmate — male or female — exhausts all appeals, the warden sets an execution date. The inmate is then moved into the death watch area of the Central Prison three to seven days prior to the execution. The death watch area is adjacent to the execution chamber and is located in the prison's custody control building.

All of the inmates' personal belongings are moved from the death row cell to one of four cells in the death watch area. Each cell in this area has a bed, a sink, and a toilet, plus a wall-mounted writing table. The cells are side by side, and except for 15 minutes a day allowed for a shower, the inmate spends the entire day there. A Corrections sergeant and a Corrections officer are stationed outside the cell 24 hours a day.

While on the deathwatch an inmate may receive visits from her/his attorney, chaplains, psychologists, and others authorized by the Division of Prisons. Inmates may receive non-contact family visits in the prisons' visiting area. An inmate on deathwatch is not allowed contact with other inmates. The inmate remains in the deathwatch area until receiving a stay or until escorted to the execution chamber.

WITNESSES

North Carolina Statute 15-190 designates the following witnesses may attend an execution:

The warden or deputy warden, or some person designated by the warden in his stead; the surgeon or physician of the penitentiary and six respectable citizens, the counsel and any relatives of such person, convict, or felon, and a minister or ministers of the gospel.

At least one week before an execution, the warden asks the prisoner whether he/she wants family members, counsel, or ministers present at his/her death. The size of the witness room restricts the number of persons allowed to sixteen.

For the six official witnesses, the District Attorney of the county of conviction and the Sheriff of the county of conviction each select two. The State Bureau of Investigation and the North Carolina Law Enforcement Officers Association are each allowed one.

In North Carolina, since 1991, crime victim families have been allowed to witness executions. In 1997, the Department of Corrections encouraged sheriffs and district attorneys to consider crime victim families in their selections of witnesses.

Five media witnesses are allowed in the witness chamber, who are then instructed to brief other reporters. Media witnesses and alternates are selected by the North Carolina Press Association, the Radio Television News Directors' Association of the Carolinas, and the Associated Press.

LETHAL INJECTION IN NORTH CAROLINA

When lethal injection is used in North Carolina, the inmate is secured to a gurney before being wheeled into the death chamber. Lined ankle and wrist restraints are used. Cardiac monitor leads and a stethoscope are attached to his/her chest and two intravenous lines of saline, one in each arm, are started. The inmate is covered with a sheet up to the neck. When the witnesses are in place the gurney is wheeled into the execution chamber by correctional officers. They then open the curtains and exit.

The condemned is given the opportunity to pray with the chaplain before execution. The warden then gives the inmate the opportunity to record a final statement that will be made public after his/her death.

Behind a curtain, trained personnel connect the cardiac monitor leads, the injection devices and the stethoscope. The warden informs the witnesses that the execution is about to begin then returns to the chamber and gives the order to proceed.

The saline intravenous lines are turned off and the thiopental sodium is injected which is supposed to put the inmate into a deep sleep. A second chemical agent, procuronium bromide (the generic name for Pavulon) follows. This is intended as a total muscle relaxant. When the inmate stops breathing he/she dies within a short period of time.

The warden pronounces the inmate dead and a physician certifies a death has occurred. The witnesses are escorted to the elevators and the body is released to the medical examiner. So far, six men and one woman have chosen execution by lethal injection in North Carolina.

WOMEN SENTENCED TO DEATH IN NORTH CAROLINA

1943

Rosanna Phillips: Black; Executed, January 1, 1943. Rosanna and Daniel Phillips were the first husband and wife executed in this century for the same crime and Rosanna was the first woman executed in North Carolina after the 1800s.

Rosanna, who was 25 at the time of the crime, was raised by her grandmother and an aunt and grew up in rural southern poverty. She left school in the 6th grade to give birth to a son and although her mother's life was unstable, she gave the baby to her mother to raise.

Eventually Rosanna met Dan Phillips and moved south with him and had another baby, a girl, who was not Phillips's child. When the rancher they worked for was found murdered and stuffed in a well, they both admitted being present at the scene of the crime. The rancher had been hit from behind with an axe. Daniel and Rosanna each blamed the other for the murder and Rosanna said Daniel forced her to marry him after the killing. They repeatedly accused each other of casting "spells."

Rosanna's face and arms were covered with scars from knife wounds, which she said Phillips had inflicted on her. No one believed that either of them was totally innocent and they were both convicted of the crime. From death row Rosanna arranged for her two children to be raised by her mother. The double execution took place on New Year's Day, 1943.

Rosanna was executed first with authorities hoping that Daniel would confess in order to save her, but he didn't and died admitting nothing.

1944

Bessie Mae Smith (Williams): Black; Executed, December 29, 1944. Bessie Mae Williams was an orphan who for the most part raised herself. She left school after the fifth grade and worked off and on as a maid. She was arrested once for drinking and disorderly conduct. One night when Bessie and a girl friend went out with two guys in a cab they didn't have any money to pay the fare so they decided they would have to get rid of the driver. Her girl friend, who was about fifteen, bludgeoned him with a brick and the two guys that were with them stabbed him when he tried to fight back.

One of the males testified that when it was over, Bessie stole two fifty-cent pieces from the taxi before leaving. He also said she did not participate in the murder. The true ages of Bessie and her girlfriend were never established, but because of how they looked it was arbitrarily decided that Bessie was the oldest and her friend the youngest. Based on this conclusion, and on the fact that Bessie had also stolen money from the cab driver, it was Bessie who was sentenced to die and her friend was given life.

Bessie's lawyer was appointed only two days before her trial and her handwritten request for clemency was answered with a form letter. She was sentenced to death at what was believed to be age 18, and was executed in December 1944 even though she had no part in the murder.

1973

Mamie Lee Ward: Black; Reversed in 1976. Mamie was convicted of first-degree murder in the death of her boyfriend, Frank Parker. She was a 52-year-old waitress at the Carolina Cafe and had been separated from her husband for nineteen years. Her three children were grown and she had known Frank for about twenty years. They had lived together for three years.

When Mamie's daughter had a baby and went home to live with her mother, Mamie and Frank talked about it. Frank told Mamie "It won't be no different between us, baby. You come to see me and I can come to see you." Mamie was used to sleeping with Frank every night and after her daughter's move, she said, they "went back and forth." Mamie still saw Frank every day and he continued to be her boyfriend. When he got off work at 6:00 p.m. he'd stop by and see her. She had been at Frank's house the night before the murder.

The night of the murder Frank was at home in the den, sitting on his couch talking to a woman named Lucy Taylor who had apparently been his girlfriend for about 5 months. The phone rang and Lucy answered it saying "Parker Residence." Whoever was on the other end hung up immediately. Ten minutes later while Lucy and Frank were still on the couch talking, Lucy heard someone come up on the front porch and walk around to the back. She later said she heard the doorknob turn, but did not see anyone come in. She told Frank to go investigate the noise, which he did.

From the den Frank could see both the front and the back door and he told her no one was there then added in a loud voice that if "Somebody was out there, they should knock." He then went back and sat down and dialed a phone number for Lucy.

Lucy was on the phone for about two or three minutes before Mamie entered the room with a shotgun. According to Lucy "She lifted it to fire" and fired the gun toward Frank who was still on the couch next to Lucy. The blast hit him directly under the chin. Mamie then opened the gun and tried to reload it as Lucy ran out of the room escaping through a back window. Lucy thought Parker was dead because he had not uttered a word before or after he was shot.

The police went to Parker's home in response to a call from Lucy. Once there, they found two shotgun shells on the floor — one live and one spent — and in the den they found Parker on the couch. There was a large amount of blood and a hole in his face. He was dead and there was no other person in the house. They found three rifles standing in one of the bedroom corners.

After the shooting, Mamie took a taxi to the police station and told them she had shot Frank. She said they'd been having trouble for over a month and she'd walked over to Frank's house and gone in the back door. She said Frank saw her when he got up to check out the noise, and he motioned her into one of the back bedrooms and then went on talking to Lucy as if nothing had happened.

That made her angry and when she saw Frank's guns in the bedroom she took one off a rack on the wall. Then she walked into the living room, aimed the gun at Frank and fired. She left the house through the front door. After making this statement Mamie, told the police she was upset and needed time to think.

During the time she and Parker lived together, she kept her personal possessions at his house, shared living expenses with him, and cooked his meals. They had also taken a bus tour to Canada together and had attended each other's family reunions.

Mamie said that on the night of the murder she heard Frank and Lucy talking and then she saw them sitting together on the couch. That upset her, but what upset her most was when Frank waved her into the back bedroom. It was then that she got so mad she couldn't think. She said she just got the gun, but didn't remember loading it. She said she didn't know what she meant to do with the gun. Frank was the man she loved, and she was not intending to shoot him. But, after she fired the gun, she saw him fall back so she just turned and walked out the door.

Mamie said she had met Lucy previously and seen her at Frank's house three other times. She said she'd talked about Lucy with Frank because she "called a lot." Much discussion in the appeals centered on whether the crime was first-degree murder or involuntary manslaughter provoked by the circumstances. Although Mamie was sentenced to death, her sentence was reversed in 1976.

1974

Rozelle Oxendine Hunt: Native American; Reversed in 1976. On the morning of August 31, 1973, Rozelle Oxendine, her common-law husband, Joe Hunt, and Brenda Jacobs, an 18-year-old girl who lived with them, went shopping in Wadesboro, North Carolina. Rozelle and Brenda left Joe in the grocery store and went to the drugstore where, Brenda testified later, she saw Rozelle buy some liquid rat poison in a small bottle and put it in her pocket.

Later, when at home, Joe went to the garden to pick okra for lunch and Brenda said Rozelle poured half of the bottle of poison into a jug of tea she prepared for Joe. According to Brenda, Rozelle prepared two separate jugs of tea, but Joe's was recognizable by a dent in the side of the jug.

At lunch, Rozelle served Joe the tea from the jug she'd put the rat poison in and Brenda drank tea from the other jug. Rozelle herself didn't have any. After lunch they laid down to rest then got up and went to the tobacco pack house to work with their tobacco. While they were working, Joe got sick and vomited several times, saying he felt like he'd been poisoned. Throughout the afternoon and into the night his condition grew worse and his hands and toes drew up in knots. Brenda said Rozelle made no attempts to help him.

Early the next morning they took Joe to the hospital in Wadesboro and the doctor in charge was not able to figure out what was wrong with him. They transferred him to a hospital in Charlotte where he died the next day, one-day after he'd been poisoned. He was buried in Rowland, North Carolina.

At the trial Brenda described the rat poison she'd seen as a white liquid in a bottle with red lettering and a skeleton on it. When she was shown a bottle of Singletary's rat poison purchased by the police, she identified it as the same kind of bottle that she had seen Rozelle purchase. According to experts, Singletary's rat poison contained large amounts of arsenic. Prior to this, Brenda testified that Rozelle had told her she'd tried to poison Joe several times, but it looked like every time she tried "God made a way for him to live" and Joe was "A hard man to kill."

Six months after Joe's death, Brenda told the FBI what she knew and Joe's body was exhumed and an autopsy performed. In the autopsy his liver was examined and found to contain arsenic. After the state rested its case, Rozelle did not present any evidence on her own behalf. The trial judge asked her if she'd consulted with her attorney about the consequences of not presenting evidence and she said that she had — and that she "only had witnesses" to testify for her. Rozelle was convicted of murder in the first-degree and sentenced to death. Her sentence was reversed in 1976.

1975

Margie Boykin: White; Reversed in 1976. Shortly after midnight on August 15, 1975, Daniel Davis, a neighbor of the Boykin family went to their home in response to a hysterical call from Margie Boykin. She said she and her husband, Chick, had been robbed and that Chick had been killed. When Mr. Davis, the neighbor, found Chick's body it was lying in a pool of blood in the bathroom and was cold. Davis said that while he was examining the body he'd heard Margie in the living room saying, "Is that goddam-son-of-a-bitch dead? I hope so."

When officers arrived on the scene Margie repeated the story that she and her husband had been robbed and in the course of the robbery she was knocked in the head. Her face was red around her left eye.

At the trial a man named Garland Sanders testified he was employed by Margie to kill her husband. Under a plea bargain, he received a life sentence for a guilty plea of second-degree murder.

Apparently Sanders was first introduced to Margie by her maid, Minnie Dublin, a year and a half before the murder. Sanders said he'd had a number of conversations with Margie at Minnie's house during which she had solicited him to kill Chick. At first, Sanders said he was not interested, so she asked if he knew anyone else who would be interested. Later, she brought him a .22-caliber pistol and said, "Here's the gun. I've got the gun for you — now I want you to kill him with it." Sanders again declined and returned the pistol to Minnie to give back to Margie. Finally, Sanders agreed to "do the job" on Thursday, August 13, for $2,000.

According to Sanders, Margie gave him a rifle and some bullets and instructed him to ring the front door bell then go around to the back of the house. She told him gloves, masking tape, and a shotgun would be at the back door. The key to her 225 Buick Electra would be in the ignition switch, the back door would be unlocked, and the floodlights would be out. Margie told Sanders to get someone to drive him to her home so he arranged to have Johnny Edmondson drop him off at 11:00 p.m.

Before going to the house that night, Sanders called Margie from a service station phone. She told him "Everything is all right; come in 30 minutes." About a half an hour later Sanders was at the Boykin home. Armed with a rifle, he went to the back door and put on the gloves he found on the doorstep. He then rang the front doorbell. Returning to the back where the floodlights were out, as Margie had told him they would be, he picked up the masking tape and the 12-guage single-barrel shotgun. Margie came to the back window, raised it and said, "Come on in, Mr. Boykin is up watching TV."

At the same time Sanders opened the storm door, Chick opened the wooden door and Margie said, "shoot," after the first shot she said "Shoot again." Chick was hit under the left arm, then fell to the floor and Sanders shot him two more times in the head.

Margie then instructed Sanders to tie her up with the tape, but Sanders refused. Instead he got in her car and drove off carrying the rifle and shotgun. Later, Sanders met Edmonson and abandoned Margie's car. Edmondson pawned the rifle and shotgun. Experts stated that the three bullets removed from Chick were fired from a rifle which was identified as belonging to Chick and which Sanders said he used for the murder.

About two weeks after the murder Margie gave Sanders an envelope with $1,100 in cash. He used $343 of it to get his car out of the garage and deposited $700 in the Micro bank. Margie made no further payments but promised to pay him the balance out of her husband's insurance proceeds. A bank cashier testified Margie had withdrawn $1,200 in cash, including ten $100 bills, at some point after her husband's death.

Margie said she had nothing to do with the murder of her husband and insisted that a large amount of money and Chick's rifle were stolen the night of the murder. She said she lent $900 of the money she withdrew from the bank to her son, but her son was unable to account for it.

Margie requested a change of venue for her trial on the grounds that too many rumors had been circulating about her. Some of them, which she brought up in pre-trial hearings, were:

- That she had hired some blacks to kill her husband.
- That she killed her first husband.
- That she killed her husband's brother-in-law and fed him to the hogs.
- That she killed someone who was formerly married to her daughter.
- That she had performed abortions and a girl had died.
- That she was instrumental in the death of her son's former fiancé who was killed in an automobile accident.
- That she was involved in the theft of television sets from Silvania.

The judge refused her change of venue plea and she was found guilty and sentenced to die for her husband's murder. Her sentence was reversed in 1976.

1976

Faye B. Brown: Black; Reversed, 1977. Faye Beatrice Brown, Frankie Squire, and Joseph Seaborn were all tried and convicted of first-degree murder during the commission of a felony bank robbery.

Around 10:00 a.m. on September 25, 1977 the Branch Banking and Trust of Jamesville, North Carolina, was held up and robbed by a black man armed with a sawed-off shotgun and a black woman with a pistol. The woman was positively identified in court as Faye Brown. Prior to the robbery, bank attendants had seen her and Seaborn in the bank parking lot. They got in a brown Pontiac parked on the street and after they got out, the car drove away thus indicating a third person drove it. Shortly afterward, the car returned and the robbery took place.

About fifteen minutes after the robbery, Trooper Guy Davis of the State Highway Patrol stopped the brown Pontiac at an intersection in Williamston, North Carolina, located 10.3 miles from the bank, for a routine traffic violation. As Davis approached the car and spoke to the driver, he was shot in the throat with a shotgun fired from the back seat where Seaborn sat. The trooper died almost instantly and the Pontiac drove off. A bystander positively identified the vehicle. Less than an hour later the car was found abandoned in a creek bottom. There were no license plates on the car, but the plates were later discovered in a nearby stream.

The owner of the car lent it to Seaborn the morning of the robbery. There were bloodstains on the outside door next to the driver's seat and fingerprints of Squire and Seaborn on the car.

That afternoon law officers began searching a field of soybeans not far from where the car was discovered. The downdraft from a search helicopter hovering over the field blew aside the bean vines and the officers saw someone lying on the ground. They ordered the person to come out with their hands up, and the three fugitives came out.

In the area where Faye had been hiding, police found a woman's purse containing a large sum of money, including a package of "bait money" identified as having been taken from the Jamesville bank. A pistol was also found lying on the ground.

When the three were interrogated, Seaborn admitted that he had robbed the bank and accidentally shot the trooper. He said he had picked the shotgun up as the Trooper approached the car and that the gun had discharged accidentally.

Faye confessed to participating in the bank robbery after which she got in the car and laid down on the front seat. Later she said she heard a siren and a loud shot and when the car stopped in a wooded area she ran and hid in the soybean field where she was found.

All three were sentenced to death. Eventually all of the death sentences were vacated and life in prison was imposed.

1978

Rebecca Detter: White; Reversed in 1979. Rebecca Case Detter was charged with the first-degree murder of her husband, Don Gene Detter. Five lay witnesses and four doctors presented the primary evidence for the state. A friend of the Detters, a woman named Joan Brooks, testified she was visiting them one day in January 1977 when Rebecca talked to her about how cruel her husband was to the family. She said she told her then that she'd done something to the brakes of his car "to either hurt him or harm him."

In late January or early February of the same year, Joan went with Rebecca to Crown Drug Store where Rebecca gave Joan some money and asked her to purchase a bottle of Terro Ant Killer, which Joan did. The chief toxicologist of North Carolina at the time, a Dr. McBay, testified that one bottle of Terro Ant killer contains 300 milligrams of arsenic — and a lethal dose of arsenic is between 100-300 milligrams. Joan said on another occasion she had visited James Holly with Rebecca and Rebecca had asked him what "lead or lead poisoning would do to someone." After Holly told her that lead would probably kill someone, Rebecca asked, "where could she get some."

When they returned home from Holly's, Joan said she saw Rebecca go to a storage area and get some lead weights from a fish tackle box and place them in a cooking pot half full of water which she boiled. When there were only a few drops of water left Rebecca poured the water into a liquor bottle. Her husband was a heavy drinker, Joan told the court, and he consumed three or four fifths of liquor a week.

About a week after that, Joan saw Rebecca pour the contents of the bottle of Terro Ant Killer into a glass of ice tea, which her husband drank. On her next visit to the house, Joan said Rebecca remarked that she had asked her husband for a divorce but he wouldn't give her one and, she'd be glad when everything was over and she wouldn't have to put up with him any more.

In March or April of 1977, Joan said she took Rebecca's son Ted to the Crown Drugstore and he purchased two more bottles of Terro Ant Killer, which he took home and gave to his mother. Joan said that on several occasions after that she observed Rebecca putting Ant Killer in ice tea and giving it to her husband and on one occasion she'd seen her pour it over his ice cream.

James Holly testified that Rebecca and her son visited him in February 1977 and she asked him then if he'd be interested in killing her husband for $5,000. Holly said he declined the offer, however, Rebecca's son bought some PCP (Angel Dust) from him and two weeks later Rebecca accused him of "ripping her off." She had put the drugs in her husband's food and they hadn't done anything except make him happy. She said she'd put PCP, cocaine, and acid in her husband's food and alcohol and nothing had killed him. She told Holly she wanted some drugs that would definitely "kill her husband."

Holly's wife testified that she'd heard Rebecca ask her husband how to kill someone with a "needle and some air" to which her husband responded that an air bubble in your vein could kill you instantly.

Gregory Wayne Boyd testified that Rebecca had talked to him in January 1977 and offered him or anyone he knew $5,000 to kill her husband. Pamela Christy, Rebecca's hairdresser, said Rebecca had asked her if she or her husband knew where she could get some dope to kill her husband. She also told Pam she'd put some stuff in her husband's food, but it didn't kill him.

Rebecca's husband was hospitalized twice — from March 30, 1977 to April 13, 1977 and from May 17, 1977 until his death on June 9, 1977. During the second hospitalization, the doctors noticed white lines across his fingernails and a thickening of the skin over his hands, in medical terminology, "hyperkeratosis" which is symptomatic of arsenic poisoning. An autopsy showed that Mr. Detter's body contained ten times the normal amount of arsenic it would take to kill a person.

Rebecca testified that neither she nor her son had ever purchased ant killer and that Joan Brooks had only taken her son to the store to pick up a prescription for her. She also said she'd never said anything to Pamela Christy about wanting her husband killed and that they had only talked about diet pills. She denied ever purchasing drugs from James Holly or ever asking him to murder her husband. She said her husband was a heavy drinker and she suspected someone at the hospital had slipped him arsenic. At the hospital one of the nurses had made a notation that Mrs. Detter had repeatedly said "I did it and I'm sorry."

There were several witnesses who knew Rebecca who said they never heard her talk about wanting to get rid of her husband and she had a good reputation in the community. She even attended the community church. Rebecca Detter was sentenced to death and her sentence was vacated in 1979 and remanded to life imprisonment.

1978

Velma Barfield: White; Executed: November 2, 1984. In his recent book *The Death Penalty: An Historical and Theological Survey* (1998) James Megivern notes that if ever a case was to be made for clemency, it would be that of Velma Barfield. As in the more recent case of Karla Faye Tucker, her lawyers brought up her religious conversion as possible grounds for clemency, the good she had done in prison, her rehabilitation, and the fact that so many people loved her. Unfortunately her case was caught up in the battle between Governor James B. Hunt (D) and the incumbent, Jesse Helms (R), to reach the U.S. Senate in North Carolina in 1984. Governor Hunt told Velma's lawyers that their argument (she was a decent human being who deserved to live because her life had meaning for a number of people) was not even relevant to clemency.

Born Margie Velma Bullard on October 23, 1932 in Cumberland County, North Carolina, her father was a loom repairman. Velma was the oldest girl, the second of nine children, and she was responsible for the care of her siblings. She later said her father beat and raped her and her siblings during their childhood, however, other members of her family disputed these claims.

Velma attended high school up to the tenth grade then dropped out and eloped with a textile plant worker named Thomas Burke when she was seventeen. At nineteen, she gave birth to a son Ron then to a daughter, Kim, three years later. Her daughter recalled her childhood with fondness saying they were the all-American family who did picnics and weekends at the beach.

In 1966 Velma's husband, Thomas, suffered head injuries in a car accident. After that, he lost his job and began to drink. Velma got a job in a textile mill and later in a department store to help support the family. It was during this time she started taking drugs. Her husband was by that time an alcoholic and she began taking prescription drugs to ease tensions. Eventually, she became addicted to a variety of tranquilizers and painkillers that a number of doctors had prescribed for her.

In 1969, Velma's husband burned to death in his bed and in 1970 Velma married Jennings Barfield. Her second husband, Jennings, died six months later. At the time, it was thought he died of natural causes, but when his body was exhumed years later it was found to be full of arsenic.

Between 1972 and 1975 Velma was treated four times for drug overdoses, although she managed to lead a religious life as a member of the First Pentecostal Holiness Church. She taught Sunday School and volunteered in the church office, and attended services twice a week.

Sometime in 1974, Velma borrowed $1,000 from a loan company to support her drug habit, by using her mother's name (Lillie Bullard) on the application papers. Eventually the loan came due and when her mother was contacted for payment, she, of course, knew nothing about it. Soon after that Velma put ant killer in her mother's Coca-Cola and Lillie died on December 30. Cause of death was listed as "natural."

Velma then got a job as a live-in nurse for an 85-year-old woman named Dollie Edwards who had a niece named Alice. Alice's father, Stewart Taylor, began dating Velma. In 1977 Velma put rat poison in Dollie's cereal and coffee and she died three days later. Velma appeared as grief-stricken as the rest of the family at the funeral.

Recommended by the pastor of her church, Velma again, took a job as a live-in housekeeper caring for 80-year-old John Henry Lee and his 76-year-old wife, Record Lee. When Velma found a blank check in the Lee's house, she forged it for $50.00. John Henry found out the forgery and within days after threatening to expose her, he died from a mysterious attack that had caused convulsions. Velma had put ant poison in his tea and beer. She also gave arsenic to Mrs. Lee before leaving her position in October 1977.

By November 1977, Stewart Taylor had made plans to marry Velma Barfield. However, they had a fight when he found out she had forged his name on a check. Then, in January of the following year Velma poisoned Stewart by putting ant killer in his beer. Taylor died four days later, and his family insisted on an autopsy. The autopsy showed his body was full of arsenic. When Velma was arrested, she admitted poisoning Taylor as well as the others.

Velma was tried for the 1978 murder of her fiancé, Stewart Taylor. His murder was the only one that took place after the new capital punishment laws went into effect. The prosecutor depicted Velma as being "callous, indifferent and malicious." Her attorney said, "I begged her to get up there and cry...instead, she did what they wanted her to, she fought back. I hate to say it but it's all a big game, and she just couldn't or wouldn't play" (Einstein, 1985). The media described Velma as a plump, hazel-eyed grandmother who spoke about her execution in a soft Southern drawl (*People Magazine*, 1983).

After her conviction, Velma claimed she did it because she wanted to "get back at them" for being "mean" to her. She was accused of poisoning her mother, her fiancee, and the three elderly people for whom she worked as a nursemaid and housekeeper. The state successfully demonstrated that Velma Barfield committed the murders for money to get drugs. She claimed she only wanted to make Taylor sick, and had nursed him for three days before taking him to the hospital where he died. Velma attended all of the funerals of those she had murder and cried for each of them.

Her cell at the Women's Prison in Raleigh, North Carolina was about the size of a small bathroom, and she was allowed to leave it once a day, accompanied by a guard. She was also allowed to talk with other women prisoners, through the bars.

Some prison personnel remembered Velma as a difficult and withdrawn prisoner. Female inmates remembered her differently. Before her execution they said "We see Mrs. Barfield as an inmate who has helped many of us while we were in segregation. She always encouraged us to change our lives. What does her execution mean for the rest of us?"

Velma claimed to have found Jesus while in the women's prison at Raleigh. As a born-again Christian she stated she did not want any appeals on her behalf since Jesus would care for her. Despite her wishes no one believed she really wanted to die and many appeals for clemency were made on her behalf. Velma's children, Kim and Ron, helped with her appeals and were supportive of her while she was on death row. They tried to get her sentence commuted on the grounds the drugs she had used had caused her to act the way she did. In pleading with Governor Hunt to spare her life, they said they had forgiven their mother for poisoning their grandmother.

In her 1998 book *Guilty by Reason of Insanity* Dr. Dorothy Lewis tells of doing a psychiatric evaluation on Velma Barfield during her appeals process. Ultimately, Dr. Lewis obtained crucial psychiatric information that she felt would have supported clemency for Velma. In the end, however, neither Velma nor her lawyers would allow any of that information to be used. According to Dr. Lewis, Velma felt that if it were brought to light she might lose the support of those who were most important to her at that time of her life.

It was six years before all of Velma's appeals were exhausted. She celebrated her fifty-second birthday in 1984, four days before her execution. For her last meal she requested Coca-Cola and Cheeze Doodles. She was executed by a lethal injection of procuronium bromide at 2:00 a.m. on the morning of November 2, 1984.

The case of Velma Barfield became a political event when her execution was set for November 2, 1984, four days before the North Carolina general elections. The setting of the date by a State Superior Court judge was seen as an attempt to embarrass James Hunt, North Carolina's governor and senate candidate. It was thought that the possibility of an execution a few days before elections would force Hunt to either grant clemency and thus appear soft on capital punishment or face an election that would take place in the atmosphere of a recent execution, not just of a woman, but of a middle-aged grandmother who had gained national attention as being deeply religious.

Governor Hunt's opponent, Jesse Helms, is a known supporter of capital punishment and was thus able to maintain his position without commenting on the case. Rather than appear soft on crime, Governor Hunt chose not to commute Velma's sentence telling a September news conference that "Mrs. Barfield should pay the maximum penalty for her crimes." Of all her victims, Velma claimed she had only wanted to make them sick until she could repay them.

In 1988, Jenny Lancaster, who was warden at the time Velma Barfield was executed, wrote of the execution of Velma Barfield as one of the most challenging and difficult experiences of her professional and personal life. She said that before Velma was executed, she worked with her and knew her for a number of years and had developed both a personal and professional relationship with her and her attorney. Velma was the only woman on death row in North Carolina at the time of her execution.

In the spring of 1984 when Ms. Lancaster realized Velma's execution was imminent, she said she knew she would have to come to grips with how she felt about the death penalty and what her role was supposed to be in the whole process. Ms. Lancaster stated that at the time she felt intense scrutiny from the powers that be about how she might manage an execution (being a woman, would she keep her feelings in perspective?), but almost no support for the human toll that it takes on the individuals involved. She said she was aware from day to day of very specific things that were clearly about the planning and the process of ending Velma Barfield's life. She and her staff had developed relationships with Velma and her family over the years that involved active listening as well as care and support for the "unbelievable stress and pressure they experienced because a person they loved lived on death row and faced execution." According to Ms. Lancaster an execution within a women's facility is one of the most highly emotional events that can occur in the life of an institution.

Velma's last appeal was filed on October 30, 1984. Her attorneys asked the North Carolina Supreme Court to stay the execution because she was incompetent at her 1978 trial as a result of withdrawal from drug addiction, but it was turned down.

Dressed in pink embroidered pajamas and her eyeglasses, Velma was executed by lethal injection at 2:00 a.m. at the Central Prison in Raleigh, North Carolina. She had dropped her appeals the previous day and requested that she be allowed to "die with dignity." Defense attorney, Jimmy Little said that Mrs. Barfield had made a "very clear-headed" decision not to take her case to the U.S. Supreme Court again, as she had already been rejected three times in the past.

Outside the prison hundreds of news reporters and technicians, as well as those who supported Velma and those who did not, awaited her execution. One paper reported there were both "jeers and tears."

After she was pronounced dead, medical workers tried but failed to restart her heart, according to the *Lexington Herald-Leader,* to keep the blood flowing to her organs since she had requested that they be donated and used for transplants. Bill Glance, spokesman for the Bowman Gray Medical Center, reported that they had removed skin and eyes for transplantation.

At 2:25 a.m. her body left the prison in a blue and white ambulance. She was buried near her childhood home in the North Carolina sandhills.

1987

Sue Cox: White; Reversed in 1992. Sue Cox was found guilty of murdering two people (her boyfriend with a lover) in Robeson County, North Carolina, in July 1986. She was given the death penalty in October 1987 and her sentence was reversed in 1992.

1989

Barbara Stager: White; Reversed in 1991. When Barbara Stager was arrested, taken from her home, and charged with murdering her husband, her neighbors were astonished. Her husband, Durham High School baseball coach, Russ Stager, was shot once in the head with a .25-caliber pistol while he was sleeping at home. Barbara said she accidentally shot him when she tried to remove the gun from under his pillow. But a Dr. Thomas Clark testified that the bullet that killed Stager was shot from above his head and about 2 feet away from him, which would seem to indicate he was lying on his side at the time of the murder. He said there was no gunpowder around the bullet wound.

Prosecutors described Barbara as a treacherous, cold-blooded murderer who shot her husband for monetary reasons and who should be put to death. During her trial there was much debate about whether a tape someone claimed they found in her husband's locker after his death could be admitted as testimony. Three people, including Stager's adopted son, Bryan Stager testified that it was not Russ Stager's voice. The issue of a number of checks that were apparently forged with Russ Stager's name was also brought up. The prosecution contended that Barbara forged her husband's signature on checks made out to her, including one for $1,500, and on his will which named her his beneficiary. A handwriting expert that was brought in testified that the forged signatures were similar to samples of Barbara's writing.

The jury deliberated less than an hour before convicting Barbara Stager of the murder of her husband. When her conviction was announced, she burst into tears and sobbed. The jury deliberated for most of the day before recommending the death penalty. Barbara was sentenced to death, and her execution date was set for July 28, 1989. A version of her story was told in the book *Before He Wakes: A True Story of Money, Marriage, Sex, and Murder* by Jerry Bledsoe. At the time of her trial, prosecutors spoke of also investigating the shooting death of her first husband in 1978. Her sentence was reversed in 1991.

1990

Patricia Jennings: White; Currently on death row. At age 47, Patricia Jennings, was sentenced to death for torturing and beating her 77-year-old husband to death in a Wilson, North Carolina, motel in September 1989.

According to court testimony, William Henry Jennings was a retired Air Force man who was visiting North Carolina in September 1989 as a member of the board of directors of an alcohol abuse center. At the local motel where he was staying Jennings was reportedly kicked, stomped and beaten to death by Patricia, his wife of three years.

The state's evidence included testimony that half of her husbands assets totaling about $150,000 had previously been transferred to Patricia. Patricia said her husband had Alzheimer's disease and that she had found him unconscious in the motel room.

A jury of 10 women and two men recommended the death penalty for Patricia Jennings after a daylong sentencing hearing in Wilson County Superior Court. She is on death row in North Carolina today.

1990

Marilyn MaHaley: White; Reversed in 1992. At age 35, Marilyn MaHaley was convicted of the strangulation death of her husband. Prosecutors agreed that she did not participate physically in the murder of her husband in the den of their home, but that she was a conspirator.

Marilyn was indicted for first-degree murder, conspiracy to commit murder and robbery with a dangerous weapon. The jury returned guilty verdicts on all counts. The court sentenced her to death for the murder conviction and arrested judgment on the other charges. Marilyn appealed her murder conviction to the North Carolina Supreme Court, which upheld the conviction but vacated the sentence. She was then given a life sentence, which she is now serving.

1990

Blanche Kiser (Taylor) Moore: White; Currently on death row. At her trial, 56-year-old Blanche Kiser Moore wore a bright blue suit, a white blouse, and a single strand of pearls. She denied all accusations that she killed the men in her life. She said she had never given arsenic to her former boyfriend Raymond Reid or to either of her two husbands, and that she took issue with witnesses who described her as cold. "I've been in jail for 16 months," Blanche told the Forsyth County Superior Court, "I've cried myself to sleep every night. I know arsenic was found in these people, but it's not because I put it there, I didn't."

Blanche was born in Tarheel, North Carolina on February 17, 1933. Her father was a minister and a gambler and early in her life Blanche was forced into prostitution to pay off her father's gambling debts. In 1952, when she was nineteen, she was able to get away from that life by marrying James Taylor who was a twenty-four year old furniture dealer. She seemed very happy with him and they had a daughter, Vanessa, a year after they were married. In 1959, Blanche had another daughter, Cindi.

After the birth of Vanessa, Blanche began working as a clerk at the local Kroeger's supermarket and by the time Cindi was born she had been promoted to head cashier. Despite her happiness with her children and the extra money she was earning, Blanche found herself in a marriage that looked very much like the life she had led with her father. Her husband, James, was a drinker and a gambler and much of the money she earned went to pay off the debts Taylor accrued.

Eventually, with her marriage falling apart, Blanche had an affair with Raymond Reid, the assistant manager of Kroeger's, who was married and had two children. Around the same time, she decided to reconcile her relationship with her father, Parker, and went to see him. Within days after she arrived, her father became ill and in less than a week, he was dead. He had all the symptoms of arsenic poisoning, although no one recognized it at the time.

Two years later after suffering a heart attack, her husband, James, turned his life around, gave up drinking and gambling, became a Christian, and began to focus on being a devoted father and husband. When his mother, Isa Taylor, became bedridden, Blanche offered to help with her care, and soon Mrs. Taylor died in much the same way as Blanche's father. No autopsy was performed.

In 1973 James Taylor died at the age of forty-five under mysterious circumstances. By this time Raymond Reid had divorced and Blanche and he began seeing each other openly. Although Raymond seemed interested in marriage, Blanche was not. Blanche had moved to Burlington after James' death and in 1985 her house there burned down. With the insurance money she received she bought a trailer home which burned to the ground the same year and for which she received more insurance money.

In 1985 Blanche received a $275,000 settlement from Kroeger's for a sexual harassment suit she had filed against them. It was the same year she met Reverend Dwight Moore who became her third husband. Within a year after meeting Reverend Moore, Raymond Reid became ill and died from what was then diagnosed as a disease of the central nervous system.

Eventually Blanche was accused of spoon-feeding Raymond arsenic-laced home-cooked food which she sneaked into his hospital room in Tupperware containers over a six month period. During that time Blanche helped him draw up a will giving her one-third of his estate and when he died, she received $50,000.

In 1989 Blanche married Reverend Dwight Moore and on their honeymoon he became violently ill and went to the hospital twice before he was finally given toxic-screening tests which revealed he had twenty times the lethal dose of arsenic in his system. The hospital informed the police, and it was only a matter of time before they became suspicious of Blanche noting the similarities in the medical files of her last two husbands.

Based on their suspicions, the police dug up the bodies of Raymond Reid and James Taylor and autopsies confirmed that there was a substantial amount of arsenic in both bodies. Later, arsenic was also found in the bodies of Blanche's father and her mother-in-law, Isa Taylor.

Blanche has always maintained she is innocent. At her subsequent trial a prosecutor told jurors that the ghost of the man who died while dating Blanche Kiser Moore was in the courtroom watching the proceedings that day. Calling Blanche a "cold, cold, calculating killer" prosecutors asked a jury to convict her of the murder of Raymond Reid.

Attorneys for Blanche requested a second look into the state's evidence against her and hired Dr. Page Hudson, a former chief medical examiner and a faculty member at East Carolina University, to analyze the evidence and tests for arsenic.

People who knew Blanche Moore remembered her as a sweet-talking gospel singer. A friend of hers said, "If she is guilty, she would have to have two different people in her body, because I haven't seen anything but good in her."

Nevertheless, according to prosecutors Blanche slowly tortured and killed one lover while she ran off with another. Ultimately, she was tried for the poisoning and death of Raymond Reid who died in October 1986 at the North Carolina Baptist Hospital in Winston-Salem. She was also charged with murder in the arsenic poisoning death of her first husband James Taylor, and assault in the poisoning of her estranged husband, the Reverend Dwight Moore.

Prosecutors used graphic details of Raymond Reid's arsenic suffering to try to persuade the jury that Blanche should be put to death while family members continued to call her a loving person. After deliberating nearly four hours, a jury sentenced her to death.

When the decision was announced, Blanche seemed stunned. As Forsyth County Superior Court Judge William Freeman announced the jury's decision, Blanche closed her eyes and said, "My God." Her lips trembled, and she shook her head. From the first row directly behind Mrs. Moore, hushed sobs rose from her family and Blanche turned to calm her two daughters. Blanche Moore joined eighty-two people on death row in North Carolina at the time. She was the fourth woman — each there for killing a husband or a boyfriend.

Blanche's brother said that daily prayers, love of family and a desire to be vindicated have helped his sister cope with life on death row. But, confinement in the un–air-conditioned prison wing in the North Carolina Correctional Institution for Women hasn't prevented Blanche, now 65, from finding ways to occupy her time. Among other things, she writes poetry.

Blanche's attorneys vowed to overturn their client's death sentence, criticizing the three-week trial as unfair and calling it "Round one of a difficult fight." Defense Attorney Mitchell McEntire said appeals would focus on "very questionable rulings" by Forsyth County Superior Court Judge William Freeman.

Blanche Moore's brother says that music she wrote during her pretrial days will be recorded. Sam Kiser of Salisbury said he plans to set his sister's words to music and record it for a radio play. During her murder investigation at least two spoof songs on Blanche's charges surfaced.

Blanche Moore's husband filed for divorce less than a month after her death-row conviction. The complaint filed by the Revered Dwight Moore in Alamance County District Court was not a surprise, since the pastor had already filed for a legal separation. Dwight Moore survived one of the largest recorded doses of arsenic, which nearly killed him and initially left him paralyzed.

In 1993, Blanche's story was portrayed in a made for TV movie, "Black Widow Murders: The Blanche Taylor Moore Story" starring Elizabeth Montgomery as Blanche.

In July 1997 Blanche Taylor Moore was back in court with her attorneys arguing for a new trial. Her hair was shorter and grayer than it was in 1990 and she sat quietly while her attorneys argued her case before Judge William Wood. She is still on death row in North Carolina.

1991

Yvette Gay: Black; Reversed in 1993. At age 27, Yvette Gay and her twin sister, Doris were arrested and charged with three counts of first-degree murder in the execution-style murders of Yvette's boyfriend's mother-in-law, Louise Farris, 40, and her children, Shamika, 16, and William, 13. The victims were found tied, gagged, and shot to death in their home. Yvette Gay was convicted on all three counts of first-degree murder and sentenced to death. At her sentencing, Yvette said, "I'd like to say, I'm real sorry this has happened to the Farris family. I know I'm very, very, sorry." Her sentence was reversed in 1993.

1996

Melanie S. Anderson: White; Currently on death row. In August 1994, Melanie Anderson and her boyfriend, Ronald Eugene Pierce, went to

Pennsylvania to visit Pierce's brother and his wife. With the consent of her parents Melanie and Ron took the Pierces' daughter Tabitha, Ron's niece, who was then 2½ years old back to North Carolina with them for a visit. Three or four weeks later the two of them brought Tabitha to the Wilkes Regional Medical Center unconscious. The extent of her injuries was severe enough in nature that she was transferred to Baptist Hospital in Winston-Salem. On August 25, life support was withdrawn and Tabitha died.

At first Ron tried to explain Tabitha's injuries by saying that a dog knocked her down and that the children in the neighborhood beat her up and that she bruised easily. Later, he changed his story and said that he had heard Melanie striking Tabitha around 8:00 p.m. on August 24. Later while he was taking a shower he said he heard Melanie bring Tabitha into the bathroom and punish her for saying she had to urinate when she didn't. He said he saw Melanie hit the little girl on the side of the head while asking her "Are you dumb? Are you stupid?" When the child did not answer Melanie put her hands on Tabitha's shoulders and began to shake her. Ron said he then slapped Tabitha and shook her hard for about a minute before she went "limp." When she went limp they took her to the hospital.

Tabitha had severe head injuries plus a torn frenulum (the piece of tissue between the upper lip and the teeth); bruises on the inside of her lips and around the gum line; a human bite mark on her thigh, and many other injuries. Photographs presented at the trial showed that Tabitha had been severely beaten and that she had bruises, grab marks, pinch marks, scratches, nicks, bumps, and other injuries on almost every inch of her body. She had distinct injuries on her head, shoulders, chin, mouth, legs, back, torso, and other portions of her body. Her death was caused by severe injuries to the brain. Doctors who treated Tabitha at Baptist Hospital testified at the trial that all of Tabitha's injuries had been inflicted during the four-week period she had been with Melanie and Ron. Two doctors stated that Tabitha was a victim of both the battered child syndrome and the shaken baby syndrome.

Both Melanie and Ron admitted punishing Tabitha for wetting her pants, wetting her bed, and refusing to eat. Melanie punished her by making her hang from a dresser by her forearms and chin and by making her wear soiled pants on her head. Ron punished her by making her stand close to a wall, place her head on the wall, and hold her leg out in the air for two or three minutes with her soiled pants on her head.

Evidence brought out in the trial showed that they had also punished Tabitha by shaking her with their hands and by beating her with their fists, with a belt, with a metal tray, with a broken antenna, and with a pair of tennis shoes. Ron admitted "smacking" Tabitha at least ten times in the three weeks prior to her death. The evidence ultimately showed that both Melanie and Ron were guilty of felonious child abuse and torture and that Tabitha's death was a probable consequence of their actions. Ron received a sentence of life imprisonment plus ten years for felonious child abuse. Melanie S. Anderson was sentenced to death and she is currently on death row in North Carolina.

24

Ohio: Gas/Lethal Injection

The state of Ohio has sentenced thirteen women to death since 1900, three of these women, Ana Marie Hahn, Blanche Smarr Dean, and Betty Butler, were executed. There are no women on death row in Ohio today.

In 1885 the Ohio State legislature enacted a law that required all executions to be carried out at the Ohio State Penitentiary in Columbus. Since then the state has used three methods of execution over a period of years.

Hanging was the first method of execution to be used and the first execution took place at the Ohio State Penitentiary on July 31, 1885. A 56-year-old man by the name of Valentine Wagner was hanged at 2:30 a.m. for the murder of Daniel Shehan. There were 27 more hangings in Ohio after Wagner.

The state next used electrocution. The first execution by electrocution was that of 17-year-old William Haas for the murder of Mrs. William Brady in 1897. In 1911, Charles Justice, the man who helped build Ohio's electric chair was also executed by electrocution. The last execution by electrocution at the Ohio State Penitentiary was that of Donald Reinbolt, a 29-year-old man from Franklin County who was executed on March 15, 1963. Over the years, a total of 312 men and 3 women were put to death in Ohio's electric chair.

One of the only two reporters allowed to witness the execution of Donald Reinbolt noted that when Warden Ernest Maxwell, briefed them before the execution, his primary concern was order. Therefore, one of the things he told them was that if anyone got sick or fainted during the execution, they would be ignored until after it was over.

The same reporter remembered the walls of the execution chamber as a "Rogue's Gallery" with pictures of the 314 people who had been electrocuted there on display (*Akron Beacon Journal*, 1963). In those days there was no viewing room that separated the witnesses from the condemned so for Reinbolt's execution two reporters, a doctor, and the warden stood about six feet away from the chair where Reinbolt sat. When he was brought in, a priest who was saying the Hail Mary accompanied him. The reporter said everything was perfunctory and quiet. Reinbolt was strapped in the chair and his head was covered with a black rubber hood. He never spoke. The warden gave a signal and the guards pulled the switches. There was a smell of singed hair and one of the reporters fainted. The whole thing took about fourteen minutes.

THE DEATH PENALTY IN OHIO

When the U.S. Supreme Court, declared the death penalty unconstitutional in 1972, 65 inmates in Ohio had their death sentences reduced to life. By 1974, the state legislature had revised its death penalty statutes. Nevertheless, in 1978, the Supreme Court again rejected Ohio's death penalty law and 100 men and four women had their sentences reduced to life.

Capital punishment was reinstated in Ohio in October 1981 and Leonard Jenkins was the first person sentenced to death under the new law. He was found guilty of killing a police officer but former Governor Richard Celeste later commuted his sentence to life.

Before August 1997, Ohio required aggravating circumstances, such as rape, robbery, or kidnapping to seek the death penalty. But in 1997 Representative Cheryl Winkler introduced what has become known as the "Kid Killers" bill, which makes the killing of children a capital offense. Winkler says she hopes using it will prevent crimes against children. She said "I hope they try a couple of these cases and find them guilty, to send a message that you don't beat little children and kill them" (*Cincinnati Enquirer*, 1997).

In 1998 a bill was signed in Ohio regarding vacating death sentences for juveniles, pregnant women, and the mentally ill.

Ohio has also joined the ranks of nearly every state that has the death penalty in introducing Life Without Parole (LWOP) as an alternative to death. According to the *Cincinnati Enquirer* (January 6, 1997) all but three of the thirty-eight states that use capital punishment now have LWOP. In Ohio the option is available only in capital cases where the crime occurred on or after July 1, 1996. However, juries are not always aware that LWOP is a possibility (ACLU Abolitionist, April 1997), as the courts are not required to inform a jury of this option.

When Ohio conducts its next execution, the first since 1963, there will be two obvious changes. The official time for execution has been changed from 12:01 a.m. to 9:00 p.m. and the inmate's final statement will be read after the execution, rather than the inmate making a statement before he/she is executed.

DEATH ROW IN OHIO

In 1995 all death row inmates in Ohio were transferred from the Southern Ohio Correctional Facility to the Mansfield Correctional Institution. The death house, however, and the execution chamber are still located at the Southern Ohio Correctional Facility. Women on death row are held at the Ohio Reformatory for Women in Marysville until a few days before their execution.

One week before a scheduled execution, the prisoner is asked to choose the way he/she prefers to die — either lethal injection or electrocution — and a ten member team is then assembled to prepare for the execution. Twenty-four hours prior to execution, the inmate is transferred from death row at the Mansfield Correctional Institution to the Death House at the Southern Ohio Correctional Facility in Lucasville.

Ohio death row inmate Wilford Berry fought for seven years to end his appeals and be executed by lethal injection. In Ohio legal circles he was dubbed "the volunteer." And in June 1997 when he announced he had fired his lawyers and wished to proceed with his execution, a Cuyahoga County judge, Judge Carolyn B. Friedland, ruled he was mentally competent to waive his appeals. However, his case is still in the courts and to date he has not been executed.

The *Akron Beacon Journal* sued the Ohio Public Defender's Office in 1998 to find out how much the office had spent on Berry's defense. Despite Berry's repeated requests to be executed the office continued to request delays on the grounds of Berry's mental incompetence. Berry's sentence was delayed again when the Public Defenders Office filed a "next friend" petition in federal court on behalf of Berry's mother and sister. The petition challenges Berry's mental competency to make decisions on his own behalf. A reporter at the paper said, "We believe the public has a right to know how much of their money is being spent on Wilford Berry."

In September, 1997 there was a riot in the death row section of Mansfield Correctional Institution that began around 5:00 p.m. when a guard was over-powered by an inmate walking through the death row housing area. Several inmates were freed from their cells with the guard's keys and two guards were overpowered. All three were let go and two were treated at a local hospital and released. Two inmates were injured when officers from the State Highway Patrol and the Ohio Corrections Department moved in. Reports said the prison was briefly under the control of thirty-seven inmates. Corrections officials said that inmate-on-inmate violence and recent drug sweeps, as well as inmate Wilford Berry's desire to abandon his appeals and become the first Ohio inmate to be executed since 1963 contributed to the upheaval. Berry, himself suffered severe head injuries in the riot when inmates held him down, kicked him, and swung chains and socks weighted with padlocks at his head. Sonny Williams, a coordinator for an inmate's rights group, the Ohio Prisoners Rights Union, said that one reason for the inmates' frustration with Berry is because historically when the first one is executed, others follow. As a result of the riot death row inmates must remain in their cells 23-hours a day.

RESIDUAL DOUBT

Paul E. Pfeifer, an Ohio Supreme Court justice, recently spoke in favor of the appeals process in Ohio explaining the concept of residual doubt. According to Pfeifer, residual doubt is a "lingering uncertainty about facts" and exists somewhere between "beyond a reasonable doubt" and "absolute certainty." In practice this means it is possible to find a person guilty beyond a reasonable doubt, yet still maintain enough uncertainty to not want to execute him/her. Pfeifer said, "Residual doubt acknowledges our humanity . . . and our ability to recognize the subtle shadings that are a part of life."

WOMEN SENTENCED TO DEATH IN OHIO

1938

Ana Marie Hahn: Executed, December 7, 1938. Ana Marie Hahn, dubbed the "beautiful blonde killer" by the press, was ultimately convicted of poisoning George Obendoerfer, an elderly gardener, in order to steal his life savings, which did not amount to much but which she needed to cover her losses at the race track.

Ana was born in Germany in 1906 and came to the United States in 1927. In 1929 she moved to Cincinnati where she married Phillip Hahn. They had one son Oscar. Her marriage to Phillip ended in divorce after he became suspicious that she was trying to poison him. She then became a self-appointed "angel of mercy" in the German immigrant community in Cincinnati by offering her services as a live-in caretaker for elderly men.

Ultimately between 1932 and 1937, Ana Marie murdered five men she had cared for by using different forms of poison. In 1937, after George Obendoerfer died, Ana was caught taking money from his account and arrested. The Cincinnati Chief-of-police ordered an autopsy on Obendoerfer's body that revealed traces of arsenic. Investigations into the deaths of the other men she had cared for showed that they, too, had died of poisoning. Though all of the deceased were in relatively good health, Ana claimed at her trial that she had killed them to relieve them of their sufferings. She was convicted of five counts of murder and sentenced to death.

Twelve year-old Oscar ("Little Oscar"), Ana's son, stayed with her in prison, almost up to the moment of her execution. Before she was executed, on his way out of death row, Oscar stopped to answer questions put to him by reporters. His parting words were "She is the best mother a person could ever have."

The night before her execution Ana did not want to see either her former husband or her son, but gave a party in her cell instead for the newsmen who had covered her trial. They were served punch and cake. Although Ana had asked for clemency it was denied and she was executed on December 7, 1938.

1954

Blanche "Dovie" Smarr Dean: Executed, January 15, 1954. Dovie Dean, nick-named the "Murderess Without Tears," grew up poor and unhappy. Her first marriage ended when her husband was incarcerated for molesting their daughter. Dovie never saw or spoke to her husband again after he went to prison.

After that marriage Dovie, spent most of her life working as a maid to support her two children. Eventually, she met Hawkins Dean and they married. They didn't love each other, but Dovie explained it by saying, "He needed a housekeeper and I needed a home." Although they apparently lived well, their marriage was not a happy one either.

Hawkins became ill and went to the hospital for a digestive disorder that was never diagnosed. After he returned home from the hospital he suddenly died. An autopsy revealed arsenic poisoning had caused his death. Dovie was immediately suspected, and at one point she told the detectives she would confess if they would leave her son out of it. Afterward she dictated a statement, which the prosecution claimed was a confession and she was sentenced to death for her husband's murder. Her daughter had been killed before all this happened and her son eventually died in an accident too.

Dovie died wearing a new cotton dress she had picked out for the occasion. Despite the grief her family told reporters they experienced at her conviction, no one visited her while she was on death row, and no one claimed her body. A representative of the funeral home accompanied her body back to West Virginia where she was buried in an unmarked grave. She was the first woman executed in Ohio in 17 years.

1954

Betty Butler: Black; Executed, June 12, 1954. Betty Butler was the second woman executed in Ohio in a six-month period in 1954. Betty was convicted of drowning Evelyn Clark, a lesbian who had apparently made advances towards her offering her money for sex. Betty did have a brief fling with Evelyn, but afterward she wanted nothing to do with her. She had married young and was pregnant at the time of her marriage, which was heavily stressed by the prosecutor in her trial, even though it was of no relevance to the case. She had separated from her husband and returned to Cincinnati to start her life over, but couldn't find work. At some point she met Evelyn Clark who approached her about a possible relationship. At first, Betty had agreed to a tryst with Evelyn, but it later repulsed her and she tried to get out of the relationship.

On the day Evelyn was murdered, both women had gone fishing with a male acquaintance and all had been drinking quite a bit. For whatever reason, Betty first tried to strangle Evelyn but didn't succeed and was pulled off when Evelyn lapsed into unconsciousness. Then, later, the same day, Betty tried again and managed to drag Evelyn's body to the edge of the water where she held her head under until she stopped breathing. She never tried to leave the scene of the crime and was arrested on the spot. She readily admitted she'd murdered Evelyn and said she'd acted in self-defense. The prosecution never presented a clear motive for the murder, but it was widely believed that Betty's race and history were both used against her.

This was a very sensational crime by any standards, but even more so in 1954. Betty Butler was sentenced to death and, although she was not isolated from the other women in prison, she kept to herself. Because of the nature of her crime and her small stature, she indicated she was afraid of being attacked by other women.

On death row, she busied herself making charcoal sketches of her children, a son age 5 and a six-year-old daughter and she sent them the sketches from prison. She became a Catholic during her incarceration; after a last visit from a priest, she was executed holding a Rosary in her hand.

1960

Edythe M. Klumpp: White: Commuted in 1961. Edythe Klumpp, a Cincinnati woman was convicted and sentenced to death for the shooting death of her lover's wife, Louise Bergen. Governor Michael V. DiSalle, who was governor of Ohio at the time, visited her on death row and questioned her about the murder after she had been given a purported truth serum, "sodium amytal." From this interview, he concluded she was not guilty of firing the fatal shot and, therefore, did not deserve execution. On January 5, 1961, he commuted her sentence to life. His constituents were so enraged by this decision that it became a major issue in his reelection campaign. Although he was defeated in the elections, on January 14, 1963, his last day in office he changed her conviction from first-degree to second-degree murder.

1975

Sandra Lockett: Black; Reversed in 1978. The case of *Lockett v. Ohio* [438 U.S. 586, 98 S.Ct. 2954 (1978)] was a landmark case involving a woman and the death penalty. Sandra Lockett, a 21-year-old black woman, was given the death penalty for a murder committed during the course of a robbery at which she testified she was not even present. The Supreme Court granted *certiorari* in this case to consider, among other questions, whether Ohio violated the Eighth and Fourteenth Amendments by sentencing Sandra to death under an Ohio statute that severely limited the consideration of the circumstances of the crime and the consideration of the record and character of the offender as mitigating circumstances (Ohio, 1975). The state's case against her was built on the testimony of another individual, Al Parker, who, it seems, was the actual triggerman in the murder.

Parker's version of the story was that he and a friend (Nathan Earl Dew) had become acquainted with Sandra, her brother, and another friend of Sandra's in New Jersey and had accompanied them back to Ohio. Once in Ohio, Parker and Dew needed money to get back to New Jersey, so Dew decided to pawn his ring. According to Parker, Sandra thought the ring was too pretty to pawn and suggested they rob a grocery store instead. She offered to get a gun for them from her father's basement. By the time their discussions about how they would get the money were over most grocery stores in the area had closed so Sandra's brother suggested they rob the pawnshop instead. No one mentioned killing the pawnshop operator. The plan was to go in the shop as if they were going to pawn the ring. Once inside Dew was supposed to ask to see a gun, and then load it with bullets he brought with him. Then they would rob the store. Parker further testified that the plan was for Sandra to take them to the pawnshop but not go in because she knew the owner.

On the appointed day, Sandra's brother and Dew went in the pawnshop. Parker followed them after giving Sandra the car keys and telling her to start the car in two minutes. The robbery went as they planned, at first, but after Dew loaded the gun the pawnbroker tried to grab it from him when Parker said it was a "holdup." The gun then went off with Parker's finger on the trigger, and the pawnbroker was killed instantly.

Parker said Sandra was waiting in the car with the engine running, and as they drove away Parker told her what had happened and she put the gun in her purse. Later, Parker and Sandra took a cab and Sandra hid the gun under the front seat of the cab when she saw the police approaching. Parker was apprehended and charged with aggravated murder with specifications, an offense punishable by death, and aggravated robbery. Before his trial, he pleaded guilty to the murder charge and agreed to testify against Sandra, her brother, and Dew if the prosecutor would drop the aggravated robbery charge and the specifications to the murder charge. By doing this the possibility of Parker getting the death penalty was eliminated, even though he admitted he was the actual triggerman.

Before the other trials, the court instructed the jury that "If the conspired robbery and the manner of its accomplishment would be reasonably likely to produce death, each plotter is equally guilty with the principal offender as an aider and abettor in the homicide. An intent to kill by an aider and abettor may be found to exist beyond a reasonable doubt under such circumstances."

In their trials, Sandra's brother and Dew were convicted of aggravated murder with specifications. Her brother was sentenced to death, but Dew received a lesser sentence because it was determined that his offense was "primarily the product of mental deficiency," one of the three mitigating circumstances specified in the Ohio death penalty statute.

Two weeks before Sandra's trial, the prosecutor offered to let her plead guilty to voluntary manslaughter and aggravated robbery, offenses which each carried a maximum penalty of 25 years and a maximum fine of $10,000 if she would cooperate with the state, but she rejected the offer. Just prior to her trial, the prosecutor again offered to let her plead guilty to aggravated murder without specifications, an offense with a mandatory life penalty, with the understanding that the aggravated robbery charge and an outstanding forgery charge against her would be dismissed. But Sandra again rejected the offer.

Ultimately, because she refused to plea-bargain, Sandra was charged with aggravated murder with the aggravating specifications that (1) the murder was committed for the purpose of escaping detection, apprehension, trial, or punishment for aggravated robbery, and (2) that the murder was committed while committing, attempting to commit, or fleeing immediately after committing or attempting to commit aggravated robbery. These were punishable by death in Ohio.

At the opening argument of Sandra's defense, her counsel summarized her version of the events leading to the murder of the pawnbroker, which were very different from Parker's. According to her counsel, as far as Sandra knew, Dew and her brother planned to pawn Dew's ring for $100 to get money for Parker and Dew to go back to New Jersey. Sandra said she did not wait in the car while the men were in the pawnshop, but went to lunch at a nearby restaurant. She met Parker returning to the car, and thinking the transaction was over, joined him. She said Parker was the one who had placed the gun under the seat of the taxi, and that she had voluntarily gone to the police when she learned they were looking for the pawnbroker's killers.

As the state's first witness in Sandra's trial, Parker gave his version of the robbery and shooting and admitted to his previous record of breaking and entering, larceny, receiving stolen goods, and bond-jumping. He also acknowledged that his plea-bargaining had eliminated the possibility of the death penalty for him and that he had agreed to testify against Sandra, her brother, and Dew as part of his plea agreement with the prosecutor. At the end of Parker's testimony, the prosecutor again offered Sandra the possibility of pleading guilty to aggravated murder without specifications and to drop the other charges against her. For a third time she refused the option.

Sandra's counsel called Dew and her brother as defense witnesses, but they invoked the Fifth Amendment and refused to testify. In the Supreme Court's review of Sandra Lockett's case it was noted that, when he was arrested, Dew told the police that he, Parker, and Sandra's brother had planned the holdup. He also said that Parker told him Sandra Lockett had not kept the car running as he told her to, but had instead gone to get something to eat as Sandra herself stated.

Sandra did not testify on her own behalf because her mother advised against it. Therefore, the defense did not introduce any evidence to rebut the prosecutor's case. The jury found Sandra guilty as charged. Once the verdict of aggravated murder with specifications was returned according to the Ohio death penalty statute the trial judge was required to impose the death sentence.

In accordance with Ohio statutes, the trial judge requested a pre-sentencing report on Sandra as well as psychiatric and psychological reports. These reports contained detailed information about Sandra's intelligence, character, and background. The psychiatric and psychological reports described her as a 21-year-old with low-average or average intelligence, who had no mental deficiency. One of the psychologists reported that her prognosis for rehabilitation if returned to society was favorable.

After considering the reports and hearing arguments on the death penalty issue, the trial judge concluded that the offense had not been primarily the product of psychosis or mental deficiency. He said he had no alternative "whether he liked the law or not" but to impose the death penalty. He then sentenced Sandra Lockett to death.

In concurring judgment when this case appeared before the Supreme Court, Chief Justice Thurgood Marshall stated:

When a death sentence is imposed under the circumstances presented here, I fail to understand how any of my brethren — even those who believe that the death penalty is not wholly inconsistent with the Constitution — can disagree that it must be vacated. Under the Ohio death penalty statute, this 21-year-old black woman was sentenced to death for a killing that she did not actually commit or intend to commit. She was convicted under a theory of vicarious liability. The imposition of the death penalty for this crime totally violates the principle of proportionality embodied in the Eighth Amendment's prohibition, *Weems v. United States*, 217 U.S. 349 (1910); it makes no distinction between a willful and malicious murderer and an accomplice to an armed robbery in which a killing unintentionally occurs.

He further stated:

I continue to adhere to my view that the death penalty is, under all circumstances cruel and unusual punishment prohibited by the 8th Amendment. The cases that have come to this Court since its 1976 decisions permitting imposition of the death penalty have only persuaded me further of that conclusion. This case as well, serves to reinforce my view.

Sandra Lockett's death sentence was finally overturned due to Ohio's unusual means of considering aggravating and mitigating circumstances in its death penalty statutes. Specifically, the Court ruled that the limited range of mitigating circumstances could be in violation of both the 8th and 14th Amendments.

In a 1982 discussion of this case Shaskolsky concluded that even though Sandra Lockett's death penalty was overturned a larger set of questions remained unanswered. How did Sandra Lockett ever reach the stage where she was condemned to die and what was the nature of the deliberations of the jury in reaching such a conclusion? Beyond that he asked what was the nature of the considerations of the prosecution in making such a deal? Did they insist on the death penalty out of anger at her because of her refusal to plea-bargain? And even further, how often have prosecutors used their power to undermine the possibility of avoiding any arbitrary decisions? These are questions we continue to consider when we look at the women who have been sentence to death throughout our history.

When Sandra Lockett was sent to prison in 1975, she was forced to say goodbye to her 5-year-old son. In 1986, her son, then seventeen, was arrested for murder.

1975

Alberta Osborne: White; Reversed in 1978. Alberta Osborne worked in a bar in Columbus, Ohio, for a man named Ross with whom she had an affair that lasted for six years. She was accused and convicted of arranging for the murder of Hermalee Ross, her lover's wife, after Ross told her he wanted to end their affair and move to Kentucky with his wife.

Alberta paid her 20-year-old son Carl and a friend of his, James Weind $325 to abduct Mrs. Ross from a parking lot in downtown Columbus which they did. They then took her to an abandoned school and Weind shot her in the head. A woman on a nearby farm witnessed part of the murder and called police. The police found the murder weapon and identified it as Alberta Osborne's and arrested her. Her son and Weind were arrested later. Alberta's 18-year-old daughter was the chief prosecution witness.

Alberta, Carl, and Weind, were all sentenced to die in the electric chair. Alberta's sentence was reversed and changed to life in 1978. She is serving a life sentence today.

1976

Patricia Wernert: White; Reversed in 1978. Patricia Wernert was convicted of aggravated murder and sentenced to die on November 26, 1976. Her sentence was reversed in 1978, and she is currently serving a life sentence at the Ohio Reformatory for Women. Her next parole hearing is scheduled for December 1, 2015.

1977

Bonita Smith: Black; Reversed in 1978. Bonita Smith was convicted of aggravated murder and sentenced to die in December 1977. Her sentence was reversed in 1978, and she is currently serving a life sentence at the Ohio Reformatory for Women.

1983

Rosalie Grant: Black; Commuted in 1991. Rosalie Grant was sentenced to die in the electric chair for starting an apartment fire in which her two children perished, allegedly so she could collect $10,000 in life insurance benefits. At her 1983 trial, Grant said someone else had started the fire to spite her. She was convicted of aggravated murder of her two children. Governor Richard Celeste commuted her sentence in 1991 because of "scanty evidence." She is currently serving a life sentence at the Ohio Reformatory for Women. Her next parole hearing is scheduled for November 17, 2004.

1983

Sharon Young: White; Reversed in 1986. Sharon Young was convicted of aggravated murder, possession of firearms, and aggravated robbery and was sentenced to die September 30, 1983. Her sentence was reversed in 1986 and she is currently serving a life sentence at the Ohio Reformatory for Women.

1985

Debra Brown: Currently serving a life sentence. Although Debra Brown has a death sentence in Indiana, she is currently serving a life sentence in Ohio. In 1998 Justice Brent Dickson signed an order setting a January 20, 1999 execution date for Debra in Indiana. The judge said she had exhausted all of her automatic appeals under the state law. (See Indiana)

1988

Elizabeth Green: Black; Commuted in 1991. Elizabeth Green was sentenced to death for the aggravated murder of a Cincinnati man, Thomas Willis, who police said she stabbed more than 100 times. Governor Richard Celeste commuted her sentence in 1991 because her IQ was determined to be below 70, and various states had enacted laws against executing mentally retarded individuals. She is currently serving a life sentence at the Ohio Reformatory for Women.

1989

Beatrice Lampkin: Black; Commuted in 1991. Beatrice Lampkin was found guilty of aggravated murder and sentenced to die in April 1989. Governor Richard Celeste commuted her sentence in 1991 on the basis of equity, since the gunman she was accused of hiring had received a life sentence. She is currently serving a life sentence at the Ohio Reformatory for Women.

25

Oklahoma: Lethal Injection

Oklahoma has sentenced seven women to death since 1900. One woman, Dora Wright, was hanged in 1903, and there are four women on death row in Oklahoma today.

In the early days of Oklahoma statehood, inmates spent less than six months on death row, but after the death penalty was reinstated in 1977, average stays have been over 12 years.

Between 1915 and 1996, Oklahoma executed 91 men—eighty-two by electrocution, one by hanging, and eight by lethal injection. Since 1976 ten men have been executed.

In 1988 the U.S. Supreme Court vacated the death sentence of William Wayne Thompson, *Thompson v. Oklahoma* [487 US. 815,108 S.Ct. 2687 (1988)] on the basis of electro-phsyiological evidence indicating that Thompson was mentally handicapped as a result of abuse. This was the first time that such scientific test results had been considered by the Supreme Court. Thompson was 15-years-old when he and three adults were accused of brutally murdering his brother-in-law. During the investigation his girlfriend told authorities that Thompson told her he was going to kill the victim, and several witnesses indicated that Thompson had admitted the murder later. The District Attorney wanted him to be tried as an adult, which he was, and he was convicted and given the death penalty.

Eventually his case was reviewed by the Supreme Court which gave the American Orthopsychiatric Association and the American Society for Adolescent Psychiatry permission to file briefs as friends of the court. Both groups presented evidence claiming all adolescents suffer psychological disturbances which increase their defenselessness against impulsive behaviors. Their data indicated that these conditions could manifest themselves as rage in some youths, with violence being the only outlet. They also provided the court with data from a survey of fourteen death row inmates who committed crimes before they were 18-years-old. All fourteen were diagnosed as mentally disturbed, showing signs of brain damage from earlier abuse. Seven of the fourteen were diagnosed as psychotic prior to their crimes, and nine showed IQs below 90.

Thompson's death sentence was overturned, and the Supreme Court ruled that "The 8th and 14th Amendments prohibit the execution of a person who is under sixteen years of age at the time of his or her offense."

Another important death penalty ruling in Oklahoma was *Eddings v. Oklahoma* [455 U.S. 104,10 S.Ct. 869 (1982)]. This case raised the question of whether the death penalty as applied to juveniles was "cruel and unusual punishment" under the Eighth Amendment. The defendant, Eddings, who was sixteen at the time of the crime, shot an Oklahoma Highway Patrol Officer point-blank without apparent cause or provocation when the officer approached the car Eddings had lost control of while driving. Eddings, who was driving a car owned by his brother, had several weapons in the car, including rifles stolen from his father.

When the case reached the Supreme Court, the Justices avoided the issue of "cruel and unusual punishment." They chose, rather, to say that the youthfulness of the offender was a mitigating factor of great weight that must be considered.

EXECUTION IN OKLAHOMA

Oklahoma was the first state to legally adopt lethal injection as a method of execution when the current death penalty law was enacted by the Oklahoma legislature in 1977. Originally, executions in Oklahoma were carried out by electrocution, but the last execution by electrocution in Oklahoma took place in 1966. Lethal injection was adopted as an alternative to spending $62,000 to repair the state's electric chair or more than $200,000 in capital investment to create a functional gas chamber. The first execution by lethal injection was on September 10, 1990 with the execution of Charles Troy Coleman.

On March 10, 1992, Robyn Leroy Parks had a violent reaction to the drugs in the lethal injection and two minutes after the drugs were administered, the muscles in his jaws, neck, and abdomen began to react spasmodically for approximately forty-five seconds. Parks gasped and violently gagged until death came eleven minutes after the drugs were administered. A reporter from the *Tulsa World* who was a witness said, "Death looked scary and ugly."

Robert Brecheen tried to save the state the time and trouble of his execution. Sentenced to die for the 1983 murder of a woman, on the morning before the execution, while waiting on Oklahoma's infamous H-Unit, Brecheen tried to take his own life with an overdose. When they found him, he was barely breathing, so they took him to the hospital and had his stomach pumped so that five hours later he would be alert and fit to be executed, which he was.

Thomas Grasso was sentenced to life in prison in New York for the murder of an elderly man, and he was given the death penalty in Oklahoma for the murder of an elderly woman. Governor Mario Cuomo, a death penalty opponent, demanded that Grasso serve his life sentence in New York before meeting his death in Oklahoma. Grasso insisted that he wanted to be executed, so when Republican George Pataki was elected over Cuomo, he returned Grasso to Oklahoma for execution as he promised he would, and restored the death penalty to New York.

Grasso's mother supported her son's decision to be executed. In an interview she said she was happy that Pataki had won the election because he was their only hope. She said having her son sit in prison was a waste of time and taxpayers money. Grasso got his wish and was eventually executed in Oklahoma.

On August 9, 1996, Oklahoma Senator Brooks Douglas, the author of the law that allows victims' relatives to watch executions, witnessed the execution of Stephen Hatch, who was sentenced to death for murdering Senator Douglas's parents even though he was not the triggerman. The alleged triggerman, Glen Ake, was also given the death penalty but had his sentence overturned on the grounds that he was denied psychiatric assistance in his legal defense. He received two life sentences at his second hearing.

On May 8, 1997, Scott Carpenter became the youngest person executed in the United States after the Supreme Court reinstated the death penalty. He was twenty-two-years old. Carpenter had pleaded no contest to killing AJ Kelley, who owned a grocery store at Lake Eufala in Oklahoma. After only one unsuccessful appeal, Carpenter told the court to forfeit his rights to continue fighting the execution. He said, "There's no chance for me to ever be out in the free world." The day of his execution, Carpenter's attorneys told prison officials at about 8:30 p.m. that no further appeals would be pursued. His was the shortest stay on death row in recent history, just 583 days. Asked if he had a final statement, Carpenter said "No."

For his execution an amendment to the state law was rushed through the state House and Senate and on to Government Frank Keating's desk in just one day. This allowed victim family members, specifically the family of AJ Kelley, Carpenter's victim, to witness the execution. About ten members of AJ Kelley's family toured the execution chamber the night before the execution. AJ Kelley's widow, Bobbie, his daughter, Deanna and son-in-law were at the prison at the time of the execution but chose not to attend.

Two minutes after being injected with the lethal chemicals Carpenter began making noises, and his stomach and chest pulsed. His body made eighteen violent convulsions followed by eight milder ones. His face first turned yellowish gray and then deep purple and gray. He was pronounced dead officially at 12:22 a.m.

DEATH ROW IN OKLAHOMA

Oklahoma's death row for women is located at Mabel Bassett Correctional Center, a maximum-security women's prison in Oklahoma City. The women are housed in a locked isolated unit upstairs where you must go through a second locked glass door to reach the row of cells. Within this triply secured isolated area, they are held for twenty-three out of twenty-four hours each day. They are not allowed to mingle with the general population or each other. Individually, they are put into the small locked outdoor exercise cage for an hour each day, if the weather permits, and if the correctional officers see fit to do so. For personal hygiene, one woman said, "We are showered three times a week." When they move from one area to another within the prison, they are handcuffed and shackled. They are never allowed contact visits with family members. The women speak of loneliness and isolation. They spend their days coming to terms with "existential death" (Jose-Kempfner, 1991).

The women speak of sense of emptiness and loss, and list being able to hug and kiss their children and have extended day visits with them as things they need the most (PRRFIT, 1991). One mother said, "Not just for us . . . the children need it too." Another said, "It's loneliness, it's cruel, it's hell" (PRRFIT, 1991).

WOMEN SENTENCED TO DEATH IN OKLAHOMA

1975
Janet Sanders aka Miller: White; Reversed, 1977. Janet Sanders (Miller) was convicted of murder and sentenced to death on August 26, 1975. Her sentence was reversed to life in 1977 and she is currently serving a life sentence in Oklahoma.

1979
Michelle Binsz: White; Reversed in 1984. Michelle Binsz was a go-go dancer when she met her husband, Steve, in 1978. At age thirty-two she found herself on death row in Lexington, Oklahoma, a little more than a year after her marriage. Michelle was accused of the contract killing of Robert Busch, a private investigator. Michelle, her husband, and a friend, Carla Rapp, went to the victim's home to "hit" him under a contract with Robert Keller, an executive of Kellco Oil Company. Using wigs for disguises, they entered the Busch home, where Steve Binsz shot and killed Busch. Carla Rapp turned state's evidence against the Binsz couple. Glasses left at the scene were tied to a prescription for Michelle. Carla Rapp's case was dismissed. Keller received life, and the Binszes were given the death penalty. Michelle insists someone else committed the murder.

1982

Lois Nadean Smith: Native American; Currently on death row. Lois Nadean Smith, a Cherokee, was born in Tahlequah, Oklahoma, in 1940 and was raised by both her mother and father, but spent most of her time with her mother. Before Lois was eighteen, the family never moved. She had two brothers. She earned a high school diploma and attended business school, completing a course in "business machines." She also took, but never completed, a course in keypunch.

By age twenty-four Lois was a bookkeeper doing monthly reports for twenty-five shoe stores. She did this for one and a half years. At age twenty-seven she went to work for a lumber company as a bookkeeper and was responsible for sending out the monthly statements. At thirty Lois was the secretary/principal bookkeeper for the company and kept that position of two and a half years. At thirty-five she became the Assistant Supervisor of Secretaries and Bookkeeper, making $12,000 a year.

Lois has four children of her own and one stepson, some were still living at home at the time of her incarceration. When she was incarcerated her parental rights were taken away from her. All her children are married now and live in Tahlequah.

Lois had never been arrested or incarcerated and was forty-two at the time of her first arrest and incarceration which was her death sentence. She did not have any health problems, but after incarceration developed high blood pressure and high cholesterol. As far as her mental health goes, Lois said she "relies on Jesus to carry me through this nightmare."

She was charged with first-degree murder along with her son in the shooting death of a 20-year-old woman in rural Sequoyah County on Tuesday, July 6, 1982. Mother and son were held in the Sequoyah County jail in Salisaw pending their arraignment. The victim, who was identified as a Tahlequah resident, Cynthia Lucille Baille, was found dead inside the house of Lois's former husband. She had been shot numerous times.

The Gans police received a call of a disturbance at the residence at 9:30 a.m. on a Sunday morning. When they arrived, the owner of the house, Lois's former husband, told police the disturbance had been settled. An hour later, police were again called to the scene by a neighbor who said he found a body inside the house. A police spokesperson said that Lois, her son, and two other women went to Gans from Tahlequah. The house was clean and the curtains shut when police arrived and no one was inside except for the victim. Lois was later found at the home of a friend and arrested along with her son. Both Lois and her son pleaded innocent and both were given the death penalty.

1989

Wanda Allen: Black; Currently on death row. Wanda Jean Allen was born in Oklahoma City, Oklahoma, in 1959 and spent her childhood there. She was raised by both parents, who were African-American. There were seven siblings in her family; she was the second oldest. Before the age of eighteen Wanda moved three times with her family and attended four different schools. She went to high school through the eleventh grade and received her GED while in prison. Before going to prison Wanda attended a vo-tech school where she studied to be a medical assistant, but did not complete her studies. She spent some time in a juvenile facility, once for six months and another time for almost a year.

Wanda worked at various jobs including construction and cleaning for which she was paid $5.25 and hour. At the time of her arrest, she was self-supporting and was not on Public Assistance or Welfare. Police arrested her in Duncan, Oklahoma, on December 6, 1988, for shooting Gloria J. Leathers, 28, who died at Mercy Hospital a couple of hours after Wanda's arrest. Gloria Leathers identified Wanda as her assailant before being taken to the hospital. A hospital spokesperson said that Gloria had undergone surgery to remove a bullet from her abdomen that had entered the right side and exited from the left. A .38-caliber handgun had been used in the shooting and was later found by a neighbor near Gloria Leathers' home.

Authorities said the two women had lived together and were involved in a dispute at a grocery store in the village fifteen minutes before the shooting, apparently over money or a check. The authorities believed the victim was trying to go to the police station to file some sort of complaint.

A police officer had escorted the two women to their home from the store and stood there while Gloria collected some of her personal belongings. After the officer received another call he left. The shooting took place a few minutes later.

Wanda was already a convicted felon. She had been sentenced to four years in prison in 1982 on a manslaughter charge. She was released in 1984 and was serving a suspended sentence when the incident occurred. Wanda remains on death row in Oklahoma today.

1989

Patricia Jones: White; Reversed in 1995. Patricia Jones was born in Oklahoma City, Oklahoma. Her father was Cherokee and her mother Caucasian. She was raised by her mother although her grandmother also lived with them. Her mother was 36-years-old when Patricia was born and had attended both high school and college. Before the age of eighteen Patricia attended four different schools. She is the youngest of four siblings.

Patricia has a high school GED and attended a vo-tech school where she completed her studies as an X-ray lab technician and as a machinist. She also took some college courses.

By age twenty-three, Patricia was in charge of the office of a window-covering company doing things such as selling, receiving, and installing windows. She also did displays at various sales-shows and held that job for four years. At twenty-seven she started working as an interior decorator and owned her own business designing show homes. She did this for six years.

Patricia has four children, three natural and one stepchild. Her first pregnancy was at seventeen. All of her children were living with her at the time of her incarceration, although she had moved out twice and left them with their father. Her parental rights were not terminated when she was incarcerated so she decided that her children should live with their father although one of them turned eighteen six months after her incarceration.

Her oldest child was involved in a burglary and she said it was because "He was spoiled. I gave him too much without teaching him the value of things." Her third and youngest child, a daughter, wasn't doing well in school at the time and she said this was because of "My being on death row and not being able to hug and kiss her" (PRFFT, 1994). About the same daughter she said "I am helpless to do much in helping her . . . she is very attached to me."

Patricia was thirty-three at the time of her first arrest and thirty-four at the time of her incarceration. She never spent any time in juvenile facilities but she was arrested three times after the age of eighteen for felonies. She said drugs and a desire to be something she was not contributed to her first three convictions. Regarding her death sentence she said, "I had no part of it and sit here innocent."

Patricia said she was sexually abused once before the age of eighteen and physically and emotionally abused frequently after eighteen "Whenever he was drunk and depending on what drugs he was on." She never said who "he" was. Although she did not drink, Patricia reported using drugs including, marijuana, crack, amphetamines, and anti-depressants. She said she received counseling for emotional problems because she was "raped at sixteen and didn't care for almost fifteen years what happened to me."

Patricia was charged with first-degree murder in the deaths of a key witness against her in a drug trial and the witness's boyfriend. The bodies of Kim Gaylene Grant, 31, and Harrell Lloyd Robinson, 37, both from Oklahoma City were uncovered side by side March 9, 1988 in a ravine near Lake Stanley Draper. Police said the evidence indicated the victims were killed at another location and transported to the Lake.

Patricia was accused of acting "with others" and paying for the killings. Kim Grant was stabbed to death with a sword, just two weeks before she was supposed to testify against Patricia at a trial. According to the police, Patricia felt that if the witness was killed after the preliminary hearing she wouldn't be prosecuted. Patricia later learned that Grant's testimony from the preliminary trial could be read to a jury and decided to plead guilty.

At the preliminary trial Kim had testified that she tried to smuggle heroin to her sister-in-law, Debra Ross, in Mabel Bassett Correctional Center in July 1987. Kim said her sister-in-law had arranged for Patricia to provide the heroin and that Patricia had given her heroin, told her how to conceal it, and stayed outside waiting for her when she went in to deliver it. But Grant was arrested inside and Patricia in the parking lot.

After her testimony Patricia and others threatened Grant in an attempt to get her to change her testimony. Her boyfriend, Robinson had unsuccessfully tried to protect her. Both were stabbed to death. After serving her sentence for drug dealing, Patricia was arrested as she walked out of the prison and taken to jail to face the murder charge. For the murders of Kim and her boyfriend she was given the death penalty. Her sentence was reversed in 1995. She is serving a life sentence today.

1989

Marilyn Kay Plantz: White; Currently on death row. Marilyn Kay Plantz was born in Oklahoma City, Oklahoma, in 1960 and lived there all her life. She did not graduate from high school but completed her studies up to the eleventh grade. She was raised by her mother and father and moved several times before the age of eighteen, attending five different schools. She had five siblings and was raised with all of them, she being the sixth and youngest.

Marilyn has two children. The oldest was eleven at the time of her arrest, and the youngest was eight. Her parental rights were taken away from her after her incarceration and her children are with her husband's relatives, who do not bring them to visit her.

She started working at the age of twenty. Her first job was as assistant manager of the Country Club Apartments where she made $350 a month plus rent; she worked there for three years. At twenty-three Marilyn got a job as manager of the Ballerina Mobile Home Park, where she worked for two years, making $250 a month. At 25 she became a part-time Teacher's Aide at a local school at $3.25 an hour. Her last job was as a retouch person at a photo shop. She made $3.45 an hour there.

Marilyn was physically abused and raped once before the age of eighteen. She was twenty-seven at the time of her first arrest, which is the one for which she received the death penalty, and she had never spent time in a correctional facility of any kind.

Marilyn Kay Plantz was arrested Monday, August 30, 1988 in connection with the death of her husband, whose body was found in his burned pickup in a secluded area of northeast Oklahoma City. She was jailed on a first-degree murder charge. Evidence led the police to believe she was involved in setting up the murder. James Plantz was an employee of the Oklahoma Publishing Company. According to the police, Plantz was attacked, then his truck was doused with a flammable liquid and set on fire. Plantz had a $300,000 life insurance policy. Marilyn Plantz was called in for questioning after which detectives decided to hold her for murder. Plantz's body had signs of head trauma consistent with a shooting, but the autopsy revealed that he might still have been alive when the truck was set on fire.

In appealing her conviction in 1994, affidavits were presented to the court describing Marilyn's relationship with her husband, in which he was characterized as being possessive, abusive, and jealous. Her three sisters presented affidavits testifying to this type of relationship and said they would have testified to this in her trial had they been asked.

In addition there was testimony from a Dr. Pamela Fischer, who examined Marilyn in the summer of 1995, more than six years after her murder trial, in which Dr. Fischer stated she found Marilyn to have a borderline intelligence quotient. She also stated that Marilyn was inhibited in personal relationships in social situations and exhibited signs of insecurity and fear of abandonment. Dr. Fischer testified that she found Marilyn's personality was not consistent with that of a typical criminal personality — and that given her limited intellectual capacity and her personality type, it would be highly improbable that she was capable of creating a scheme to murder her husband. The court found no merit in any of these claims and upheld Marilyn's death sentence. She is on death row in Oklahoma today.

1995

Delpha Spunaugle: White; Currently on death row. Court records state that Delpha Spunaugle had tried to find someone to kill her husband for at least two years before the evening of August 14, 1993. That evening she asked her friend David Woodward to come over, to be there when her husband, Dennis, came home from a night of drinking. She apparently believed that her husband would not verbally abuse her with Woodward there, because she had invited him over on other occasions for the same reason. Woodward and Delpha had been friends for years. He worked occasionally at the Spunaugle's T-shirt shop, and for a time he and Delpha had been lovers. Woodward disliked Dennis Spunaugle because Delpha had told him many times that Dennis abused her physically and had molested her daughter. Delpha had asked Woodward to kill Dennis before, but he had ignored her request.

That night Woodward was intoxicated. By his own account he had spent the afternoon drinking beer and vodka at a friends house and someone had driven him home because he was too drunk to drive. At home he continued drinking beer and Delpha called him several times asking him to come over, which he eventually did.

When Dennis Spunaugle came home, Woodward and Delpha were sitting on the edge of the Spunaugle's swimming pool. After Dennis "bitched at her" for a while, he went inside and went to bed. A short time after that Woodward went to sleep in the Spunaugle's motor home that was parked in their driveway.

Later Delpha awakened Woodward and said, "It's time." Then she and Woodward went to the bedroom where Dennis was sleeping and Woodward hit him with a baseball bat so hard it partially severed his ear and knocked him off the bed. To their surprise Dennis got up and started to fight. In the struggle that ensued Woodward stabbed Dennis several times. When it looked as if Dennis might still survive, Delpha hit him again with the bat. When it appeared that Dennis was not dead and was not going to die easy, Delpha went outside, got a rope and Woodward put it around Dennis's neck. Then Woodward tried to strangle him with it, but he was too exhausted from the struggle so Delpha helped. Each pulled one end of the rope and kept pulling until Dennis was dead. Later, Woodward estimated it took about five minutes.

Delpha and Woodward loaded Dennis's body into Woodward's Mercury Lynx and drove out to the country and dumped the body into a dry creekbed. After disposing of the body, they drove back to Oklahoma City and Delpha got rid of the murder weapons. Then she gave Woodward a $20 bill to buy a beer and told him to keep the change.

The next day Woodward drove to Kansas. Meanwhile Delpha reported Dennis "missing." Dennis's body was found five days later in the creekbed near the intersection of 164th St. and County Line Road in Oklahoma County where Woodward and Delpha had dumped it.

When he heard the body had been found, Woodward confessed, but said he would not have done it if Delpha Jo hadn't manipulated him into it while he was intoxicated. Delpha also confessed to her part in the murder, but said she was under duress. She told the police that Woodward was "possessed" during the attack and threatened to harm her or her children if she did not help kill Dennis. She also told the police that Woodward was a devil-worshipper who licked Dennis's blood from his knife and threatened her by saying his followers would hurt her if she reported the crime. Delpha and Woodward were tried jointly and convicted.

During the trial Delpha's defense counsel set forth a motion to remove a juror who was sleeping contending that in a capital murder case in which guilt means punishment of death, a juror who dozes through parts of the trial is an unacceptable degradation of due process. The trial judge did not agree, however, and said on record that the juror had paid attention "for the most part" even though he had been seen dozing in some parts. So the juror was not replaced.

Delpha Jo Spunaugle was tried for the crimes of first-degree murder, conspiracy to commit murder, and solicitation to commit murder in the first degree. The jury returned a verdict of guilty and gave her death for first-degree murder, ten years imprisonment and a fine of $5,000.00 on the conspiracy count; and life imprisonment for solicitation. Woodward was sentenced to life without parole.

Woodward later argued that life without parole was an excessive punishment because he had no prior criminal record. The court, however, did not find it excessive given the evidence that Woodward beat, stabbed and attempted to strangle Dennis Spunaugle over the course of several hours. There was also evidence presented that Dennis knew he was dying during the attack and asked

Woodward to allow him to put his pants on and to take him out to the country where he could die alone.

Delpha Jo Spunaugle was granted a new trial in September 1997 by the state Court of Criminal Appeals because she claimed she was not allowed to offer evidence of being under duress from her co-defendant Woodward, during the crime. She is currently awaiting trial on death row at the Mabel Bassett Correctional Center in Oklahoma City, Oklahoma.

26

Pennsylvania: Lethal Injection

The state of Pennsylvania has sentenced ten women to death since 1900. Two women, Irene Schroeder and Corrine Sykes were legally executed, and there are four women on death row in Pennsylvania today.

The first penitentiary in the United States, Eastern State Penitentiary, was built in the state of Pennsylvania by the Quakers around 1820. Located on the outskirts of Philadelphia, it was, at first, surrounded by open fields. By the time it finally closed its doors to prisoners in 1970 the city had built itself around it to such an extent that today it can be found still standing in the heart of Philadelphia. Now a tourist attraction with its own website, the penitentiary is listed as one of seven American cultural heritage sites on the World Monuments Fund's most endangered list of 100. By signing a waiver, putting on a hard hat, and paying a $7.00 fee, anyone can now walk the broad cold corridors of the old prison past rows and rows of tiny cells, which, though gutted, still contain artifacts of a way of life we can now not even imagine.

In this formidable castle-like structure, the Quaker model, known as the "isolation model" (also called the "Pennsylvania model") was first used to replace the punishment model of correction and rehabilitation that was being practiced everywhere at the time the prison was built. The Quaker model favored isolation, reflection, and work, based on a belief that solitude could better reform criminals. It was postulated that strictly enforced solitude would prevent the spread of criminality as well as provide prisoners time for reflection and penance.

The Quaker model gained worldwide fame as a "radical experiment" in incarceration and people traveled great distances to visit the prison and learn what it was about. In 1842 Charles Dickens visited Pennsylvania, coming all the way from England for the specific purpose of seeing Eastern State Penitentiary. Dickens was ultimately appalled by what he saw and wrote: "I hold this slow and daily tampering with the human mind worse than any torture of the body."

Although executions never took place at Eastern State, there was a wing referred to as "death row" where prisoners who were given the death penalty were held until they could be transferred to another prison.

THE DEATH PENALTY IN PENNSYLVANIA

In 1970 when state Attorney General Fred Speaker visited the Pennsylvania death chamber at Rockview State Prison he was so appalled by what he saw that he declared Pennsylvania's death penalty law unconstitutional on the spot and ordered the electric chair dismantled. By that time 350 inmates had already been executed there, but none since 1962.

Then in 1972, in accordance with the Supreme Court's ruling in *Furman v. Georgia*, all executions were halted in the state. From this ruling, two women, Sharon Wiggins and Marilyn Dobrolenski, who were on death row at the time, had their sentences commuted to life.

The death penalty resumed in the state in 1977, but no executions took place until 1995. In April 1989, the state Senate passed a bill legalizing the use of lethal injection as the official method of execution. After Governor Robert P. Casey signed the bill into law in 1990 he stopped issuing death warrants for a while to give prison officials time to establish a procedure for this process. Casey's predecessor, Governor Dick Thornburgh had signed six death warrants for four men and Casey had previously signed ten warrants for eight men. The old oak electric chair was turned over to the state Historical Museum Commission where museum officials said they have no plans to exhibit it in the near future.

In 1995 Governor Tom Ridge made a promise to take no longer than 90 days to sign death warrants once inmates completed all of their appeals. Then that same year he approved the legislation that made it a law. After that Governor Ridge signed 35 death warrants in 1995. This was more death warrants in one year than were signed by all the previous governors in the 17-year history of the Pennsylvania death penalty statute.

A new law went into effect on January 16, 1996 that requires all inmates on death row to file their state appeals within one year or lose their right to file appeals. The new law also stipulates that an inmate is not entitled to a stay of execution unless he/she files a petition. This means that any inmate who does not have a lawyer to file a petition for him/her and doesn't know how to do it themselves has no possibility of ever getting a stay.

Any case affirmed before 1994 cannot get a stay of execution even if a petition is filed unless the petition demonstrates a substantial likelihood of success. In other words, if an inmate cannot show that his/her claim has any legal merit they cannot get a stay.

In March 1998, a bill was approved by a 41–7 vote with no debate in the Pennsylvania legislature, that gave the governor sixty days to choose an inmate's date of execution after he signs a death warrant. Previous Pennsylvania law required that the governor choose the date when he signed a warrant. The stated purpose for the legislation was to avoid the possibility of multiple executions in one day.

With 215 inmates on death row today the Pennsylvania Supreme Court has over eighty cases for which it has not yet completed automatic reviews. Once the automatic reviews are completed the case goes to the Governor's Office.

In other death penalty developments the state Attorney General, Mike Fisher, recently asked the Pennsylvania Supreme Court to reconsider its order to suspend the Capital Unitary Review Act (CURA) which, according to Fisher, was designed to establish a "unified means" to appeal death sentences at the state level. Before CURA, inmates with death sentences had to exhaust their direct appeals to the state Supreme Court and the U.S. Supreme Court before seeking a "collateral review" of their case. CURA required courts to consider collateral issues and the issues raised in direct appeals at the same time. According to Fisher, it expedited the review process, which really means it expedites executions. In his petition Fisher said the court had not developed any rules regarding the pre-appeal collateral review of death penalty cases, therefore, the court had no constitutional right to suspend a law for being inconsistent with rules that don't exist. The Attorney General also maintained that the court had violated the limits on its constitutional authority.

Fisher's petition specifically asks the court to vacate the suspension of CURA and to adopt rules consistent with the policies set by the General Assembly during its Special Session on Crime. Fisher's petition was filed on September 26th, 1997 in Pittsburgh.

In order for a state to "opt-in" to the expedited rules for submitting state and federal habeas appeals, under the 1996 federal Anti-terrorist and Effective Death Penalty Act (AEDPA), the state must show by a formal commitment that it provides all death-sentenced prisoners with competent and adequately-reimbursed counsel, which Pennsylvania does not.

Currently, the Pennsylvania Post-Conviction Defender Office has two lawyers with approximately 125 cases pending that must file appeals within a year. The federal courts have done a study and have estimated that one lawyer working full-time on nothing but capital cases can handle 4–6 cases a year. That means that two lawyers working full time can handle 8–12.

Pennsylvania has no statewide system of funding indigent defense services or legal services for the poor. Robert Dunham, Executive Director of the Pennsylvania Post-Conviction Defender Organization said, "In Pennsylvania there is a silent crisis. Because people who can't present their claims this year are going to lose their right to present them in the future. The death penalty is moving forward like a train moving towards a cliff." Dunham said one of the reasons there are so many people on death row in Pennsylvania is because of bad lawyers. Lawyers are untrained in death penalty litigation and there is no money, he said.

Only about eighty of Philadelphia's 8,000 attorneys are willing to represent indigent defendants with capital-charges hanging over their heads. For those who do handle these cases all up front expenses are their own and they have to wait for months and even years to get paid.

In 1997, 300 delegates present at a meeting of the Pennsylvania Bar Association, called for a moratorium on the death penalty in the state. The Bar Association voiced its concern over fairness, racism, and the lack of minimum standards for legal representation as relevant issues. The resolution came from the association's Civil Rights Committee, which began looking at the death penalty in Pennsylvania in 1994. In reviewing the death penalty they found a disparity from county to county in the amount of money available for the defense in capital cases. Many court appointed lawyers were found to be well intentioned but inexperienced and poorly compensated. In its response, the Attorney General's Office said the Pennsylvania Bar Association is "out of touch" with the people (Amnesty International, 1997).

In November, 1997 Pierre Sane, of Amnesty International, visited death row inmates in Pennsylvania and later told the Philadelphia Bar Association that Pennsylvania was "Worse than Georgia, worse than Mississippi, worse than Alabama" in applying the death penalty almost exclusively to racial minorities and the poor. He called for a moratorium on capital punishment in Pennsylvania until such time that fairness in its administration can be assured.

DEATH ROW IN PENNSYLVANIA

Unlike other states, death row prisoners in Pennsylvania are not all held in the same prison. They are distributed in seven different prisons throughout the state, with 112, the largest number, at the SCI Greene in Waynesburg, Pennsylvania. The Pennsylvania Department of Corrections (DOC) continues to issue new and more severe standards for death row inmates.

Under new regulations access to condemned inmates is more severely restricted and falls into two categories: AC or DC status. Under AC status an inmate is permitted one two-hour visit a week. Under DC status an inmate is permitted one visit per month, immediate family only, for one hour in duration. According to the DOC this is a move to stop death row advocates from offering legal counsel to inmates who neither want nor need it.

In 1998 the men on death row at SCI Greene went on a hunger strike to protest the DOC taking custody of their legal papers and documents. The men said they felt very strongly that the state agency that signs their death warrants and that is ultimately their executioner should not be custodians of documents that may potentially free them of their repression.

A copy of a letter to the prison Superintendent from one of the women currently on death row in Pennsylvania best expresses how some of the recent changes in prison policies regarding death row inmates affects the women condemned to death in this state:

I am writing to you to address some of the issues in the new policy #802-4, specifically for Phase I capital cases. I wanted to speak to you personally about these things when you came to visit our unit, but was told you would be back later. Since you never returned I have decided a letter might be best.

I have some concerns about the new policy and how it applies to us as women on death row. I know that the purpose of the policy is to make whatever happens fair for all of the death row inmates throughout the state of Pennsylvania. But since there are over 200 men and only 4 women in that situation some things do not seem fair because, as women, we have different needs.

For example, regarding clothing and hygiene needs. We will only be permitted one jumpsuit and three showers in a seven day period. We are young women with female issues that men do not have. When a woman is on her menstrual cycle daily hygiene is the most important thing. Three pairs of panties may be fine for men, but women have hygienic problems on a daily basis men do not deal with and which we have no control over. We should be allowed a change of underwear every day. One pair of thermal underwear and one pair of pajamas fit into this category also. Women have to wash underwear daily and even more often during our menstruals.

For the Fall and Winter, if our one pair of thermal underwear is in the wash we cannot go outside because we have nothing to wear to keep warm. If our pajamas are in the wash then we have nothing to wear that night. This does not seem fair. Could you function with one pair of underwear or one pair of pajamas?

Two personal bras and three state-issued bras are not suitable for me personally because my doctor has said I must wear a strong supportive bra. This will help prevent cysts and breast cancer. My family is willing to buy these. State issued bras are not supportive strong bras. To deny our most basic needs is cruel and unusual punishment.

Right now we are allowed to purchase cocoa brown shorts sold on our commissary, but when we buy these we have to give back our state issued sweat suit. Is there any logical reason we can't have enough clothes to wear? Why can't we have one pair of shorts and our state issued sweat suit too? Is this excessive?

I am also concerned about the new rules regarding the visiting room and non-contact visits. Right now, we have to share the room with everyone who does not have contact visits. We are only allowed longer visits if no one else needs the room. Therefore all our visits are cut short. Why can't we have a visiting non-contact area of our own?

Soon we will only be allowed one, one to two-hour visit a month. I have no immediate family that lives in this state. All of my visitors drive from Virginia, Maryland, Oklahoma, and California for a one-hour visit. I will be denied visits because my family cannot afford to drive or fly all of that distance for one hour. It is already devastating enough that I cannot touch or hold my children. Why must I be denied permission to see them altogether?

As far as phone calls go. You have reduced our calls from three a week to one. I can understand that with 200 men wanting to use the telephone this would be necessary in order to allow everyone phone calls. But we are four women. We are all minorities and all mothers. I know that some men on death row are fathers, but women are the ones who keep in close contact with our children. I have three children that live in Virginia and two in Oklahoma. The new policy means that each week I have to choose between my children and have no calls to anyone else. It is already difficult for my children to know that their mother is on death row, is there a reason I will be denied even that type of access?

The new policy will also take away nail polish, polish remover, emory boards, barrettes, and tweezers. Prohibiting men from having these items makes sense because, for the most part, they do not use them. But for women, is it because we are on death row that you think we should not care about our appearance? We do care. If not for anyone else, at least for ourselves. We would still like to be allowed to feel like women in some way. Please don't strip of us that also.

Along these same lines, we are allowed hair appointments once every six months which can only be a cut or trim. Our unit lieutenant offered to escort us to Cosmetology to have our hair really done and I spoke with the Cosmetology Instructor, and she has no problem with giving us a real hair appointment with a perm or relaxer. We would like to have the same thing that lifers are allowed. The only difference between the sentences of the lifers and ours is that we will die by unnatural causes and they will die by natural causes.

It appears that in Pennsylvania the system is telling us if you are a woman sentenced to death then you are no longer women but caged animals. And you have no right to try to feel like a woman.

I can only speak for myself, but when the judge sentenced me to death he did not put a clause in that stated that SCI-Muncy has the right or responsibility to punish you again and again and again until the day you die.

I ask that you please take the things I have written in this letter into consideration. We are only four women who wish to remain women on death row in this state. What I am asking for myself and the other women are very small things that you have the power to grant. Yes, we are condemned to death, but you don't have to kill us every day.

Thank you very much for your time and consideration of these matters. I look forward to hearing from you in the near future.

EXECUTIONS IN PENNSYLVANIA

Under Pennsylvania Law executions take place at the State Correctional Institution at Rockview and both of the two prisoners executed since 1977 chose to abandon all appeals and sought execution. Governor Ridge himself presided over Pennsylvania's first execution in thirty-three years. The inmate, Keith Zettlemoyer begged the courts to let him die because "brain disease" made his prison life hell. He was what is referred to as a "volunteer."

Volunteers fire their lawyers, drop their appeals, and tell the state they want to be executed. Zettlemoyer spent fourteen years on Pennsylvania's death row for the 1980 murder of a friend who was going to testify against him. Zettlemoyer said "I see my execution as an end to my imprisonment, a blessed, merciful release from all the health problems I'm constantly suffering with." The mother of his murder victim filed an appeal to save his life, but Zettlemoyer was found competent to make his own choice and was executed. Three months later Leon Jerome Moser was also executed.

In July 1995 Superintendent Joseph F. Mazurkiewicz of the state Correctional Institution at Rockview announced that he was soliciting applications from Pennsylvanians who wanted to witness an execution. Pennsylvania law requires that six representatives of the media and six "reputable adult citizens" witness an execution. Witnesses are not paid and must be Pennsylvania residents who are at least twenty-one years of age. The superintendent selects volunteer witnesses and the State Department of Corrections selects the media witnesses. The state was ultimately overwhelmed by thousands of applicants expressing their desire to witness an execution.

A new proposed legislation would also bring an end to the practice of having a physician pronounce an executed inmate dead and would replace the physician with a coroner. Health professionals have cited the physician's mandate to heal in their opposition to physician participation.

PARDON AND PAROLE IN PENNSYLVANIA

In the past few years, serious concerns have been raised about the composition and voting of the Pennsylvania Board of Pardons. Up until November 1997 the governor could not commute or pardon a person serving a life sentence or a death sentence without a majority vote of the five-member Board of Pardons. Membership on the Board of Pardons is through appointment by the governor and approval of the state senate. Until recently it consisted of the lieutenant governor, the attorney general, a prison warden, an attorney and one other penologist. The lieutenant governor and the attorney general are obvious allies of the governor, and the attorney general handles all death penalty appeals, both direct and post-conviction. In his term of office, Governor Ridge has pardoned no one, and Governor Casey before him pardoned only two people, both lifers.

Since, November 1997, however, a constitutional amendment, which passed by a 3–2 margin, states that commutations can be considered by the governor only with a unanimous vote of the board, and the board will now include a crime victim in its membership, replacing the previous penologist.

THE CITY OF PHILADELPHIA AND JUDGE SABO

The city of Philadelphia's Court of Common Appeals accounts for over half of all the active death sentences in Pennsylvania. The mayor of Philadelphia has said that the outcome of a trial depends literally on what judge the case is assigned to. First elected to the Philadelphia Court of Common Pleas in 1974, Judge Albert Sabo of the Philadelphia Court of Common Pleas was said to have had a "personal death row larger than the death rows of thirteen of the 38 states with the death penalty." From 1978 to 1990 Judge Sabo served with a select group of judges who only heard homicide cases. In that capacity he sentenced more people to death than any other judge in the country. One of his most famous cases was that of Mumia Abu-Jamal, a former radio journalist convicted in 1982 of the murder of a Philadelphia police officer. Abu-Jamal appealed for a new trial in 1995 on the grounds that he did not receive a fair trial from Judge Sabo. His case had wide media attention and more that 500 people marched on city hall on his behalf.

In his time Judge Sabo sentenced 32 people to death and all but two were people of color. Judge Sabo, who denied he was unproductive or had a difficult temperament in court, was forced to retire in 1997.

STATE CORRECTIONAL INSTITUTION FOR WOMEN

From 1991 to 1998, Mary V. Leftridge Byrd was the Superintendent at the State Correctional Institution at Muncy (SCI), where the four women on death row in Pennsylvania are imprisoned. In this position she was responsible for an average daily population of 900 female inmates in custody levels ranging from minimum to maximum security, and approximately 400 staff. Of her personal philosophy in this area, Superintendent Leftridge Byrd said:

What's essential is to manage correctional facilities with head and heart, an environment in its totality where respect for humanity is non-negotiable. This idea includes teaching, expecting and modeling behavior that is about responding to the offense and the offender. I have heard, and entirely believe, that inmates are sent to prison as punishment . . . not for punishment. I go into this acknowledging that these women are inmates, but we should still regard them as individuals, human beings, whose fears and needs are, at essence, like most people we know.

With twenty years experience in Corrections Management, which have included appointments in the District of Columbia and Maryland, Superintendent Leftridge Byrd has particular expertise in program development and evaluation, correctional leadership development, domestic violence, cultural diversity, communication, designing and administering correctional programs, and the historical role of women in corrections.

In offering some of the history of SCI Muncy, once State Industrial Home for Women under the auspices of the Pennsylvania Department of Public Welfare, Superintendent Leftridge Byrd pointed out a section of a 1928 "Report of the Board of Trustees and the Superintendent of the State Industrial Home for Women." The Superintendent at the time requested "a new cottage, a central heating and laundry plant, a new cannery building, a greenhouse, and a slaughterhouse."

In the 1964 *Manual of Information for Muncy Girls* it states:

Muncy is for the rebuilding of character and the restoring of one's self to a better condition. Girls are admonished to respect the decision of the person in charge; reply politely to any question asked; stand in respect when a visitor or matron enters the room; girls must be quiet in the dining room; dance only in an approved manner; obedience is expected at all times and girls are expected to be able to go from one end of the campus to the other within a very short time, so you do not have time to go slowly or to stop to talk along the way.

Superintendent Leftridge Byrd tells about reading somewhere that this history of "differential care based on gender" is the reason terms like girls, campus grounds, and matron still exist in the field of corrections and "continue to be part of the changing culture and mission at SCI-Muncy."

On the table in the Superintendent's office is a plaque that reads "In my father's house there are many mansions, I hope yours is next to mine" and another "Where there is life, there is hope." Superintendent Leftridge Byrd is animated and smiles as she speaks about her concept of "prison as community" and the model for management of women's prison which she has been developing over the years and calls *In the Company of Women* (book forthcoming).

As women in our positions (prison management) we often do things differently than our male counterparts. Having celebrations, open houses, graduations in prison is not an oxymoron. Having memorial services when inmates pass away while they're with us is for us a natural and important thing to do. Approving women to go the infirmary to be with each other and to read and pray with a woman who's dying is accepted and encouraged.

Superintendent Leftridge Byrd, who speaks throughout the country at events sponsored by community based civic organizations as well as institutes of higher learning has been honored by the Pennsylvania Coalition Against

Domestic Violence, the National Organization of Black Law Enforcement Executives and was recently named to the Pennsylvania Honor Roll of Women. She is also a gubenetorial appointee to the Pennsylvania Commission for Women. Of women on death row, Superintendent Leftridge Byrd says:

It has been my experience that women who are locked up deal with incarceration as a continuation rather than an interruption of their lives. This reality provides prison administrators and staff an opportunity to create initiatives, even on death row, that deal with the truth that waiting for an execution date should not be equated with living as a doomed person.

Indicating a large portrait of Patti La Belle hanging on one wall in her office, Superintendent Byrd says, "Patti La Belle is one of my personal s/heroes. I've written and invited her to come and sing for the women and am still hoping, she will one of these days."

WOMEN SENTENCED TO DEATH IN PENNSYLVANIA

1931

Irene Schroeder: White; Executed. Irene Schroeder, nicknamed "Iron Irene," was the first woman executed in Pennsylvania in modern times. She was a 22-year-old former waitress who along with her lover and brother robbed a grocery store and killed a highway patrolman who attempted to stop their car. After leaving her four-year-old son, who was with them during the robbery, with relatives, Irene, her lover, Glenn, and her brother Tom fled to Arizona. In a gunfight there they killed an Arizona deputy. After being captured, Irene and her lover were extradited to Pennsylvania. Her brother was never found although Irene said he had died of gunshot wounds and they had buried him along the way.

Irene's four-year-old son was instrumental in identifying his mother and in giving details of how the robbery-murder had taken place. When he was six, Donnie Schroeder went to see the governor of Pennsylvania to plead for his mother's life, but the governor did not grant his request.

Irene spent her last days on death row writing her life story that was to be sold after her death to raise money for her son. Before being executed Irene told her father not to feel bad, and she told her son she was going to die, but was not afraid, and that he should be a good boy and be brave too. Leaving her death row cell the night before she was executed, Donnie told reporters, "I think Mom would make a nice angel."

1935

Grace Giovanetti: White; Commuted. At age 45, Grace Giovanetti was one of a group of more than 24 defendants in a mass poisoning ring who were tried for murder. She was convicted of murdering her husband and sentenced to death.

Her motive was said to have been financial gain. Her sentence was later commuted.

1936

Josephine Romualdo: White; Commuted. At age 41, Josephine Romualdo, along with Grace Giovanetti was one of a group of more than 24 defendants in a mass poisoning ring in Pennsylvania. She was convicted of murdering her husband and sentenced to death. Her motive was said to have been financial gain. Her sentence was later commuted.

1946

Corrine Sykes; Black; Executed, 1946. Corrine Sykes, described in her trial as having the mind of an eight-year-old, was accused of murdering and stealing from a wealthy white woman for whom she worked as a maid, when she was twenty-one years old. The woman was stabbed to death with a butcher knife. Money, jewels, and furs amounting to $2,000 were taken. A male accomplice who received the stolen goods was suspected of having masterminded the crime, but ultimately, he was sentenced to only seven years in prison. Although her case was appealed to the Supreme Court, Corrine was not granted clemency. Her last meal was prepared in the superintendent's home. At 21, she was the youngest woman ever to be executed in Pennsylvania.

1969

Sharon Wiggins: Black; Commuted. Sharon Wiggins was only a teenager when she was given the death penalty for killing someone in a bank robbery. When she and her co-defendants entered the bank, one of the patrons who was deaf didn't hear the command to freeze and lunged at her. Sharon shot him and when he fell on her, she shot him again. One of the other co-defendants jumped over the counter and shot the same man four more times. Sharon was on death row for two years before the Supreme Court eliminated the death penalty in 1972. She is now serving a life sentence in Pennsylvania.

1972

Marilyn Dobrolenski: White; Commuted. Marilyn Dobrolenski was a teenager from Ohio when she went on a bank-robbing spree with a man she'd known for only a week. They called themselves Bonnie and Clyde and, in the course of events, they killed two Delaware State troopers. Marilyn's accomplice was also killed. Eventually, Marilyn was arrested and given the death penalty in Pennsylvania plus two more death sentences in Delaware. All of her death sentences were changed to life as a result of the Supreme Court's decision in *Furman v. Georgia* in 1972. She is now serving a life sentence in Pennsylvania and still has two life sentences in Delaware.

1989

Dolores Rivers: Black; Currently on death row. At age 34, Dolores, a home health care worker, was charged with murder, burglary, robbery and related offenses in the death of Violet Burt, a 77 year-old woman for whom she had provided care. She was found guilty and sentenced to death in 1989. She is currently on death row in Pennsylvania.

In September, 1998, Dolores, who is called "Precious" by her friends received word that her son had been murdered. She described being told of his death in this way:

On September 1, 1998, around 11:00 AM, I was told that I was supposed to go to the day room. I assumed it was for my one on one counseling with the chaplain which had finally been approved. They came and put me in chains and took me there where I saw three male officers, two female officers and the chaplain waiting. I knew then something was not right. So, my first thought was that my death warrant had been signed.

They told me to sit down and when I did the officers surrounded me with their arms outstretched like they were going to grab me. This really scared me and made me very nervous. The chaplain then said "I have some terrible, terrible, terrible, terrible bad news for you." When she said this, the officers were so close to me with their arms outstretched that I thought to myself "I must remain calm. If I don't they are going to jump me and strip me down." I immediately braced myself with every ounce of control I had so that whatever was said I would not show any emotions or react in a way that would make them grab me or strip me down.

Then the chaplain said "Right now our concern is for your safety." Then she pulled out two pieces of paper and told me my son had been murdered. She said my son had been arguing with another guy on the front steps just before he was going to eat. Then the young man he was arguing with left and my son went to eat, but the young man soon returned with a 9mm gun and started arguing again. My son got up and said "Hold on" and as he did the man shot him in the hand. When my son started to run the guy shot him in both legs so he fell to the ground. And as my son was pleading for his life, the man walked over and shot him in the head. My son was taken to the hospital where he died.

After she described every detail of this nightmare to me, I did not react because I knew they were ready to strip me and put me in isolation. So, they escorted me back to my cell where I cried quietly afraid to show my pain. I've never hurt so bad in my life. My baby was gone and there was no one to tell. At recreation, the officers advised me to stay in. I wanted someone to hug me at that point, but I was not allowed any human contact. Only women on the row can understand the pain I am feeling and it is only to them that I can express my pain and fear.

As hard as I try, I cannot find any reason why those in charge would want me to go through such a heartbreaking tragedy alone. They would have felt better, I think, if I had cried and screamed and given them a reason to strip and restrain me. But the way I see it, I had no choice but to react the way I did.

I am not suicidal and never have been. And, I have never acted out in the ten years I have been on death row. I was horrified to hear the details of my son's death in front of all those strangers. When they said they were concerned with my safety it meant they wanted to make sure I was around long enough to be executed.

I had asked to see the psychiatrist but when she came she saw the other women for their scheduled appointments, but I was told she had no time in her schedule for me. They said it wasn't necessary for me because I had showed no reaction to the news of my son's death. And because I showed no reaction they were uncompassionate and inconsiderate. I suppose they thought I didn't care, but they overlooked how they had scared me into silence.

A mother on death row learns of the death of her son without compassion. What she receives instead, is ignorance and contempt.

Dolores remains on death row in Pennsylvania today.

1992

Donetta Hill: Black; Currently on death row. At age 23 Donetta Hill was sentenced to death for the murders of two males, one Asian, and one black. She is on death row in Pennsylvania today. Donetta has had two death warrants signed so far.

Donetta had this to say about her life right now:

I have two little girls at home (7 and 11 years old) wondering when I'm going to be coming home to be with them. So, right now, I'm fighting to get off death row, to have a life, a very long life at home with my two daughters. This is where my heart is. I have had two death warrants signed and I am sure, if I sit here and do nothing, the third one will cost me my life.

I have been going through a lot to get back into court. I was told that if they can get the false statements that were made in my trial thrown out, I might be able to walk out of here. I was told they have no evidence against me and that I was convicted only on false statements. One that they made up and threatened me into signing.

What I am trying to do is get a DNA test. My lawyer doesn't agree with me — but she is speaking from the other side of this door. There was blood and hair found at the crime scene that did not belong to the victim. But, the state refuses to give me a DNA test to see if there would be a match with me. They prefer not to know.

I have heard of cases where people were proven innocent by DNA testing — even people on death row. So I would like to find a lawyer or some lawyers who are willing to help me with this.

I am innocent. God knows that. I did not kill anyone. If you had been at my trial, you would have seen it was a set-up. The person who did the killings is now serving three to seven years for robbery/cutting someone up. I told my lawyers that this person should also have a DNA test.

The twenty-third of this month I will be 32-years-old. And in three more years I will have spent ten years here for something I did not do. To tell you the truth, I don't know if I can fight another three years. My soul/mind are tired and worn out. By the grace of God and for my two daughters I have held on this long.

Donetta remains on death row in Pennsylvania today.

1993

Kelley O'Donnell: White; Currently on death row. At age 25, Kelley O'Donnell and her boyfriend/common-law husband were both given the death penalty for the murder of Eleftherios "Terry" Eleftherios, a 50-year-old pizza parlor owner in Philadelphia, in 1992. After bludgeoning him to death it was believed they took his body to the apartment where Kelley was living at the time and sawed it to pieces; stuffed it in trash bags and distributed the bags in various trash containers along Delaware Ave. in Philadelphia. At the time of their arrest, both Kelley and her boyfriend said they alone were responsible for the murder. Both were charged with murder, robbery, theft, receiving stolen property, unauthorized use of a vehicle, and arson.

Today Kelley says she did not commit the murder but admits being present when her husband committed it. She said she panicked at the time and confessed to it partly to protect her husband.

In recalling what happened Kelley spoke about the trial in which she and her husband were found guilty saying that at first it didn't impact her when she was given the death sentence because she was focusing more on what sentence her husband would receive. So when the judge asked her if she had anything to say after sentencing, she said "No."

When her husband was also sentenced to death and the judge asked him if he had anything to say, Kelley said he got up in the courtroom and tearfully told everyone how sorry he was. She said that as she listened to him speak, she kept waiting for him say, "But my wife had nothing to do with this," which he never said. And since that moment her life has been a nightmare.

Kelley has five children. Their ages were 9 years, 7 years, 5 years, 3 years, and 8 months when she was given the death sentence. Three are now with relatives, one is with a friend, and the youngest child was put up for adoption. Kelley said she also had a child who was stillborn and is buried in Pennsylvania. She does have visits with her children occasionally, but since they are non-contact visits, it is very difficult and, as time goes on, she says, "the children are pulling away." She says she misses hugging and kissing them, remarking poignantly, "No one has touched me in years."

Before all of this, Kelley was a go-go dancer who loved music and dancing. Her hands and arms were severely burned in a fire when she was a child, the same fire in which her mother died. Kelley remembers being teased about her scars by other children as she was growing up. She said she loved being a go-go dancer because she was a good dancer and when she was on the stage dancing people applauded her for what she was doing and no one could really see her scars. In November 1997 Kelley wrote of her mother's death and the fire:

As far as the fire goes, this is a very difficult time of year for me. It will be 25 years ago November 19. My mother and I were the only two they couldn't get out. I had second and third degree burns over 20 percent of my body, including my hands, arms, face, and head. My mother died of third degree burns over 80 percent of her body. We were visiting friends that had just built a new house on the property. It burnt to the ground. My mother was 24 when she died.

On death row in Pennsylvania today, Kelley says her life now is "like hanging from a cliff with someone stepping on your fingers."

Of grief, Kelley says "I've been grieving since I was five over everybody in my life who has died and especially in 1986. I just have never gotten over any death. This includes the victim I did not kill." "Most of all," she says, "I grieve for my children."

In March 1998, Pennsylvania Governor Tom Ridge signed a death warrant for William R. Gribble, Kelley's companion. His execution was scheduled for 10:00 p.m., Tuesday, March 31, 1998, but he was given a stay to pursue his appeals. He has been given a new execution date for January 9, 1999.

1994

Carolyn King: Black; Currently on death row. Born in 1970, Carolyn King and her boyfriend were given the death penalty in Pennsylvania in November 1994 for robbery and the murder of 74-year-old man in Lebanon, Pennsylvania. She was also given a life sentence for the kidnapping and murder of a woman in Nevada. Carolyn is on death row in Pennsylvania today.

27

South Carolina: Lethal Injection

South Carolina has sentenced four women to death since 1900. Two of these women, Sue Logue and Rosa Marie Stinette were executed. There are no women on death row in South Carolina today.

In 1912 the state began using the electric chair and on June 16, 1944, 14-year-old George Stinney earned his place in the annals of criminal history by becoming the youngest person executed in this century in the United States. He was strapped into the electric chair at the South Carolina State Prison for raping and murdering two young girls in a South Carolina town.

The 76-year-old electric chair was moved from the Central Correctional Institution (CCI) to the Broad River Road Correctional Institution in 1988. For seventy-six years the chair was housed in the same room at CCI. Two hundred and forty one men and two women were executed there.

In 1997 South Carolina's death row inmates lost their option to have a family member or friend present when they are executed. The only people allowed under a law passed in 1997 are a lawyer and a minister. In November 1997, when Earl Matthews was executed, his attorney Michael O'Connell was the only witness. O'Connell said, "I didn't want to be there but he asked me to. He couldn't have anyone else." Fifteen people have been executed in South Carolina since the death penalty was reinstated in 1976.

State Attorney General Charlie Condon proposed making people charged in certain domestic killings eligible for the death penalty in South Carolina in 1998. State law requires that aggravating circumstances, such as the victim being a child, be involved in a murder before the death penalty can be sought. The Condon proposal would include any murder committed in violation of a valid protection order or a murder committed in the presence of a household member of the victim.

EXECUTIONS IN SOUTH CAROLINA

When Donald "Pee Wee" Gaskins was put to death in Columbia, South Carolina in 1991, it was the first time in nearly a half-century that a white person was executed for killing a black. Not since 1944, when a Kansas man was executed for killing a black in an attempted robbery had a white person in the United States received the death penalty for killing a black. In South Carolina it had only happened in 1880.

Then in 1998 two white men, John Arnold and his cousin John Plath were executed by lethal injection four months apart for the murder of 33-year-old Betty Gardner, a black woman, in April 1978. The two men tortured, raped, stabbed, and strangled Betty after they picked her up as she was hitchhiking to see her father. Before leaving her corpse, Arnold carved "KKK" into her body.

Sylvester Adams was the first person in South Carolina to be given a choice between the electric chair and lethal injection. All the prior executions were by electrocution.

Recently, prison officials announced a change in the time schedule for executions saying it was felt that executions should be carried out during the day to make it easier on victims' families, judges, prison officials and others involved in the process.

WOMEN SENTENCED TO DEATH IN SOUTH CAROLINA

1931
Beatrice Snipes: White; Commuted. At age 29, Beatrice Snipes was given the death penalty for the murder of a police officer who was trying to arrest her husband. Her sentence was commuted to life.

1943
Sue Stidham Logue: White; Executed. Sue Logue, a former schoolteacher, was the first woman in modern times to be executed, in South Carolina. Her husband had a dispute with a neighbor over a mule that kicked one of the Logues' calves to death. Mr. Logue wanted to be paid for the calf and while her husband was arguing over the price the neighbor killed him. The neighbor was acquitted of the crime, but was mysteriously murdered later.

When the neighbor showed up dead a posse went out to the Logue home and several of the members of the posse were killed. At age 43, Mrs. Logue, her brother-in-law, and another man were all arrested for the deaths and executed.

1947
Rosa Marie Stinette; White; Executed, January 17, 1947. Rosa Marie Stinette was convicted and ultimately executed for arranging the murder of her husband

whose mutilated body was found beside a railroad track. It was said that her motive for the murder was her husband's insurance policy. Three men who participated in the killing were also tried for murder.

Two of the men received life sentences and the third was sentenced to death with Rosa, but just before the execution he was granted a reprieve and she was executed alone.

When Rosa was electrocuted, the surge of energy that was caused when the switch was pulled blew a fuse, and everyone was left in total darkness. The only light was a shower of sparks that outlined her body giving everyone present an eerie feeling. Her body, as it were, was outlined in death. No woman was ever executed in South Carolina again. She was buried in Potter's Field because her daughter had no money with which to claim her body.

1990

Rebecca Smith: White; Reversed, 1992. Witnesses testified at her trial that 40-year-old Rebecca Smith was into witchcraft. This was apparently why she beat her 49-year-old husband to death with her son's Louisville Slugger baseball bat at their North Myrtle Beach mobile home in July 1989.

She became the first woman to receive a death sentence in South Carolina in forty-seven years. A jury of six men and six women who decided she'd first robbed her husband and then killed him took a little more than an hour to decide that Rebecca should die in the state's electric chair. Rebecca and her relatives cried when her sentence was announced.

In 1992 the state Supreme Court reversed the conviction of Rebecca Smith saying the Horry County circuit judge had made two errors during her trial.

28

Tennessee: Electrocution/Lethal Injection

The state of Tennessee has sentenced two women to death since 1900 and no woman has been legally executed in Tennessee. There are two women on death row in Tennessee today.

In early Tennessee law, once the jury found a defendant guilty of murder they went ahead without any additional evidence and decided whether or not to impose the death penalty. This procedure was made official in 1838 (Nakell & Hardy, 1987).

In 1909 Tennessee began using the electric chair and between 1930–1977 there were ninety-three executions. In 1915 Tennessee abolished capital punishment for murder, but retained it for rape. The last execution in Tennessee was on November 7, 1960 when William Tines was electrocuted for rape. Since 1977 there have been no executions.

THE DEATH PENALTY IN TENNESSEE TODAY

In 1997, State Representative Chris Newton said juries should be allowed to choose between lethal injection and the electric chair as the method of execution for a particular criminal. Of the states that have lethal injection, eleven states make it an option available to the condemned. Newton said she prefers giving the jury the choice because "The victim didn't have a choice how they were murdered and the inmate shouldn't have the right to choose how he or she dies." Currently, there is no state that gives the jury such a choice. This legislation was passed in 1998.

After the Supreme Court's decision in *Furman v. Georgia,* Tennessee adopted the bifurcated trial system for death penalty cases. In 1990 a new section was added to the death penalty statute which prohibits the imposition of a death sentence on defendants convicted of first degree murder who are found to have been mentally retarded at the time of the offense. It also provides for consideration of diminished intellectual capacity as a mitigating circumstance.

In 1995, the Tennessee Supreme Court ruled that indigent defendants appealing death sentences may be entitled to state-funded expert witnesses and investigative resources to aid their appeals. This ruling gives capital defendants the right to petition the courts to authorize fees for experts and investigators in their post-conviction appeals when they cannot afford them.

Recently, in Tennessee, two prospective jurors who were excluded from a capital trial in Tennessee because of their religious objections to the death penalty have filed a temporary injunction against the state charging that barring them violates the state constitution. They cited Article 1. Section 6 of the document, which says "The right to trial by jury shall remain inviolate, and no religious or political test shall ever be required as a qualification of jurors." Although a trial court ruled against the injunction, the two — Gerald Bowker, a Southern Baptist, and Janet Wolf, a United Methodist — are appealing the case. They are citing the writings of Thomas Jefferson, whose views influenced the framers of Tennessee's constitution, and who held that no citizen should be deprived of a civic trust or duty because of the exercise of religious conscience.

In December, 1997 the State Supreme Court Justices in Tennessee laid out seventeen factors to help determine whether the death penalty is warranted or not. The rules were part of a 43-page opinion in the case of a Memphis man who was sentenced to death for shooting another man repeatedly. Nashville lawyer, David Raybin, who wrote Tennessee's death penalty law in 1977, said "Up until this time, it was more of a case-by-case analysis with very little rationale as to why or how they were upholding a death penalty case as compared to other death penalty cases."

Since 1979 justices in Tennessee have used the "precedent setting" approach that compares the case before them to other cases in which the defendants were convicted of the same or similar crimes. By examining the facts of the crimes, the characteristics of the defendants and the aggravating and mitigating factors involved, judges make their decisions.

WOMEN SENTENCED TO DEATH IN TENNESSEE

1986

Gaile Owens: White; Currently on death row. At age 32 Gaile Owens, a woman from Bartlett, Tennessee was sentenced to death. She confessed to offering three men $15,000 to kill her husband in Shelby County in 1985. He was beaten to death in his home with a tire iron by Sydney Porterfield, who was also given the death penalty.

Gaile appealed her death sentence on the grounds that her lawyers did not provide an appropriate defense. The Tennessee Supreme Court upheld her conviction and death sentence in May 1998. Gaile remains on death row in Tennessee today.

1996

Christa Gail Pike: White; Currently on death row. Christa Gail Pike, a native of Durham, North Carolina, who called herself the "Lil Devil," was only eighteen when she was sentenced to death for the murder of 19-year-old Colleen Slemmer in Knoxville in 1995. Both Christa and Colleen were students at the Knoxville Job Corps Center when Colleen was murdered.

Christa apparently believed that Colleen was trying to seduce her boyfriend and decided to teach her a lesson one evening. With that in mind, she got a box cutter and a meat cleaver and, accompanied by her boyfriend and another student at the Job Corps, she invited Colleen to walk to a local video store with them.

On the way, Christa told Colleen she had some marijuana stashed in a nearby park that she wanted to go get. When they got to a secluded area in the park Christa started fighting with Colleen and accusing her of trying to take her boyfriend. When Colleen tried to fight back, Christa sliced her in the stomach with the box cutters and Christa's boyfriend cut her across the chest. Later, Christa said that at this point she decided they'd have to kill Colleen because she knew she would tell someone what had happened if they didn't.

Christa said she couldn't stand hearing Colleen beg for her life so she took off her hair-band and shoved it in Colleen's mouth to keep her quiet and then cut her neck several times. But even with her throat slit Colleen kept trying to talk. Seeing that they were not going to listen to her Colleen got up and tried to run away. It was then that Christa picked up a rock and threw it hitting Colleen in the back of the head. Colleen fell down as soon as she was hit and Christa picked up a loose piece of asphalt and started crushing Colleen's skull. When Colleen was finally quiet Christa and her boyfriend carved a pentagram in her chest, and then Christa took a piece of her skull for a souvenir.

Later that night Christa bragged to some other students in the Job Corps that she had killed Colleen and cut a pentagram in her chest. She also bragged about carrying around a piece of her skull.

When Colleen Slemmer's body was found, Christa showed up at the crime scene and asked the officers who had roped off the area what was going on. But Christa and her accomplices were arrested within thirty-six hours because their boasting had made it easy for the authorities to link them to the murder. In the Community of Knoxville it soon became known as the "Job Corps Murder." The Knoxville Job Corps was subsequently closed at the insistence of the people of Knoxville.

The prosecutors in the case decided almost immediately to seek the death penalty for Christa Pike. Although they had no problem producing evidence, the most damaging piece of evidence was the skull of Colleen Slemmer. The medical examiner testified that it was the blows to the head and the crushed skull that had killed Colleen. The fragment of Colleen's skull that Christa kept was found in the pocket of her jacket. At the trial, the prosecutor brought in Colleen's skull and showed a mesmerized jury how the fragment fit perfectly into the skull.

The jury also heard Christa's taped confession where she described every detail of the murder even down to the color of Colleen's skin and her final act of leaning over Colleen's dying body and asking her if she knew who had done that to her.

After 2½ hours of deliberation the jury found Christa Pike guilty of first-degree murder and conspiracy to commit murder and sentenced her to death. But her sentencing for the conspiracy conviction was held over until June 6, 1996. On this day, Christa went to court confident and calm and totally unprepared for the evidence presented by one of the women who worked at the Knoxville County Jail where Christa had been held.

According to the jail employee after Christa had been sentenced to death she was returned to the Knoxville County jail where she immediately wrote a letter to her boyfriend and gave it to the jailer to mail. In the letter, which was read in court, Christa asked her boyfriend to lie about what had happened to make their statements the same. But, the most chilling part of the note was a flippant remark Christa made saying she had done the "ho" (Colleen Slemmer) a favor by bashing her skull in because she would have bled to death anyway and "look what I get for being nice," the note read.

Christa Pike was given twenty-five years for the conspiracy conviction and the judge issued an order that she was prohibited from the sale or distribution of her story. Christa Pike is on death row in Tennessee today.

In a 1998 television interview Christa said she wasn't afraid to die. But, she said she was afraid to die in the electric chair. She said that she knows when two people touch each other and there is static electricity that hurts a little. So, she said, she already knows that the electricity going through her body will hurt "real bad."

29

Texas: Lethal Injection

The state of Texas has given the death penalty to twelve women since 1900. On February 3, 1998, Karla Faye Tucker became the first woman to be executed in Texas since 1863 and in the United States since 1984. The last woman executed in Texas was a woman named Chipita Rodriguez who was hung for murdering a horse trader. There are seven women on death row in Texas today.

The story of Chipita Rodriguez has been told in 2 operas, a poem, several books, and a host of ghost stories. In 1985, on the 100th anniversary of her execution, the Texas legislature gave her case "symbolic redress" by unanimously voting into the record that she did not have a fair trial.

Legend has it that Chipita ran an inn of sorts for travelers in South Texas on the road between Refugio and San Patricio at a ford in the Arkansas River. Today, the location is about five miles downstream from where U.S. 77 crosses the river.

John Savage was a horse trader who sold some mustangs and mules to the Confederate Army in San Antonio and who stopped at Chipita's place in 1863. Since it was after his business with the Army, he was carrying about $600 in gold coins in his saddlebags. The next time he was seen or heard from was when his body was found stuffed in gunnysacks in the Arkansas River. He had apparently been hacked to death with an axe.

Prosecutors said the motive was robbery, although his saddlebags were found in the river with him still full of gold. Chipita was indicted for his murder along with a retarded man who worked for her named Juan Silvera. Silvera was found guilty of helping Chipita kill Savage and was sentenced to five years of hard labor. Chipita was found guilty of the murder, although she denied it, saying only "No soy culpable" (I'm not guilty). A San Patricio county historian said it was widely believed she was protecting someone else, perhaps her illegitimate son.

The jury recommended leniency for Chipita, but the judge sentenced her to death. She was hanged on the banks of the Arkansas River because that was the only place there was a tree big enough. Geraldine McGlain of Corpus Christi, Texas, said recently "Chipita was hung in my great-grandmother's wedding dress. She didn't have a decent dress for her hanging, so my great-grandmother gave her her wedding dress." After the hanging they buried her beside the river in an unmarked grave which has never been found. San Patricio residents claim Chipita's ghost roams the river banks and her soul will forever be in limbo because she never should have been hanged and was not buried in a cemetery.

From 1889 to 1918 Texas ranked third in terms of the number of lynchings carried out in the country, with a total of 335 (Marquart et al., 1994). In the early years convicted capital offenders were executed in the county of their conviction under the supervision of the local sheriff. Hangings were, by design, public spectacles open to rich and poor alike. Capital crimes in those days included treason, piracy, murder, kidnapping of slaves, selling free persons as slaves, rape, robbery, burglary, counterfeiting, and arson (Marquart et al., 1994).

In 1923, Texas changed its official method of execution from hanging to electrocution and began executing people in earnest behind closed doors in 1924 when five men were electrocuted in one day. Two reasons for the change were that lawmakers felt that having the electric chair would clearly distinguish legal executions from vigilante justice, and the electric chair was believed to be more progressive and humane. Texas law at the time was fairly specific and spelled out the procedures for a variety of things pertaining to executions, such as the timing of executions (after midnight and before sunrise), the amount of money allocated for the construction of the electric chair ($5,000), and the size of the nine death row cells and one shower.

In Texas, prisons are called "Units." The Texas electric chair, "Old Sparky," was embedded in the concrete floor of the death chamber in the Huntsville Unit in December 1923. Texas executions have been carried out at the Huntsville Unit commonly called "the Walls" because of its tall brick walls, since then.

Between 1923 and 1972, 510 capital offenders were sentenced to die in the Texas electric chair and, 361 were electrocuted. Before the first scheduled electrocution in Texas in 1924 Captain R. F. Coleman, the warden of the Huntsville prison, resigned his position, stating, "A warden can't be a warden and a killer, too. A penitentiary is a place to reform a man, not kill him." The first prisoner executed in Huntsville was Charles Reynolds, a convicted murderer from Red River County. He claimed to have found God in prison and said in his final statement, "I'm not afraid to meet my maker" (Ward, 1998).

Three women were sent to death row during the years Texas used the electric chair, but none of them were executed. Emma Oliver and Maggie Morgan were both black women convicted of murder who had their sentences commuted to life. Both died in prison. Carolyn Lima, a white woman convicted of murder, won a new trial in 1966, got a 15-year sentence, served her time, and was released.

By the 1930s death sentences were routinely appealed in the Texas Court of Criminal Appeals. Until the initial appeal was decided, inmates remained in the county jail. If the conviction was affirmed, the offender was brought a second time before the trial judge, who pronounced a sentence and set a date of execution, which could not be less than 30 days later. Once a date was set it was an "unbroken custom" from 1936 to 1972 for Texas governors to grant a 30-day stay of execution beyond the initial date set; the offender was then transported to Huntsville to await execution.

After July 1964, a moratorium suspended all executions in Texas until June 1972. Then, on May 11, 1977, Governor Dolph Briscoe signed into law a bill mandating the use of lethal injection as a means of execution in Texas. Briscoe praised lethal injection, saying it was a "more dignified, humane means of carrying out the death penalty." The new law took effect on September 11, 1977, but it was not until December 7, 1982, that Charles Brooks became the first person executed by lethal injection in Texas.

THE DEATH PENALTY IN TEXAS

Known as the Death Penalty Capital of the Western World, Texas is the state with the largest number of executions since 1977. There have been 155 executions since 1982, nineteen in 1995, thirty-seven between January 1st, 1997 and December 31, 1997, eleven as of July 1998.

Perhaps the attitude of most Texans toward the death penalty was best expressed in 1993, when Judge Charles J. Hearn signed the warrant for Robert Nelson Drew's execution on October 15, 1993 with his name and a happy face (Makeig, 1993). According to former Attorney General Jim Mattox, "Executions have gone from being a novelty (in Texas) to something that is more a matter of fact." Crowds of 200 to 300 reporters, prison employees and college students used to clog the sidewalks between the back door to the prison administration building and the front door of the Walls Unit on the day of an execution, said Mattox. However, in recent times, numbers have dwindled to the point of no one showing up at all.

Be that as it may, the 1998 execution of Karla Faye Tucker, who had been on death row for 14½ years, seemed to have changed this sense of ennui. Reportedly, a crowd of 500 people showed up for her execution, and those present described it as a bizarre, surrealistic, circus atmosphere with singing, praying, shouting, and a large TV screen playing a video of Karla Faye. Karla was seen dancing and signing, in the video, to the music "When Jesus, my precious savior comes to take me away." A sign in a music store in downtown Huntsville on the day of her execution read "Karla Faye Tucker Sale — Killer Prices — Deals to Die For!" One person in the crowd held a sign "Forget

Injection — Use a Pickax." A man dressed as the Grim Reaper held a banana, mocking Karla's request for a last meal of fruit and salad. And a member of the College Republicans of Texas held a placard illustration of a dripping hypodermic needle under which was written "Karla Faye, this is your last shot." Another sign read "Hollywood elite, Euro-Trash Socialists, Pope John Paul: Stay out of Texas Politics!" Some people shouted "She sliced, she diced, and now she's got to pay the price!" When the news reached the crowd that Karla was dead a cheer rose from the death penalty advocates as some sang "Na Na Na Na…say goodbye" (Associated Press, 1998). On February 3, 1998, in Huntsville, Texas, at least, it seemed that everyone had an opinion about executions.

When asked if the death penalty is an ethical form of punishment, James A. Farren, the Randall County, Texas, district attorney, said, "I most definitely believe execution is an ethical form of punishment as long as we can agree on a definition of how it's carried out." He went on to say that he believes that the death penalty is a deterrent to violent crime, and that executions should be conducted without lengthy delays. Rebecca King of the 47th District said, "When I ask for the death penalty I ask for it because there's a future danger to society" (*Amarillo Globe-News*, 1997). King said she and other prosecutors look at all the ramifications of a person's case and attempt to answer the one fundamental question, which is, is this person a danger to society? She said if we find he/she is not a danger to society, then maybe something else can be done.

In Texas, capital murder is defined as a murder that is committed under any of the following special circumstances:

- If the victim is a peace officer or fireman;
- If it is during a kidnapping, burglary, robbery, aggravated sexual assault, arson, or obstruction or retaliation;
- If it is for remuneration;
- If it is while escaping or attempting to escape from prison;
- If it is of a penal institution employee while incarcerated;
- If it is while incarcerated for murder or serving life or 99 years for kidnapping, aggravated sexual assault, or aggravated robbery;
- If it is of more than one person, either during the same act, or during different acts but pursuant to the same scheme or course of conduct;
- If it is of a person under six years of age.

Fourteen-year-olds may be prosecuted as adults in Texas and seventeen-year-olds are always prosecuted as adults. Of the eleven juveniles executed in the United States since capital punishment was restored, seven have been from Texas.

When the Texas State Legislature meets in January 1999 Representative James Pitts, a Republican from Waxahachie will introduce legislation to lower the age for death penalty eligibility in Texas to 11 years old. Of his proposal Pitts said, of course, no one would be executed until they were 17, nor would they be housed in the state prisons. Other ideas that may result in proposals for the 1999 Texas legislature include:

Requiring judges to inform juries the true and full meaning of life imprisonment — 40 years incarceration before parole eligibility;

Offering juries the option of life without parole;

Requiring the Texas Board of Pardons and Paroles to have full, in person, open hearings for all executive clemency requests;

Giving full and complete executive clemency responsibility to the Texas governor;

Providing oversight to determine competency of legal counsel appointed by the Texas Court of Criminal Appeals;

Providing the means to have mental and emotional competency hearings for death row inmates who request them.

Currently, Texas has a bifurcated trial procedure for capital punishment where the sentencing phase is separate from the guilt-innocence phase of the trial. The same jury presides for both phases and for capital punishments the judge is not required to explain anything about the defendant's parole eligibility to the jury.

Rules also state that neither the court, the state, the defendant, nor the defendant's attorney can inform a juror or a prospective juror of the effect of a failure by the jury to agree on sentencing. Questions the jury must consider in the sentencing phase of a capital trial include:

Is there a probability that the defendant would commit criminal acts of violence that would constitute a continuing threat to society?

Is the defendant criminally responsible for the death of the deceased?

Taking into account all of the evidence, including the circumstances of the offense, the defendant's character and background, and the personal moral culpability of the defendant, is there sufficient mitigating circumstance or circumstances to warrant that a sentence of life imprisonment rather than death be imposed?

In 1995 a bill mandating that a prosecutor must seek the death penalty for someone convicted of "an act of terror" passed the Texas Senate unanimously, but did not pass the House. The bill was proposed in response to the Oklahoma City bombing.

In October 1997 the U.S. Supreme Court rejected a challenge to the Texas rule that bars a jury from being told when a defendant will be eligible for parole if given a sentence other than death. According to Justice John Paul Stevens "The Texas rule tips the scales in favor of a death sentence that a fully informed jury might not impose." Stevens noted that in a number of states that had been polled, support for the death penalty decreases when life imprisonment is presented as an alternative, with the defendant not being eligible for parole for at least 25 years.

A study by Marquart and Eckland-Olson (1989) looked at the post-*Furman* death penalty statute in Texas which addresses the punishment phase of the trial, and the question of whether or not the defendant presents a continuing violent threat to society. According to the study, from 1874 to 1988, 92 capital murderers had their sentences commuted to life imprisonment. The authors analyzed these commutations and the predictions made by the jurors that these individuals would present a future violent threat to society. They also looked at patterns of institutional and post-release behavior of this group and compared them to similar patterns for 107 defendants convicted of capital murder who were not predicted to be dangerous and who received life imprisonment over the same 15-year period. The authors found that, although most capital offenders were model inmates, two commuted offenders committed second murders, one while in prison and the other in the community. This study is helpful in considering the validity of current death statues that require jurors to predict future dangerousness in all capital cases.

Recently the Catholic bishops in Texas issued a statement through the Texas Catholic Conference reiterating their opposition to the death penalty. The bishops said that the need for the death penalty today is "practically non-existent." Their statement went on to say that it is unfortunate that so many Americans still support capital punishment despite evidence of its ineffectiveness, racial bias, and staggering costs, both materially and emotionally. Bishop John McCarthy of Austin said the bishops are appalled at the rapid rise in the number of executions in Texas.

A death row case in Texas costs on average $2.3 million which is about 3 times the cost of imprisoning someone in a single cell at the highest security level for 40 years (*Dallas Morning News*, 1992).

In 1998, U.S. Representative Henry Gonzalez, the senior member of the Texas Congressional delegation, announced his resignation after thirty-six years in Washington. Gonzalez, who was eighty-one at the time, was the first Hispanic elected from Texas. He introduced a bill in every recent congressional session to abolish the death penalty in the United States.

DEATH ROW IN TEXAS

The average time an inmate spends on death row in Texas is nine years, although there have been exceptions such as Kenneth Granville, who was on death row for 21 years, Pamela Perillo, who has now been on death row for nineteen years, and Clarence Lackey, on death row in Texas for 17 years. In 1995, Lackey argued [*Lackey v. Texas* 115 S.Ct. 1421 (1995)] that the execution of a prisoner who has been on death row for seventeen years violates the Eighth Amendment's prohibition of cruel and unusual punishment. Among other things, Lackey contended that years of death row confinement plus the extreme psychological anguish caused by such confinement, constitutionally deprived Texas of the power to carry out his death sentence. The Supreme Court, however, did not agree, and Clarence Lackey was executed on May 20, 1997. Currently (1998) the inmate who has been on death row the longest in Texas is Robert Excell White, who has been on death row for twenty-three years and his execution date has not been set.

The average age of inmates executed in Texas is thirty-seven, and 60 percent of the individuals on death row in Texas are Black, Latino, Asian, or Native American (NAACP, 1996). The oldest woman on death row in Texas, Betty Lou Beets, is sixty-one.

When the Secretary General of Amnesty International, Pierre Sane, visited the death row in Huntsville in October 1997 he spent two hours touring and chatting with condemned inmates. After he left, he said "I found the prisoners calm. I don't know what they do in order to cope." He went on to say that the officers appeared to be professional, but it is what that professionalism reflects that he found frightening. He said, "You have here a machinery of death, a conveyor belt of death, and you have professionals manning it." This is very reminiscent of another historical era which no one should ever forget (Amnesty International, 1997).

A garment factory in the Huntsville, Texas, prison is the only such prison enterprise in the country designed for and operated exclusively by a death row community. The factory is a booming workplace, with 115 workers and places for eighty-five more being planned. The prisoners view the work as a final chance to confound society's judgment of their lives as utterly worthless.

The Gatesville women's death row Mountain View Unit is a one-story red brick bungalow separated from the rest of the prison by a 12-foot high chain-link fence topped with curly razor wire. The women live in 6 by 9 cells that have a bunk, a small bookshelf, a sink, a commode, a two-drawer dresser, and a chair. The floor of the cells is dark red.

There is a TV outside the cells in the day room where the women eat their meals at a table. A carpet gives the room a sort of living-room look. Next to the TV is a bookshelf. There is also a sewing shop where some of the women make Cabbage-Patch dolls known as "parole buddies." The dolls are hand-painted and hand-sewn for prison employees who provide the material and order custom-made dolls. Outside, the inmates have a vegetable garden along one wall. There is a volleyball net on the front lawn and a wooden bench near the front gate.

Texas death row inmates are allowed one two-hour visit a week from approved family and friends, with a maximum of two people at a time and four visits a month. Every three months inmates are allowed to make a list of ten people for the prison authorities approval. Media do not count as a weekly visit.

CLEMENCY IN TEXAS

The governor of Texas does not have the power to grant clemency and can only grant a 30-day stay of execution, recommending that the attorney general review the case. Clemency in Texas is a 2-step process and is in the hands of the 18-member Board of Pardons and Paroles. Members of the Board are at widely scattered locations in Texas. They rarely meet and make decisions mostly by mail. No one can meet with them all at once and they have never granted a clemency. The Texas Board of Pardon and Paroles and its methods were widely debated before the execution of Karla Faye Tucker. In one of Karla's last minute appeals to the Supreme Court, her lawyers questioned the "Policy and practice of the Board of Pardons and Paroles" and whether or not they were in accord with procedural due process. Their document stated in part:

It would appear that the Board members usually do not meet the person upon whose life they are voting, that the Board members usually do not meet as a group before making their decisions, and that they vote, not upon meeting as a group, but by faxing, calling, or mailing in their vote to the Austin Office of the Board. These facts are not only common knowledge, but are also confirmed by a representative of the Board of Pardons and Paroles. (*Texas v. Tucker*, 1998)

Despite this appeal, on Monday, February 2, 1998, Victor Rodriguez, then chair of the Texas Board of Pardons and Paroles, announced that the Board had denied Karla Faye Tucker's plea for mercy in a 16–0 vote with two abstentions, one of the abstentions being an individual who always abstains in death penalty decisions.

In 1998, in a controversial and unprecedented move, Governor George Bush commuted the death sentence of Henry Lee Lucas, a former mental patient who killed his mother and who admitted killing hundreds of others, to life. This was the first time that Texas has taken such action at an inmate's request since the death penalty was reinstated. The Texas Board of Pardon and Paroles voted 17–1 in favor of commutation. Lucas was sentenced to death in Texas for the murder of an unidentified female hitchhiker nineteen years earlier. Lucas's confession was the only thing that linked him to the murder. But in 1996 he told a U.S. district judge that he did not murder the hitchhiker and only knew the facts of the case because he had seen the case file. Governor Bush said that the jurors who heard his case did not know Lucas had a pattern of lying and confessing to crimes he did not commit.

Besides the death penalty, Lucas was serving six life terms, two 75-year terms, and one 60-year term for other murders. His execution date was set for June 30, 1998.

Former Attorney General Jim Mattox, who conducted a detailed study of Lucas's case, said it was highly improbable that Lucas committed the crime for which he was scheduled to be executed.

EXECUTIONS IN TEXAS

Texas is among a growing number of states who now allow victim witnesses or members of victim's families to witness executions. The execution of Leo Jenkins on February 9, 1996 became the first to be watched by the victim's relatives. Richard Thornton, whose wife was killed by Karla Faye Tucker and her companion in 1983, and his children witnessed Karla's execution in 1998. Thornton said then "I want to say to all victims in the world: Demand this. Don't ask for it, demand this, it is your right."

In Texas, the execution area for witnesses is divided by a soundproof wall that separates the family of the victim from the prisoner's witnesses. On the side for witnesses invited by Karla Faye to her execution was the brother of the woman Karla murdered, Ron Carlson, who held the opposite view of his brother-in-law. Carlson, a Christian who is active in the anti death penalty movement, said he had forgiven Karla. "They only killed her body, but her spirit still lives on," he said.

The identity of the executioner who stands behind a one-way mirror in Texas executions is kept a secret. But, there have been several notable cases of executions that were botched in the state.

In March 1985 authorities had to probe Stephen Peter Morin in both arms and legs with needles for forty-five minutes before they found a suitable vein.

For the execution of Raymond Landry on December 13, 1988, the syringe came out of his arm and had to be reinserted. During the time the reinsertion was taking place the curtain was pulled and witnesses were not allowed to observe the procedure. After the syringe was reinserted, it took twenty-four minutes for Landry to die.

In 1998, when Joseph Cannon was being executed, he had said goodbye to everyone and asked forgiveness of the victim's family, then closed his eyes, but within seconds he opened them again and said, "It's come undone." The vein where the needle had been inserted in his left arm had collapsed. The curtain in front of the witnesses was closed and the prison chaplain told everyone Cannon was doing fine, they just had to reinsert the needle. Witnesses were taken outside for 15 minutes until the needle was reinserted. When they returned to view the execution, Cannon apologized saying he'd "Lost his cool." He again asked forgiveness from the victim's family and was pronounced dead seventy minutes after he was taken from his cell.

Justin Lee May on May 7, 1992, had an unusually violent reaction to the lethal drugs and according to a reporter who witnessed the execution, he gasped, coughed, and reared against his heavy leather restraints, coughing one last time before his body froze. Of the same execution, another reporter wrote, "He went into a coughing spasm, groaned and gasped, lifted his head from the gurney and would have arched his back if he had not been belted down. After he stopped breathing, his eyes and mouth remained open."

The use of the chemicals in lethal injections has been fraught with debate. Edward Shaughnessy, chief of the appellate division for the Bexar County district attorney's office says there is no proof that the chemicals have ever been inadequately administered in a Texas execution. "Certain things," he says, "You're never going to know. This holds true of any method of execution. If you use the electric chair, you can never call them back and say, 'Did that cause you pain?' That evidence can never be produced. That holds true of the gas chamber, hanging, and firing squads."

George Lott was on death row for only eighteen months before he was executed. During that time he begged the state to execute him, which they did, making his the shortest stay on death row in Texas. Lott was given the death penalty for the 1992 shooting deaths of two attorneys in a Ft. Worth courthouse. He also wounded three others. Lott was an attorney and he blamed his violence on the unfairness he received at the hands of the legal system while going through a divorce.

Perhaps one of the strangest aftermaths of an execution in Texas was that of Paul Jernigan, who was executed on August 5, 1993. According to the *Houston Chronicle* after his execution, his body was sent to the University of Colorado, where it was put in cold storage at 50–60 degrees below zero until it was completely frozen, after which it was sliced from head to toe into 1,871 pieces. Each piece, which was thinner than a slice of bread, was photographed and stored digitally. The layered images were then stacked on top of each other electronically in a computer database and the executed Paul Jernigan was reborn as the "Visible Man" to be transmitted on-line on the Internet computer network.

Michael Ackerman came up with the idea and headed the "Visible Man" project. According to Ackerman the multidimensional map of Jernigan's body would be used to help teach and enhance surgery skills to medical students and help doctors explain surgery to their patients. The high-tech idea, which is supposed to take up fifteen gigabytes in storage space, would be equivalent to about five million typewritten pages of text.

After examining Jernigan's corpse, Ackerman said it was the "perfect cadaver" because unlike other corpses they had examined there were no injuries or debilitating illnesses. Questions were later raised as to whether this type of death row donor procedure violated any state or federal laws. What will ultimately come of Jernigan is yet unknown.

REPRESENTATION OF DEATH ROW INMATES

All death sentences are automatically appealed in the Texas Court of Criminal Appeals. This is mandatory. If the Court decides against the inmate, then a Writ of Certiorari may be filed directly to the U.S. Supreme Court. If the U.S. Supreme Court decides against an inmate, then they must file an application for a Texas State Writ of Habeas Corpus. If a defendant decides to file an application for a Writ of Habeas Corpus it cannot be filed later than 180 days after the date the Court of Criminal Appeals appoints counsel, or not later than 45 days after the date of the appellant's original brief was filed on direct appeal.

If the Texas Court of Criminal Appeals decides against the death row inmate, then the application for a Federal Writ of Habeas Corpus may be filed. If the defendant decides to file, it must be filed in the appropriate Federal District Court. The deadline is one year from the time the conviction was final, less the time the Texas Court of Criminal Appeals takes to render its decision on the state habeas.

If the Federal District Court decides against the Death Row inmate, then an appeal may be filed with the U.S. Court of Appeals at the Fifth Circuit. If the U.S. Court of Appeals at the Fifth Circuit decides against the death row inmate, then a Writ of Certiorari, may be filed directly in the U.S. Supreme Court.

By all accounts there are not enough attorneys in Texas to cover the need. Senator John Montford sponsored a bill that took effect in September, 1995 that tightened the time limits for filing appeals in capital cases in Texas (Best, 1993). The new law requires that direct appeals (arguing errors in trial procedures) and the state post-conviction habeas corpus appeal (arguing constitutional issues) be filed at the same time. Previously habeas appeals were filed after all direct appeals were exhausted.

A first for Texas in this new law is a provision requiring the state to pay for appellate representation of death row prisoners. Initially, the Texas courts allotted $7,500 per case for appellate attorneys, but most qualified lawyers refused to take such a small amount for such time consuming casework. According to Vincent Perinin, chair of the State Bar Committee on Death Penalty Representation, the lowest figure they've come up with from various studies is $25,000 in attorney fees and $6,000 for investigative fees. Currently there is $1 million in the pot to cover legal fees for the 400+ inmates currently on death row in Texas.

When lawyers didn't appear voluntarily to represent inmates in the appellate process, the Texas Courts assigned them to cases. But, as soon as assignments were made, many lawyers filed motions to be removed from cases. Lawyers contend that judges and prosecutors are not asked to donate hundreds of hours of their time to make the Criminal Justice System work, so why should defense and appellate attorneys be asked to do so?

In July 1998 a representative of the Texas Criminal Defense Lawyer's Association (TCDLA) said they were advising their members not to accept certain death-row appeals assigned by the Texas Court of Criminal Appeals because judges are not fully reimbursing attorney's expenses.

Kent Schaffer, a Houston defense attorney and president of TCDLA, said the appeals court is ruining the practices of defense lawyers. According to Schaffer most lawyers pay investigators and expert witnesses out of their own pockets because the state won't fully reimburse them.

One attorney who worked on indigent defense before the death penalty resource centers were done away with said people who take these cases better be prepared to do hundreds of hours of pro bono work. They should also have up to $20,000 of their own money to put into an investigation, he said.

Schaffer said, "When lawyers around the state see that other lawyers who have taken these cases are financially devastated, they take that into consideration."

WOMEN SENTENCED TO DEATH IN TEXAS

1924

Emma Oliver: Black; Commuted to life in prison. Emma Oliver had a criminal history of vagrancy, prostitution, four arrests for murder, seven for aggravated assault, and one for attempted murder long before she was given the death penalty. She was convicted of her first murder in 1924 and served 1½ years in the state penitentiary before being released.

A year later she was arrested three times for aggravated assault, then in February 1949 she was charged with another murder and sentenced to die. This time it was for killing a forty-year-old black man in San Antonio in a dispute over three dollars. According to court testimony, after discovering the body of the victim, the police found Emma who reportedly yelled, "I killed him" after she was arrested.

Emma was the first woman to be sentenced to death by electrocution in Texas. She made numerous appeals for clemency and one was on the grounds that there were no blacks on the commission that selected the grand jurors, nor on the grand jury that indicted her. She also claimed the district attorney was biased which the Court of Criminal Appeals denied.

Once Emma was on death row, a psychological evaluation report found Emma was psychotic, had severe organic brain damage and only a limited contact with reality. The parole board recommended her sentence be commuted in a 2–1 vote. R. A. Schmidt, the dissenting board member, said he was disturbed by the fact that Emma had been previously convicted of murder. He also noted that she had a record of 59 other arrests.

Nevertheless Governor Allan Shivers commuted Emma's death sentence to life imprisonment on June 29, 1951. He said the reason was simply "letters and petitions signed by numerous citizens of Bexar County requesting a commutation." Emma died in prison of cancer, twelve years later, in February 1963 (Marquart et al., 1994).

1961

Maggie Morgan: Black; Commuted to life. Maggie Morgan was sentenced to death in May 1961 for the murder of 48-year-old Wilma Selby, a white woman from Austin. Maggie, who worked at a massage parlor, was a fortune-teller on the side. The story goes she was paid $1,600 by one of her customers, Joseph Selby, to get rid of his wife. Maggie, Selby, and a man named Clarence Collins, the triggerman, were all convicted of the murder, but Maggie was the only one sentenced to death. Another massage parlor worker, Patra Mae Bounds, who turned state's evidence, was also found guilty. Maggie always denied her guilt and claimed she had a minor role in the crime.

In an interview with a prison doctor, Maggie was cooperative, but told him her trial was not conducted the way she would have liked and she objected to not being allowed to take the stand on her own behalf. The doctor said she smiled a lot and denied being sad, depressed, or suicidal. She said she'd been "framed" and had some doubt about her lawyer's competence.

Letters recommending clemency for Maggie were written by various trial officials, in part because her co-defendant was sentenced to life imprisonment. The parole board recommended that her sentence be commuted to life, which Governor Price Daniel granted on July 25, 1961. Maggie died in prison nine years later, on September 12, 1970.

1963

Carolyn Lima: White; Commuted to five years, released from prison. Carolyn Lima was sentenced to death in January 1963 in Houston for the 1961 murder of a 45-year-old male acquaintance with whom she had had a sexual relationship. In February 1961, Carolyn and Leslie Ashley (a male prostitute) went to the victim's office, where the victim suggested that Ashley take part in a three-way sexual act. Ashley refused, and a scuffle took place between Carolyn and the victim. Ashley then took a gun from Carolyn's purse and shot the victim once. After the injured man threatened Carolyn with a "bayonet," she grabbed the pistol from Ashley and shot him five more times.

Ashley and Carolyn then took the body to an open field, doused it with gasoline, and set it on fire, after which they fled Texas. They were later apprehended in New York City. While on death row, Carolyn received six reprieves. Her sentence was finally commuted in April 1965, to five years imprisonment on the rationale that the offense was in part precipitated by the victim and was thus a matter of self-defense. Carolyn was discharged from prison the day of her commutation. Her co-defendant's sentence was commuted to fifteen years on January 14, 1966.

1978

Mary Anderson: White: Reversed, 1982. Mary Anderson was given the death penalty in Texas in 1978 for murder. Her sentence was reversed in 1982 after spending four years on death row.

1979

Linda Burnett: White; Reversed; Sentenced to life in 1983. Linda May Burnett spent four years on death row for the murder of 3-year-old Jason Phillips, one of five family members who were abducted, bound, shot, and buried in a mass grave near Fannett, west of Beaumont, Texas. Elmer and Martha Phillips and their son Jason, from Woodward, Oklahoma, were visiting Jason's grandparents, Bishop and Esther Phillips, when all five were driven to a pre-dug grave and shot in the head, in July 1978.

Linda, the mother of three children, claimed she was innocent and that her only mistake was agreeing to serve as an alibi for her lover, Joseph Dugas. Bishop and Esther Phillips were Dugas's former in-laws, and he blamed them for the break-up of his marriage to their daughter. Both Linda and Dugas were convicted and given the death penalty for the killing of Jason. They were also charged with the other four deaths. Joe Dugas was shot and killed by detectives who were accompanying him from death row to testify at Linda's trial. They said he was trying to escape.

Linda denied being present at the killings, but tape recordings of various versions of the murders, she gave while under hypnosis, were used extensively by the prosecution. In one version Linda admitted, on tape, killing all four of the adults, then later she claimed she had only killed two, Dugas's ex-parents-in-law. The prosecution argued that although the second version of the tapes was a result of hypnosis, Linda was not under hypnosis in the first version and the tapes were, therefore, admissible in court.

In October 1982, Linda asked that all appeals in her case be dropped and that she be executed. Now, she says this was a decision she made while deeply depressed. Three weeks after this decision, the Texas Court of Criminal Appeals threw out her conviction and gave her a new trial, saying some of the evidence allowed at her trial was improper. In her second trial, Linda was again convicted of murder, but the jury gave her life in prison. Of her feelings at the sentencing Linda said, "My legs turned to jelly. My knees got weak. I was trying to look at my mom, but all I could see were tears. Most people are sent back to death row at a second trial and I was prepared to go back" (*Dallas Morning News,* 1997). In 1997, on December 26, Linda became eligible for parole. She is the only "former" female death row inmate still incarcerated in Texas, which has approximately 10,200 women in its general population.

When asked about her parole, Linda said, "I expect to get it. I'm not a threat to anyone. I've lived by all of the TDC's rules. I have a Christian base I'm going to. I'm working with people who have dealt with inmates a great deal and will be in their company" (*Dallas Morning News,* 1997). She said she has worked with younger inmates and counseled them on the value of getting an education while they are doing time. She got her GED while in prison and now lacks only nineteen hours for a college degree.

Of her case, Linda now says she's innocent. She says she wasn't at the scene of the shootings and that she was beaten and raped by Dugas and a companion, whom she met at the doughnut shop where she worked. They also threatened the lives of her three children, she said. Linda says she was the typical abused woman who wouldn't fight back, but now she has changed and stands up for what she believes in.

Most recently, in 1998, Linda spoke out on behalf of Karla Faye Tucker opposing her execution. She said "I think Karla is a better person than I am, she's a crusader . . . person who can reach out and talk to you, and if you even think of going in the wrong direction, she can pull you back. If I can do this, come into the prison system and live in peace with other people and reach out and help people around me, I believe in my heart Karla can. Even if you believe in the death sentence, surely you can see that this woman could be locked up for the rest of her life if the parole board doesn't want her out. She can do nothing to anyone in the free world if she's locked up. Give her a chance."

The Jefferson County former assistant prosecutor who tried Linda said he knew nothing about her eligibility for parole, and when asked if he thought she should be released, he said, "Based on what I saw at the trial my answer would be *definitely not.*"

1980, 1984

Pamela Lynn Perillo: White; Currently on death row. Pamela Lynn Perillo has been on death row in Texas longer than any other woman. She first arrived in August 1980 convicted of the strangulation murder of Bob Skeens in Houston. After that first death sentence her conviction was reversed because of an error during the questioning of jurors. She was retried and convicted a second time in 1984 and resentenced to death. In November 1997 a federal judge turned down her request for a new trial, saying she had adequate representation in her first trial. But, in 1998 she was granted the opportunity for a third trial.

In 1997 Pam argued that her capital murder conviction should have been thrown out because one of her two attorneys in her second trial, Jim Skelton, also represented Linda Fletcher, her co-defendant, and a witness for the prosecution. He had been hired to assist Pam's primary counsel for her second trial after her 1981 conviction was overturned. Skelton had convinced Linda Fletcher, who had moved to California, to return to Texas to testify about her husband's influence over her and Pam. Therefore, Pam contended, Skelton had a conflict of interest. However, U.S. District Court Judge Ewing Werlein ruled that, if anything, the attorney's close relationship with Linda Fletcher was only a help to Pam's case.

Pam grew up in a poor family in California and was raised by an abusive father. She began using drugs at age ten; heroin was her drug of choice. As soon as she could pass for twenty-one she began dancing in bars. Then in 1980, Pam, James Briddle, and his wife, Linda Fletcher, left California to avoid arrest for a robbery they had committed to support their drug habits. They were hitchhiking in Texas when a man named Bob Banks gave them a lift near the Houston Astrodome. Banks was moving furniture from an apartment to a new house and offered to put them up for a couple of days in exchange for their help. He took them home and the next day a friend of his, Bob Skeens, arrived from Louisiana. Banks and Skeens went out to get coffee and doughnuts for breakfast and by the time they returned the decision had been made to rob and kill them.

Briddle forced the two men to the floor at gunpoint, and he and Pam tied their hands and feet. Then they put a rope around Banks's neck, and with Briddle on one end and Pam on the other, they pulled for ten minutes or more until Banks stopped writhing on the floor and was strangled to death. His friend, Bob Skeens, was forced to watch. No one but the killers know for sure when the three of them ate the doughnuts. It might have been after the first killing, but Bob Skeens was killed the same way as Banks an hour later. In the crime scene photos, the doughnut box was empty.

After the crime, the three of them left the two bodies in the house, took Skeen's car, $800, a tape player, three guns, and a camera, and drove to Dallas. From there they took a bus to Denver. By the time they reached Denver, Pam's drug-induced state had apparently worn off and she flagged down a Denver police officer and confessed to the killings. According to her attorney, this demonstrated Pam's first step towards rehabilitating herself and resulted in the arrests of the other two defendants. She told the police, "I want to stop running and get my son back." Pam was returned to Texas, where both she and James Briddle were convicted of the murders and given the death penalty.

Pam has never denied her part in the killings. In a 1995 Associated Press interview, she said the media likes to pound away at the "gruesome facts" of crimes committed by death row inmates. "All I can say is it's hard to live knowing what I did. I took two people's lives. I'm sorry it happened." She told the interviewer that "Everyone wants exclusive rights to my story" but "I don't like reliving it over and over and over. And I don't want to hurt the victims any more than I already have."

Linda Fletcher, who was with them, was also charged with capital murder initially. But her charges were lowered to aggravated robbery and she was sentenced to five years probation in exchange for testifying against Pam.

Today, Pamela Perillo, has been on death row for eighteen years. In her years on death row, she became a Christian and claims Christ as her source of strength. She was scheduled to be executed in 1995, but received an 11th hour reprieve. She is now in her last stages of appeals. In June 1998, the court overturned Pam's death sentence and gave the state 180 days to contest it or release her. Pam has a 19-year-old son who, she says, is the happiest part of her life.

1984

Karla Faye Tucker: White; Executed, February 3, 1998. Karla Faye Tucker, who will always be remembered as the pickax murderer, was executed by lethal injection on February 3, 1998, in Huntsville, Texas. A born-again Christian who had found God on death row, Karla will also be remembered for sparking a worldwide debate over redemption and retribution. Two weeks before Karla's execution, Pat Robertson appeared on CNN's "Larry King Live" and asked that her life be spared. He told the world that the death penalty is not about vengeance. The pope, Karla's prosecutors, Bianca Jagger representing Amnesty International, and even House Speaker Newt Gingrich all took up Karla's cause to no avail.

Minutes before her execution, people outside the Huntsville prison facility were standing should-to-shoulder facing a big screen video image of Karla translating into sign language the lyrics of a gospel song being sung on tape by the daughter of her minister, David Kirschke. As one group chanted "No Mercy" another sang "Amazing Grace." There were signs in English, Italian, French, and Spanish pleading for mercy. A crime victim's advocate for the Houston mayor's office said the only reason Karla was receiving so much attention was that she looked like one of the Brady Bunch.

Professor David Dow of the University of Houston Law School, who has represented more than 20 capital defendants, said, "You had a unique convergence of factors in Karla Faye Tucker . . . once it's possible to execute someone like her, there's almost nobody you can't execute."

Inside, prison officials said that Karla did not ask for a sedative, so that she was fully conscious when the execution took place. She wore prison whites with white sneakers. After her last words, she gasped once and coughed twice before dying. Her eyes remained open. She was pronounced dead at 6:45 p.m. Karla's last words were:

I would like to say to all of you, the Thornton family and Jerry Dean's family that I am so sorry. I hope God will give you peace with this. Baby I love you (to her husband). Ron (Deborah Thornton's brother), give Peggy a hug for me. Everybody has been so good to me. I love all of you very much. I am going to be face to face with Jesus now. Warden Baggett, thank all of you so much. You have been so good to me. I love all of you very much. I will see you all when you get there.

Some believed that Karla Faye had led a life that could only end in some type of tragedy. By the age of eight she was doing hard drugs and by eleven she was mainlining heroin. According to Karla, she was never without drugs from around ten years of age until four months before her 24th birthday, when she was incarcerated. Karla had dropped out of school before completing the seventh grade and she had her first sexual encounter around twelve or thirteen. She started shooting heroin while living with her father around the age of twelve. When she was thirteen her mother first let her travel with the Allman Brothers Band on tour, and it was on these trips that she first used cocaine. When Karla was fifteen or sixteen she moved in with Steven Griffith, a man she later married. They were together for about five years, and after their break-up Karla took up prostitution to earn a living. She continued working as a prostitute until a few months before the murders.

Karla had known Shawn Dean, the wife of the man she murdered, for sixteen years. Shawn had also traveled with the Allman Brothers Band, and Karla said she and Shawn were like "Siamese twins." She and Shawn got an apartment together and that was how she met Jerry Dean. All of them used drugs heavily, and Karla met Danny Garrett through a doctor from whom they got illegal prescriptions. Karla said that on one occasion Jerry Dean took the only photographs she had of herself with her mother and destroyed it by stabbing it with a knife. She only saw Dean once after that, before the night of the murders.

In 1983 Karla moved in with Danny Garrett and her sister Kari Burrell, who was married to Ron Burrell at the time. They were all using speed. Two or three weeks before the murders, Shawn Dean came to live with them because Jerry, who was her husband, was beating up on her. They all talked about Jerry Dean and how he had treated them and how Karla was angry at him for parking his motorcycle in her living room where it dripped oil all over the carpet. It was Danny Garrett who brought up the idea of stealing Dean's motorcycle to get even with him.

With this in mind, Karla got the key to his apartment from Shawn's pockets one night when she was doing the laundry. Karla said she was jumpy and hadn't been able to sleep the night she, Danny Garrett, and Jimmy Leibrant (another friend) decided to go over to Garrett's to "case the place out." They planned to return another night to break in.

Garrett took his shotgun and when they got to Dean's apartment, Karla opened it with the key she had taken from Shawn's pocket. Dean was on a mattress on the floor and Karla immediately sat on him and woke him up. He recognized Karla and told her "We can work things out." She started wrestling with him until Garrett intervened by hitting Dean repeatedly over the head with a hammer.

Karla turned on the lights and saw Dean lying face down on the mattress, making gurgling sounds. She said she wanted to stop him from making that noise so she took his pickax that was leaning against the wall and hit him in the back with it several times. She told Garrett that Dean wouldn't stop making that noise so Garrett took the pickax and hit him with it until the noise stopped.

It was then that Karla noticed someone else underneath the covers. She took the pickax again and hit that person in the shoulder, not knowing whether it was a man or a woman. At that point Deborah Thornton stood up and tried to take the pickax out of her shoulder. When Garrett came back in the room, Karla left and she said that when she returned she saw Garrett kill Deborah Thornton. He left the pickax embedded in her chest, which is where the police found it the next day.

After the murders, neither Garrett nor Karla Faye bothered to leave town. In fact, they continued living at home and occasionally bragged about what they had done. Ultimately, about eight months down the line, they were turned in by their siblings, Garrett's brother and Karla's sister. Doug Garret recorded Karla on tape telling him how she was sexually aroused every time she swung the axe that killed Jerry Dean. She later recanted that statement saying she had only spoken that way to impress him.

Over the years of her incarceration Karla received a lot of support from Christian groups and even from relatives of the victims. In 1993 she told Leah Darotkin of the *Houston Press:*

Because I was taken out of an environment where drugs and violence were the norm, and put in here and given a chance to really kind of stop and realize what's right and good. It's been great for me.

In 1995 she was married while still on death row to prison ministry worker, Dana Brown. Brown was present at Karla's execution and said "Her gain today was our loss . . . she was someone who literally reached thousands of people for Jesus and probably will continue to do so through her testimony. Even though she cried out for forgiveness, God gave her just what she needed. That was love."

After the execution Brown took her body to an undisclosed funeral home and said he had not decided where she would be buried.

1985

Betty Lou Beets: White; Currently on death row. Betty Lou Beets was a cashier and waitress convicted of the shooting death of her fifth husband, Dallas firefighter Jimmy Don Beets at the couple's home near Gun Barrel City in East Texas. She buried his body in their yard. At the time, the murder was believed to be a scheme to collect $500,000 in life insurance benefits.

The body of her fourth husband, Doyle Wayne Barker, was also found on her property buried behind a tool shed. She was charged with killing him too, but never stood trial.

In 1984 the Texas Court of Criminal Appeals ruled that Betty's crime technically did not fit the capital offense of murder for remuneration, since she did not hire a third party to kill her husband. Later, however, the State Supreme

Court reversed this decision. Betty Lou Beets is currently on death row in Texas.

1988

Frances Elaine Newton: Black; Currently on death row. Frances Newton worked in accounting and was convicted of the murders of her 23-year-old husband and two children, a 7-year-old son and a twenty-one-month-old daughter, to collect insurance benefits. When she was sentenced to death, at twenty-four, she was the youngest woman on death row in Texas at the time of her incarceration.

1995

Cathy Lynn Henderson: White; Currently on death row. Cathy Lynn Henderson was sentenced to death for the murder of Brandon Baugh, a 3-month-old baby boy from Austin. His body was found by the police using a map Cathy had drawn. Cathy was arrested in Kansas City, Missouri eleven days after she disappeared while babysitting at the child's home. Although she denied knowing anything about Brandon at first, she later admitted killing him, saying it was an accident and that she had kidnapped him because she wanted to sell him.

Cathy lost her most recent appeal (December 1997) when the Texas Court of Criminal Appeals upheld her capital murder conviction. During the appeals Cathy raised seventeen points dealing with trial error. Most had to do with the court ordering her attorney to turn over the map showing where Brandon was buried in a wooded area near Waco. Cathy also claimed that her confession to an FBI agent was involuntary.

The appeals court indicated that the order to produce the map was not illegal because it was part of the evidence of a crime. The court also rejected her claim of an involuntary confession.

1995

Erica Sheppard: Black; Currently on death row. Erica Sheppard, the youngest of the women on death row in Texas, was sentenced to death for her role in the murder of Marilyn Sage Meagher, a real-estate agent in Houston. Mrs. Meagher was attacked while carrying clothing from her car to her apartment. Graphic trial testimony showed that Erica, who was nineteen at the time, and her co-defendant, James Dickerson, accosted Marilyn inside her apartment near the Houston Galleria with the intention of stealing the keys to her car. They slashed her throat with a butcher knife as she begged for her life, then wrap ed her head in a plastic bag and clubbed her to death with a 10-pound statue. After that they left the scene in Marilyn's black Mazda.

Erica confessed to the crime after her arrest and in her appeal argued that the trial court should have suppressed the statements she made. She was a high school graduate and was studying to be a medical assistant at the time the murder took place. At trial, Erica's attorneys argued that it was James Dickerson who actually killed Marilyn and that Erica had only provided the weapon, a butcher knife. They also argued that the evidence during the penalty phase of the trial wasn't sufficient to show that Erica deserved death. But, in the end, it took the jury an hour and twenty minutes to decide that Erica should die for her part in the crime.

According to Erica's mother, a drug counselor, she was raised in a God-fearing household by her mother and grandmother in South Central Houston. In an interview in 1998, she said Erica didn't "get religion in prison. She was raised in the church and always knew God."

In June 1997 the Texas Court of Criminal Appeals upheld Erica's capital murder conviction and in January 1998 Erica asked State District Judge J. Lon Harper to dismiss all her appeals so that she could be executed. The judge granted her request and after a psychiatric evaluation, set an execution date for Erica for April 20, 1998. He also told her that she could change her mind any time before the date.

At the time Erica said she talked to her three children, ages 5, 6, and 8, who are being raised by their 88-year-old great-grandmother about her upcoming execution. She said she did not feel they understood what she was trying to tell them. After her decision, people tried to persuade her to change her mind, especially her mother who wrote to Reverend Jesse Jackson and asked him to intervene.

At her mother's request, Reverend Jackson visited Erica and prayed with her at the prison. Reverend Jackson, who arrived for the visit with state Senator Rodney Ellis (D-Houston), and three state troopers, said he was mindful of the pain of everyone on all sides, those whose lives were lost and those whose lives were destroyed. Erica's mother, grandmother, brother, and her three children, were all present during Reverend Jackson's visit. Upon leaving, Jackson urged Governor George Bush to take a more compassionate approach to inmates who are sentenced to death especially those who express sincere remorse.

Because of her impending execution, Erica was moved to the Huntsville Unit and put in an isolated cell a few weeks prior to her execution date. She had her Bible and a typewriter. During that time, Erica said she prayed, wrote letters and thought about her death.

Erica received letters every day from death penalty opponents all over the world, including Bianca Jagger telling her not to give up. But, she said it was God who changed her mind. She was doing some cleaning in her cell one day and talking to God, when God spoke to her and told her to keep fighting and it was then that she decided to go on with her appeals.

At the end of March 1998, one of her attorneys, Kristine Woody, told Judge Harper that Erica had changed her mind. The brother of the murder victim said that he had originally understood Erica wanted to drop her appeals so that she could be executed while her children are still young. Erica's mother said she hoped the family of the victim would forgive her daughter. She said she wished them peace and offered apologies for what her daughter had done to cause them pain.

Erica said she was close to Karla Faye Tucker and regrets that she did not have the opportunity to say good-bye to her since she was in Houston at a hearing at the time Karla was taken away. She now keeps a picture of Karla, whom she sometimes called "Mom" in her room. Erica Sheppard is on death row in Texas today.

1997

Darlie Routier: White; Currently on death row. Darlie Routier was convicted of murdering her two sons, Damon and Devon, although she was only tried for the stabbing death of Damon, who was five at the time. On the night her two sons were killed, Darlie told police an intruder broke into their house in the Dallas suburb of Rowlett, and fatally stabbed both Damon, 5, and Devon, 6, while they slept. The same intruder then slashed her neck and shoulders before escaping through a garage window. Darlie and the two boys had fallen asleep downstairs in the living room while watching TV prior to the intrusion. Ultimately, however, it was Darlie whom the police charged with the murders.

Darin Routier, Darlie's husband, who was upstairs sleeping at the time of the assault, testified on her behalf saying that his wife was asleep through the fatal stabbings of their two sons and her own wounding. Tearfully, he insisted his wife was close enough to the wounded boys to get their blood spattered on her but it was not she who killed them.

Weeks before the fatal stabbing of her two sons, Darlie had written in her diary that she was "miserable" and had apologized in advance for her plan to commit suicide. "I hope that one day you will forgive me for what I am about to do" she wrote on May 3, the day of her last entry. Her suicide attempt was never carried out because although she had unwrapped some pills and was writing her suicide note, her husband came home before she could follow through with it.

A police evidence expert testified that soon after viewing the crime scene he knew that the murders couldn't have happened the way Darlie claimed. On the other hand, an expert witness for the defense testified that Darlie didn't fit any of the psychiatric profiles of mothers who kill their children. Dallas psychiatrist Lisa Clayton said Darlie suffers from "traumatic amnesia" which prevents her from remembering important details about the stabbings of her sons and herself. After interviewing Darlie for twelve hours in jail, Clayton was convinced that Darlie was telling the truth.

A police expert who confronted Darlie with the murder said that she didn't deny stabbing her sons but said, "If I did, I don't remember it." The defense psychiatrist said that Darlie may have had memory lapses about the slaying and might have made contradictory statements to police if the police suggested answers to her.

More than 200 items of evidence were presented during Darlie's trial including a kitchen knife described as the murder weapon, the nightshirt Darlie was wearing with traces of her sons blood, and Darlie's ten-page handwritten statement to the police. A bloodstain expert said the blood found on her nightshirt led him to believe that Darlie was the killer because there were stains of Devon's blood on the back right shoulder of the nightshirt which, in his opinion, could only have been caused by a knife coming over her shoulder. He said he doubted that the blood was a result of Darlie's being near when her husband tried to resuscitate their son.

Prosecutors described Darlie as a vain status-seeker who was driven to murder her sons because her looks and lavish lifestyle had started to crumble under financial and family pressures. They said she was a "self-centered, cold-blooded, evil-hearted killer" and that she had murdered her children because "they got in the way of what she wanted," namely, a life free of parental responsibilities. Dramatically, in closing arguments, the prosecutor held the knife up to the jury and knelt down over an imaginary body showing with stabbing motions how he imagined Darlie fatally attacked her sons. In winding up his case, Dallas prosecutor Greg Davis told the jury to just "imagine the horror the boys felt when they looked up at their killer and saw it was their mother." Darlie reacted quietly to his portrayal of her as a woman so caught up in her own vanity and materialism that she felt she had to kill her sons. But, when Darlie took the stand she testified tearfully that she dearly loved her sons and did not kill them. "I did not murder my children, sir," Darlie told the prosecutor.

Because of the way it was played out, one of the most damaging pieces of evidence was a video from a local TV station showing Darlie, her husband, their families and friends holding a birthday party at the graves of the two murdered children. According to most who saw the tape, Darlie did not demonstrate the proper amount of grief or trauma for a mother who had so recently lost two sons in such a tragic way.

Darlie was already crying by the time the jurors returned to the courtroom after ten hours of deliberation. When the guilty verdict was announced she sobbed "I did not kill my babies."

At the punishment phase of her trial Darlie was described as a woman who spent Mother's Day with male strippers, publicly humiliated her children, and supplied a sixteen-year-old babysitter with marijuana. On Darlie's behalf relatives, including her husband, said she was a loving mother with strong family values and begged the jurors to spare her life. When the punishment of death was announced Darlie cried, as did several members of her family who were in the courtroom wearing T-shirts with the pictures of the two victims, Damon and Devon.

The death sentence for infanticide today is extremely rare. According to the Death Penalty Information Center in Washington, DC only five women in the country are now on death row for killing their children. And no woman has actually been executed for this crime since the Supreme Court cleared the way for the reinstitution of the death penalty in 1976.

Darlie's family supports her claim of innocence and her in-laws say they are refinancing their Lubbock, Texas, home to put up a reward for the "real killer" of her sons. Sarilda and Leonard Routier say their son Darin has no money left to defend his wife and Sarilda said the reward is for "the arrest and conviction of the real killer of Devon and Damon." They have also hired a private investigator to look into the case, and they want to hypnotize Darlie to try to learn more about the crime.

Darlie was convicted under a Texas law that allows the death penalty for murdering children younger than 6. She was not tried in the death of Devon, 6, although police said she killed both of her sons. The family's surviving son, Drake, who was, eighteen-months-old at the time, lives in Lubbock with his paternal grandparents.

Darlie's cell is #6 at the Mountain View Unit in Gatesville. In an interview for ABC-TVs "Prime Time Live" she said, "I had one inmate call me a baby killer, but it doesn't bother me too much because they're not in here for good behavior." Her family members were invited to appear on several news programs including "Good Morning America" and the "Maury Povich Show." In 1998, *Cosmopolitan* ran her story in two successive issues.

Sarilda Routier, Darlie's mother-in-law, said, "As long as she's breathing, she's going to fight . . . she says that she would rather be innocent and in prison than guilty and out."

A 1989 state law allows prosecutors to seek forfeiture of any payments Darlie or others might derive from their accounts of the murders. The money would go to the victims or into the Texas Crime Victims' Compensation Fund. The law allows seizure of "income a person accused or convicted of a crime...receives from a movie, book, magazine article, tape recording, phonographic record, radio or television presentation or live entertainment in which the crime was re-enacted."

A state district judge denied a new trial for Darlie. The defense motion for the new trial marked the first step in the appeals process. Her attorneys argued that the evidence presented at her trial in Kerr County was not sufficient to justify convicting her. Appeals lawyer John Hagler said he expected the decision by retired state District Judge Mark Tolle. Hagler said he remains confident Darlie can win a new trial when the Texas Court of Criminal Appeals reviews her case.

The most recent turn of events in Darlie's case came about in 1998 when members of her family approached Texas millionaire Brian Pardo and asked him to investigate her situation after they saw an interview with him on Dateline NBC." Pardo agreed to look into the case, but said he would seek truth and justice wherever it leads.

In June, 1998 Pardo announced that Darlie's husband, Darin, was "a very significant suspect in his investigation." He then made public the results of a lie-detector test administered to Darin Routier. He said the same test was given to Darin three times and each time he gave deceptive answers to four questions about his knowledge of the crime.

Pardo's theory is that Darin was involved in planning the attack but didn't kill his sons. He thinks there may have been as many as three intruders, which may have included Darin. The plan was to kill Darlie, but the children were killed because they witnessed the crime. Pardo believes the motive was a $250,000 life insurance policy on Darlie in which Darin was the beneficiary.

Prosecutors in Darlie's trial said there has always been suspicions about Darin Routier's knowledge and involvement, but that they never had enough evidence to go forward with an indictment.

Darlie has said she believes Darin is innocent, but she asked Pardo to go ahead with his investigation. Don Davis told Darlie's story in a 1997 book, *Hush Little Babies*. Darlie is on death row in Texas today.

1998

Brittany Marlowe Holberg: White, Currently on death row. Brittany Marlowe Holberg was convicted of capital murder and sentenced to death, at age twenty-five for the murder of AB Towery Sr. of Amarillo, Texas, on November 13, 1996. A Randall County, Texas jury, rendered the verdict on March 13, 1998. They deliberated eleven hours before sentencing her to death saying that she constitutes a continuing threat to society and lacks mitigation to warrant life in prison.

When State District Judge Pirle sentenced Brittany to death she cried "Oh my God" and collapsed. Guards escorted her from the courtroom but she returned a few minutes later and said, "You cannot take away my soul. It is going to heaven." Criminal District Attorney James Farren later said Brittany was irrational and speaking from emotion. Brittany's family and friends were crying and declined to comment on her sentence.

The son of the victim, Russell Towery, said he was happy with what the jury decided. During the closing arguments District Attorney Farren said all human life is important, and the loss of anyone is a tragedy. But the value of each human being differs depending on how that human being lives. He said, "there are some values higher than human life." Assistant Randall County Criminal District Attorney Robert Love said, "there is no amount of mitigation that would excuse or warrant a life sentence in this case."

The body of AB Towery Sr. was found by his son in his southwest Amarillo apartment on November 14, 1996, the morning after his murder. His body had fifty-eight stab wounds, blunt-trauma to his head and a foot-long lamp pole shoved halfway down his throat.

Brittany Holberg was arrested for the murder of 80-year-old AB Towery Sr. on February 17, 1997 in Memphis, Tennessee after *America's Most Wanted* aired a show dubbing her "Public Enemy # 1." Before she returned to Texas she confessed to Towery's murder to Memphis Police. As a result, her lawyers filed a motion to bar the jury from knowing about her confession during the trial. Her attorney said she was ill from a beating and/or intoxicated the day she was arrested, and, therefore, her statements were not entirely voluntary.

Brittany told the police when she was arrested that she was coming down from a ten-day high on crack cocaine when she killed Towery and that she acted in self-defense.

On arrest, Brittany admitted stabbing Towery, hitting him with a claw hammer and leaving a lamp pole embedded in his throat to silence his gurgling. A knife was protruding from Towery's torso when his son found the body. Prosecutors say Towery was also stabbed with a paring knife, a butcher knife, a grapefruit knife and two forks. Further blood was found on a skillet and iron.

The prosecution rested its case against Brittany on March 11, 1998 after a forensic pathologist said it had taken "significant force" to get a foot-long lamp pole down the throat of the victim. Dr. Jeff Barnard, chief medical examiner in Dallas, testified that the fifty-eight stab wounds Towery suffered were in his head, face, chest, back, neck, arm, hand, and wrist. One stab went into Towery's nose and broke it, and there was a cluster of nine wounds in his chest and stomach. Two of the nine wounds punctured his liver, Barnard said.

Brittany's former cellmate, Vicki Kirkpatrick, testified at the trial that Brittany told her she enjoyed killing Towery. "The blood was just amazing" Vicki said Brittany told her when both of them were in the Randall County Jail, "I don't know how you would say it . . . it was pretty, just like a fountain." She said she knew Brittany before the killing and that they had lived the same sort of "street life." She said she saw Brittany the day of the killing when she returned from a visit with a "sugar daddy" with some money. But Vicki said she didn't know who the man was or where he lived. Brittany later went back for more money, she said, and apparently when AB Towery Sr. refused to give her any, Brittany tried to reach into his shirt pocket for it. Vicki said, Brittany told her a struggle broke out between them, and she couldn't stop stabbing him. She said, "she stuffed that lamp thing down his throat because she got tired of hearing him making noises." She commented that Brittany showed no remorse when she was talking about it.

According to testimony by Towery's apartment manager, he was a friendly man. She said Brittany Holberg came into the apartment offices on November 13, 1996 to use the restroom then went out into the courtyard where she was seen by at least one of the maintenance men. Around 7:00 p.m. the same day Brittany paid two people $200 for a ride.

"She didn't just kill AB Towery" Randall County District Attorney James Farren told the jurors, "She butchered him. She slaughtered him." Brittany testified on her own behalf that she was high on crack the day AB Towery was killed.

In the penalty phase of her trial Candace Norris, Brittany's attorney, urged the jury to consider her upbringing, family life and past experience, not as an excuse but as an explanation. According to her attorney, Brittany had suffered from post-traumatic stress disorder, battered woman syndrome and a drug addiction at the time of Towery's death. The attorney said Towery became violent when he found a crack pipe on Brittany. He struck her twice with a metal pan and threatened her with a knife. So she stuck the lamppost in Towery's mouth and stabbed him once with his knife to repel his attack. Afraid that no one would believe a drug-abusing prostitute, she fled to Tennessee. Brittany Holberg is on death row in Texas today.

30

Vermont: No Death Penalty

Although Vermont is one of the twelve states that does not have capital punishment today, from 1905 to 1965 fourteen people were sentenced to death in Vermont. In the 1930s when death sentencing peaked in the United States, only one person was sentenced to death in the state. For the most part, the people of Vermont have opposed capital punishment and have refused to impose death sentences on convicted felons.

By 1965 Vermont had practically abolished capital punishment and the homicide rate in the state was very low. Eventually the state legislature decided that the penalty for first-degree murder would be life in prison except in cases where the victim was a warden, a prison employee, or a law enforcement officer killed in the "performance of the duties of his office." In those cases, the jury could decide on a death sentence or life imprisonment. According to Roth (1997) between 1965 and 1987 several law enforcement officers were killed in the line of duty, but none of the perpetrators received the death penalty.

In 1987 the Vermont Legislature recognized the fact that Vermont jurors were no longer willing to hand out death sentences and abolished capital punishment.

WOMEN SENTENCED TO DEATH IN VERMONT

1905

Mary Mabel Rogers: White; Executed. Mary Mabel Rogers, the only woman ever executed in Vermont in this century, was born in Bennington, Vermont in 1883. She was executed by hanging at the age of 21 on December 8, 1905, three years after being convicted of murdering her husband. Her accomplice was given life in prison.

In her adolescence, Mary was remembered (Smith, 1996) as having "large dark eyes, jet black hair, and white unblemished skin." Her husband, Marcus Meritt Rogers, whom she married at age fifteen in 1898, was ten years older than she and always called her "May."

Mary gave birth to her first stillborn child in 1901 although she had a reputation of being a "fast woman" in the community. When she was nineteen, she left her husband and went to work as a maid for a family that had two sons, both of whom she became involved with while apparently also having an affair with a boarder that the family had taken in. When she became pregnant out of these alliances, she tried to have an abortion and when the doctor refused, she became so enraged that from her rantings and ravings, he concluded she was insane.

Since she was destined to have a child who was not her husband's, Mary began to think about the $500 life insurance her husband held with her as the beneficiary. She seemed to think she could use the money to elicit a proposal of marriage from the boarder she had been having the affair with at her place of employment. Of all the men she'd been with, she seemed to feel the most affection toward him and talked about wanting to set up housekeeping with him and her new baby. She even began pricing furniture in Bennington stores and telling the clerks she was preparing to marry.

When she asked one of her employer's sons and the boarder to help her kill her husband, for the insurance money, they both thought she was joking. But, when she asked the other son, Leon Perham, he said he'd do it. At that point she wrote a note to her husband telling him to meet her at a picnic grounds near the Little Walloomsac River on August 12, 1902. When Marcus arrived, she greeted him with a kiss and he said he was "awfully glad" to see her again. Once they were seated on the ground and began to talk her husband said he'd heard she was seeing a lot of men. Mary simply responded by saying that people should mind their own business and stop gossiping. Then she suggested he lay down and put his head in her lap, which he did.

As he lay there she told him how a girlfriend of hers had recently seen Houdini perform at the Rutland Opera House and how he'd done some marvelous rope tricks, and she offered to show him one. When he agreed, she tied his hands behind his back, and immediately covered his face with a chloroformed handkerchief. As soon as she did this Leon jumped out to help her. By the time the two of them were done, Marcus had a crushed skull, a severe contusion over one eye, a badly torn ear, and swollen wrists. To finish him off they rolled his body down to the river and dumped him in.

Since her idea was to make his death look like suicide, Mary tied a man's hat to a nearby tree with a note on it. The note said "Blame no one as I have at last put an end to my miserable life, as my wife knows I have threatened it…everyone knows I have not any thing or nobody to live for, and so blame no one as my last request, Marcus Rogers. Mary, I hope you will be happy."

Even before the autopsy, Mary applied for the insurance money, which was never given to her because when the police questioned Leon, he told them everything that had happened. As a result, Mary was tried and convicted of her husband's murder. When she gave birth to the child she was expecting, it was stillborn.

When Mary was sentenced to die by hanging, many people took up her cause and wrote to President Roosevelt asking him to intervene, but he refused. Both the Vermont Supreme Court and the U.S. Supreme Court declined to intervene on her behalf.

The governor of Vermont, Charles Bell, received over forty thousand requests from all over the world asking for Mary's life to be spared. Even the sheriff and his deputies asked the Governor not to force them to hang her. Over eight hundred people from Bennington alone signed a petition for clemency. Despite all of this, Governor Bell said he felt duty-bound to see her hang, and that if the sheriff or any of the deputies had a problem with it, they could resign. During her incarceration Mary received thousands of letters as well as candy and food from hundreds of supporters. She was given two reprieves during that time.

When the day of her execution finally arrived and Mary was brought down from her cell on the top floor of the prison, she told the authorities that she was pregnant again by another inmate, a convicted rapist at the prison. Apparently, that did not change anyone's mind. The sheriff had decided against using the rope that had been used for eight previous hangings and had taken it upon himself to prepare a new one. Mary ascended the scaffold wearing pince-nez glasses, which she took off and gave to the sheriff, requesting that he see that they were given to her sister. After the hood and noose were put on, the trap door opened and, to everyone's horror, the rope turned out to be too long. The tips of Mary's toes touched the ground before she shot up again and dropped, her toes again touching soil.

The sheriff and a doctor who was assisting at the execution grabbed the rope and yanked it so that her feet were off the ground and held it there until she died fourteen minutes later swinging back and forth like a pendulum.

Exactly why Mary Rogers was given the death penalty is a question still being debated in Vermont. There had been others who had committed similar crimes and been given life in prison. One idea is that Mary Rogers alienated the public by her claims of innocence and also by conceiving a child with a convicted rapist while still in prison.

31

Virginia: Lethal Injection

The state of Virginia has given the death penalty to only one woman, Virginia Christian, since 1900. She was executed in 1912. There are no women on death row in Virginia today.

Fifty-two people have been executed in Virginia since the death penalty was reinstated. Historically, the record year for executing people in Virginia was 1909 when the state executed seventeen. But in recent years the numbers have begun to climb. In 1997 nine inmates were executed in Virginia. And, as of July 1998, five inmates had been executed.

Virginia is second next to Texas in its number of executions. And twice, the state of Virginia has executed people on International Human Rights Day. Governor George Allen was responsible, during his term of office for twenty-four executions.

In 1977, a year after the Supreme Court reinstated the death penalty, Virginia lawmakers passed a capital murder statute. This new statute divided capital trials into the bifurcated guilt phase, where guilt or innocence is determined, and the sentencing phase where prosecutors try to prove the "future dangerousness" of a defendant or that the crime was heinous enough to deserve death. In the sentencing phase, the defense may present mitigating factors, however, Virginia does not allow jurors in death penalty cases to know when a defendant sentenced to life would be eligible for parole.

Prosecutors are never required to seek the death penalty in a capital case and by law they can only seek it if (1) there is a probability the defendant will constitute a continuous, serious threat to society. This is referred to as the "Future dangerousness precept" or (2) the crime is outrageously or wantonly vile, horrible or inhuman. This is known as the "Vileness Standard."

When the death penalty was reinstated in Virginia it was modeled after the Texas statutes which provide an automatic review of death sentences and in which the convicted person has 30 days to seek a new trial based on new evidence. However, in Virginia, the defendant has only 21-days to present new evidence.

J. Samuel Glassock (D-Suffolk), who was involved in the Virginia debates to bring it's capital punishment statutes in line with the 1976 Supreme Court Rulings, recalls that there was no conscious consideration of the 21-days. According to Glassock, it was felt that that was the standard length of time it takes for a judge's order to be final. Glassock also felt that the reason the 21-day rule has never been changed is because most politicians like being perceived as tough on crime.

But Richard Dieter of the Death Penalty Information Center has said that because of its 21-day rule, Virginia is the most restrictive state in the nation for death penalty appeals. Of the nation's top five states for executing prisoners, Virginia is the only one that has never released inmates after reviewing new evidence. Virginia's appeals courts have the lowest rate in the country for overturning cases on appeal because, according to the NAACP Legal Defense Fund, it enforces its 21-day rule religiously and excludes evidence of innocence.

Suppressed evidence fits under what is considered "new" evidence, in Virginia. And, even though the suppression of evidence by prosecutors is a denial of the defendants basic rights, in actual fact, once evidence has been suppressed it takes years to discover it and few states grant access to prosecutor's files either before or after a conviction.

Dieter believes that most prosecutors think of withholding evidence as a matter of judgment rather than an attempt to hide anything. According to Dieter (Jackson & Arenas, 1994), death penalty cases are full of abuses and mistakes, but there have never been any sanctions against prosecutors who have broken the law, even where wrongdoing has been proven.

Rules of evidence are based on theoretical assumptions that the police, prosecutors and defense attorneys bring all the known facts of a crime and all the available evidence to court and that the judge and jury seated for that trial hear all of these facts and evidence. But this is only an assumption. In actual fact it does not always happen. Nevertheless, it is on the consideration of the facts and evidence that judges and/or juries reach their decisions.

Legal experts have called Virginia the worst state in the nation for both unfair trials and a lack of due process (Jackson & Arnes, 1994). In several capital murder cases in Virginia prosecutors withheld or failed to explain critical lab tests, they omitted physical evidence, key witnesses lied or changed their statements, and prosecutors kept quiet about deals they had made with witnesses.

One such case is that of Mario Murphy, who was executed on September 17, 1997. Murphy, 25 was a Mexican citizen. He was accused of being part of a hit squad hired to kill James Radcliff, a Virginia Beach man beaten to death with a steel pipe in July 1991. Murphy was said to have been hired, along with the others, by the victim's wife and boyfriend. Of the six people charged in the murder, Murphy was the only foreigner and the only one not offered a plea bargain to spare his life.

After his arrest he was denied the right to contact the Mexican consulate, as required by a 1963 treaty. By way of explanation, Governor George Allen said neither Murphy nor his attorneys sought contact with Mexican officials until years after his conviction. Virginia Beach authorities said they did not tell Murphy about his rights under the treaty because they did not know he was a Mexican citizen. Mexico, which has not executed anyone in decades, offered to put Murphy in a Mexican prison for what probably would have been a 50-year prison term. But instead, Murphy became the 43rd inmate put to death in Virginia since the death penalty resumed there in 1982.

William H. Wright, a former staff attorney for the Virginia Capital Representation Resource Center in Richmond said, "If we're going to have the death penalty, we've got to have a criminal prosecutorial system that is beyond excellent in determining guilt or innocence...we don't have that in Virginia. We're not even close to that."

William S. Geimer, a law professor at Washington & Lee University described Virginia as a state without meaningful appellate review for capital crimes. According to Geimer (1994) the Virginia Supreme Court and the 4th Circuit Court of Appeals are in the habit of supporting the death penalty. He said it's worse than the Virginia Lottery because if you get a prosecutor who's roughshod or a defense who doesn't understand the death penalty law, or a biased judge, there's nothing anyone can do about it.

Defense lawyers who represent Virginia's indigent defendants are among the worst paid in the nation. They get $60 an hour for their work in the courtroom and $40 per hour for work outside the court. And Virginia caps the fee for the worst felonies at $575. A proposed legislation would raise that to $735 to take effect in 1998. One delegate, the chairman of the Virginia Crime Commission, said, "They (lawyers) are so grossly underpaid that it's really unbelievable."

A nationwide survey by the American Bar Association showed that several states including Maryland, Tennessee, and Mississippi, set the cap at $1,000, but the limit can be waived if court-appointed defenders can show they have incurred high expenses or have worked excessive hours. Seventeen states have no maximum and in nine states the amount varies locally. In Virginia, the result has been that lawyers do not accept as many capital-cases as they have in the past because they cannot afford it.

One lawyer with the Virginia Capital Resource Center said capital cases are just an extension of what's happening in other cases. It's just that "the stakes are higher" when the result is death. Prosecutors are pressured to get convictions and a death sentence acts as a symbol of "tough on crime."

The Anti-terrorism and Effective Death Penalty Act included a new federal filing deadline for death row inmates appeals. The statute requires death row inmates to file their federal appeals — also known as petitions or writs of habeas corpus — within 180 days of the final denial of their state appeals. They can also have an extra 30 days if a district court judge decides they need it. Virginia was one of the states that decided to impose it retroactively. This meant that several death row prisoners in Virginia missed their filing deadlines because the deadlines didn't exist when they missed it. This practice was challenged in Virginia by the case of a convicted murderer named Johnile Dubois of Portsmouth.

Dubois was sentenced to death for the 1991 murder of a Portsmouth store clerk who was mentally and physically impaired. Apparently, Dubois, who was on parole at the time, felt the clerk was not moving fast enough and shot him. Prior to this new law there had been no filing deadline. The day before Dubois's execution a panel of judges from the U.S. Court of Appeals for the Fourth Circuit Court ruled that the law setting the deadline could be applied to "pending" cases but not cases in which the filing deadline had already been missed.

The Virginia's Capital Litigation Unit, formed in 1995, exists for the purpose of ensuring that the state's condemned are executed. The Unit works mostly on habeas appeals. Recently they were successful in persuading the Fourth Circuit Court of Appeals to deny the appeals petition of Joseph O'Dell.

On January 19, 1993 Charles Stamper was executed in Virginia's electric chair for murdering three people in 1978. Stamper, who began using a wheelchair after his spinal cord was injured in a 1988 fight with other prisoners, was the first disabled person to be executed since capital punishment was reinstated in 1976.

EXECUTIONS IN VIRGINIA

Virginia, recently changed its time of execution from 11:00 p.m. to 9:00 p.m. Six official witnesses are allowed to attend executions at the Greensville Correctional Center. This number includes members of the victim's family as well as up to 5 members of the media.

The minimum age for execution in Virginia is fifteen and in 1996 a Circuit Court jury recommended that Chauncey Jackson, who was sixteen at the time of his crime, be sentenced to death. Jackson was convicted of capital murder, conspiracy, attempted robbery, possession of stolen good and two firearms charges. When a court technicality let Jackson out on bond just before the start of his trial he committed several crimes during that time. These included abduction, robbery and use of a firearm. There were a total of fourteen felonies for which he was later convicted.

The prosecution argued that if Jackson would commit such crimes while he was out on bond for capital murder, then it was clear that he would surely commit crimes in the future. Prosecutors said Jackson fell into "the category of human beings that don't change." Thus, they contended he posed a future threat to other human beings. He had turned sixteen just a few weeks before committing the murder for which he was tried.

Virginia currently has eleven capital crimes on the books. In 1997 the Senate voted 34–4 to make it a capital crime to kill someone to prevent them from testifying against you. There is also a proposal to make it a capital crime to kill a neighborhood watch volunteer or torture a child to death.

WOMEN SENTENCED TO DEATH IN VIRGINIA

1912

Virginia Christian: Black; Executed. Virginia Christian, a 17-year-old teenager, who worked as a maid and a washerwoman, was the only woman legally executed in Virginia. From a poor family, Virginia worked for a white woman in Hampton as a laundress. The woman accused her of stealing a shirt and they got into an argument followed by a fight.

Virginia was convicted of murdering the woman by beating her and then suffocating her by forcing a towel and her hair down her throat with a broom handle. Virginia said her employer had attacked her first, and appeals were made to spare her life because of her gender, but no mention was made of her age. Nevertheless, she was electrocuted on August 16, 1912, the day after her 17th birthday. Virginia confessed to the fight and robbery but said she didn't realize she'd killed the woman.

Appendix A

Women on Death Row, 1998

Alfaro, Maria del Rosio (CA)
Allen, Wanda Jean (OK)
Anderson, Melanie (NC)
Ballenger, Vernice (MS)
Beets, Betty Lou (TX)
Brown, Debra D. (OH)
Cardona, Ana (FL)
Carrington, Celeste Simone (CA)
Coffman, Cynthia (CA)
Copeland, Faye (MO)
Dalton, Kerry L. (CA)
Ford, Priscilla (NV)
Frank, Antoinette (LA)
Harris, Louise (AL)
Henderson, Cathy L. (TX)
Hill, Donetta (PA)
Holberg, Brittany (TX)
Jennings, Patricia (NC)
King, Carolyn Ann (PA)
Larzelere, Virginia (FL)
Lyon, Lynda (AL)
McDermott, Maureen (CA)
Milke, Debra J. (AZ)
Moore, Blanche K. Taylor (NC)
Neelley, Judith (AL)
Nelson, Leslie (NJ)
Newton, Frances E. (TX)
O'Donnell, Kelley (PA)
Owens, Gaile (TN)
Perillo, Pamela L. (TX)

Pike, Christa (TN)
Plantz, Marilyn K. (OK)
Pulliam, Latasha (IL)
Riggs, Christina (AR)
Rivers, Dolores (PA)
Routier, Darlie (TX)
Row, Robin (ID)
Samuels, Mary E. (CA)
Sheppard, Erica (TX)
Smith, Geraldine (IL)
Smith, Lois Nadean (OK)
Spunaugle, Delpha (OK)
Thompson, Catherine (CA)
Williams, Dorothy (IL)
Williams, Jacqueline (IL)
Wuornos, Aileen (FL)
Young, Caroline (CA)

Appendix B

Women with Death Sentences by State

Alabama

1930	Selena Gilmore	executed
1953	Earle Dennison	executed
1957	Rhonda Belle Martin	executed
1978	Debra Bracewell	reversed
1981	Patricia Thomas	reversed
1983	Judith Neelley	on death row
1988	Judie Haney	life
1988	Altione Walker	reversed
1989	Louise Harris	on death row
1994	Lynda Lyon Block	on death row

Arizona

1928	Eva Duggan	executed
1933	Winnie Ruth Judd	reversed
1991	Debra Jean Milke	on death row

Arkansas

1984	Patricia Hendrickson	reversed
1998	Christina Riggs	on death row

California

1941	Ethel Juanita Spinelli	executed
1947	Louise Peete	executed
1955	Barbara Graham	executed
1962	Elizabeth Ann Duncan	executed
1970	Susan Denise Atkins	life
1970	Leslie Van Houten	life
1970	Patricia Krenwinkel	life
1975	Mabel Glenn	reversed
1989	Cynthia Coffman	on death row

1990	Maureen McDermott	on death row
1992	Maria del Rosio Afaro	on death row
1993	Catherine Thompson	on death row
1994	Celeste Carrington	on death row
1994	Mary Ellen Samuels	on death row
1995	Kerry Lynn Dalton	on death row
1995	Caroline Young	on death row

Connecticut
1914	Bessie Wakefield	commuted

Delaware
1935	May Carey	executed

Florida
1926	Bertha Hall	commuted
1927	Billie Jackson	commuted
1953	Ruby McCollum	overturned
1962	Irene Laverne Jackson	life
1968	Maria Dean Arrington	life
1976	Sonia Jacobs aka Linder	released
1984	Andrea Hicks Jackson	reversed
1985	Judi Buenoano	executed
1987	Carla Caillier	reversed
1987	Dee Dyne Casteel	life
1987	Kaysie Dudley	reversed
1990	Deidre Hunt	on death row
1992	Ana Cardona	on death row
1992	Andrea Jackson	reversed
1995	Andrea H. Jackson	reversed
1992	Aileen Wuornos	on death row
1993	Virginia Larzelere	on death row

Georgia
1945	Lena Baker	executed
1958	Anjette Lyles	life
1975	Rebecca Smith	life
1979	Emma Cunningham	reversed
1979	Shirley Tyler	reversed
1981	Janice Buttrum	life
1982	Teresa Whittington	reversed

Idaho
1984	Karla Windsor	life
1993	Robin Lee Row	on death row

Illinois
1938	Marie Porter	executed

1991	Geraldine Smith	on death row
1991	Dorothy Williams	on death row
1992	Guinevere Garcia	life
1993	Marilyn Mulero	released
1994	Latasha Pulliam	on death row
1998	Jacqui Williams	on death row

Indiana

1985	Lois Thacker	reversed
1986	Debra Denise Brown	life
1986	Paula Cooper	life
1989	Cindy Landress	reversed

Kentucky

| 1980 | La Verne O'Bryan | reversed |
| 1987 | LaFonda Fay Foster | life |

Louisiana

1929	Ada LeBoeuf	executed
1935	Julia Moore	executed
1942	Toni Jo Henry	executed
1975	Catherine Dodds	reversed
1995	Antoinette Frank	on death row

Maryland

1981	Annette Stebbing	life
1982	Doris Foster	reversed
1984	Doris Foster	life

Massachusetts

| 1912 | Lena Cusumano | reversed |

Mississippi

1920	Carrie McCarty	executed
1922	Pattie Perdue	executed
1922	Anna Knight	executed
1937	Mary Holmes	executed
1944	Mildred Johnson	executed
1982	Attina Canaday	life
1984	Cecilia Williamson	reversed
1985	Judy Houston	revered
1989	Susie Balfour	life
1990	Sabrina Butler	reversed
1993	Vernice Ballenger	on death row

Missouri

| 1953 | Bonnie B. Heady | executed |
| 1988 | Nila Wacaser | suicide |

1989	Virginia Twenter	life
1991	Faye Copeland	on death row
1991	Maria Isa	life
1992	Shirley Jo Phillips	life

Nevada
| 1982 | Priscilla Ford | on death row |
| 1983 | Sheila Summers | reversed |

New Jersey
1913	Madeline Ciccone	commuted
1935	Marguerite Dolbrow	commuted
1984	Marie Moore	reversed
1997	Leslie Ann Nelson	on death row

New York
1909	Mary Farmer	executed
1928	Ruth Snyder	executed
1934	Ana Antonio	executed
1935	Eva Coo	executed
1936	Frances Creighton	executed
1944	Helen Fowler	executed
1951	Martha Jule Beck	executed
1953	Ethel Rosenberg	executed

North Carolina
1943	Rosanna Phillips	executed
1944	Bessie Mae Smith	executed
1973	Mamie Lee Ward	reversed
1974	Rozelle O. Hunt	reversed
1975	Margie Boykin	reversed
1976	Faye B. Brown	reversed
1978	Rebecca Detter	reversed
1978	Velma Barfield	executed
1987	Sue Cox	reversed
1989	Barbara Stager	reversed
1990	Patricia Jennings	on death row
1990	Marilyn MaHaley	reversed
1990	Blanche T. Moore	on death row
1991	Yvette Gay	reversed
1996	Melanie S. Anderson	on death row

Ohio
1938	Ana Marie Hahn	executed
1954	Dovie Smarr Dean	executed
1954	Betty Butler	executed
1960	Edythe M. Klumpp	commuted
1975	Sandra Lockett	life

1975	Alberta Osborne	reversed
1976	Patricia Wernert	reversed
1977	Benita Smith	reversed
1983	Rosalie Grant	commuted
1983	Sharon Young	reversed
1985	Debra Brown	on death row
1988	Elizabeth Green	commuted
1989	Beatrice Lumpkin	commuted

Oklahoma

1903	Dora Wright	executed
1975	Janet Sanders	reversed
1979	Michelle Binsz	commuted
1982	Lois Nadean Smith	on death row
1989	Patricia Jones	life
1989	Wanda Jean Allen	on death row
1989	Marilyn Plantz	on death row
1995	Delpha Spunaugle	on death row

Pennsylvania

1931	Irene Schroeder	executed
1935	Grace Giovanetti	commuted
1936	Josephine Romualdo	commuted
1946	Corrine Sykes	executed
1972	Marilyn Dobrolenski	life
1972	Sharon Wiggins	life
1989	Dolores Rivers	on death row
1992	Donetta Hill	on death row
1993	Kelley O'Donnell	on death row
1994	Carolyn King	on death row

South Carolina

1931	Beatrice Snipes	commuted
1943	Sue Stidham Logue	executed
1947	Rosa Marie Stinette	executed
1990	Rebecca Smith	reversed

Tennessee

1986	Gaile Owens	on death row
1997	Christa Pike	on death row

Texas

1924	Emma Oliver	commuted
1961	Maggie Morgan	commuted
1963	Carolyn Lima	released
1978	Mary Anderson	life
1979	Linda Burnett	life
1980	Pamela Perillo	on death row

1984	Pamela Perillo	on death row
1984	Karla Faye Tucker	executed
1985	Betty Lou Beets	on death row
1988	Frances Elaine Newton	on death row
1995	Cathy Lynn Henderson	on death row
1995	Erica Sheppard	on death row
1997	Darlie Routier	on death row
1998	Brittany Holberg	on death row

Virginia

| 1912 | Virginia Christian | executed |

Vermont

| 1905 | Mary Mabel Rogers | executed |

Appendix C

Length of Time on Death Row

Name	Date of Sentencing	Time
Pamela Perillo (TX)	September 2, 1980	17 years
Priscilla Ford (NV)	April 29, 1982	16 years
Lois Nadean Smith (OK)	December 29, 1982	16 years
Judith Neelley (AL)	April 18, 1983	15 years
Betty Beets (TX)	October 14, 1985	13 years
Gaile Owens (TN)	January 15, 1986	12 years
Debra Brown (OH)	June 18, 1986	12 years
Frances E. Newton (TX)	November 7, 1988	10 years
Wanda Allen (OK)	April 26, 1989	9 years
Cynthia Coffman (CA)	August 30, 1989	9 years
Louise Harris (AL)	August 11, 1989	9 years
Marilyn Plantz (OK)	March 31, 1989	9 years
Dolores Rivers (PA)	March 16, 1989	9 years
Maureen McDermott (CA)	June 15, 1990	8 years
Patricia Jennings (NC)	November 5, 1990	8 years
Blanche Moore (NC)	November 16, 1990	8 years
Debra Jean Milke (AZ)	January 18, 1991	7 years
Geraldine Smith (IL)	February 20, 1991	7 years
Dorothy Williams (IL)	April 18, 1991	7 years
Faye Copeland (MO)	April 27, 1991	7 years
Aileen Wuornos (FL)	January 31, 1992	6 years
Ana Cardona (FL)	April 1, 1992	6 years
Donetta Hill (PA)	April 9, 1992	6 years
Maria del Rosio Alfaro (CA)	July 14, 1992	6 years
Vernice Ballenger (MS)	January 13, 1993	5 years
Virginia Larzelere (FL)	May 11, 1993	5 years
Catherine Thompson (CA)	June 10, 1993	5 years
Kelley O'Donnell (PA)	July 1, 1993	5 years
Robin Lee Row (ID)	December 16, 1993	5 years

Latasha Pulliam (IL)	June 15, 1994	4 years
Mary Ellen Samuels (CA)	September 16, 1994	4 years
Celeste Carrington (CA)	November 23, 1994	4 years
Carolyn King (PA)	November 30, 1994	4 years
Lynda Lyon Block (AL)	December 21, 1994	4 years
Erica Sheppard (TX)	March 3, 1995	3 years
Delpha Spunaugle (OK)	March 31, 1995	3 years
Kerry Lynn Dalton (CA)	May 23, 1995	3 years
Cathy Lynn Henderson (TX)	May 25, 1995	3 years
Antoinette Frank (LA)	September 13, 1995	3 years
Caroline Young (CA)	September, 1995	3 years
Christa Gail Pike (TN)	October, 1996	2 years
Melanie Anderson (NC)	June, 1996	2 years
Darlie Routier (TX)	February 4, 1997	1 year
Leslie Ann Nelson (NJ)	May, 1997	1 year
Jacqui A. Williams (IL)	March, 1998	
Brittany Holberg (TX)	March, 1998	
Christina Riggs (AR)	July, 1998	

Appendix D

Women's Death Sentences Since 1900

State	Death Sentences
Alabama	10
Arizona	3
Arkansas	2
California	16
Connecticut	1
Delaware	2
Florida	15
Federal Jurisdiction	2
Georgia	7
Idaho	2
Illinois	7
Indiana	4
Kentucky	2
Louisiana	5
Maryland	2
Massachusetts	1
Mississippi	11
Missouri	5
Nevada	2
New Jersey	4
New York	7
North Carolina	15
Ohio	13
Oklahoma	7
Pennsylvania	10
South Carolina	4
Tennessee	2
Texas	12
Vermont	1
Virginia	1
Total	175

Appendix E

Ages of Women on Death Row, 1998

Name	Date of Birth	Present Age
Alfaro, Maria del Rosio (CA)	1970	28
Allen, Wanda J. (OK)	8/17/59	39
Allen, Wanda J. (OK)	8/17/59	39
Anderson, Melanie (NC)	1977	21
Ballenger, Vernice (MS)	1937	61
Beets, Betty L. (TX)	3/12/37	61
Brown, Debra (IN)	11/11/62	36
Cardona, Ana (FL)	1961	37
Carrington, Celeste (CA)	1961	37
Coffman, Cynthia (CA)	1/19/62	36
Copeland, Faye (MO)	1919	79
Dalton, Kerry (CA)	1960	38
Ford, Priscilla (NV)	2/10/29	69
Frank, Antoinette (LA)	1970	28
Harris, Louise (AL)	6/16/53	45
Henderson, Cathy (TX)	1957	41
Hill, Donetta (PA)	1967	31
Holberg, Brittany (TX)	1973	25
Jennings, Patricia (NC)	8/24/42	56
King, Carolyn (PA)	12/9/65	33
Larzelere, Virginia (FL)	12/27/52	46
Lyon, Lynda (AL)	1949	49
McDermott, M. (CA)	5/15/47	51
Milke, Debra J. (AZ)	3/10/64	34
Moore, Blanche (NC)	2/17/33	65
Neelley, Judith (AL)	6/7/64	34
Nelson, Leslie (NJ)	1960	38
Newton, Frances E. (TX)	4/12/65	33
O'Donnell, Kelley (PA)	1969	29

Owens, Gaile (TN)	9/22/52	46
Perillo, Pamela (TX)	12/3/55	43
Pike, Christa (TN)	1967	21
Plantz, Marilyn (OK)	10/19/60	38
Pulliam, Latasha (IL)	1972	26
Riggs, Christina (AR)	1972	26
Rivers, Dolores (PA)	12/25/53	45
Row, Robin (ID)	1957	41
Routier, Darlie (TX)	1969	29
Samuels, Mary Ellen (CA)	1949	49
Sheppard, Erica (TX)	1974	24
Smith, Geraldine (IL)	1948	50
Smith, Lois N. (OK)	9/12/40	58
Spunaugle, Delpha (OK)	8/10/49	49
Thompson, C. (CA)	1948	50
Williams, Dorothy (IL)	1954	44
Williams, Jacqueline (IL)	1967	31
Wuornos, Aileen (FL)	2/29/56	42
Young, Caroline (CA)	1944	54

Bibliography

Abrahamson, A. (1990, August 30). Divided court upholds Harris death penalty. *Los Angeles Times,* p. 1.

ACLU Abolitionist. (1997, June).

ACLU Abolitionist. (1997, April).

Amnesty International Annual Reports, 1992, 1996, 1997.

Anderson, C. & McGehee, S. (1991). *The true story of Judias Buenoano, Florida's serial murderess.* Carol Publishing: Lyle Stuart Books.

Anderson, E. (1990, July 8). Old Sparky headed for trash. *Times-Picayune,* p.1B.

Applebome, P. (1993, March 3). Alabama releases man held on death row. *New York Times,* p. 8A.

Applebome, P. (1989, July 15). 2 electric jolts in Alabama execution. *New York Times,* p. 6A.

Auerbach, S. (1974). Common myths about capital criminals and their victims. *Georgia Journal of Corrections, 3*(2), 41–54.

Azbell, J. (1957, October 12). Waitress' final wish rejected by relatives.   *Montgomery Advertiser,* p. 1A, 10A.

Azbell, J. (1956, October 10). Governor holds murderess' fate. *Montgomery Advertiser,* p. 1A, 2A.

Bailey, W. C. (1991). The general prevention effect of capital punishment for non-capital felonies. In R. M. Bohm (Ed.), *The death penalty in America: Current Research* (pp. 21–38). Cincinnati, OH: ACSJ.

Baird, C. & Taylor, G. (1995, February). A historical overview of the Texas capital sentencing scheme. *Texas Bar Journal, 58,* 118.

Baird, R. M. & Rosenbaum, S. E. (1995). *Punishment and the death penalty.* New York: Prometheus.

Baldus, D. (1990). *Equal justice and the death penalty: A legal and empirical analysis.* Boston: Northeastern University Press.

Barber, P. (1980, November 28). Car rams Reno crowd. *Reno Evening Gazette,* p. 1, 5.

Bardwell, S. K. (1995, June 28). New bride can't leave death row. *Houston Chronicle,* p. 17A.

Barnum, A. (1995, October 3). Woman on death row wants to die now. *Chicago Tribune*, p. 1D.

Beck, E. M. & Tolnay, S. E. (1990, August). The killing fields of the deep south: The market for cotton and the lynching of blacks, 1882–1930. *American Sociological Review, 55*(4), 526–539.

Bedau, H. (1984). *The case against the death penalty.* Washington: ACLU.

Best, K. (1993, January 26). High court narrows death row appeals. *St.Louis Post Dispatch*, p. 1A.

Blakely, R. (1990, Fall). The cost of killing criminals. *Kentucky Law Review, 1*(61).

Blankenship, M. et al. (1997). Jurors' comprehension of sentencing Instructions: A test of the death penalty process in Tennessee. *Justice Quarterly,* 14(2), 325–346.

Bolton, P. (1977, December 5). Poisoner of child dead. *Macon Telegraph News*, p. 1.

Bowman, C. (1993, June 23). Arraignment in death of 2 grandchildren. *San Francisco Chronicle*, p. 13A.

Bowman, C. & Wilson, Y. (1993, June 19). Children killed: Grandma accused. *San Francisco Chronicle*, p. 16A.

Brown, E. (1989). *Public justice, private mercy: A governor's education on death row.* New York: Weidenfeld & Nicolson.

Brown, W. (1963). *Women who died in the chair.* New York: Collier.

Bruning, F. (1987, October 26). Countdown to the electric chair. *Macleans*, p. 13.

Bryant, T. (1997, June 21). Maria Isa given new sentence; life in prison. *St. Louis Post-Dispatch.*

Bryant, T. (1997, May 16). Jurors deliberate punishment for mother in teen's slaying. *St. Louis Post-Dispatch.*

Bryant, T. (1997, April 30). Officials try to shorten time between sentence, execution. *St. Louis Post-Dispatch.*

Bryant, T. (1993, April 2). Four indicted as terrorists. *St. Louis Post-Dispatch.*

Bryant, T. (1991, December 20). Parents get death in teen's murder. *St. Louis Post-Dispatch.*

Bureau of Justice Statistics. (1990). *Capital punishment 1989: Report #124545.* Washington, DC: Bureau of Justice.

Caldwell, G. (1996, Spring). Florida capital cases: July 1, 1994, June 30, 1995. *Nova Law Review, 20,* 1255–1298.

Carmichael, V. (1993). *Framing history: The Rosenberg story and the cold war.* Minneapolis, MN: University of Minnesota Press.

Carter, R. & Smith, L. (1969). The death penalty in California. *Crime and Delinquency, 15,* 62–76.

Casteneda, C. (1996, January 17). Death row woman gets reprieve. *USA Today,* p. 11A.

Casteneda, C. (1996, January 16). Activists fight to save woman facing execution. *USA Today,* p. 3A.

Casteneda, C. (1993, April 1). 'I had faith' I wouldn't be executed. *USA Today,* p. 2A.

The Charlotte Observer. (1990, December 26). More women convicted of murder are being put on death row.

The Charlotte Observer. (1990, December 8). Blanche Moore's husband files for a divorce.

The Charlotte Observer. (1990, November 30). Verses Blanche Moore wrote in jail.

The Charlotte Observer. (1990, November 19). Cruelty of death convinced jurors Moore should die.

The Charlotte Observer. (1990, November 17). Moore sentenced to death.

The Charlotte Observer. (1990, November 16). Moore painted as torturer, loving Christian.

The Charlotte Observer. (1990, November 15). North Carolina woman guilty of poisoning.

Chicago Tribune. (1991, January 5). Judge: No deal for accused killer of 5. pp. 1, 14.

Christian, S. & Barnum, A. (1996, January 4). Activists petition Edgar to stop Garcia execution. *Chicago Tribune,* p. 20.

Cicero, L. (1979, May 29). These are death row's five women. *The Miami Herald.*

Clancy, P. (1989, March 1). Indiana death row teen appeals case today. *USA Today,* p. 2A.

Corwin, M. (1992, April 19). Death's door: State's only condemned woman awaits her fate. *Los Angeles Times,* p. 3A.

Corwin, M. (1991, January 25). Waiting in isolation. *Los Angeles Times,* p. 3A.

Coward, C. L. et al. (1984). The effects of death qualification on the tendency to convict and on the quality of deliberation. *Law and Human Behavior, 8,* 167–183.

Crites, L. H. (1965, Fall). A history of the Association of Southern Women for the Prevention of Lynching, 1930–1942. *Masters Abstracts International, 3*(3), 7.

Curriden, M. (1991, September 24). Lethal injection now a preferred method. *Atlanta Constitution,* p. 22A.

Davis, D. B. (1957, October). The movement to abolish capital punishment in America: 1787–1861. *American Historical Review,* p. 63.

Dieter, R. (1997). *Innocence and the death penalty: The increasing danger of executing the innocent.* Washington, DC: Death Penalty Information Center.

Dietz, D. (1992, April 17). One who saw the state's last execution. *San Francisco Chronicle,* p.12A.

Dizon, L. (1992, July 15). Judge orders death penalty for woman. *Los Angeles Times,* p. 3A.

Dolan, M. (1993, July 17). High court to review case of death row inmate. *Los Angeles Times,* p. 8B.

Dougan, M. (1992, April 12). Gas chamber knows no gender. *San Francisco Chronicle,* p. 1A.

Doyle, J. (1993, October 28). Gas chamber death is painless, state experts says. *San Francisco Chronicle,* p. 8A.

Dubray, R. W. (1968, October). Mississippi and the proposed federal anti-lynching bills of 1937–1938. *The Southern Quarterly, 7*(1), 73–90.

Duffy, C. & Hirshberg, A. (1962). *88 Men and 2 women.* Garden City, New York: Doubleday.

Duke, J. (1987, April 25). Foster sentenced to electric chair: Powell received life prison term. *Lexington Herald Leader,* p. 1A, 5A.

Espy, M. W. & Smykla, J. (1987). *Executions in the United States 1608–1987: The Espy File.* Ann Arbor, MI: Inter-university Consortium for Political and Social Research.

Everhart, S. (1996, Spring). Precluding psychological experts from testifying for the defense in the penalty phase of a capital trial. *Florida State University Law Review, 23*(4).

Feldman, P. (1992, April 20). Humane death by gas had history of doubters. *Los Angeles Times,* p. 19A.

Fernandez, G. & Cooper, T. (1987, July 22). Kids who kill: Lost rites of passage. *San Francisco Examiner,* p. 4.

Flood, M. (1980, August 22). Woman sentenced to death in strangulation. *Houston Post.*

Foo, R. (1980, November 29). Ford profile emerges in autobiography. *Reno Evening Gazette,* p. 1A, 16A.

Frankel, M. C. (1973). *Criminal sentences: Law without order.* New York: Hill and Wang.

Freedman, E. (1981). *Their Sisters Keepers: Women's prison reform in America 1830–1930.* Ann Arbor, MI: University of Michigan Press.

Freeman, S. (1958, July 12). Chain of coincidences broke in famous caper. *Macon Telegraphy and News,* p. 1A, 6A.

Frisman, P. (1996, July 29). Connecticut Supreme Court leaves no doubt. *The Connecticut Law Tribune.*

Gaines, J. (1986, May 6). Woman told cellmate of 5 killings, official said. *Lexington Herald Leader,* p. 5A.

Ganey, T. (1990, August 1). Court overturns death sentence. *St. Louis Post-Dispatch.*

Ganey, T. (1989, January 7). Mercer's long wait comes to a swift and efficient end. *St. Louis Post-Dispatch.*

Garber, M. & Walkowitz, R. (1995). *Secret agents: The Rosenberg case, McCarthyism, and fifties America.* New York: Routledge.

Gatrell, V. (1994). *The hanging tree: Executions and the English people:1770–1868.* New York: Oxford University Press.

Gill, J. (1990, August 1). Official executions, then and now. *Times-Picayune,* p. 9B.

Ginzburg, R. (1962). *100 years of lynching.* New York: Lancer Books.

Gonzalez, J. (1997, February 2). Jury convicts Routier of murder. *Houston Chronicle,* p. 1A.

Graddess, P. (1988, May 2). Which is more expensive: Execution or a life sentence? *The Washington Post National Weekly Edition,* p. 23.

Gregory, T. (1995, September 9). Woman on death row to undergo new tests. *Los Angeles Times,* p. 19A.

Groner, J. I. (1995, July/August). Murder by medicine. *The Free Press,* p. 10–12.

Gross, S. R. & Mauro, R. (1983). Patterns of death: An analysis of racial disparities in capital sentencing and homicide victimization. *Stanford Law Review, 37,* 27–153.

Guardian. (1992, April 22). California sends a shiver through 2500 on death row. p. 6.

Hackett, J. (1987, September 21). Indiana killer, Italian martyr. *Newsweek,* p. 37.

Hager, P. (1992, March 26). Justices will recruit death row lawyers. *Los Angeles Times,* p. 3A.

Haney, C. et al. (1994, Summer). Deciding to take a life: Capital juries, sentencing instructions, and the jurisprudence of death. *Journal of Social Issues, 50*(2), 149–176.

Haney, C. et al. (1994, August). Comprehending life and death matters: A preliminary study of California's capital penalty instructions. *Law and Human Behavior, 18*(4), 411–436.

Harris, P. (1986). Over-simplification and error in public opinion surveys on capital punishment. *Justice Quarterly, 3,* 429–435.

Hiskey, M. (1989, September 22). Woman on death row to get new sentencing. *Atlanta Journal Constitution,* p. 6E.

Hodson, S. (1998, May 21). Waiting on death row. *The Augusta Chronicle.*

Honeycutt, V. (1987, February 26). Powell-Foster witnesses describe chain of events. *Lexington Herald Leader,* p. 1A, 7A.

Howlett, D. (1990, November 15). NC woman guilty in arsenic murder. *USA Today,* p. 3.

Huie, W. B. (1957). *Ruby McCollum: Woman in Suwanee jail.* New York: Signet Books.

Huie, W. B. (1954, November). Strange case of Ruby McCollum. *Ebony,* p. 16–22.

Ingle, J. B. (1989). Final hours: The execution of Velma Barfield. *Loyola of Los Angeles Law Review,* 221.

Jackson, J. (1996). *Legal lynching: Racism, injustice, and the death penalty.* New York: Marlowe.

Jackson, J. & Arney, J. (1994, June 26). Sentenced to die without fair trials. *The Virginia Pilot.*

Jet. (1990, August 13). Blacks fight to save life of Mississippi teen on death row. p. 12.

Johnston, D. (1993, April 15). Justice Department to investigate hangings. *New York Times.*

Jose-Kampfner, C. (1991). Coming to terms with existential death: An analysis of women's adaptation to life in prison. *Social Justice, 17*(2), 10–23.

Katz, I. (1996, January 16). Mother to die tonight. *Guardian,* p. 11.

Klemm, M. (1993). The determination of capital sentencing in Louisiana, 1979–1984. *Dissertation Abstracts International, 47*(12), 4502.

Kunci, T. (1985). *Ladies who kill.* New York: Pinnacle.

Lacoy, R. (1992, June 1). You don't always get Perry Mason. *Time Magazine,* p. 38–39.

Lafferty, L. (1995, Winter). Florida's capital sentencing jury override: Whom should we trust to make the ultimate ethical judgment? *Florida State University Law Review, 23*(2).

Lancaster, J. (1993). Management issues for female inmates on death row. In E. Watts (Ed.), *Female offenders: Meeting needs of a neglected population* (pp. 89–93). Laurel, MD: ACA.

Landry, G. (1958, May 11). State can show intent to kill in arsenic death, Wood says. *Macon Telegraphy and News,* p. 1A.

Lanier, C. (1994, April 16). Review of *The Execution Protocol. Journal of Criminal Justice and Popular Culture, 2*(2), 17–31.

Lee, H. (1995, June 7). Woman found guilty of killing grandchildren. *San Francisco Chronicle,* p. 2A.

Lerner, P. (1990, June 9). Nurse gets death in murder case. *Los Angeles Times,* p. 4B.

Levin, E. (1984, October 29). Cunning prisoner — or redeemed Christian? *People Magazine,* p. 85–86, 89.

Lewis, D. (1998). *Guilty by reason of insanity: A psychiatrist explores the minds of killers.* New York: Fawcett.

Lexington Herald Leader. (1991, May 19). If we want executions, we should watch them.

Lhotka, W. (1997, July 27). For state's death penalty team, every day is a fight for life.

St. Louis Post-Dispatch.

Liebrum, J. (1994, May 18). 20-Year-old found guilty in slaying. *Houston Chronicle,* p. 20A.

Liebrum, J. (1994, March 2). Woman found guilty in slaying. *Houston Chronicle,* p. 27A.

Lindecke, F. (1996, March 31). Rice launches bid to end executions. *St. Louis Post-Dispatch.*

Linebaugh, P. (1992). *The London hanged: Crime and civil society in the eighteenth century.* New York: Cambridge University Press.

Los Angeles Times. (1991, October 26). Parents convicted in taped killing of girl. p. 21A.

Los Angeles Times. (1990, February 11). Woman sentenced to gas chamber. p. 35A.

Los Angeles Times. (1980, November 28). 5 killed by car on Reno sidewalk. p. 1, 4.

Lowry, B. (1992). *Crossed over: A murder, a memoir.* New York: Alfred A. Knopf.

Mackey, P. (1976). *Voices against death: American opposition to capital punishment, 1787–1975.* New York: Burt Franklin.

Magee, D. (1980). *Slow coming dark: Interviews on death row.* New York: Pilgrim Press.

Makeig, J. (1993, July 27). Happy face on execution letter. *Houston Chronicle,* p. 11A.

Mann, C. R. (1996). *When women kill.* Albany, NY: State University of New York Press.

Mann, C. R. (1984). *Female crime and delinquency.* Huntsville, AL: University of Alabama Press.

Manning, C. (1994, February 22). Copeland seeking new trial. *St. Louis Post-Dispatch,* p. 2C.

Marquart, J. & Eckland-Olson, S. (1989, August). Gazing into the crystal ball: Can jurors accurately predict dangerousness in capital cases? *Law and Society Review,* 23(3), 449–468.

Marquart, J. et al. (1994). *The rope, the chair, and the needle: Capital punishment in Texas, 1923–1990.* Austin, TX: University of Texas Press.

Masur, L. P. (1989). *Rites of execution: Capital punishment and transformation of American culture.* New York: Oxford University Press.

McGowan, J. (1984, October 29). Facing the executioner. *Maclean's.*

McGuire, J. (1996, August 4). Widow of 'Tiny' Mercer recalls bloodthirstiness. *St. Louis Post-Dispatch.*

Mecoy, D. (1988, August 30). Wife arrested in death of man found in pick-up. *Oklahoma Times,* pp. 1–4.

Meeropol, R. & Meeropol, M. (1986). *We are your sons.* Urbana: University of Illinois.

Megivern, J. (1997). *The death penalty: An historical and theological survey.*

Mello, M. (1995, Winter). Adhering to our views: Brennan and Marshall and the relentless dissent to death as a punishment. *Florida State University Law Review,* 22(3).

Meyers Sharp, J. (1980, September 13). A different case: Woman is first in state sentenced to die. *The Louisville Courier Journal.*

Moran, D. (1993, August 24). California has largest death row population. *Los Angeles Times,* p. 18A.

Moran, D. (1992, April 22). Witness to the execution: A macabre, surreal event. *Los Angeles Times.*

Moran, D. (1992, April 11). A precise procedure for killing. *Los Angeles Times,* p. 1A.

Mosley, J. (1989, November). Farm couple are charged with murder. *St. Louis Post-Dispatch,* p. 1A.

Mosley, J. (1989, October 26). Fourth body found in Northern Missouri. *St. Louis Post-Dispatch,* p. 1A.

Mosley, J. & Ganey, T. (1989, January 9). Ashcroft refuses to block execution. *St. Louis Post-Dispatch.*

Mosley, J. & Ganey, T. (1989, January 6). Missouri's death row: A final step. *St. Louis Post-Dispatch,* p. 14A.

Muallem, A. (1996). Harris v. Alabama: Is the death penalty in America entering a fourth phase. *Journal of Legislation, 22*(1), 85–101.

Nakell, B. & Hardy, K. A. (1987). *The arbitrariness of the death penalty.* Philadelphia, PA: Temple University Press.

Nelson, L. (1994, July/August). Is there a doctor in the house? *The Angolite,* p. 18–20.

New York Times. (1995, September). Death row for ex-policewoman who killed partner. p. 16A.

New York Times. (1991, December 20). Missouri couple sentenced to die in murder of their daughter. p. 13A, 14A.

New York Times. (1991, October 28). Terror and death at home are caught on FBI tapes. p. 13A, 14A.

New York Times. (1991, July 24). Inmates protest building of execution table. p. 17A.

New York Times. (1991, May 23). Farmer, 76, gets death sentence in slaying of five. p. 26A.

New York Times. (1991, April 28). Missouri woman faces death in slayings. p. 12, 20.

New York Times. (1991, March 22). Death penalty urged in slayings of 5 drifters. p. 16A.

New York Times. (1991, March 19). 76-year-old farmer guilty of killing five drifters. p.18A.

New York Times. (1991, January 25). Judge spurns plea bargain in Missouri killings. p. 12A, 16A.

New York Times. (1991, January 24). Farmer to plead guilty in slaying of 5 drifters. p. 12A, 16A.

New York Times. (1990, November 18). Woman is sentenced to death on poisoning. p. 28.

New York Times. (1990, November 15). Suspected of poisoning her mates, woman is guilty in friend's death. p. 16.

New York Times. (1990, November 14). Death penalty recommended in slaying of five transients. p. 30A.

New York Times. (1990, November 13). Woman, 69, may face execution in 5 killings. p. 25A.

New York Times. (1990, November 12). Jury finds woman guilty in killings of ten men in Missouri. p. 13.

New York Times. (1989, November 15). Farm couple charged in deaths of drifters. p. 22A.

New York Times. (1989, September 4). Death sentence in California given first woman since 1962. p. 9A.

New York Times. (1984, November 2). Woman executed in North Carolina. p. 11A, 20A.

New York Times. (1982, March 30). Reno woman who killed six with auto sentenced to die. p. 13B.

New York Times. (1980, November 28). Car hits Reno pedestrians, killing 5, hurting 7. p. 20.

Nizer, L. (1973). *The implosion conspiracy.* Garden City, NY: Doubleday.

Noack, D. (1998, May 2). Death chamber photos? Florida prohibition challenged. *Editors & Publishers.*

O'Connor, M. (1991, February 21). Illinois woman on death row: 1st since 1938. *Chicago Tribune,* p.1.

Oklahoma Times. (1982, July 6). Tahlequah man, mother charged in shooting death. p. 4.

O'Neill, A. (1994, September 17). Woman sentenced to death in paid killings. *Los Angeles Times,* p. 3B.

O'Neill, A. (1994, July 22). Jury urges execution of woman. *Los Angles Times,* p. 1B.

O'Neill, A. (1994, March 21). Wife faces charges of hiring assassins — twice. *Los Angeles Times,* p. 1B.

Paddock, R. (1993, August 25). Just before dying, killer refused to make an appeal. *Los Angeles Times,* p. 1A.

Parsons, C. (1996, February 9). Keep 'outsiders' out of death row clemency matter, law makers urge. *Chicago Tribune,* p. 2.

Pearsall, T. (1978, December 3). Barfield jury calls for death. *The News Observer,* p. 1, 20.

People Magazine. (1984, October). Woman to be executed. p. 85.

Phillis, M. (1982, March 20). Ford's future: Execution or prison. *Reno Evening Gazette,* p. 1A, 12A.

Phillis, M. (1982, March 6). Ford defense rests. *Reno Evening Gazette,* p. 1A, 12A.

Phillis, M. (1980, November 28). I'm thankful I'm alive. *Reno Evening Gazette,* p. 3.

Pinsky, Mark (1992, March 24). Woman found guilty of killing girl, 9. *Los Angeles Times,* p. 3A.

Pollack, J. (1995, May 11). The killing field. *St. Louis Post-Dispatch.*

Poor, T. (1991, February 4). Accept the Copelands' plea bargain. *St. Louis Post-Dispatch,* p. 2B.

Potter, H. (1993). *Hanging in judgment: Religion and the death penalty in England.* New York: Continuum.

Raber, T. (1991, May 7). She's 69 and sentenced to die. *USA Today,* p. 3A.

Raber, T. (1990, January 3). Couple plead in 5 killings *USA Today,* p. 3A.

Radelet, M. & Bedau, H. (1992). *In spite of innocence: Erroneous convictions in capital cases.* Boston: Northeastern University Press.

Radford, J. & Russell, D. (1992). *Femicide: The politics of woman killing.* New York: Twayne Publishers.

Radosh, R. (1983). *The Rosenberg file.* New York: Holt, Rinehart, & Winston.

Reidy, D. (1991, January 6). 'Graves' tracks sordid road to death row. *Atlanta Journal*

Constitution, p. 10N.

Roderick, K. (1990, March 28). Last steps, last words on the row. *Los Angeles Times*, p. 1A.

Root, J. (1963). *The betrayers: The Rosenberg case: A reappraisal of an American crisis*. New York: Coward-McCann.

Rosenberg, J. (1994). *The Rosenberg letters*. New York: Garland.

Rosenberg, T. (1996, February). Dead woman walking. *Harper's Bazaar*, 110–122.

Roth, R. (1997, Winter-Spring). "Blook calls for vengeance!" The history of capital punishment in Vermont. *Vermont History*, p. 21–25.

Rupert, L. (1980, Fall). Woman in North Carolina fights to stay alive. *Southern Coalition Report on Jails and Prisons, 7*, p. 1–8.

Russell, K. (1993, April). Trial by jury, death by judge: An empirical and legal analysis of jury override in Alabama. *Dissertation Abstracts International, 53*(10), 3684A.

San Francisco Chronicle. (1995, July 13). Death penalty urged for slayer of grandkids. p. 16A.

Schneider, V. & Smykla, J. (1991). A summary analysis of executions in the United States, 1608–1987: The Espy file. In R. M. Bohm (Ed.), *The death penalty in America: Current research* (pp. 1–20). Cincinnati, OH: Anderson Publishing.

Schreiber, M. (1995). *Somewhere in time: A 160 year history of Missouri Corrections*. St. Louis, MO: Missouri Department of Corrections.

Sharp, M. P. (1956). *Was justice done: The Rosenberg-Sobell case*. New York: Monthly Review Press.

Shaskolsky, L. (1982). *Ultimate penalties: Capital punishment, life imprisonment, physical torture*. Columbus, OH: Ohio State University Press.

Sievers, S. (1996, January 17). Edgar spares life of woman on death row. *St. Louis Post-Dispatch*, p. 1A.

Simpson, K. (1997, September). Debate swirls over lethal injection. *Denver Post*, p. 1.

Smith, B. (1991, January) Farmer and his wife 'never killed nobody.' *St. Louis Post-Dispatch*.

Smith, G. (1996). In Windsor prison. *American Heritage*, p. 100–105.

Smith, G. (1980, June 17). Only woman in Texas condemned to die calls prison a zoo. *The Houston Chronicle*.

Snyder, D. (1991, July 24). Angola inmates refuse to build 'death bed.' *Times-Picayune*, p. 1A.

Squitieri, T. (1990, November 12). Jury deciding fate of Missouri serial killer. *USA Today*, p. 3A.

Stasny, E. et al. (1998, June). On fairness of death-penalty jurors. *Journal of the American Statistical Association, 93*(442), 464–477.

Steinbrook, R. (1992, April 11). Cyanide gas kills by blocking the body's ability to use oxygen. *Los Angeles Times*, p. 24A.

St. Louis Post-Dispatch. (1996, January 20). Governor comments on death penalty law. p. 6A.

St. Louis Post-Dispatch. (1991, May 24). No. 1 on death row. p. 2C.

Strausberg, C. (1996, May 2). Burroughs fights for death row inmate. *Chicago Defender*, p. 3.

Streib, V. (1993). *A capital punishment anthology*. Cincinnati, OH: Anderson Publishing.

Streib, V. (1990a). *Capital punishment of female offenders: Present female death row inmates and death sentences and executions of female offenders, January 1, 1973 to June 30, 1996.* Cincinnati, OH: University of Ohio Press.

Streib, V. (1990b). Death penalty for female offenders. *University of Cincinnati Law Review, 58*(3), 845–880.

Streib, V. (1988). *American executions of female offenders: A Preliminary inventory of names, dates, and other information.* Cleveland, OH: Cleveland State University.

Sufrin, R. (nd). "Everything is in order, Warden": A discussion of death in the gas chamber. *Suicide and Life Threatening Behavior, 6*(1), 44–56.

Tabor, R. (1958). *I want to live.* New York: Signet Books.

Tackett, M. (1991, March 8). Trial starts in farmhand slayings. *Chicago Tribune,* p. 10.

Terry, D. (1996, January 8). After a life of desperation, a female inmate asks to die. *New York Times,* p. 8A.

Time. (1990, November 6). Grandma's last roundup. p. 39.

Time. (1984, November 12). Death of a grandmother. p. 41.

Times-Picayune. (1995, September 13). Frank wouldn't be 1st.

Tolliver, T. (1987, April 27). Powell says she not Foster incited killings. *Lexington Herald Leader,* p. 1A, 6A.

Tran, M. (1989, July 15). Electric chair death bungled. *Guardian,* p. 6.

Treen, J. (1992, January 20). Die, my daughter, die. *People Weekly,* p. 71–72.

Tribble, B. (1958, May 14). Mrs. Anjette Lyles faces hearings today on four murder charges. *Macon Telegraph and News,* p. 1A.

Tribble, B. (1958, May 7). Mrs. Lyles held in deaths. *Macon Telegraph and News,* p. 1A.

Tucker, D. M. (1971, Summer). Miss Ida B. Wells and Memphis lynchings. *Phylon, 32,* 112–122.

Urban, J. (1994, May 6). Scheduled execution of woman, 38, remote. *Houston Chronicle,* p. 33A.

Varney, J. (1995, October 21). Ex-cop gets death in triple murder. *Times-Picayune,* p. 1A.

Von Drehle, D. (1996). *Among the lowest of the dead: The culture of death row.* New York: Dimension Books.

Von Drehle, D. (1988). Judicial override bogs system down. *The Miami Herald.*

Voyles, S. (1980, November 29). 6th person dies in holiday rampage. *Reno Evening Gazette,* p.1A, 6A.

Walsh, B. (1993, November 3). Dodds rebuilding life after murder. *Times-Picayune,* p. 1B.

Walsh, B. (1993, January 26). First execution-by-injection date set for state. *Times-Picayune,* p. 3B.

Walsh, B. (1991, August 20). Execution delay kills electric chair. *Times-Picayune,* p. 1.

Walsh, B. (1991, January 27). Electric chair OK, judge decides. *Times-Picayune,* p. 1B.

Walsh, B. (1991, January 26). Electric chair ruling is expected today. *Times-Picayune,* p. 8.

Walsh, B. (1991, January 25). Judge hears testimony on state's electric chair. *Times-Picayune,* p. 1B.

Walsh, B. (1990, December 19). Electric chair put on trial. *Times-Picayune,* p. 1B.

Walsh, B. (1990, October 29). LA's electric chair needlessly brutal. *Times-Picayune,* p. 1A.

Ward, M. (1998, February 4). Death chamber dispute from start. *American Statesman.*

Wardlaw, J. (1991, September 13). State museum will get electric chair. *Times-Picayune,* p. 1A.

The Washington Post. (1993, October 23). Ray Copeland. p. 4D.

The Washington Post. (1984, June 14). Judge sets August 31st for execution. p. 19A.

The Washington Post. (1980, November 29). Priscilla Ford charged with murder. p. 8A.

The Washington Post. (1980, November 28). Priscilla Ford drives car onto sidewalk in Reno. p. 20A.

Weschsler, H. (1959). Model Penal Code § 201.6 at 59-63, Tentative Draft, No. 9.

Wexley, J. (1995). *The judgment of Julius and Ethel Rosenberg.* New York: Cameron & Kahn.

William, W. H. (1984, November 28). Death in North Carolina. *Christian Century,* p. 1116.

Williams, D.T. (1970). The lynching records at Tuskegee Institute. In *Eight Negro Bibliographies.* New York: Kraus.

Woolfolk, J. (1994, June 17). East Palo Alto woman convicted of killing 2. *San Francisco Chronicle,* p. 22A.

Woolfolk, J. (1993, June). Inmate wins ruling in bid to be executed. *San Francisco Chronicle,* p. 19A.

Yaffe, D. (1996, April 22). Habeas bill may boomerang at first. *Court TV Library: Death penalty.*

Young, V. (1990, September 25). Death row woman to get new trial. *St. Louis Post-Dispatch,* p. 12A.

Zimring, F.E. & Hawkins, G. (1986). *Capital punishment and the American agenda.* New York: Cambridge University Press.

CASES CITED

Batson v. Kentucky [47 US 79, 106 S. Ct. 1712 (1986)]

Cooper v. State, 504 N.E. 2d 1216 (Indiana, 1989)

Eddings v. Oklahoma [455 US 104,10 S.Ct. 869 (1982)]

Fierro v. Gomez [790F Supp. 966 CA (1992)]

Furman v. Georgia [408 US. 238, 92 S.Ct. 2726 (1972)]

Gregg v. Georgia [428 US 153,96 S.Ct. 2909 (1976)]

Haney v. Alabama, [603 So. 2d 368 (Al. Crim. App.1991)]

Harris v, Alabama [632 So.2d 503 (1992)]

Herrera v. Collins [506 US 390,113 S.Ct. 853 (1993)]

Lackey v. Texas [115 US S.Ct. 1421 (1995)]

Lockett v. Ohio [438 US 586,98 S.Ct. 2954 (1978)]

McCleskey v. Kemp [481 US 279,107 S.Ct. 1756 (1987)]

Tedder v. State [322 So. 2d, at 908 Fla. (1975)]

Texas v. Karla Faye Tucker [388.428-B.(1998)]

Thompson v. Oklahoma [487 US 815,108 S.Ct. 2687 (1988)]

White v. Commonwealth [671 S.W.2d 241 (1984)]

Witherspoon v. Illinois [391 US 510,88 S.Ct. 1770 (1968)]

Index

About the Author

KATHLEEN A. O'SHEA is a social worker who does criminal justice research on female prisoners, with a focus on the death penalty. She is an activist and advocate for women on death row, as well as coauthor (with Beverly R. Fletcher) of *Female Offenders*: *An Annotated Bibliography*, published by Greenwood Press in 1997.

ISBN 0-275-95952-X

90000>

EAN

9 780275 959524

HARDCOVER BAR CODE